THE Painter Wow! 6 BOOK

Cher Threinen-Pendarvis

Peachpit Press

The Painter 6 Wow! Book

Cher Threinen-Pendarvis

Peachpit Press
1249 Eighth Street
Berkeley, CA 94710
(510) 524-2178
(800) 283-9444
(510) 524-2221 (fax)

Find us on the World Wide Web at: http://www.peachpit.com/books/wow.html

Peachpit Press is a division of Addison Wesley Longman.

Series Editor: Linnea Dayton
Peachpit Press Editor: Cary Norsworthy
Cover design: TMA Ted Mader + Associates
Cover illustration: Cher Threinen-Pendarvis
Book design: Jill Davis
Art direction and layout: Cher Threinen-Pendarvis
Editing: Linnea Dayton
Copyediting and proofreading: Susan Bugbee
Index: Jackie Estrada
Production and prepress manager: Jonathan Parker

This book was set using the Stone Serif and Stone Sans families. It was written and composed in Adobe PageMaker 6.52. Final output was computer to plate at Graphic Arts Center, Indianapolis.

ISBN 0-201-35449-7

0 9 8 7 6 5 4 3 2 1
Printed and bound in the United States of America.

To my husband Steven,

for his friendship,

encourage   ⌐ ᵤnderstanding;

and to o⌐

from wʰ

— Che

Brush Control
General
Dab type : Circular
Stroke type : Simple
Method : Cloning
Subcategory : Soft cover cloning

Brush :
Cloners – soft cloner
Setup for clone
Layers :
Method : Default
Composite depth : Ignore

Mark Zimmer created the original Paint Can *image for the Painter 1.0 program.*

ACKNOWLEDGMENTS

The Painter 6 Wow! Book would not have been possible without a great deal of help from some extraordinary people and sources.

My heartfelt thanks go to Linnea Dayton, the *Wow!* Series Editor and a treasured friend and colleague. During the first, second, third and *fourth* editions, her inspiration, wisdom and encouragement proved invaluable. Thank you, Linnea, for editing *The Painter 6 Wow! Book.*

Warmest thanks go to my friends at Peachpit Press, especially Ted Nace for his inspiration, Nancy Ruenzel for her guidance, Cary Norsworthy—our *Wow!* Peachpit editor—for her advice that came when it was needed most, and the rest of the publishing team for their support. Thank you Peachpit, for giving me the opportunity to do this book.

A big "thank you" goes to the creators of Painter: Mark Zimmer, Tom Hedges and John Derry, for creating such a *Wow!* program and for their inspiration, enthusiasm and openness; to Kim Kern and Lori Whallen for their support with communications; to Shawn Grunberger, for answering Web-related questions, and to the outstanding technical support team, especially Stanley Vealè and Elizabeth Mitchell for answering questions about the program.

I am grateful to the talented Painter artists who contributed their work and techniques; their names are listed in Appendix D in the back of the book. I would especially like to thank Daryl Wise who helped me locate artists who use Painter.

I'd also like to thank the companies who supplied the *Wow!* book team with supporting software during the development of the book—Adobe Systems for supplying me with Photoshop, Illustrator, Premiere and GoLive; and Macromedia, for contributing

This Paint Can *illustration was created for the Painter 3 poster by John Derry.*

Painthenge, *was illustrated by Chet Phillips for Painter 5's poster.*

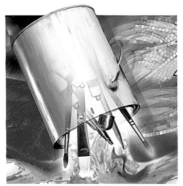

Brian Moose illustrated Creative Journey, *shown here as a detail, for the Painter 6 program. To see the complete image, turn to page 229.*

Director, Dreamweaver, Fireworks, and Flash so I could demonstrate how nicely these programs work with Painter, and Baseline Publishing for Screenshot.

Thanks to Corbis Images and PhotoDisc for their support during all four editions of the book; these two "stock on CD-ROM and Web" companies allowed us to use their photos for demonstration purposes in the book. I am also grateful to the other companies who provided images or video clips for *The Painter 6 Wow!* CD-ROM; their names are listed in Appendix A in the back of the book.

Additionally, the following companies donated, loaned or gave us a good deal on hardware that helped to create the book: Wacom, for their great pressure-sensitive tablets, Mitsubishi Electronics America, for their monitors; Hewlett-Packard and Epson for color printers for the testing of printing techniques.

I'm grateful to Linnea Dayton, Jack Davis, Victor Gavenda, Chris (Boz) Jennings, Donal Jolley, Shawn Grunberger, Cary Norsworthy and Lance Williams for their helpful technical reads. My warmest thanks go to Carol Benioff for her expertise in traditional and digital printmaking, Michele Lill for sharing her knowledge about reflection maps, and Steven Gordon for his experience with terrain maps. Special thanks also go to Dorothy Krause and Bonny Lhotka for sharing their knowledge of experimental printmaking, Jon Lee and Geoff Hull of Fox Television for sharing their experience in designing for broadcast television; Cindy and Dewey Reid of Reid Creative for sharing their expertise in animation and film; and Lynda Weinman for sharing her knowledge about designing graphics for the Web.

Warmest thanks go to my friend Mary Envall for permitting me to use her photograph of lilies as one of the references for the book's cover illustration.

I'd like to thank my co-workers "behind the scenes" on the Wow! book team. Warmest thanks go to Jill Davis for her brilliant book design; Susan Bugbee for her friendship and helpful copyediting and proofreading; Jackie Estrada for her careful indexing; and PageMaker whiz Jonathan Parker for his production and prepress expertise. His calm assurance during the deadlines of all four editions of this book was much appreciated!

My very special thanks go to Victor Gavenda at Peachpit Press for his fine work on the *Painter Wow!* CD-ROM.

A heartfelt thank you to these special "co-workers;" to my husband Steve, for his encouragement, tasty meals and reminders to take breaks during the project; and to our cat Little Doll, the close companion who has warmed my office chair.

Finally, I would like to thank all the other family, friends and colleagues who have been so patient and understanding during the development of four editions of this book.

Cher Threinen-Pendarvis

Mark Zimmer, creator of Painter

FOREWORD

"So Mark. . . *Painter SIX Wow!* Can you believe it?"

"Wow is right! Where does the time go?"

"I don't know, but Cher sure must have used a lot of it writing this book!"

In some respects, it seems like such a short time ago since Painter first appeared. Using the natural-media concept as a central theme, Painter has grown and matured into a powerful environment for creative expression on the computer. Cher and her *Painter WOW! Books* have expertly chronicled this growth over the years. Seems like we talk with her quite often.

Writing about something that is exclusively visual presents a formidable challenge. It's one thing to view an artwork or design piece as an aesthetic experience; it's an entirely different thing to dissect it and divine its internal construction. Cher takes this task and turns it into a highly informative and entertaining experience for her readers. *The Painter 6 WOW! Book* is the written equivalent of looking over an artist's shoulder as he paints, or draws, or airbrushes or. . .

Painter 6 WOW! is based on a step-by-step instructional premise. A finished artwork example is introduced as the final result of applying a set of techniques. With the example as a starting point, individual image-making concepts are introduced to the reader. These singular concepts are then used like building blocks to construct the final image. This is a very powerful method of

John Derry, co-creator of Painter

instruction, particularly for image-making. It's often difficult, if not impossible, to visualize the creative journey the artist goes through to arrive at a final design. *WOW!* does this with dozens of examples.

These instructional examples will appeal to both the beginning and experienced Painter user. For the beginner, it's akin to being shown the secret to a magic trick; for the experienced user, it's an enriching fuel for boosting creativity. Cher also seasons her examples with tidbits of art history and traditional technique. There are no empty calories in this visual and instructional feast!

Painter is a tool for personal creative expression. There is no better way to illustrate this than by showcasing high-quality examples created by Painter users. *WOW!* is lushly illustrated throughout with these examples. The Gallery sections amply demonstrate what can be accomplished through a mastery of Painter's tools.

And without a good teacher, mastery of any kind is often an elusive goal. Through *The Painter 6 WOW! Book*, Cher offers users a key for unlocking this mastery within themselves. (Use the brush, Luke! But don't force it!)

"Note also, Mark, how once again we're surprised at the variety and quality of the work produced with Painter!"

"Yeah, and we're also surprised at completeness of Cher's cohesive compendium of creative content in *The Painter 6 WOW! Book*."

"That's a mouthful of words about an eyeful of art! Let's go make some art!"

"Right! After reading this, I think I'm going to work on my next Painter poster image!"

Mark Zimmer and John Derry
Scotts Valley, California

March, 2000

CONTENTS

WELCOME TO *PAINTER 6 WOW!*

SOME PEOPLE EMPHASIZE THE DIFFERENCES between traditional and digital art tools—almost as if "real" art and the computer are not compatible. But during the early development of this book, we discovered many working artists who had bought computers specifically because they were thrilled by the promise of Painter. It seemed logical that *The Painter Wow! Book* should become a bridge connecting conventional tools and techniques with their electronic counterparts. Early chapters of the book, in particular, touch on color theory, art history and conventional media, and explain how to translate foundational art theory using Painter's tools.

This book addresses the needs of a wide variety of creative professionals: artists making the transition from traditional to digital media; photographers looking to expand their visual vocabulary; screen or print graphic designers hunting for special effects to apply to type; even creative explorers out for some fun. For those of you with a long history in a traditional art form and a short history with computers, we've done our best to guide you through Painter's interface, making it as simple as possible for you to achieve the results you want. And if you've spent more time with a keyboard and mouse than you have with an artist's palette and paintbrush, you may learn a lot about conventional art terms and techniques as you read the book.

The creative team that invented Painter—Mark Zimmer, Tom Hedges and John Derry—are famous for their brilliant innovation and dedication to improving and expanding their software tools. Along with Painter 6 features such as speedy rendered brushes, redesigned palettes, new industry-standard layers, the exciting capabilities of dynamic text, and tools that make it easy to prepare graphics for use on the Web, the team has also made changes to Painter's interface that make it easier to use.

Painter 6's new Impasto interface and Impasto brushes let Chelsea Sammel paint with realistic three-dimensional strokes, creating bristle marks and thick paint on the surface of her painting Dying Orchids, *shown in this detail.*

Painter 6's new brushes and industry-standard masks and layers let you paint on the Canvas and layers with realistic brushstrokes and create layered composite images to produce results like Debi Lee Mandel's Angelfish, *shown here.*

Painter 6 offers several brush variants designed specifically for photographers, such as the Add Grain brush used here.

ORIGINAL PHOTO: CORBIS IMAGES

WHAT'S NEW IN PAINTER 6?

To make *The Painter 6 Wow! Book* complete and up-to-date for Painter 6, we've revised every page. And we've expanded the book—adding many pages of brand-new real-world tips, techniques and galleries that specifically profile features added in version 6. We've also added a brand-new chapter about using type in Painter. Here's a quick overview of some of Painter 6's exciting new features and a description of where in this book you can find information about them.

Among the changes that make Painter easier to use are these: Painter 6 features a sleeker, leaner, meaner, redesigned interface that's easier to navigate. Three new **expandable palettes**—the Art Materials, Brush Controls and Objects palettes—allow easier access to many resources. Notably, the new Brush Controls palette makes it easier to **customize brushes** to your heart's content. Also important in the redesign, Painter 6 makes better use of large amounts of RAM when working with big images.

An area of the program that's most likely to change the way you work is Painter 6's industry-standard **masks and layers** model, which will be familiar to users of Adobe Photoshop. With Painter 6, you can make selections and save them as masks into the Masks section of the Objects palette, much like saving selections as masks into the Channels palette in Photoshop. Painter's updated masking tools also include a more versatile **Magic Wand**. To find out about these useful new functions, turn to Chapter 4, "Selections, Shapes and Masks." The new layers operate much more like Photoshop's layers, and are true transparent layers (with Preserve Transparency) that you can paint on with most any brush. You can also use a selection with any layer you target. And Opacity and Compositing Methods controls are included in the Layers section of the Objects palette.

Users of previous versions of the program will be pleased to find Painter's familiar Brushes palette, stocked with brand-new **rendered brushes** that paint more naturally than ever before, and faster, too. The new rendered brushes bring great versatility: for instance, the new Camelhair brush can lay down paint or smear it, and each brush hair has the capability to carry its own color. The rendered brushes also contribute to **more realistic cloning** capabilities. And you can paint with new **special effects brushes**—for instance, the Shatter brush helps you break an image up into icy shards.

Painter's easier-to-use **Impasto** feature has been integrated into the image canvas. See "Working With Thick Paint" on page 88 for a step-by step tutorial using Impasto. Also, dynamic lighting controls allow you to modify Impasto lighting settings and adjust the thickness of the paint. Turn to "Brushing Washes Over Live Canvas" on page 86 to read more about these features.

In addition to new painting tools, Painter 6 includes many tools designed specifically for photographers. Photo brushes (such

Painter 6's new features help prepare images for use on the World Wide Web. For instance, Painter can convert colors to Web-friendly palettes, slice images and export coding for interactive buttons.

SHAWN GRUNBERGER

1

You'll learn real applications for Painter's tools in the Basics sections of each chapter.

2
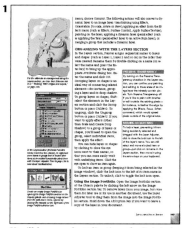

Each chapter includes step-by-step technique sections.

as **Add Grain**) and dynamic layers such as **Brightness and Contrast** allow you to make adjustments to an image without actually changing the original image. See Chapter 6, "Enhancing Photos, Collage and Montage," to read about these tools.

In addition to setting type shapes with the Text tool, Painter 6 offers improved, editable Dynamic Text, with live drop shadows and other effects you can apply. You'll find information about how these **type tools** work and techniques for using them in the Chapter 8, "Working with Type in Painter."

Designers preparing graphics for display on the Web love Painter's ability to make **client-side image maps.** You can even export **sliced images** with **JavaScript rollovers** with the Image Slicer. Add motion to your Web pages with Painter 6's improved export of **GIF animations**. See the beginning of Chapter 10, "Multimedia and Film with Painter," and Chapter 11, "Using Painter for Web Graphics," for more about animation, video and Web graphics using Painter. With Painter's updated GIF Options, you can now export images with constrained Web-safe color palettes.

If you need to prepare images for print, Painter 6 offers a useful updated **Kodak Color Management System**. Turn to pages 322–323 in Chapter 12, "Printing and Archival Concerns," to read about this system.

DO YOU USE MAC OR WINDOWS?
Painter works similarly on Macintosh and PC/Windows platforms. We've taken the path of least resistance by using primarily Macintosh screenshots. (Just to make sure of our techniques, though, we've tested them under Windows 98, and we've included key commands for both Mac and Windows users.) The few differences between running Painter on Mac and PC are covered in Chapter 1.

ARE YOU A BEGINNER OR A POWER-USER?
If you're new to Painter, welcome! We've worked very hard to make this edition of Painter Wow! more friendly to beginners by adding more cross-references and by including complete, unabbreviated directions to the techniques in the book. We've also added more basics to the chapter introductions. For intermediate and advanced users, we've included new power-user tips throughout, many new techniques and inspiring galleries.

We've assumed that you're familiar with the basic Mac or Windows mouse functions and that you know how to open and save files, copy items to the clipboard and navigate through the Mac's hierarchical file system or through Windows directories. We suggest reading Chapter 1, "Getting to Know Painter," Chapter 4, "Selections, Shape and Masks," and Chapter 5, "Using Layers and Shapes," before jumping into the more advanced techniques. It's also a good idea, though it isn't essential, to have worked with the *Painter 6 User Guide* and to have completed the tutorial that comes with the program.

SAMPLING PAINT

You can temporarily switch to the Dropper tool and sample colors by holding down the Ctrl/⌘ key while you're using many of Painter's other tools.

Each chapter includes an inspiring gallery of professional work.

You'll find helpful resources in the Appendix.

A HELPFUL SOFTWARE PATCH

The Painter development team has built a software patch (Painter 6.03) that fixes problems in the Painter 6.0 Windows/Mac programs. The patch is available for free download at http://www.painter6.com or http://www5.metacreations.com/ cgi-bin/downloads/index.cgi.

HOW TO USE THIS BOOK

In chapters 2 through 11, the information we're presenting generally progresses from simple to complex. We've organized these chapters into four types of material: "Basics" sections, techniques, practical tips and galleries. In addition, useful hardware, software and other resources are listed at the back of the book.

1 The **Basics** sections teach how Painter's tools and functions work, and give real-world applications for the tools. *The Painter 6 Wow! Book* wasn't designed to be a replacement for the *Painter 6 User Guide* that comes with the program. We've focused on the tools and functions that we think are most useful. In some cases we've further explained items covered in the manual, and, where important, we've dug deeper to help you understand how the tools and functions work. In other cases, we've covered undocumented functions and practical applications, either shared by contributing artists or uncovered in our own research.

2 Within each **Technique** section, you'll find step-by-step, real-world methods that give you enough information to re-create the process yourself. In the *Wow!* format, pictures illustrating the stages of the process are positioned alongside the appropriate step in the project. Browse the pictures in the art column within a technique for a quick overview of the development of an image. We've done our best to give you enough information so that you won't have to refer to the manual to follow the steps.

3 The **Tips** are easily identified by their gray title bar. We've placed them in the Basics and Technique sections where we thought they'd be the most helpful, but each tip is a self-contained tidbit of useful information, so you can learn a lot very quickly by taking a brisk walk through the book, reading only the tips.

4 The **Galleries** are there for inspiration, and one appears at the end of every chapter. With each gallery image, you'll find a short description of how the artwork was produced.

5 No book is an island, so in the **Appendixes** in the back of this one, we've included lists of other resources for your use. If you want to contact a vendor, an artist, or a fine art print studio, or locate an art-related book or other publication, you'll find the information you need there.

The Painter 6 Wow! Book was created to share useful techniques and tips and to provide creative suggestions for using the program. We hope that you'll use it as inspiration and a point of departure for your own creative exploration. Above all, don't be overwhelmed by Painter's richness. . . Just dig in and enjoy it!

Cher Threinen-Pendarvis

www.peachpit.com/peachpit/meetus/authors/ cher.threinen.pendarvis.html

Painter Wow! Web site: http://beta.peachpit.com/wow/painter

GETTING TO KNOW PAINTER

John Derry's illustration, Paint Can, *was inspired by the abstract expressionist artist Robert Rauschenberg.*

SIT RIGHT DOWN AND POWER UP! This chapter explores Painter's basic needs and functions, as well as its unique strengths and idiosyncrasies. If you're new to Painter, you'll benefit the most from this chapter if you've already spent some time with the *Painter 6 User Guide* that ships with the program.

PAINTER'S REQUIREMENTS FOR MAC AND PC

Here are Painter's *minimum* requirements: If you use a Macintosh you'll need a Power Macintosh running System 8 or later with a minimum of 32 MB of application RAM (64 MB is recommended). To run Painter on Windows 95, 98 or Windows NT 4, you'll need at least 32 MB of application RAM (64 MB is recommended). For both platforms you'll need a hard disk with approximately 100 MB of free space to perform a minimum installation.

When you open an image in Painter—for example, a 5 MB image—and begin working with it, Painter needs three to five times that file size in RAM in order to work at optimal speed—in our example, that would be 15–25 MB of RAM. Opening more than one image, adding layers or shapes, or increasing the number of Undos (under Edit, Preferences, Undos) adds further demands on RAM. When Painter runs out of RAM, it uses the hard disk chosen in Edit, Preferences, General as a RAM substitute. This "scratch disk" holds the Painter Temp file you may

QUICK COPIES

Here are two ways to make quick copies without going through the clipboard and using valuable RAM. To make a copy of your entire document, use File, Clone. (This is also a quick way to make a "flat" copy with the layers in the document merged.) To quickly duplicate a layer, select the layer in the layers section of the Objects palette, choose the Layer Adjuster tool, press the Alt/Option key and click in the image to make a copy in register, or drag off a copy.

THE FONT RENDERING ENGINE

Painter 6 uses a unique method to display type on its palettes. This technology helps the program boot more quickly, but for the palettes to display correctly, these default System fonts must be present in your System folder: The Mac uses Helvetica; Windows uses Arial.

On the Mac, Painter runs faster with Virtual Memory turned off in the Memory Control Panel. (It interferes with Painter's own virtual memory scheme.)

Setting the Maximum Memory for Painter in Windows

have seen. Since hard disks operate much slower than RAM, performance suffers accordingly—even if you have a fast hard disk.

Ideally, to work with Painter, you would use a computer with a speedy processor; a large, fast hard disk; and lots of RAM. In addition, you'll want a large, 24-bit-color monitor—probably no less than 17 inches—and perhaps a second monitor on which to store palettes. Also highly recommended—some might say *essential*—is a drawing tablet with a pressure-sensitive stylus. Not only is it a more natural drawing and painting tool than a mouse, but many of Painter's brushes lose their personality without a pressure-sensitive input device.

Mac memory allocation. To allot maximum RAM to Painter on a Mac, first quit all open applications. In the Finder, under the Apple menu, choose About This Macintosh. Write down the number next to Largest Unused Block. This is the total amount of RAM in which you can run applications. Subtract 500 or 1000 K (as a buffer) from this number. Now, in the Painter folder, click once (not twice!) on the Painter application icon and choose File, Get Info. Enter the result of your math in the Preferred Size box. This method won't let you open any other applications of significant size while Painter is running, but it assures you of the use of nearly all available RAM while you're in Painter.

Windows memory allocation. To make maximum RAM available for your Windows 98–based PC, choose Edit, Preferences, Windows to access the Windows Preferences dialog box. Under Physical Memory Usage click the "Maximum Memory for Painter"

HARD DISK TIPS

You can speed up your scratch disk by using hard disk driver software to make a separate partition just for the Painter Temp file. Additionally, use a hard disk utility program like Norton Utilities, Mac Tools or PC Tools (all from Symantec) to regularly defragment the partition. Over time, hard drives become fragmented (space is broken into smaller and smaller blocks)—and thus slower—so the file data has to be split up in order to be written to them.

| Largest Free Contiguous | 24.8 M |
| File Fragmentation | 23.62% |

APS 2 — Files: 1,634 / Used: 1,372.6 M / Free: 160.7 M / Total: 1,533.3 M

FASTER STARTUP

Painter reads all open fonts and loaded plug-in filters when it starts up. For faster startup, consider organizing your fonts with a utility (Suitcase or MasterJuggler) that enables you to turn them on and off. And, if you have a large number of third-party filters, create several plug-ins folders. To change to an alternate plug-ins folder, choose Edit, Preferences, Other Raster Plug-ins, and navigate to the folder. Restart Painter, and the alternate filter set will appear under the Effects, Plug-in Filters menu.

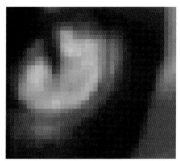

This scan of a photograph is a pixel-based image. Enlarging it to 1200% reveals the grid of pixels.

Cher Threinen-Pendarvis's Tienda Verde *in progress. Using the Rectangular Selection tool, we selected an area of the image's sky and deleted the area to reveal the new purple Paper Color.*

button. Quit all applications and relaunch Painter. Painter will run faster if you let Windows manage the virtual memory scheme.

FILE SIZE AND RESOLUTION

If you're new to the computer, here's important background information regarding file sizes: Painter is primarily a *pixel-based* program, also known as a *bitmap*, *painting* or *raster* program (see "Painter's Vector Capabilities" below), not a *drawing* program, also known as an *object-oriented* or *vector* program. Drawing programs use mathematical expressions to describe the outline and fill attributes of objects in the drawing, while pixel-based programs describe things dot-by-dot. Because its components are mathematically described, object-oriented art can be resized or transformed with no loss of quality. Not so with Painter, Photoshop and other pixel-based programs. Increasing the size of an existing image in these programs means that additional pixels must be created to accommodate the larger size by filling in spaces as the existing pixels spread apart. As a result of the interpolated (manufactured) pixels, resized images can lose their crispness.

There are ways of working around this "soft image" dilemma. One solution is to do studies using a small file size (for instance, an 8 x 10-inch image at 75 pixels per inch), then start over with a large image to do final art at full size (for instance an 8 x 10-inch file at 300 pixels per inch). You can also block in the basic form and color in a small file, then scale the image up to final size (using Canvas, Resize) to add texture and details (textures seem particularly vulnerable to softening when enlarged). You'll notice that many of the artists whose work is featured in this book use another efficient method: They create the components of a final piece of art in separate documents, then copy and paste the components into a final "master" image. Painter 6 offers yet another solution for working with large file sizes—composing with reference layers (small "stand-in" versions of larger images that are kept outside the document). Because data for the large image is not kept in the working file, performance improves. Turn to "Using Reference Layers" in Chapter 5 on page 144, to learn about this feature.

Painter's vector capabilities. Although it's primarily a pixel-based program, Painter does have some object-oriented features— shapes, shape paths and outline-based selections. Painter's shapes exist as floating elements above the image canvas and have mathematically described outlines with stroke and fill attributes. And Painter's selections (areas of the image designated for work) are versatile; they can be used as pixel-based selections (similar to Photoshop's selections), or they can be transformed into outline-based selections or converted into shapes. (Other elements in Painter—the image canvas, masks and layers—are pixel-based.) Chapters 4 and 5 tell more about selections and shapes.

Expressing width and height in "pixels" in the New Picture dialog box keeps the file size the same, regardless of how you change the Resolution.

Whether the Constrain File Size checkbox in the Canvas, Resize dialog box is checked or unchecked, if you're using "pixels" as the units, the file size stays the same, regardless of how you change the Resolution.

Click the Browse button in the Open dialog box to preview all of the images in a folder. The watercolor studies in Mary Envall's "Lilies" folder are shown here. (Some files may not have a preview—for example, some PICT or JPEG files created by other programs.)

Pixel size and resolution. There are two commonly used ways of describing file sizes: in terms of their pixel measurements, or in a unit of measure (such as inches) plus a resolution. An image is a fixed number of pixels wide and tall—like 1200 x 1500—or a measurement combined with a resolution—4 x 5 inches at 300 ppi. (Either way it's expressed, the full-color file is 7 MB.) If you use pixels as a measurement for Width and Height in the New File dialog box, notice that the file size doesn't change, regardless of the numbers you type into the Resolution box. The pixel number does not change unless you resize the image using Canvas, Resize. Increasing or decreasing the number of pixels in the Width and Height fields in the Canvas, Resize dialog box to add (or reduce) pixel information in the picture automatically unchecks the Constrain File Size box.

INCREASING FILE RESOLUTION WITH SCRIPTS

You can use Painter's Scripts function to record your work at low resolution, then play it back at a higher resolution. This technique gives you a much crisper result than simply resizing the original image to a new resolution. Here's how to do it: Start by opening the Scripts section of the Objects palette. Click the right triangle on the Scripts section bar to open the menu and choose Script Options. In the Script Options dialog box check the Record Initial State box, then click OK. Open a new file (File, New) and choose Select, All (Ctrl/⌘-A). From the Scripts section menu, choose Record Script (or press the round red button on the Scripts section) to begin recording. Then begin painting. When you're finished, from the menu on the Scripts section bar, choose Stop Recording Script (or click the square black button on the Scripts section). Open a new document two to four times as large as the original (this

Choosing Script Options from the pull-down menu on the Scripts section

technique loses its effectiveness if your new file is much bigger than this), press Ctr/⌘-A, then choose Playback Script from the menu, or click the black triangle button (to the left of the red button) on the Scripts section. Painter will replay the script in the larger image, automatically scaling brushes and papers to perfectly fit the new size. A word of caution—scripts can be quirky: Your higher-resolution image may not match the lower-resolution one if you use imported photos, complex selections, shapes or the Image Hose, for instance.

OPENING FILES

Images in Painter are 24-bit color, made up of RGB (red, green and blue) components consisting of 8 bits each. Painter will recognize and open CMYK TIFF and grayscale TIFF images, but it will convert both CMYK and grayscale TIFF files to Painter's own RGB mode. Layered files saved in Photoshop format must be converted to RGB mode before they can be opened in Painter. CIE LAB, Kodak Photo CD format and other color formats will need to be converted to RGB in a program such as Adobe Photoshop or Equilibrium's Debabelizer before Painter can read them.

You can preserve layers in files by saving in either RIFF or Photoshop format, but RIFF (even uncompressed) is usually significantly smaller. Rick Kirkman's 663 x 663-pixel image with 150 layers weighs in at 1.7 MB as a compressed RIFF, 6.1 MB as an uncompressed RIFF, and 7.1 MB when saved in Photoshop format.

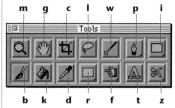
SAVING FILES

Painter offers numerous ways to save your image under File, Save or Save As. If you've created an image with a mask (Chapter 4 tells how to create masks), some of the formats will allow you to preserve the mask (by checking the Save Alpha box in the Save or Save As dialog box), while others won't. Here's a list of the current formats that includes their "mask-friendliness" and other advantages and disadvantages:

RIFF. Thrifty (files are saved quite small) and robust (allows for multiple layers), RIFF (Raster Image File Format) is Painter's native format. Few other programs recognize RIFF, so if you want to work with a Painter image in another program, save a copy in a different format. If you're using elements unique to Painter, such as Wet Paint, reference layers, dynamic layers, shapes, selections or mosaics, saving in RIFF format will preserve them. (Selections, masks, layers and shapes are described in depth in Chapters 4 and 5.) If you have *lots* of free hard disk space, check the Uncompressed box in the Save dialog box when you're saving in RIFF: Files will become many times larger, but will save and open much more quickly.

Photoshop format. Saving files in Photoshop format gives you nearly all the flexibility of RIFF, and is ideal if you frequently move data between Painter and Photoshop. When you use Photoshop to open a file saved in this format, Painter's layers become Photoshop layers (Chapter 9, "Using Painter with Photoshop," contains more information about working with Painter and Photoshop); Painter's masks (explained in depth in Chapter 4) become Photoshop channels; and Painter's Bézier paths translate perfectly to Photoshop's paths and subpaths, appearing in Photoshop's Paths palette.

TIFF. Probably the most popular and widely recognized of the bitmap file formats, TIFF allows you to save a mask with your image (check the Save Alpha checkbox). Unfortunately, unlike Photoshop, Painter's Save As dialog box gives you no option to

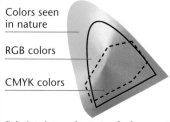

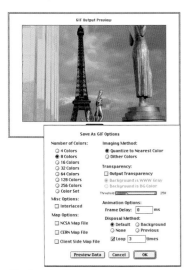

The Save As GIF Options dialog box includes GIF Animation Options.

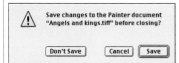

compress the TIFF file—the Uncompressed check box is checked and grayed-out.

PICT. PICT is the format of choice for many multimedia programs and other on-screen display. Painter's PICT format lets you save a single mask (but not layers), and save a Painter movie as a sequence of numbered PICT files to export and animate in another program (described in Chapter 10, "Multimedia and Film with Painter"). Painter also opens PICT files very quickly.

JPEG. When you save a file in JPEG format, a dialog box will appear with four choices: Excellent, High, Good and Fair. You'll get the best results by choosing Excellent. The advantage of saving a file in JPEG format is that you get superb space savings: a JPEG file is usually only one-tenth as large as a TIFF file of the same image if you choose Excellent, and only one-hundredth the size if you choose Fair. The drawbacks: No mask, layers or paths are saved; and the compression is a lossy compression—which means that some data (color detail in the image) is lost in the compression process. While JPEG is a good way to archive images once they're finished (especially images that have no sharp edges), many artists prefer not to use JPEG because it alters pixels. Don't save in JPEG format if you're continually opening and resaving an image—you'll lose more data every time you do so.

JPEG is also useful for preparing 24-bit images with the tiny file sizes that are needed for graphics used on the World Wide Web. (See Chapter 11 for more information on JPEG use in projects created for the Web.)

GIF. GIF is the graphics format of choice for the World Wide Web on the Internet. Like TIFF, PICT or JPEG, saving in GIF format combines layers with the background. It also reduces the number of colors to a maximum of 256, so remember to Save As in a different file format first, if you want to be able to access the original image structure again. When you save in GIF, a dialog box appears that gives you a number of options for saving your file. Click the Preview Data button to see how your choices will affect your image. For more information about using Painter's GIF format turn to Chapter 11, "Using Painter for Web Graphics."

EPS. Saving in this format drops layered elements into the background and ignores masks, so it's best to choose Save As in another format if you'll want to make changes to your document at a later time. Saving in EPS format also converts the file into a five-part DCS file: four separate files for the four process printing colors, and a fifth file as a preview of the composite image. Check Chapters 2 and 19 in the *Painter 6 User Guide* for a complete explanation of the EPS Options dialog box.

PC formats. BMP, PCX and Targa are formats commonly used on DOS and Windows platforms. BMP (short for "bitmap") is a

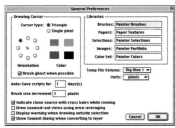

The General Preferences dialog box lets you specify default libraries, cursor type and orientation, Temp File Volume (location of the scratch disk) and Units, among other features.

To view Painter 6's new brush footprint cursor (shown here when painting a brushstroke with the Captured Bristle variant of Brushes), turn on the "Brush ghost when possible" checkbox in the General Preferences dialog box.

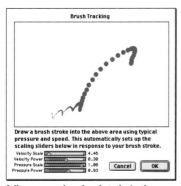

When you make a brushstroke in the Preferences, Brush Tracking dialog box, Painter adjusts the range of pressure-sensitivity based on the stroke.

Windows-based graphics file format, and PCX is the PC Paintbrush native format. Neither of these two formats supports shapes or masks. Targa is a popular format used for creating sophisticated 24-bit graphics; it was originally developed by the Truevision company as a proprietary format for use with its video capture boards. The Targa format is often used (in place of PICT) when preparing numbered files for import into Windows animation applications.

Movie formats. Movies in Painter (described in Chapter 10, "Multimedia and Film with Painter") are saved as Frame Stacks, but you can choose Save As to export the current frame of your movie, export the entire Frame Stack as a QuickTime or AVI/VFW (on the PC) movie, or export the entire Frame Stack as numbered PICT files. See Chapter 10 for more about multimedia formats.

Pyramid files. The Pyramid file structure is useful for composing high-resolution documents. A file with Pyramid data structure is capable of containing multi-resolution information. When an image is placed into a document (File, Place), it comes in as a reference layer (a low-resolution *reference* to the original image). To read more about working with reference layers and Pyramid files, turn to page 144 in Chapter 5.

SETTING PREFERENCES

Painter's Preferences (under the Edit menu) go a long way in helping you create an efficient workspace. Here are a few pointers:

Brush tracking. Before every work session, it's a good idea to first choose Edit, Preferences, Brush Tracking. Make a brushstroke with your stylus using a typical amount of pressure. Painter accepts this as the average stroke and adjusts to give you the maximum amount of range and pressure-sensitivity based on your sample stroke. Unfortunately, Painter doesn't remember your custom setting after you quit the program; so it's a good idea to re-establish your typical brushstroke every time you launch.

Multiple undos. Painter lets you set the number of Undos you want under Edit, Preferences, Undo. It's important to note that this option applies cumulatively across all open documents within Painter. For example, if the number of Undos is set to 5

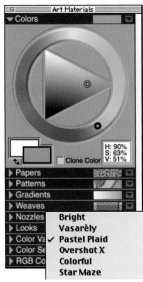

The new expandable Art Materials palette has section swatches that display the current color, paper, gradient and weave. Clicking on a swatch allows you to choose another material from a pop-up list.

DOCKING THE PALETTES

Painter's new expandable palettes are designed to snap together when one is dragged close to the side, top or bottom of another. This design helps to keep your desktop tidy, and there's a bonus: The palettes are designed not to overlap each other. If you dock a palette, then open its sections, they will open but will not cover the palette below it, unless you drag the bottom corner to expand it.

COLORS WON'T CHANGE?

If you choose a new color in the Colors section of the Art Materials palette (or sample a new color from your image with the Dropper), but your brush still paints with the old color, you've probably chosen the back color rectangle in the Colors section when setting the new color. Click on the arrow icon to toggle the back color to the front, and begin painting.

Back color rectangle
Front color rectangle

(the default) and you have two documents open, if you use two Undos on the first document, you'll be able to perform only three Undos on the second document. And, since a high setting for the number of Undos will burden your RAM and scratch disk, unless you have a good reason (such as working on a small sketch where you'll need to make many changes), it's best to leave the Undo setting at 5.

PAINTER BASICS

Here's a guide to some of Painter's basic operating procedures.

Navigating the new expandable palettes. Painter 6's three expandable palettes (the Art Materials, Brush Controls and Objects palettes) have several sections that you can open so that you can see and access the tools you need easily. When closed, the expandable palettes display a stacked series of section bars. To open a section of a palette, (for instance, the Colors section of the Art Materials palette), click the left triangle on the section bar. Click the name of a section to open that section and close all other sections in the palette.

Additionally, the Art Materials and Objects palettes have pull-down menus that contain commands. To use an alternate color set, for instance, choose the Load Color Set command by clicking the right triangle on the Colors section bar.

In the Art Materials palette, a swatch on the Colors, Papers, Patterns, Gradients or Weaves, section bar displays the current resource choice—for instance, the current color chosen in the Colors section. Each of these swatches (except color) allows you to access a resource list. For instance, click on the Papers swatch, and you can view the list of Papers in the loaded library.

Opening drawers. The Brushes palette and some sections of the Art Materials palette (the Papers, Patterns, Gradients, Weaves, Looks and Nozzles sections), display a push bar when they are open, with an arrowhead in the

HIDE AND SHOW PALETTES

To hide all of Painter's open palettes press Ctrl/⌘-H. The key command works as a toggle—press Ctrl/⌘-H to show the palettes again.

UP AND DOWN A PALETTE

To move up or down an open expandable palette:

• Drag up and down in any gray area of a section.

• To use any palette surface to scroll, press Alt/Option, then drag.

• Click or drag the interactive scroll bars on the right side of the palette.

CONTROLLING ALL SECTIONS

To use palette sections efficiently:

• Click the left triangle on a section bar to open that section.

• Press Shift and click the left triangle on one of the section bars to close or open all of the sections in a palette at once.

• Click the name of a section to open that section and close all other sections in the palette.

• Click the right triangle on a section bar to open its pop-up menu.

For Thistle, *Jinny Brown used many of Painter's natural media effects in her image. She began by setting a type shape in the Fleuron font. After filling the shapes with colors, she used Apply Lighting to add depth to the layers and painted with brushes, including Airbrushes, Photo brushes and the Just Add Water variant of Liquid.*

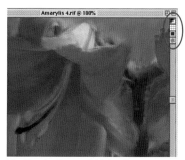

The Tracing Paper, Grid Overlay, Output Preview and Impasto icons reside at the top of Painter's vertical scroll bar.

A. Rafinelli Vineyard by Cher Threinen-Pendarvis. The Drawing Mode icons will pop up if you click the icon in the lower left corner of the image window. They are, from left to right: Draw Anywhere, Draw Outside and Draw Inside. To read more about them, turn to Chapter 4.

center that you can click on to open (the arrow turns green) or close a drawer. An open drawer gives you access to a wide choice of brushes, gradients, papers and so on from whatever library is active for that section at the time. A closed drawer (you see only the "front" of the drawer) shows your five most recent choices and may give you additional controls.

Screen management shortcuts. Like other programs, Painter offers lots of shortcuts designed to cut down on your trips to the menus, palettes or scroll bars. To *scroll* around the page, press and hold the spacebar (a grabber hand appears), then drag on your image. To *zoom in* on an area of your image at the next level of magnification, hold down Ctrl/⌘-spacebar (a magnifier tool appears) and click in your image. Add the Alt/Option key to *zoom out*. (You can also use Ctrl/⌘-plus to *zoom in* one magnification level and Ctrl/⌘-minus to *zoom out*.) These are the same zooming shortcuts used in Photoshop and Adobe Illustrator.

To *rotate the page* to better suit your drawing style, press Spacebar-Alt/Spacebar-Option (the Rotate Page icon appears) and click and drag in your image until the dotted outline preview shows you the angle you want. (The Rotate Page command rotates the view of the image only, not the actual pixels.) Restore your rotated image to its original position by holding down Spacebar-Alt/Spacebar-Option and clicking once on your image.

Two other frequently used screen-management shortcuts are Ctrl/⌘-M (Window, Screen Mode Toggle), which replaces a window's scroll and title bars with a frame of gray (or toggles back to normal view), and Ctrl/⌘-H (Window, Hide Palettes), which hides (or restores) all palettes.

Helpful icon buttons. Just outside the Painter image window are two sets of very helpful icon buttons. At the top right on the Painter Window scroll bar are four icon buttons: the Tracing Paper icon (allowing you to toggle Tracing Paper on and off), the Grid Overlay icon (which turns the Grid View on and off), the Output Preview icon (to toggle between the full-color, RGB view and a preview of what your image will look like when printed) and the Impasto icon (which you can click to hide or show the highlights and shadows on thick paint). Turn to Chapter 12, "Printing and Archival Concerns," for information about Painter's Output Preview.

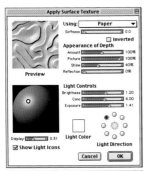

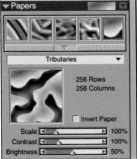

The Apply Surface Texture dialog box preview window, here shown Using Paper, updates when a new choice is made in the Papers section of the Art Materials palette.

Positioning the baseline of active letterform shapes with the help of the Ruler and horizontal Guides pulled from the ruler. The circled items here are the Ruler Origin field (top) and a triangular guide marker (bottom).

To the left of Painter's bottom scroll bar are the Drawing Mode icons, which allow you to control where you paint—anywhere in the image, outside of a selection, or inside of a selection. Turn to the beginning of Chapter 4, "Selections, Shapes and Masks," to read more about the Drawing Modes.

PREVIEW SURPRISE

Don't panic if a dialog box's Preview window is empty; Painter commonly displays the upper-left corner of your working window. Click and drag in the Preview (a grabber hand appears) to find your image.

Interactive dialog boxes. In most programs, clicking to make choices outside of a dialog box will reward you with an error beep, but Painter's interactive dialog box design encourages you to continue to make the choices you need. As an example, you can open a piece of artwork or a photo, then choose Effects, Surface Control, Apply Surface Texture and click and drag in the Preview window until you see a part of the image that you like. If you then choose Paper in the Using pop-up menu you can go outside the dialog box to choose a different paper (even a paper in another library) in the Papers section of the Art Materials palette. You can even move the Scale, Contrast and Brightness sliders in the Papers section and watch as the Preview image in the Apply Surface Texture dialog box updates to reflect your choice. When you've arrived at a result that you like, you can click OK in the Apply Surface Texture dialog box. The Effects, Surface Control, Color Overlay dialog box behaves in a similar way, allowing you to choose Uniform Color in the pop-up menu and test different colors from the Colors section of the Art Materials palette before you click OK. The Edit, Fill dialog box (Ctrl/⌘-F) is also interactive, giving you the ability to preview your image before it's filled with the current color, a pattern, a gradient or a weave.

Measuring and positioning elements. The Ruler, Guides and Grid Overlay can help you measure and position shapes and layers. The commands for these features reside in the Canvas menu. They are especially helpful for aligning type shapes and selections.

To set up a guide using precise measurements or to change the default guide color, double-click on the Ruler to access the Guide Options. Double-click on a triangular marker on the Ruler to access options for an individual guide. Delete guides by dragging their triangles off the document window or by pressing the Delete All Guides button in Guide Options.

To easily measure the exact *width* of an item, try moving the Ruler Origin. Press and drag it from the upper-left corner of the Ruler, where the horizontal and vertical measurements meet, to the left end of the item you want to measure. Then see where the right end falls on the ruler.

The Grid Overlay is useful for aligning items. Choose Canvas, Grid, Show Grid or click on the checkered Grid icon above the

Using the Grid overlay to help when positioning text shapes

scroll bar. To change the grid's appearance (for example, to create a grid of only horizontal lines), choose Canvas, Grid, Grid Options and adjust the settings.

The Align dialog box (Effects, Objects, Align) is helpful for lining up several shapes or layers (or a combination of the two). To align a series of items, start by selecting the Layer Adjuster tool, pressing the Shift key and clicking on each item's name in the Layers section (Objects palette). When all the items are selected, go to the Effects menu and choose Objects, Align, and choose your settings. The dialog box preview will update to show you how your horizontal and vertical choices will affect alignment of the objects, and you can click OK to accept, or Cancel. The elements below in the center, are aligned using Horizontal: Center, and Vertical: None. The elements below on the right, were aligned using their tops. The settings were Horizontal: None, and Vertical: Top.

  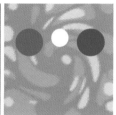

The Objects, Align dialog box with settings for the shapes

CUSTOMIZING YOUR WORKSPACE

Painter 6 makes it easy to customize your workspace. You can change the order of sections of the three expandable palettes (such as dragging the RGB Color section to a new position directly under the Colors section of the Art Materials palette). And the program allows you to build your own custom palettes to store favorite menu commands (brushes and textures, for instance).

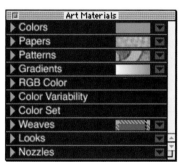

The Art Materials palette with sections closed, showing a custom stacking order for the sections

Arranging palette sections. Painter lets you move palette sections up or down within the palette. Close all sections of the palette you want to modify. To see this work easily, click on a palette and close all of its sections, then click on a blank area of a section bar and drag it up or down. For instance, we rearranged our Art Materials palette in this order: Colors, Papers, Patterns, Gradients, RGB Color, Color Variability, Color Set, Weaves, Looks and Nozzles. Painter will remember the changes you made to the palette. To save your palette layout permanently, choose Window, Arrange Palettes, Save Layout and when the Save Layout dialog box appears, name it and click OK. As your needs change, it's easy to rearrange the sections.

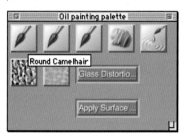

The new Oil Painting palette with favorite brushes, textures and effects. You can use Tool Tips in the custom palette to display the name of the brush. Tool Tips are turned on by default; if you've turned them off, choose Show Tool Tips from the Help menu.

Building a custom palette. You can make your own palettes to store menu commands and art materials for your work. For instance, to make a custom palette for oil painting, begin by selecting the Brushes icon in the Brushes palette and choose a brush variant

CHER THREINEN-PENDARVIS

Waterlilies, a detail of which is shown here, was painted with several of Painter 6's new Brushes variants, including the Round Camelhair and Smeary Flat, which we included in our custom Oil Painting palette (shown on page 16). The full illustration can be seen on the front cover of this book.

that you prefer (we chose the Opaque Round variant of Brushes). Drag the Brushes icon off the Brushes palette—this action will create a new custom palette with a copy of the Brushes icon in it. To add another item, select another brush variant and drag it directly over the new palette; the palette will expand automatically. (We added the Smeary Flat and Round Camelhair variants of Brushes.) We needed blending tools to mix colors, so we added the Grainy Water variant of the Liquid brush and the Palette Knife variant of the Impasto and dragged them onto our new custom palette.

Now for the texture: We clicked on the Raw Silk texture from Painter 6's default Papers library and dragged it into our palette, then clicked on the Big Grain Rough texture and dragged it into the new custom palette.

To add a menu command to a custom palette, choose Window, Custom Palette, Add Command, then select the menu item that you'd like to add to the palette. We added two commands that are useful for adding texture to paintings after the brushwork is complete: Effects, Focus, Glass Distortion and Effects, Surface Control, Apply Surface Texture.

SAVING PALETTE LAYOUTS

You can drag a palette anywhere on your desktop, and Painter will remember the palette arrangement until you choose to return to the default palette arrangement. To save a layout permanently, choose Window, Arrange Palettes, Save Layout and when the Save Layout dialog box appears, name it and click OK. (We saved a layout that included our Pastel Painting custom palette and a favorite arrangement of the Art Materials palette, so that we could choose it by name from the Window menu.) To delete a layout, choose Window, Arrange Palettes, Delete Layout and choose the layout you want to remove from the list. To return to Painter's default palette arrangement, choose Window, Arrange Palettes, Default.

KEEPING FAVORITE ITEMS ON THE FRONT OF DRAWER

Clicking on an item inside a drawer may be an easy way to select a new tool, but if you want *total* control over the arrangement of items on the front of the palette's drawer, don't click on items. Instead, drag them from the drawer directly to the desired positions on the front. (Dragging to the front of the drawer—or clicking on an item inside the drawer—causes the previous occupant of the space to be displaced by a new occupant.)

To keep a frequently used item on the front of a palette's drawer, click and hold the item for one second. When the tiny green light appears below the item, it's locked, meaning it's kept out of the drawer-to-front cycle. Click and hold again for a second to unlock and return the item to the rotation.

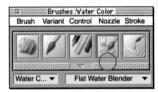

A green light indicates a locked item.

CHANGING A CUSTOM PALETTE

You can add items to an existing custom palette, delete items from it or change the palette's layout. To *add* an art material (such as a brush, a texture or a grad), drag it directly into the palette. And a bonus: You can also drag items from one custom palette to another.

To *add* a menu command choose Window, Custom Palette, Add Command, then select the menu item. To delete *any* item, press the Ctrl, Shift and Alt/Option keys, and when the trash can cursor appears, click on the item to delete it. To move an item, press the Ctrl and Shift keys, and when the four-arrowed cursor appears, drag the item to a new location in the palette.

We arranged our pastel painting palette horizontally, so we could keep it along the bottom of our image canvas. We included the Square Chalk, Sharp Chalk and Oil Pastel variants of Dry Media and the Ribbed Pastel, Hand-Made and Basic Paper textures.

You'll find the Load Library command at the bottom of the resource list on the Brushes palette and on some sections of the expandable Art Materials and Objects palettes.

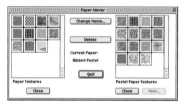

Dragging an item into the Pastel Painting Textures library

The open Papers section's drawer showing the newly created Pastel Painting Textures library, filled with interesting textures

LIBRARIES AND MOVERS

Painter uses *libraries* and *movers* to help you manage the huge volume of custom textures, brushes and other items that the program can generate. Libraries are the "storage bins" for those items, and movers let you customize those bins by transferring items into or out of them.

How libraries work. You'll find the Load Library command at the bottom of every palette that has a resource list—for instance, the brush list on the Brushes palette, the paper list on the Papers section of the Art Materials palette and the Script list on the Scripts section of the Objects palette. Scroll down to the bottom of the list and choose Load Library to display the standard Mac or Windows Open dialog box so you can search through folders on any hard disk or CD-ROM (like the Painter 6 CD-ROM or the Wow! CD-ROM) until you find the library you want; then double-click to open it. Fortunately, Painter is smart enough to show only libraries that can be opened in the palette of origin. For instance, if you clicked on the Library button in the Papers section, you'll see Paper libraries only, not the Gradients or Brushes libraries.

Using movers to customize your libraries. If you find that you're continually switching Paper texture libraries, it's probably time to use the Paper Mover to compile several textures into a single library for your work. For instance, you can create a Paper texture library containing favorite textures that work well with Painters's grain-sensitive Dry Media brushes and the Chalky Brushes library on the Wow! CD-ROM—such as Raw Silk, Hand-Made and Big Grain Rough (from Painter's

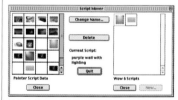

The Script library containing special effects "macros" that can be applied to images

CHER THREINEN-PENDARVIS

For this illustration of a Queen Parrotfish, we used brushes included in the custom Oil Painting and Pastel Painting palettes (described on pages 16 and 17) .We laid in color for an underpainting with the oil-painting brushes (including the Round Camelhair), then we added texture to areas of the image by painting with grain-sensitive brushes (the Square Chalk variant of Dry Media, for instance), which was included in the Pastel Painting palette.

EXPRESSIVE MOUSE-PAINTING

Painter 6 offers more expressive painting for mouse users using Stroke Data that was recorded using a pressure-sensitive stylus.

To use the Painter 6's default Stroke Data, choose Use Stroke Data from the Stroke menu and select a saved brushstroke from the list. Make a new brushstroke with your mouse. The resulting brush-stroke will vary with pressure based on the information saved in the stroke data file.

default paper texture library), Big Canvas, and Small Canvas (from the More Paper Textures library in the Paper Texture librar-ies folder on the Painter 6 CD-ROM), and Ribbed Deckle and Sandy texture, both from the Drawing Paper Textures library (in the Content Sampler folder within Painter 6's application folder).

Here's how to build this custom paper library: On the Art Materi-als palette, click the right triangle on the Papers section bar to open the pull-down menu and choose Paper Mover. In the Paper Mover, create a new, empty Paper library by clicking on the New button on the right side of the mover, then name your Paper Texture file and save it. (We named ours Pastel Painting Textures.) To copy a texture from the left side of the mover (your currently active library) into the new library, select a texture's icon on the left side of the mover: The name of the selected texture will appear in the center of the mover window; drag the texture icon from the origi-nal library (left side) and drop it into the new library (right side).

Continue adding textures to the new library in this fashion. We selected each of the four textures from the More Paper Tex-tures library and dropped each icon into the new Pastel Painting Textures library. Next, we added the Sandy texture from the Draw-ing Paper Textures library to our new library. To add a texture from another library to your new library, click on the left-hand Close button, then click again when it changes to an Open but-ton and open the next library that you want to draw from. (Don't forget the libraries on the Wow! and Painter 6 Application CD-ROMs!) We selected the Sandy texture and dragged and dropped it to our new library. When you've finished, click Quit. Now open your new library by choosing Load Library from the Papers section's paper list menu. If you want your new library to open every time you launch Painter, choose Edit, Preferences, General and type its exact name in the Papers box.

All movers work in the same way, so you can follow the above procedure to, say, create a new Brushes library that contains the only five brushes that you ever use. (See "Expressive Custom Brushes" in Chapter 3 on page 91, for an example of using the Brush mover.)

WET PAINT AND CROPPING

If you've been painting with Water Color brushes, and attempt to crop your image or increase its canvas size (by choosing Canvas, Canvas Size), you'll be greeted with a polite dialog box that says "You must turn off Wet Paint before changing your canvas size." To turn off the Wet Paint, choose Canvas, Dry. On the other hand, if you'd like to continue to paint using Water Color brushes in the wet-into-wet style without drying the paint, wait until your image is complete before changing its size.

2

THE POWER OF COLOR

Margaret Sweeney used reds, oranges and yellows with stark shadows to depict warmth at midday in Sketchers, *as shown in this detail. To see more of Sweeney's work, turn to the gallery at the end of Chapter 3.*

Colors section bar

Color (Hue) ring

Color triangle

Color rectangles

HSV/RGB color readout

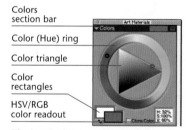

The Standard Color picker with Hue ring opened by expanding the Colors section bar

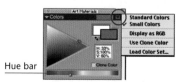

Hue bar

The Colors section command menu opens so you can switch between the Standard and Small Color pickers

"COLOR, THE FRUIT OF LIGHT, is the foundation of the painter's means of painting—and its language." Abstract painter Robert Delaunay's observation mirrors our own appreciation of color as an expressive and essential element of the visual arts. Getting the most out of Painter's powerful color tools is an important first step for those of us who work with "the fruit of light."

HUE, SATURATION AND VALUE

Painter's interface for choosing color is built around a model that uses *hue*, *saturation* and *value* (HSV) as the three basic properties of color. The program is designed so that you'll typically first choose a hue, then alter it by changing its saturation or value. Painter's Standard Color picker and Small Color picker are designed to work with these properties, but the program also allows you to work in RGB (red, green, blue) color space if you prefer. Clicking the triangle on the left end of the Colors section bar in the Art Materials palette (Window, Show Art Materials) opens the HSV Colors section. To switch between Standard and Small Color pickers, click the triangle at the top right of the Colors section bar to access the pull-down menu. To specify RGB rather than HSV, open the RGB Color section of the Art Materials palette by clicking the triangle on the RGB Color section bar.

> ### QUICK SWITCH TO RGB
> Click on the HSV color readout on the Standard or Small Colors picker to show color readings in RGB mode. Click again to switch back to HSV.

Hue. The term *hue* refers to a predominant spectral color, such as red or blue-green. Hue indicates a color's position on the color wheel or spectrum, and also tells us the color's temperature. A red-orange hue is the warmest color; a blue-green hue is the coolest. (Keep in mind, though, that temperatures are relative.

The RGB Color section with Red, Green and Blue sliders. (We moved the RGB Color section nearer to the Colors section in Art Materials. To move it, drag the RGB section bar.)

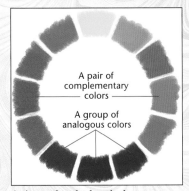

A pigment-based color wheel

Saturating a color

Desaturating a color

Creating a shade of a color

Creating a tint of a color

Blue-violet is a cool color, but it warms up when it's placed next to blue-green.)

In the traditional pigment-based color system, red, yellow and blue are *primary* hues—colors that cannot be obtained by mixing. *Secondary* hues—green, orange and violet—are those colors located midway between two primary colors on the color wheel. Yellow-green, blue-violet and red-orange are examples of *tertiary* hues, each found between a primary and a secondary color.

Analogous hues are adjacent to each other on the color wheel and have in common a shared component—for instance, blue-green, blue and blue-violet. *Complementary hues* sit opposite one another on the color wheel. Red and green are complements, as are blue and orange. (Painter's Hue ring and bar are based on the RGB components of the computer screen, so it doesn't exactly match a traditional pigment-based color wheel.)

To change hues in Painter's Standard Color picker, drag the little circle on the Hue ring or click anywhere on the ring. Dragging and clicking also work with the Hue bar in the Small Color picker.

Saturation. Also known as *intensity* or *chroma*, *saturation* indicates a color's purity or strength. The most common way of changing a color's saturation is by adjusting the amount of its gray component. In the Color triangle, move the little circle to the left to desaturate a color, or to the right to saturate it. Fully or very saturated colors—those at or near the tip of the Color triangle—won't print the way they look on the screen. If you want to see colors closer to their printed equivalents while you paint, the Canvas, Output Preview, Kodak Color Correction command can help. (See Chapter 12, "Printing and Archival Concerns" and Chapter 19 of the *Painter 6 User Guide.*)

Value. A color's lightness or darkness is its *luminance* or *value.* To create a *tint* of a color

SAMPLING PAINT

While you're using many of Painter's other tools, you can temporarily switch to the Dropper tool and sample colors by holding down the Ctrl/⌘ key.

A COLOR PREVIEW

As you drag the circle in the HSV triangle or Hue ring (or slider on the Hue bar), Painter 6 compares the previous color you'd clicked on (right) with the new color (left) in the front Color rectangle. The entire color rectangle updates when the mouse or stylus is lifted. The front rectangle in the RGB Color section also updates as you drag in the Color section, but not if you drag the RGB Color sliders.

Dragging to choose a new color in the Small Color picker; the RGB Color picker updates automatically in response.

An example of atmospheric perspective. The illusion of distance is enhanced in Mendocino Point *because the distant coastal hills are painted with reduced saturation and less value contrast.*

As you can see in this detail of 1872, *Richard Noble used saturated color, clear detail and strong contrast to paint a bright morning. To see more of Noble's work turn to the galleries at the end of Chapters 2 and 3.*

A study in value contrast, based on a drawing by Michelangelo

Inspired by Monet, Dennis Orlando modulated shadows with complementary color in Bend in the Epte.

(lightening it, or increasing its value), move the little circle higher in the Color triangle. To create a *shade* of a color (darkening it, or decreasing its value), move the little circle lower in the Color triangle.

PUTTING HSV TO WORK

Here are several practical suggestions and creative solutions for solving artistic problems using hue, saturation and value.

Reduce saturation and value to indicate distance. Artists have been creating *atmospheric* (or *aerial*) *perspective* in their work for thousands of years. The wall paintings of Pompeii in the first century B.C. show this technique. Hills we see in the distance have less intensity than nearer hills, and they also have less variation in value. This effect increases in hazy or foggy conditions. To depict this in your art, you can reduce the color saturation and value range as the landscape recedes from the foreground.

Use saturation to indicate time of day. At dawn or dusk, colors appear to be less saturated, and it becomes more difficult to distinguish colors. At noon on a bright sunny day, colors seem saturated and distinct.

Use color temperature to indicate distance. The eye puts warm colors in front of cool colors. For example, orange flowers in the foreground of a hedge appear closer than blue ones.

Create drama with light-to-dark value contrast. Baroque and Romantic period artists as diverse as Caravaggio, Zurbarán, Géricault and Rembrandt are known for their use of extreme light-to-dark contrast. They accomplished this by limiting their palette to only a few hues, which they either tinted with white or shaded by adding black. A close look at the shadows and highlights that these artists created reveals complex, modulated tone. Digital artists can use Painter's Apply Lighting feature (from Effects, Surface Control) to add a dramatic splash of contrast to an image and also to unify a painting's color scheme, although achieving genuine tonal complexity requires additional painting.

Use complementary colors to create shadows. The Impressionists Monet, Renoir and Degas frequently avoided the use of black in the shadow areas of their paintings. They embraced a more subjective view of reality by layering complementary colors to create luminous shadows.

Neutralize with a complement or gray. One way to tone down a hue is to paint on top of it with a translucent form of its complement. El Greco painted his backgrounds in this manner to draw attention to more saturated foreground subjects. Try painting with a bright green hue, then glaze over it with a reduced opacity of red. The result will be an earthy olive. You can also neutralize a hue using shades of gray, as did the French artist

For a look of soft watercolor washes, we blended color on the hills using the Grainy Water variant in Punta San Antonio.

Simultaneous contrast at work. Notice how the gold looks brighter next to the dark blue than it does next to pink.

Janet Martini used color to express intense emotion in Red Mask.

A landscape with figures, based on Mahana no atua (The Day of the God) *by Paul Gauguin*

Ingres. Although he often limited his palette to red, blue, gold and flesh tones, he created the illusion of a larger palette by adding varying proportions of gray and white.

Blending, pulling and thinning colors. Subtle changes in hue and saturation take place when colors are blended in a painting. You can use the Just Add Water or Grainy Water variant of the Liquid brush (from the Brushes palette) to blend, for instance, two primary colors (red and blue) to get a secondary color (violet). For a more dramatic blending, you can pull one color into another by using the Smear variant of the Liquid brush. Artists using traditional tools often thin paint by mixing it with an extender. In Painter, you get a similar effect by reducing a brush's Opacity in the Controls:Brush palette.

Draw attention with simultaneous contrast. If two complementary colors are placed next to one another, they intensify each other: Blue looks more blue next to orange, and white looks more white next to black. In the 1950s, Op artists used the principle of simultaneous contrast to baffle the eye. Advertising art directors understand the power of simultaneous contrast and use it to gain attention for their ads.

Use a family of colors to evoke an emotional response. You can create a calm, restful mood by using an analogous color theme of blues and blue-greens. Or develop another family of hues using reds and red-oranges to express passion and intensity. You can also use a color family to unite the elements of a composition.

Create your own color world. Post-Impressionist Paul Gauguin (among others) created a powerful, personal color language by combining several of the above techniques. He used warm, bright colors to bring a subject forward in his composition, and used cool, dark colors to convey distance and mystery. He also made the bright foreground colors seem brighter by surrounding them with darker, more subdued colors.

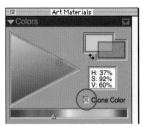

When the Clone Color box is checked, the Color picker is disabled

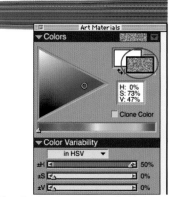

These brushstrokes were painted with the Round Camelhair variant of the Brushes and Color Variability: top, Hue slider only set to 50%; middle, Saturation slider only set to 50%; bottom, Value slider only set to 50%.

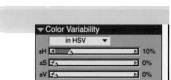

Both of these brushstrokes were painted with the Broad Water Brush variant of the Water Color brush and increased Hue variability of 10%.

PAINTING WITH MULTIPLE COLORS

Painter has several brushes that can paint with more than one color at a time if you use the settings in the Color Variability section of the Art Materials palette (Window, Show Art Materials). Brushes with the Rake or Multi stroke type or the new Bristle Spray, Camel Hair or Flat dab types have the capability to paint with multiple colors. The Van Gogh variant of the Artists brush and the Round Camel Hair variant of the Brushes are examples.

Randomize colors with Color Variability. To see how multicolor works, open the Color Variability section of the Art Materials palette by clicking the triangle on the Color Variability bar. In the Brushes palette, choose the Round Camelhair variant of the Brushes; its Camel Hair dab type has the potential to carry a different color on each brush hair. In the Color picker choose a color and begin painting. Then experiment by adjusting the Hue (± H), Saturation (± S) or Value (± V) slider and painting again.

Also try the Broad Water Brush variant of the Water Color brush. The Broad Water Brush incorporates the Rake stroke type; each "tine" of a Rake brush can paint with a different color. In the Color Variability section, set Hue to 10% (for a subtle variation) or much higher (for a rainbow-like effect) and make brushstrokes on your image. For a graphic version of this method try adding Color Variability to the Scratchboard Rake variant of the Pens.

Using Color Variability based on a gradient. With Painter 6, you can paint with multiple colors from a gradient instead of using completely random Color Variability. To begin, set all the Color Variability sliders

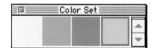

Brushstroke painted with the Opaque Bristle Spray variant using Color Variability based on the current gradient. Note that the front rectangle in the Color picker updates to include both colors from the active two-point gradient.

The Pastel Colors set

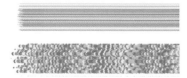

Brushstrokes painted with the Smeary Flat (above) and the Dry Ink (below) variants of the Brushes using Color Variability based on the Pastel Colors set.

to 0; open the Colors section of the Art Materials palette and set up the colors for a two-point gradient by clicking on the front color rectangle and selecting a color, then clicking on the back color rectangle and selecting a color. In the Gradients section, choose Two-Point from the pop-up menu. From the Brushes palette select the Opaque Bristle Spray variant of the Brushes. In the Color Variability palette, choose From Gradient from the pop-up menu, then make brushstrokes on your image. (This is a useful feature, but there are some inconsistencies as of this writing. If the brush does not immediately paint using the Color Variability from the gradient, click the little circle in the Color picker to help it to update.)

Using Color Variability based on a color set. You can create a special Color Set containing a few colors and then use those colors when painting. Begin by opening the Color Variability section of the Art Materials; set Color Variability to "in HSV" and the ± H, ±S, and ±V sliders to 0. Open the Color Set section and click on the New Set button. A very small Color Set title bar will appear. Choose a color in the Color picker. Click on the Add Color button to add the current color to the Color Set. Continue to select and add more colors by using the Color picker and clicking the Add Color button. To save your colors, click on the Library button in the Color Set section, then click Save, name the set and Save. We named ours "Pastel Colors." Choose the Smeary Flat variant of the Brushes, and in the Color Variability section, set Color Variability to "from Color Set." Paint brushstrokes on your image. To learn more about color sets turn to "Keep Colors in Color Sets," on page 28 and to "Capturing a Color Set," later in this chapter.

Change colors with stylus pressure. Use your pressure-sensitive stylus to paint in two colors. Start by choosing the Captured Bristle variant of the Brushes. In the Expression section of the Brush Controls palette choose Pressure from the Color pop-up menu. In the Standard or Small Color picker, click on the front color rectangle and choose a bright blue color. Click the back Color rectangle and select a rose color. If you paint with a light touch, you'll be painting in rose. If you press heavily, the stroke turns blue. (If the balance between the two colors seems uneven,

> **MORE COLORFUL STROKES**
>
> To paint with two colors using criteria other than pressure, open the Brush Controls:Expression palette and move the Color pop-up menu to Velocity. Once you get started, moving slowly paints using the color in the front color rectangle; speeding your strokes to paints with the back color. Now change the Color menu to Direction. Start drawing horizontal brushstrokes (front color) and then gradually turn the strokes vertical (back color).

choose Edit, Preferences, Brush Tracking. Make a typical brushstroke in the Scratch Pad area, click OK, and try the graduated version of the Captured Bristle variant again.)

Before and after: Sampling in the image with the Dropper to determine the color cast of a bright highlight on the aluminum foil reveals these values: Red: 227, Green: 241, and Blue 213 (left); the corrected image (right) with pure white highlights shows Red, Green and Blue values of 255.

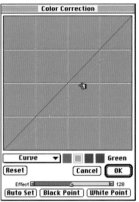

Pulling the Green color curve in the Color Correction dialog box to lessen the green cast in the image above. The biggest change in color occurs at the point where you pull the curve. If you pull the dot, the color you sampled will be affected most. The Effect slider controls how much of the curve will change when you pull on it. Move the slider to the right to affect a broad range of tones. Move the slider to the left to affect a narrower range of tones.

MAKING COLOR ADJUSTMENTS

Painter offers several ways to modify color in scanned photos or in your art work *after* you have created it. To see the results of your choices in many of the dialog boxes that are involved in color adjustments, you'll need to click and drag in the Preview window.

Correct Colors. Do you see an unnatural color cast in your image? The Correct Colors, Curve feature can help you fix this problem. This feature is especially useful when working with scanned photos, for instance.

To adjust an image so that the brightest highlights are pure white, begin by analyzing the color cast. (To ensure that the front Color rectangle in the Color picker will show the color you are about to sample, make sure that "in HSV" is chosen from the pop-out menu in the Color Variability section.) Use the Dropper tool to sample a bright highlight in your image. In the Colors section, click on the HSV values box to toggle to RGB values. Check the RGB values in the Color palette. In our example, the color and numbers show that the unwanted color cast is green. A bright white should have R, G and B values of 255 in the Color picker. Choose Effects, Tonal Control, Correct Colors and choose Curve from the pop-up menu. Curve will allow you to adjust the individual RGB values. Click on the small square icon for the color that you want to adjust. (We clicked on the Green color icon—to constrain the adjustment to *only* the green values in the image.) Then, position the cross-hair cursor over the diagonal line, and when you see the hand cursor appear, pull down and to the right. Pulling down (as shown) will decrease the selected color in the image. Click the Reset button to try out another adjustment without leaving the dialog box.

Adjust Colors. To change the hue, saturation or value of all of the colors in an image, choose Effects, Tonal Control, Adjust Colors. Experiment with the sliders and view the changes in the Preview window. Adjust Colors is also useful for quickly desaturating a full-color image—making it black-and-white. To desaturate an image, move the Saturation slider all the way to the left.

Adjust Selected Colors. You may want to make color adjustments in particular color ranges of your image. Painter's Adjust Selected Colors feature lets you make dramatic changes (turning a blue sky yellow) or more subtle ones (removing the red cast from a subject's face). Choose Effects, Tonal Control, Adjust Selected

COMPLEMENTARY COLORS

The Curve mode of the Color Correction dialog box (Effects, Tonal Control, Correct Colors, Curve) and some other dialog boxes let you increase or decrease the Red, Green and Blue components of color. You can also adjust cyan, magenta and yellow by applying the opposite adjustments to their complements—Red, Green and Blue: To decrease yellow, increase blue; to decrease magenta, increase Green; and to decrease cyan, increase Red.

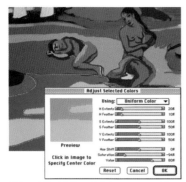

Using Adjust Selected Colors to neutralize a bright blue

We added colored texture to this photo with Color Overlay.

Susan LeVan used Effects, Tonal Control, Negative on the right side of the background of Two Birds in Hand *as shown in this detail.*

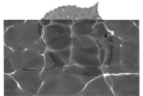

In this image, we applied the Darken composite method to the leaf layer.

Colors. When the dialog box opens, click in your image (*not* in the Preview window) on the color you want to change. Adjust the Hue Shift, Saturation and Value sliders at the bottom of the dialog box. When the basic effect is in place, use low settings on the Extents sliders to limit the range of colors that are adjusted. Use the Feather sliders to adjust transitions between colors: 100% produces soft transition, 0% gives abrupt ones.

Color Overlay. Found under Effects, Surface Control, the Color Overlay dialog box lets you tint an image with a color using either a Dye Concentration model (which applies *transparent* color) or a Hiding Power model (which covers the image with the *opaque* color). With either model you can add texture by choosing Paper in the pop-up menu, as we did in the illustration at the left. When using the Dye Concentration model, adjust the Amount slider to control the density of the color: 0% for no effect; to 100% or –100% for full transparent coverage. The Hiding Power model operates differently. You can add color using a plus value, or pull color out of an image using a minus value. Try this to see how it works: open a new image and make a rectangular selection. Choose a yellow-green in the Color picker (approximately H 58%, S 92%, V 43%). Fill the selection using Effects, Fill, Current Color. Choose yellow in the Color picker (ours was H 50%, S 94%, V 70%) then choose Effects, Surface Control, Color Overlay, Using Uniform Color and Hiding Power. Move the Opacity slider to 100% to see the yellow completely cover the yellow-green. Finally, move the Opacity slider to –100% to the see some of the yellow disappear from the green.

Dye Concentration. With Effects, Surface Control, Dye Concentration you can add or remove pigment from your image. Setting the Maximum slider above 100% increases the pigment density. When you choose Paper in the Using menu, the Maximum slider controls the amount of dye on the peaks and the Minimum slider controls the amount of dye in the valleys of the texture.

Negative. Creating a negative of all or part of an image can have dramatic, artistic purposes—such as in the detail of Susan LeVan's illustration, at left. Choose Effects, Tonal Control, Negative to convert your image.

Coloring using layer compositing. With Painter's Composite Methods you can change how a layer interacts with the image underneath, affecting the color in your image. For more about layers and to see examples of how Painter's 21 Composite Methods affect color, turn to page 151 in Chapter 5, "Using Layers and Shapes."

Output Preview and Video Colors. Your monitor can display more colors than can be reproduced in the four-color printing process, and if you are creating images for video, some highly saturated colors will not make the transition to video. It's a good idea to convert your out-of-gamut colors while you're in Painter

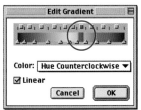

This is how Painter 6's Expressive Greens gradient appears in the Gradient Editor. When you click a square hue box in the Gradient Editor, the Color Hue pop-up menu appears, here it's set to Hue Counterclockwise, resulting in a small spectrum below the square hue box.

While painting Love Connection, *Kathy Blavatt filled areas of her pen drawing with color using the Paint Bucket.*

NAMING AND FINDING COLORS

To name your colors so you can search for them by name, double-click on the color in the Color Set that you want to name, type a name and click OK. To view color names, click on the Display Text button at the bottom of the Color Sets palette. To search for a named color in a set, click the Find Color button.

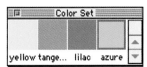

The Pastels Color Set (from page 25) with names displayed

RESTORING DEFAULT COLORS

To restore the default Color Set (called Painter Colors) after you've used or created another Color Set, click the Library button and find the Painter Colors file in your Painter 6 folder on your hard disk.

so there won't be any surprises. Choose Canvas, Output Preview, Kodak Color Correction or Effects, Tonal Control, Video Legal Colors, depending on whether your image is destined for paper or video. For more information about Kodak Output Preview, turn to Chapter 12, "Printing and Archival Concerns."

MORE COLOR TOOLS

Adding color with Gradations. Painter's powerful Gradients palette lets you fill selected areas with preset gradations or ones that you've created. (See "Adding Color and Gradations to Line Art" later in this chapter.) You can also colorize an image with a gradation using Express In Image from the pop-up menu in the Gradients section of the Art Materials palette. To see an example of this technique, turn to "Making a Sepia Tone" in Chapter 6.

The gradient editor is a powerful tool for creating custom color ramps. You can't use this tool to alter all of Painter's existing gradations, however, it is used primarily for creating new ones. On the Art Materials palette, click the left triangle on the Gradient section bar to open the section, then click the right triangle, and choose Edit Gradient from the pop-up menu to bring up the gradient editor. Select one of the triangular color control points and choose a color from the Color picker. The color ramp will update to reflect your choice. Add new color control points by clicking directly in the color bar; the control points are sliders that can be positioned anywhere along the ramp. To delete a control point, select it and press the Delete key; Alt/Option-click on the color bar to add a new control point in the current color. Clicking on any of the squares above the ramp brings up the Color menu; experiment with the options available there to get quick rainbow effects in the section of the gradient indicated by the square. To store the new gradient in the Gradients section, choose Save Grad from the Gradient pop-up menu.

Coloring images. You can color images or selected parts of images using either Effects, Fill (Ctrl/⌘-F) or the Paint Bucket tool. The Fill command lets you fill your image with a color, a gradient, a clone source (if one is available), a pattern (if no clone source is available) or a weave. The Paint Bucket gives you the same fill options. (The Paint Bucket options appear on the Controls palette when you select the Paint Bucket tool.) Cartoonists and others who fill line art with color will want to explore the Lock Out Color feature (to preserve black line art, for example) made available by double-clicking on the Paint Bucket tool icon in the Tools palette.

Keeping colors in Color Sets. Painter can store your most frequently used colors in the Color Sets section of Art Materials. Painter Colors is the default set. Switch Color Sets by clicking on the Library button in the Color Sets section. You'll find more Color Sets (including a full Pantone set) in the Color Sets folder on the Painter 6 application CD-ROM. For more about Color Sets, turn to "Capturing a Color Set" on page 36.

Colorizing Scratchboard

Overview *Create black-and-white art; float it and apply the Gel Composite Method; view the black-and-white art as you paint on the background in color.*

CHET PHILLIPS

Phillips' black-and-white scratchboard art

Choosing the Gel Composite Method

Color added to the image background viewed with visibility of the black-filled layer turned off.

HERE'S AN EFFICIENT WAY TO ADD COLOR to black-and-white art, a favorite technique of artist Chet Phillips. To paint *The Three Bears*, Phillips used a layer and the Gel Composite Method, which makes the white areas of the layer appear transparent.

1 Creating black-and-white art. Start a new document with a white background. Choose black for the front color square in the Color picker, then Effects, Fill (Command-F) using Current Color. Click OK. Use white and the Scratchboard Tool variant of the Pens brush to "etch" into the black fill.

2 Making a layer. Select All (Ctrl/⌘-A), choose the Adjuster tool and click once on the image to float it. The black-and-white image is now floating over a white background. In the Controls palette, choose Gel from the Composite Method pop-up menu. This method makes the white areas of the layer transparent, which will allow any color you will add to the background in step 2 to completely show through without affecting the black in the layer.

3 Painting on the background. In the Layers section of the Objects palette, click the canvas layer's name. This makes sure that you'll be painting on the background. Choose a brush and a color and begin painting. To view either without the other, toggle the eye icon to the left of the layer name. Phillips used the Digital Airbrush variant of the Airbrushes in varying sizes and colors. In addition to painting freehand with the brush, he also made selections and filled the selections with color (Effects, Fill). If you need to edit the black areas, click on the black-filled layer's name in the Layers palette and then paint.

Coloring a Scanned Illustration

Overview *Scan a traditional black-and-white pen drawing; clean up the scanned line art; use the Paint Bucket to fill areas with flat color; create texture and energy with a variety of brushes.*

WENDY MORRIS

The raw scan of the Rapidograph pen drawing

WENDY MORRIS'S WHIMSICAL DRAWING STYLE appears to be a quick, spontaneous expression; but her illustrations begin by drawing carefully with traditional pen and ink. In Morris's *Beeman*, the sky is vibrant and charged with frenetic bee energy. *Beeman* was colored with Paint Bucket fills and a variety of brushes.

1 Creating a pen drawing and scanning. Morris chose a bright white recycled drawing paper with a smooth finish and created a black-and-white line drawing using a conventional Rapidograph pen. She intended to use the *Beeman* illustration for a 6 x 8-inch greeting card design that would be printed with off-set lithography so she scanned the line drawing using grayscale mode at 100% magnification with a resolution of 300ppi. She saved the scan as a TIFF file and opened it in Painter, which automatically converted the grayscale art to RGB. To learn more about scanning and resolution, see Chapter 1, "Getting To Know Painter" and Chapter 12, "Printing and Archival Concerns."

2 Cleaning up the scan. Morris adjusted the contrast of the scanned line work using Brightness/Contrast. To make the adjustment on your scan, choose Effects, Tonal Control, Brightness/

Adjusting the Brightness and Contrast
"beef up" the line work

Cleaning up specks of black on the scan

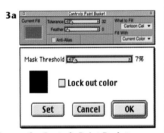

Setting up the Controls:Paint Bucket
palette and the Mask Threshold dialog box
to make Cartoon Cel fills

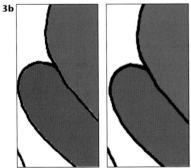

Color fills with halos (left), and color fills
made with the Cartoon Cel method,
showing no halos (right)

Contrast. When the dialog box appears, you can thicken or thin the line work by moving the Brightness slider (the bottom one of the two) to the left or to the right, respectively. Then, to get rid of any fuzziness along the edge that resulted from the Brightness change, increase the Contrast by moving the top slider to the right. (Keep in mind that moving it too far to the right can create a pixelated edge rather than a smooth one.) Each time you move one of the sliders, you can see the tonal adjustment on your image.

Then Morris cleaned up the specks of black on the scan by choosing white in the Color picker, and touching up areas with the Pen and Ink variant of the Pens, found in Painter 5.5 Brushes, in the Brushes folder on the Painter 6 Application CD-ROM. (To read about loading libraries, turn to "Libraries and Movers" in Chapter 1, "Getting To Know Painter.") She switched to black color, and used the pen to repair any breaks in the black lines. (The lines must be completely solid to constrain the Paint Bucket fills that follow in step 3.)

3 Filling areas with flat color. After Morris had adjusted the contrast of the line art, to establish the color theme, she used the Paint Bucket tool to fill the flower petals, stems and sky with flat color. When the Paint Bucket is used to fill areas within scanned black-and-white line art, halos (partially unfilled areas) can appear along the edges of the anti-aliased black lines. In Painter 6 there are at least two ways to prevent these halos: One approach involves layering a copy of your original line work over a thinned version of the lines and filling the thinner lines with color. This way any halos that develop on the layer below will be hidden by the original, thicker lines in the layer above. This method is easy to understand and carry out, and it makes it easy to change colors later if you want to. The technique is described in the "Trapping Fills Using a Transparent Layer" tip on page 33. However, if you feel that using extra layers would get in the way of the "painterly" experience of applying color to a single layer of canvas, the Cartoon Cel method may be the technique for you. It works by allowing the fill color to "seep into" the anti-aliasing pixels at the edge of the line work, leaving no halo. This method is described next.

There are three essential parts to the Cartoon Cel fill method: (1) making a selection based on luminance, (2) setting the Paint Bucket's Mask Threshold and filling criteria and (3) choosing a color and filling.

First select the black lines in the image using Select, Auto Select, Using Image Luminance, and click OK.

Second, in the Tools palette, double-click the Paint Bucket to open the Mask Threshold dialog box and set the Mask Threshold low—moving the slider to a point between 7% and 14% usually works well. Click OK to close the dialog box. In the Controls:Paint Bucket palette, under What to Fill choose Cartoon Cel, and under Fill With, choose Current Color.

The petals and stems filled with color

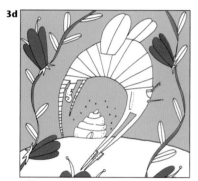

Filling the image with flat color fills

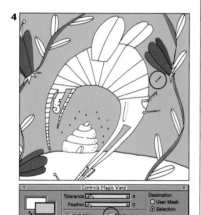

Using the Magic Wand to select the sky

Third, open the Color Variability section of the Art Materials palette, choose "In HSV" from the pop-up menu and set the (± H), (± S) and (± V) sliders to 0, this will allow you to choose a flat color in the Colors section. Click with the Paint Bucket in one of the white spaces enclosed by the black lines. Then examine the resulting color fill. (To get a better look at the edge, you can choose Select, Hide Marquee. You can also zoom in by clicking on the image with the Magnifier tool.) If the fill has overrun the lines, the Mask Threshold is set too low. On the other hand, if you see a halo at the edge, the setting is too high. If you need to refill, first undo then fill—Edit, Undo—and then change the Mask Threshold setting and fill again. Once you have a satisfactory fill, you should be able to use the same Mask Threshold setting throughout your drawing.

Morris filled the flower petals with three shades of a purple-pink color. Then she filled the stems and sky with other colors.

4 Making a selection with the Magic Wand. In preparation for the next step, when she planned to paint lively brushstrokes across the sky, Morris isolated the entire sky area (based on its color) by making a selection using the Magic Wand. To select all of the blue sky areas at once, she chose the Magic Wand in the Tools palette, unchecked the Contiguous check box on the Controls: Magic Wand palette, and clicked on a blue sky area in her image. To read more about the Magic Wand and selections, turn to the beginning of Chapter 4, "Selections, Shapes and Masks."

5 Painting with brushes. Morris used the Dropper tool to sample sky color in her image, then she used the Variable Flat variant of the Brushes to paint "helter-skelter style" brushstrokes across the sky. The Variable Flat incorporates enhanced Color Variability, which allowed the value of the color to change subtly as she painted. For more subtle brushstrokes, she lowered the opacity using the Opacity slider on the Controls:Brush palette.

6 Adding texture and details. After completing the flat color fills and the brushwork in the sky, Morris used the Dirty Marker variant of the Felt Pens to modulate color in the plant stems, then she used a low-opacity Digital Airbrush variant of the Airbrushes to paint soft shadows on the leaves and stems. To add texture to the ground, she used the Scratchboard Rake variant of the Pens.

Next, Morris added movement and energy to the bee swarm and the beeman's stinger. She chose black in the Colors section and used the Pixel Dust variant of the Pens to paint spiraling strokes behind the bee's stinger and above the hive. (The Pixel Dust pen is located in the Painter 5.5 Brushes library, on the Painter 6 Application CD-ROM.)

5

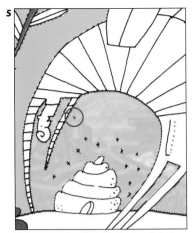

Painting on the sky with free brushstrokes

6a

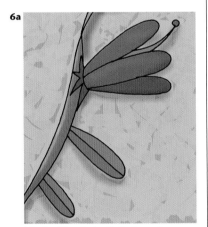

Morris airbrushed soft shadows along edges of the foliage.

6b

The image with fills and brushwork texture, prior to adding the bee swarm

Morris finished the piece using the Digital Airbrush to add more highlights and shadows to the bee, plants and flowers. She airbrushed a soft drop shadow along some of the edges on the beeman and the flowers. For more subtle brushstrokes, she lowered the opacity of all of the brushes (except the Pixel Dust pen), using the Opacity slider on the Controls:Brush palette.) The completed illustration can be seen at the top the page 30.

TRAPPING FILLS USING A TRANSPARENT LAYER

This method of coloring line art uses a transparent layer that contains slightly thicker lines to trap or hide the edges of the fills on the image canvas below. First, correct the contrast of your line art using Effects, Tonal Control, Brightness/Contrast, and retouch any black specks, as described in step 2 of "Coloring a Scanned Illustration" on pages 30 and 31.

Select the black line art by choosing Select, Auto Select Using Image Luminance. When the selection marquee appears, hold down Alt/Option (to copy), and choose Select, Float to make a transparent layer containing only the line art. (Layer 1 will appear in the Layers section of the Objects palette.) In the Layers section, turn off the visibility of the Layer 1 by clicking its eye icon off, then target the Canvas layer by clicking on its name. Make the lines thinner on the canvas, by choosing Effects, Tonal Control, Brightness/Contrast, and move both sliders to the right enough to thin the lines but not enough to make breaks in them (you may have to experiment with settings, depending on the thickness of your lines).

Now choose the Paint Bucket tool, and in the Controls:Paint Bucket palette, choose Image under What To Fill and Current Color under Fill With. Turn on Anti-Alias. Use the Dropper to sample black color from your line work. Open the Colors section of the Art Materials palette. Choose a new color, then click the Paint Bucket in a white area of the canvas. To complete the "trap" on your fill, toggle Layer 1's visibility back on by clicking its eye icon, and choose Multiply in the pop-up Composite Method menu at the top of the Layers section. You can inspect the result with the Magnifier tool. (To read more about Layers, turn to Chapter 5, "Using Layers and Shapes.")

The Objects:Layers section

Image canvas showing the flat color fills with halos

Image with Layer 1 in Multiply mode and with its visibility turned on

COLORING A SCANNED ILLUSTRATION   **33**

Adding Color and Gradations to Line Art

Overview *Use the Pens brush to create line art; use the Paint Bucket to fill areas with flat color and gradations; add highlights with the Airbrush.*

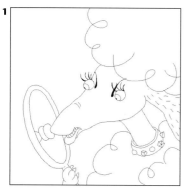

Line art created with the 1-Pixel variant of the Pens brush

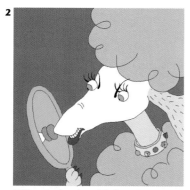

Filling the drawing with flat color

A TOLERANT PAINT BUCKET

To fill an area of modulated color with the Paint Bucket, use the Tolerance slider on the Controls:Paint Bucket palette to increase the amount of Tolerance. To sample a narrower color range, decrease the Tolerance setting.

LINDA DAVICK

FILLING LINE ART WITH COLOR AND GRADATIONS is slick and efficient in Painter, using what children's book illustrator Linda Davick calls "the coloring-book technique." Davick employed the Paint Bucket tool to create the vain, arrogant Zuba, the protagonist in Debbie Smith's *Beauty Blow-Up.*

1 Creating a black-and-white line drawing. Choose the Pens brush, 1-Pixel variant, and choose the Flat Cover submethod from the General section of the Brush Controls palette. Flat Cover lets you draw a solid-color line, a necessity for this technique that fills all neighboring pixels of the same color. Choose black (in the Color picker) and draw your line art, making sure all your shapes are completely enclosed with black lines. If you need to correct your work, switch the color to pure white in the Color picker and erase.

2 Filling with flat color. To test color choices and tonal values, you can fill areas of your illustration with flat color. First open the Color Variability section of the Art Materials palette, choose "in HSV" from the pop-up menu and set the ± H, ± S and ± V sliders to 0. Choose the Paint Bucket tool, and in the Controls:Paint Bucket palette (Window, Show Controls), choose Image under What To Fill and Current Color under Fill With. Turn off Anti-Alias. Choose a color, then click in the area of your drawing that you want to fill. Since the Paint Bucket fills all neighboring pixels of the same color, you can refill by choosing another color and

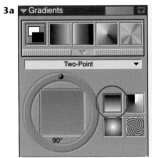

Setting up the Two-Point linear gradient

Filling the background with the gradient

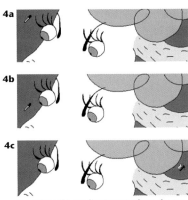

Sampling the gradient across from the top of the area to be filled (a); sampling across from the bottom of the area to be filled (b); filling the area with the gradation (c). Repeat this process for each flat color (negative) area to be filled.

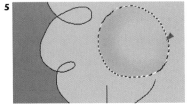

Adding dimension to Zuba's hair using the Digital Airbrush inside a selected area

clicking again. If you're filling small areas, it's important to know that the Paint Bucket's "hot spot" (where it fills from) is the tip of the red paint in the icon. Davick filled all areas except Zuba's face using this method.

3 Adding color ramps. To fill the background with a gradation, open the Gradients section of the Art Materials palette. Click the Two-Point icon at the top of the section (or choose Two-Point from the pop-up menu). Choose the Linear button (from the four Types buttons to the right of the direction ring), and set an angle for your fill by rotating the red ball around the direction ring. In the Art Materials:Colors section, choose colors for both the front and back Color rectangles. (Click on the front Color rectangle and select a color, then click on the back Color rectangle and select a color.) With the Paint Bucket chosen, in the Controls palette, choose Fill With Grad. Finally, to apply the gradation, click in the area that you want to fill. Davick filled the largest background area and the mirror with linear gradations.

4 Duplicating color ramps. To duplicate the large background gradation in each of the smaller background shapes—under Zuba's chin and below and above her ear—Davick created a new gradation using color sampled from areas in the background gradation. She then filled the smaller background shapes with the new gradation. If you need to do this on the "negative" shapes in your image, first check the Color palette to make sure that the Color rectangle that contains the starting color of your original gradation is selected. Choose the Dropper tool and position it over the gradation in your image at approximately the same height as the top of the negative area that you want to fill. Click in the gradation to sample the color. To sample the bottom portion of the gradation, select the opposite Color rectangle, then position and click the Dropper at about the same height as the bottom of the area to be filled. Click in the negative area using the Paint Bucket to fill with the new sampled gradation. (If you need to refill, undo the fill—Edit, Undo—before you fill again.)

5 Adding airbrush details. Davick finished the piece by painting with the Digital Airbrush variant of the Airbrushes within circular selections to add dimension to Zuba's hair and fur. You can make roughly circular selections using the Lasso tool by choosing the Lasso tool and dragging in your image. (To read more about selections, turn to the beginning of Chapter 4, "Selections, Shapes and Masks.") Now use the Airbrush to add dimension. Choose the Digital Airbrush and paint along the edge of the animated selection marquee. Davick used the same Airbrush with unrestricted strokes on Zuba's face and ear.

Capturing a Color Set

Overview *Capture color from a reference image using the Dropper; build and customize a Color Set; use the Color Set to paint a new image.*

1a

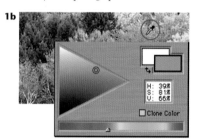

The reference photograph

1b

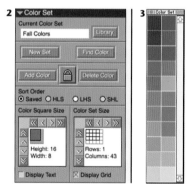

Using the Dropper to sample color from the image

2

The Color Set section

3

The Fall Colors Set

4

Applying colored brushstrokes with the Square Chalk using the Fall Colors Set

If you're planning a series of illustrations based on the same color theme, you'll find Color Sets invaluable. Use this technique of sampling color from a photo or painting to quickly build a full palette of colors as we did here to create the pastel painting *Tienda Verde*.

1 Sampling the color. Open your first image that contains the color range you want. Before you sample the color open the Color Variability section of the Art Materials palette, choose "In HSV" from the pop-up menu and set the (± H), (± S) and (± V) sliders to 0, then choose the Dropper tool and click it on a colored pixel in the image. The Colors section of the Art Materials palette will display the color. If the displayed color isn't the one you want, you can click and drag the Dropper around your image. The Colors section will update to show the new color as you drag.

2 Creating a Color Set. In the Art Materials palette, click on the Color Set section bar to open the Color Set section, and click on the New Set button. A very small Color Set title bar will appear. Click on the Add Color button to add the selected color to the Color Set. Continue to sample and add more colors by clicking Dropper and the Add Color button. To save your colors, click on the Library button in the Color Sets palette, then click Save, name the set and Save. We named ours "Fall Colors."

3 Arranging the Color Set display. You can arrange your colors in the Color Set to fit your drawing environment. To change the shape of the individual color squares, click on the Color Square Size arrow buttons, or click on Color Set Size arrow buttons to change the shape of the layout. We built our Color Set of 32-pixel-wide squares with 2 columns and 11 rows.

4 Using your new colors. To paint with the new Color Set, start a new file, click on a color in the set, choose a brush and begin painting. We drew a sketch using a dark blue-gray from our set with the 2B Pencil variant, and added brushstrokes in other colors using the variants of the Dry Media brush.

■ Creative use of saturated color, loose, illustrative strokes and an eclectic mix of brushes and paper textures let **Susan LeVan**, of LeVan/ Barbee Studio, create a strong emotional quality in her work.

In the Christmas card illustration *Two Birds in Hand* (right), LeVan used a palette composed primarily of moderately saturated colors, including many warm oranges and yellows, accented by pastels—creams, greens, blues and pinks. LeVan roughed in the image with the Large Chalk variant of the Dry Media brush, then added more color with the Opaque Flat and Smeary Flat Brushes variants. To "create balance, a stillness of motion and the beauty and magic of dark and light," LeVan made a loose Lasso selection of the "sky" area to the right of the figure and used Effects, Tonal Control, Negative to turn the colors negative. Then she used the Large Chalk, Square Chalk and Waxy Crayons (Dry Media) and the Scratchboard Tool (Pens) tools for the details, switching between a variety of subtle and coarse paper textures.

■ **Wendy Morris's** illustrations begin with a traditional Rapidograph pen drawing on smooth-surfaced recycled paper. Known for her whimsical drawing style and unique color sense, Morris creates illustrations for editorial spots, greeting cards and jewelry designs.

Downhill Racer (right), was created for a holiday card commissioned by Tom Bottman Designs. Morris scanned the original black-and-white pen-and-ink drawing, then she opened it in Painter. She used the Paint Bucket to fill areas with flat color, as described in "Coloring a Scanned Illustration" earlier in this chapter. To suggest a cloudy winter day she used muted, less-saturated, colors. She added details with the Digital Airbrush variant of the Airbrushes: she gave the racer's cheek a rosy glow, painted the lavender shadow and soft swirls on the background, and she airbrushed subtle shadows on the snow. Then she used the Pixel Dust pen variant to add a black motion trail behind the racer and to add golden flecks in the sky behind the racer's head. (The Pixel Dust variant of the Pens is located in the Painter 5.5 Brushes library, in the Brush Libraries folder on the Painter 6 Application CD-ROM.)

Artist **Richard Noble** has successfully re-created the look of traditional acrylic using Painter. He generally begins by importing a reference photograph into Painter to use as a template. For these two paintings of Mendocino, he roughed in the color with the Sargent Brush variant of the Artists brush and the Round Camelhair Brushes variants. Both of these brushes allowed Noble to move paint around on the canvas; he also blended color using the Palette Knife variant of the Brush. He added details with Artist Pastel Chalk (Dry Media) and a tiny Digital Airbrush (Airbrushes). Noble prints his pieces on canvas, then stretches and finishes them with a clear glaze and touches of acrylic paint.

In *Fog* (above), Noble used a rustic, low-saturation palette and expressive brush work to create the foggy atmosphere. He painted highlights and shadows with subdued color and with looser detail.

In *1872* (right), Noble depicted the bright light of a sunny morning. Using the Sargent Brush and the Round Camelhair Brushes variants, he developed strong light-to-dark contrast. Then he used a small brush to paint fine detail in the shaded areas of the foreground flowers as well as in the sunlit areas of the painting.

■ **Dennis Orlando's** sensitive use of light combined with layered color in the shadowed areas in his paintings has earned him the name "The Modern Impressionist." For the two paintings on this page Orlando used very different color palettes and contrast to depict different lighting and time of day.

To paint *The Palace of Fine Arts* (top) Orlando began by sketching with a Pencils variant, then he laid in expressive color with the Smeary Bristle Spray variant of the Brushes. Orlando used saturated color and dramatic contrast in highlights and shadows to depict a sunny, clear San Francisco morning. To paint the sparkling reflections on the water, he used a custom Chalk brush that contains a small amount of Color Variability, which helps to modulate the color. Orlando rendered architectural details with the Artist Pastel Chalk (Dry Media), then used a tiny Just Add Water variant (Liquid) to blend colors in the water and foliage and on the buildings.

Inspired by a Chinese painting on silk, Orlando painted *The Pond with Low Branches* (bottom) with the Artist Pastel Chalk variant of Dry Media. He used the Grainy Water variant of the Liquid brush to pull and blend colors into each other. To establish a mood of late day, he used muted colors and an analogous palette with deep shadow colors but without bright highlights.

3

PAINTING
WITH
BRUSHES

This detail of Dennis Orlando's New Martinique Beach *shows his expressive digital oil painting technique, achieved by using Dry Media, Liquid and Brushes variants. See more of Orlando's work later in this chapter.*

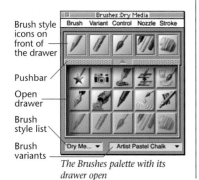

Brush style icons on front of the drawer

Pushbar

Open drawer

Brush style list

Brush variants

The Brushes palette with its drawer open

PAINTER'S BRUSHES ARE THE PROGRAM'S HEART: Without them, Painter would be a lot like other image editors. What sets Painter apart is the way it puts pen to paper and paint to canvas—the way its brushes interact with the surface below them. Here's a primer on getting the most from Painter's brushes.

Painting basics. If you're new to Painter, follow these steps to jump right in and begin painting. Create a new file (File, New). If the Brushes palette is not open, choose Window, Show Brushes to open it; or double-click the Brush tool in the Tools palette. (For more choices, you can click the palette push-bar to open the brush drawer.) Click the Dry Media icon. Then to select a color, choose Window, Show Art Materials and click on the word Color or toggle the triangle at the left of the Colors section bar to open a Color picker. Click in the Color picker's Hue ring or bar and in its triangle to choose a color for your painting. In the Art Materials palette, you'll also find the Papers section bar. Click its left triangle to open the Papers section, click the push-bar to open the drawer, then click a paper swatch to change the texture from Painter's default. Paint a few strokes on the image canvas. Experiment by changing brushes, colors and paper textures as you paint. It's also possible to paint on a layer or a mask. Painting on masks is covered in the introduction of Chapter 4; for information

covered in the introduction of Chapter 4; for information

YOUR FAVORITE BRUSHES

Choosing a brush icon from the inside of the Brushes palette's drawer moves it to the front of the drawer, replacing a less recently used brush. You can keep the icon for a favorite brush style on the front of the drawer by clicking and holding on it for 1 second. A tiny green light will appear below the brush, signaling that it's locked in place. To unlock the brush, click and hold again until the green light goes out.

This detail of Roses *shows brushstrokes painted with custom variants based on the Captured Bristle, Round Camelhair and Opaque Flat variants of the Brushes.*

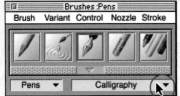

Above: Script drawn with a pressure-sensitive stylus and the Calligraphy variant of the Pens. Below: Choosing the Calligraphy variant of the Pens from the variant pop-up menu.

A lower-opacity brush will allow you to build up color slowly with more sensitivity, as demonstrated here on the coastal hills in Punta San Antonio.

regarding painting on layers, turn to "Painting on Layers" on page 53 and to Chapter 5 "Using Layers and Shapes."

Brush styles. Brush styles are shown as the mark-making tool icons on the Brushes palette, both on the front of the drawer and inside it. (You can also choose a new style by selecting it from the resource list in the bottom left corner of the Brushes palette). Brush styles are at the top level of organization for mark-making tools in Painter; they are like the *containers* that hold the individual brushes, pens, chalk and other painting and drawing implements. To choose a brush style, click one of the icons, such as the Pens.

Brush variants. Every brush has its own *variants*, so every time you choose a different brush style, the list of variants changes. Brush variants appear in the pop-up menu in the bottom right corner of the Brushes palette drawer. For instance, within the Pens are several variants (or varieties), such as Calligraphy, Smooth Ink Pen, Grad Pen and Pattern Pen. To choose the Calligraphy variant of the Pens, click the variant pop-up menu and choose Calligraphy.

Saving and restoring variants. While many artists will be content to use a few of the many brush variants that come standard with the program, others will create dozens of their own. Even if you're an intuitive artist, you'll probably find yourself wanting, for instance, "that scrubby-edged oil brush." (For in-depth information on creating your own brushes, turn to "Building Brushes" on page 54.)

When you make modifications to a brush, Painter 6 remembers the custom settings. Still, it's a good idea to save your custom brushes under their own names and to preserve Painter's default brushes. If you've changed settings and want to switch back to the default, choose Restore Default Variant from the Variant menu at the top of the Brushes palette. To *replace* a default brush with your custom settings, choose Variant, Set Default Variant. **Caution:** After this choice, the only way to restore the original variant is by reinstalling the Painter Brushes file as described in "Resetting Default Brushes," below.

RESETTING DEFAULT BRUSHES

To delete *all* cached variants and restore brushes to their original state, hold down the Alt/Option key and from the Brushes palette menu choose Variant, Restore Default Variant. (Keep in mind, if you've used Set Default Variant to save your own defaults, this command will restore to the *new* default you set.) If you'd like to preserve the Painter Brushes library with modifications and also have access to the original default set, open your Painter application folder and rename the Painter Brushes file. We typed "Painter Brushes 2." Then to reinstall the default Painter Brushes file from the Painter 6 Application CD-ROM, double-click on the Painter 6 Installer icon and navigate to the Painter 6 Installer dialog box. Choose Custom Install from the pop-up menu and uncheck all of the boxes that you can see. Click the triangle next to the Painter 6 Default Files checkbox and choose Brush Library. Navigate to your Painter 6 folder to install the brushes.

Although it's fun to assign whimsical names (such as Monster Airbrush) to variants you save, informative names are more useful. Try listing brush size, color variability, percentage of opacity, and any change in Method or Subcategory (Submethod) in your variants.

Switch Methods to make dramatic changes in brush characteristics. Here we've applied the Waxy Crayons variants of Dry Media over a gradient using the default Buildup method (top), Cover method (center) and Eraser method (bottom).

The Gritty Charcoal variant of Dry Media was applied using various Subcategory settings: the antialiased default Grainy Hard Cover (top); the pixelated Grainy Edge Flat Cover (middle); and the soft-edged Soft Cover (bottom).

If you've made changes to a brush variant, and you'd like to store it in the Brushes palette, first check that all your settings are the way you want them. Then choose Save Variant from the Variant pull-down menu on the Brushes palette, name the variant and click OK. Your new variant will appear in the variant list for that brush style and will stay there, even after you leave the program, until you remove it by selecting it and then choosing Variant, Delete Variant.

Methods. *Methods* are the backbone of many brush variants, including brushes that users of earlier versions of Painter know and love. To see the method for a specific brush variant, such as the Artist Pastel Chalk, open the Brush Controls palette's General section by choosing Window, Show Brush Controls and then clicking the left triangle on the General section bar. A brush variant's method controls how the paint will interact with the background and with other paint. For instance, the Pencils variants use the Buildup method, meaning that overlapping strokes will darken. The Chalk variants of Dry Media use the Cover method, which means that strokes—even light-colored ones—will cover other strokes. You can, however, switch the method for the variant that you design. For example, you can save a Cover method variant of the Pencils.

Subcategories. While each method gives a radically different effect to a brush, the *subcategories*, or submethods, make more subtle changes, affecting the edges of brush strokes. Subcategories that include the word *Flat* produce hard, aliased strokes with

To quickly check settings for the current variant, check out the Brush Controls palette's collapsed "score card" view (Windows, Show Brush Controls). Settings for the Soft Charcoal variant of the Dry Media brush category are displayed below:

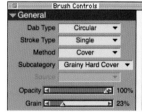

Soft Charcoal default settings. Settings not available for this brush are grayed out.

For Painter users familiar with versions prior to Painter 6, Brush Methods and Subcategories have moved from the expanded Brushes palette to the Brush Controls palette's General section. To access the Method and Subcategory for the current variant, choose Window, Show Brush Controls; when the Brush Controls palette appears, click the left triangle on the General section bar to open it.

The General section of the Brush Controls palette contains Dab Type, Stroke Type, Method, Subcategory, Opacity and Grain settings for the current variant, in this case, the Artist Pastel Chalk.

Janet Martini added interest to her India *painting—maximizing the interaction between brush and virtual texture in Painter—by exaggerating the size of the texture. Before painting with Water Color and Pens variants, she adjusted the Scale slider in the Papers section of the Art Materials palette.*

In this location study for Path to Water 1, *two grain-sensitive variants, the Square Chalk and the Large Chalk, were used on Sandy paper texture. (Sandy paper texture can be found in Drawing Paper Textures, in the Paper Texture Libraries folder on the Painter 6 Application CD-ROM.)*

pixelated edges. Those that include the word *Hard* give smoother strokes. Strokes made using *Soft* submethods appear with feathered edges. Strokes with the word *Grainy* in their subcategory setting will be affected by the active paper texture. Strokes that contain the word *Edge* give a thicker, stickier look; *Variable* refers to strokes that begin with a slight transparency.

Paper textures. "Grainy" brush methods will reveal the paper texture you've selected in the Papers section of the Art Materials palette. You can use Painter's standard papers or create your own (see "Applying Scanned Paper Textures," on page 78). Adjust the Grain slider on the Controls:Brush palette to vary the intensity of the grain on your brush strokes. For all of Painter's brushes except the Water Color brushes, a lower Grain setting means that less of the color will penetrate the grain, so your strokes will actually look grainier (See "The Grain Paradox" below.)

THE GRAIN PARADOX

For almost all of Painter's brushes, the lower the Grain setting, the "grainier" your strokes will look. That's because the Grain setting actually describes *grain penetration*. A lower Grain setting means that less of the color will penetrate the grain. The paint is hitting only the "peaks" of the paper surface. In contrast to the way it behaves for most brushes, the Grain setting works the opposite way for Water Color variants: To make grain more prominent when using a Water Color brush, increase the Grain setting.

The Grain slider in the Controls: Brush palette

NEW COMPUTED BRUSHES

Using a brand-new *computed brush* technology, Painter 6 paints faster than you could in previous versions. Another exciting brush improvement enables each brush hair to carry its own well of color. When an artist uses a traditional brush, the bristles often get contaminated by the colors of wet paint on the canvas. When the brush touches a neighboring color, it affects the paint along the edges of the brushstroke. When using traditional media, we often use this technique to mix color on a conventional color palette, or on the canvas itself. In Painter this technique is known as *brush loading*. Some new brushes (the Round Camelhair variant of the Brushes, for instance) have this capability built into them. When painting with dab-based brushes without the built-in loading capability, you can also activate Brush Loading in the Well section of the Brush Controls palette by checking the Brush Loading checkbox. (You can also activate Brush Loading with brushes created in earlier versions of Painter.)

In addition to the speed and brush-loading enhancements, Painter 6 incorporates new advanced input technology (such as

Detail of Agave Shawii, *painted with the Round Camelhair variant. New in Painter 6, the Round Camelhair allows for more color "activity" when painting because each brush hair can paint with its own color. For more information turn to "Painting an Expressive Color Study" later in this chapter.*

Wisteria flowers created with Painter 6's new Pattern Pen variant of the Pens

Sketch created with the 2B Pencil variant of the Pencils

tilt and bearing) from pressure-sensitive tablet manufacturers such as Wacom. Most brushes in Painter 6 are able to take advantage of this new capability.

New rendered dab type brushes. The new Painter 6 brushes that incorporate a *rendered dab* can produce smoother, more realistic brushstrokes than other brushes can. Here are just a few of the new Painter 6 variants that use rendered dabs: Round Camelhair and Loaded Palette Knife (Brushes variants), Scratchboard Tool and Smooth Ink Pen (Pens variants), and Line Airbrush and Pixel Airbrush (Airbrushes variants). For more detailed information about using rendered dab types turn to "Building Brushes" on page 54.

New Special Effects brushes. In addition to painting with color, Painter 6 introduces several new kinds of media application—for instance, brushes that paint with gradients or patterns. To sketch the Wisteria example at the left, choose the Pattern Pen variant of the Pens and load the Watercolored Patterns library: You'll find the Load Library command at the bottom of the Pattern list in the Patterns section of the Art Materials palette. Scroll down to the bottom of the list and choose Load Library to display the standard Mac or Windows Open dialog box. Navigate to the Pen Pattern Libraries folder within the Content folder on the Painter 6 Application CD-ROM; choose the Watercolored Patterns library; then double-click to open it. For more information about special effects brushes that paint using a pattern or other source turn to "Building Brushes" on page 54, and to Chapter 7, "Exploring Special Effects."

AUTOBUILDING BRUSHES

Artists who used earlier versions of Painter will be happy to hear that Auto Build Brush is a default in Painter 6. To toggle Autobuild on and off, choose Brush, Auto Build Brush from the Brushes palette menu.

EMULATING TRADITIONAL TECHNIQUES

Here's a brief description of several traditional art techniques and how to re-create them in Painter. One or two techniques for each medium are outlined as a starting point for your own experimentation. But there are a number of ways to obtain similar results.

Pencil. Pencil sketches using traditional materials are typically created on location. Tools include soft-leaded graphite pencils (HB to 6B), various erasers and white paper with a smooth to medium grain. To create a pencil sketch in Painter, select a relatively smooth paper such as Regular Fine paper texture and choose the Pencils brush, 2B Pencil variant. Select a black or dark gray and begin sketching. To erase or add white highlights, choose a white

The Artist Pastel Chalk and Large Chalk variants were used on Big Canvas texture to paint Coastal Meadow. *(Big Canvas texture is located in More Paper Textures, in the Paper Texture Libraries folder on the Painter 6 Application CD-ROM.)*

Detail of Tienda Verde (The Green Store). *This colorful painting was created using custom brushes based on the Square Chalk and Oil Pastel variants of the Dry Media brush.*

Harp Shell *study. A custom Conté crayon was used to draw this study on Ribbed Pastel paper.*

color and switch the method from Buildup to Cover.

Colored pencil. Conventional colored pencils are highly sensitive to the surface used: Layering strokes with light pressure on a smooth board will create a shiny look, while switching to a rougher surface creates more of a "broken color" effect (color that doesn't completely cover the existing art). To closely match the grainy, opaque strokes of a soft Prismacolor pencil on cold-pressed illustration board with Painter, select a fine medium-grained paper such as Plain Grain (found in the Drawing Paper Textures library in the Paper Texture Libraries folder on the Painter 6 Application CD-ROM). Choose the Colored Pencils variant of Pencils. Switch the Method from Buildup to Cover and change the Subcategory to Grainy Edge Flat Cover. See "Drawing with Colored Pencils," later in this chapter for a full description of this technique.

Pastel. Pastels encourage a bold, direct style: Edgar Degas preferred pastels for his striking compositions because they simultaneously yield tone, line and color. A great variety of hard and soft pastels are used on soft or rough-grain papers. Pastel artists often use a colored paper stock to unify a composition.

Use Painter's Sharp Chalk, Large Chalk, Artist Pastel Chalk and Oil Pastel variants from Painter 6's Dry Media category to mimic traditional hard or soft pastels, and if you want to use a colored paper, click on the Paper Color box as you open a new document and choose a color. The Chalk and Pastel variants are among Painter's most popular; turn to "Blending and Feathering with Pastels," "Painting With Pastels" and "Spontaneous Pastels," later in this chapter for three different techniques using them.

Conté crayon. Popular in Europe since the 1600s and used today for life drawing and landscapes, Conté crayons have a higher oil content than conventional chalk or pastel; as a result, they work successfully on a greater variety of surfaces.

To get a realistic Conté crayon look in Painter, start with the Sharp Chalk variant of Dry Media. Reveal more paper grain in the brushwork by moving the Grain slider in the Controls:Brush

BRUSH RESIZE SHORTCUT

To resize your brush on-the-fly, press Ctrl-Alt (Windows) or ⌘-Option (Mac) and drag in the image window. You will see a circle representing the current brush size. Drag to resize the brush to your liking.

Brushstrokes made using the Graphic Paintbrush, Soft variant of the Brushes. In the upper left, its default size; upper right, the resized brush size cursor; lower right, a stroke made with the resized brush.

Charcoal study after Raphael Sanzio. This study was drawn with the Charcoal and Soft Charcoal variants (Dry Media), then blended with the Just Add Water variant (Liquid).

Crab, by Mary Envall. To draw this spot illustration, Envall used the Smooth Ink Pen and Scratchboard Tool variants of the Pens. Both of these Pens incorporate Painter 6's new rendered dabs.

Study of a Nude after Rembrandt Van Rijn. We sketched with the Fine Point variant of Pens, then added translucent washes using the Broad Water Brush variant of Water Color.

palette to 14%. On the Brush Controls palette (Window, Show Brush Controls), open the Spacing section by clicking its name. Set the Spacing at 25%. Now open the Size section of the Brush Controls, palette and choose the upper right brush tip. Begin drawing. This custom Conté variant works well over Ribbed Pastel paper texture. To blend color, while revealing the paper texture, choose the Smudge variant of the Liquid brush. To see another Conté variant, turn to "Spontaneous Pastels," later in this chapter.

Charcoal. One of the oldest drawing tools, charcoal is ideal for life drawing and portraiture in *chiaroscuro* (high value contrast) style. Renaissance masters frequently chose charcoal because images created with it could be transferred from paper (where corrections could be made easily) to canvas or walls in preparation for painting. To create a charcoal drawing in Painter, select a rough paper (such as Big Grain Rough) and the Charcoal variant of the Dry Media brush. Create a gestural drawing, then blend the strokes—as you would traditionally with a tortillion, a tissue or your fingers—with the Smudge variant of the Liquid brush. For a smoother result with less texture try blending with the Just Add Water variant of Liquid. Finish by adding more strokes using a Charcoal brush, this time using the Gritty Charcoal variant of the Dry Media brush.

Pen and Ink. Many artists use Painter's Pens variants to draw editorial and spot illustrations. To create a black-and-white pen-and-ink drawing in Painter, choose the Fine Point variant of the Pens and choose 100% black in the Color picker. Sketch your composition. To draw with lines that are expressively thick and thin based on the pressure you apply to your stylus, switch to the Smooth Ink Pen. To etch white lines and texture into black areas of your drawing, select pure white in the Color picker and draw with the Fine Point or Smooth Ink Pen. For a sense of spontaneous energy try drawing with the Nervous Pen.

In Baseball Memories, Chet Phillips used the Scratchboard Tool variant of the Pens, as shown in this detail. To see the full image, turn to the gallery at the end of Chapter 5.

DYNAMIC WET FRINGE

You can use the Wet Fringe slider in the Brush Controls:Water section to dynamically adjust the Wet Fringe of all "wet" Water Color brushstrokes.

For this watercolor study of a Pelican, we increased the Wet Fringe of "wet" brushstrokes painted on the sky. (Note the darker edge of the blue brushstroke where it meets the white image canvas.) Paint on the bird was not affected, because it had been previously "dried" (Canvas, Dry).

A glazing technique was used for a watercolor portrait study of Sabina Gaross.

Scratchboard illustration. Scratching white illustrations out of a dark (usually black) background surface became popular in the late 1800s. Illustrations created in this manner often contained subtle, detailed tone effects, making them a useful alternative to photographic halftones in the publications of that era. Modern scratchboard artists use knives and gougers on a variety of surfaces, including white board painted with India ink. To duplicate this look in Painter, start with the Flat Color variant of the Pens and increase its size in the Controls:Brush palette. Choose black from the Color picker and rough out the basic shape for your illustration. To "scratch" the image out of the shape with hatch marks, switch to white and change to the Scratchboard Tool variant. Use the Scratchboard Rake to add texture. Turn to Chapter 5's gallery to see Chet Phillips's Painter-generated scratchboard work, or check out John Fretz's blending of traditional and digital scratchboard in the gallery at the end of Chapter 4.

Calligraphy. With the exception of "rolling the nib" and a few other maneuvers, you can imitate nearly all conventional calligraphic strokes in Painter. To create hand lettering similar to the example on page 41, choose the Calligraphy variant of the Pens and begin your brushwork. To make guides for your calligraphy, select Canvas, Rulers, Show Rulers and drag guides out from the ruler, or you can use Painter's Grid overlay (choose Canvas, Grid, Show Grid and then Canvas, Grid, Grid Options, Transparent Background). If you want a rougher edge to your strokes, try switching the subcategory to Flat Cover or Grainy Edge Flat Cover. To fine-tune the "nib," open the Brush Controls by choosing Window, Show Brush Controls, then click on Angle to open the Angle section. Create a flatter nib by setting a smaller value on the Squeeze slider; if you want to adjust the angle of the brush, drag the Angle slider until you like what you see in the preview in the Size section of the palette.

Watercolor. Landscape artists like Turner and Constable helped popularize watercolors in the nineteenth century, and the medium's portability lends itself nicely to painting on location. Traditional watercolor uses transparent pigment for color, and the paper is often moistened and stretched prior to painting.

Painter 6 lets you achieve many traditional watercolor effects—without paper-stretching! Choose the Broad Water Brush variant of the Water Color brush, a rough paper (such as Big Grain Rough) and a color, and begin painting. To blend color, switch to the Flat Water Blender or Round Water Blender variant. If you want your strokes to appear to *diffuse* into the paper, switch to the Diffuse Water variant. (If the color created with this variant is too intense, reduce the opacity in the Controls:Brush palette.) You can also diffuse all existing strokes in the Wet Layer using the Post-diffuse command: Shift-D. Repeat the keystroke to increase

A pen and watercolor wash study of the king of beasts. Washes were added with the Simple Water and Broad Water Brush variants of Water Color.

To paint Porcelain Morning Glory, *Kathy Blavatt used several Airbrushes variants.*

AIRBRUSH MEDIA POOLING

Several of Painter 6's new Airbrushes—the Coarse Spray, the Fine Spray and the Graffiti variants for example—allow media to pool when the stylus (or mouse) is held down in one position. In contrast, the Digital Airbrush and Inverted Pressure variants must be moved before they apply color to the image. To enable these two variants to apply color at the first touch, turn on Continuous Time Deposition in the Spacing section of the Brush Controls palette.

the effect. To erase only the color painted with Water Color variants, use the Wet Eraser variant.

Pen and wash. Tinted, translucent washes over pen work has been a medium of choice of Asian painting masters for many centuries. Painter's Wet Layer lets you add a wash to any drawn (or scanned) image without smearing or hiding it. Choose the Simple Water or Broad Water Brush variant of the Water Color brush, pick a color and a medium-textured paper (such as Basic Paper) and begin painting on top of line work.

Airbrush. The trademark of most traditional airbrush work is a slick, super-realistic look; photo retouching is a more subtle use of the tool. A traditional airbrush is a miniature spray gun with a hollow nozzle and a tapered needle. Pigments include finely ground gouache, acrylic, watercolor and colored dyes, and a typical support surface is a smooth illustration board. Airbrush artists protect areas of their work from overspraying with pieces of masking film, or flexible friskets cut from plastic.

In Painter, choose one of the Airbrushes variants and begin sketching or retouching. To get the most from the tool, make selections with the Lasso tool and use them to limit the paint just as you would traditional airbrush friskets.

Several of Painter 6's Airbrushes (such as the Fine Spray, Pixel Spray and Graffiti variants) spray paint onto the image canvas differently than earlier Airbrushes. These Airbrushes take advantage of new input technology available from manufacturers such as Wacom. They respond to angle (tilt) and bearing (direction). For instance, as you paint, particles of color land on the image canvas reflecting the way the artist tilts the stylus. And with Painter 6's Fine Wheel Airbrush variant, you can adjust the flow of paint by adjusting the wheel on a special Airbrush stylus. For those accustomed to the Airbrushes in earlier versions of Painter, the Digital Airbrush variant is most similar to these early Airbrushes.

Turn to "Selections and Airbrush" in Chapter 4 and the gallery in Chapter 8 to see John Dismukes's masterful airbrush work using selections and layers.

Gouache. Roualt, Vlaminck, Klee and Miro were a few of the modern artists who experimented with this opaque watercolor, used most frequently in paintings that call for large areas of flat color. Gouache contains a blend of the same type of pigment used in transparent watercolor, a chalk that makes the pigment opaque, and an extender that allows it to flow more easily.

WET PAINT

When you choose any Water Color brush, the paint stays "wet" until you choose Canvas, Dry. (*Note*: Painter documentation calls this feature the *Wet Layer* but it is not a true layer like those listed in the Layer hierarchy in the Layers section of the Objects palette.) For more details about repeatedly drying the Wet Layer for a *glazing* (translucent layering) effect, turn to "Glazing with Watercolor" later in this chapter.

This detail of Nancy Stahl's Mercury *shows her gouache technique. To see the full image, turn to "Gouache and Opaque Watermedia," later in this chapter.*

This detail of Coast *by Richard Noble is an example of the artist's digital acrylic technique. The full image is presented in the gallery at the end of this chapter.*

Detail of Amaryllis. *This study was painted with the Opaque Bristle Spray and Smeary Bristle Spray variants of Brushes, then blended with the Smudge variant of Liquid.*

Artist Nancy Stahl has modified several brushes in Painter to emulate traditional gouache applied to cold-pressed illustration board. To learn her secrets, turn to "Gouache and Opaque Watermedia" later in this chapter.

Oil paint and acrylic. These opaque media are "standards" for easel painting. Both can be applied in a thick impasto with a palette knife or stiff brush, or they can be *extended* (thinned) with a solvent or gel and applied as transparent glazes. They are typically applied to canvas that has been primed with paint or gesso.

Try the following methods to get the look of oil or acrylic in Painter. For a technique that incorporates the texture of brush striations and a palette knife, begin by choosing the Big Grain Rough paper texture and the Opaque Round variant of the Brushes and begin painting. To paint brushstrokes with varied color, switch to the Variable Flat variant. Blend colors using short strokes with the Distorto variant of Liquid. To scrape back or move large areas of color on the image canvas, use the Palette knife variant of the Brushes. When working on smaller areas of your image, adjust the size of the Palette knife using the Size slider on the Controls: Brush palette.

For an oil painting technique with the feel of wet paint on canvas, use the Sargent Brush variant of the Artist's brush. The Sargent Brush allows you to move color as well as apply it while painting. As you pull the Sargent Brush through pools of color on the image canvas, the brush carries some of the neighboring color with it as you paint.

For a painting method reminiscent of the texture of canvas, begin by choosing the Canvas 2 texture from the More Paper Textures library (in Paper Texture Libraries, on the Painter 6 Application CD-ROM). Now choose the Opaque Bristle Spray variant of the Brushes and lay color into your image. To smear existing paint as you add more color, switch to the Smeary Bristle Spray variant. To reveal the texture of the image canvas, while you blend colors, switch to the Smudge variant of Liquid. For yet another digital oil method, see Dennis Orlando's version of a traditional oil look in "Painting With Oils," later in this chapter; to see more examples of Richard Noble's digital acrylic paintings, turn to the gallery in Chapter 2 "The Power of Color."

To get textured brushstrokes (a "3D paint" look) with any of these methods when you're finished, choose Effects, Surface Control, Apply Surface Texture. Choose Image Luminance from the pop-up menu, and an Amount setting of 20–30%. If you want to

BRUSHES FOR BLENDING

The Liquid brushes and Water brushes in earlier versions of Painter have been combined in the Liquid category in Painter 6.

LIQUID BRUSH STRENGTH

To control the strength of the Bulge, Pinch, Smear and Turbulence variants of the Liquid brush, adjust the Opacity slider in the Controls:Brush palette.

In Portrait of Seafth, *Phil Howe mixed media while painting. As shown in this detail, he used Chalks (Dry Media), Airbrushes, blenders—the Grainy Water and Distorto (Liquid),—and finally the Gritty Charcoal (Dry Media) and the Thick and Thin Pencils variant to define details.*

In Harley, *Richard Noble blended color with a variant of Liquid to get the look of conventional acrylic.*

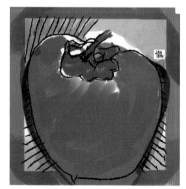

Mixing Media. To complete Speedy Persimmon *Janet Martini used the Calligraphy variant of the Pens on top of Water Color variants and Oil Pastel strokes (Dry Media).*

mimic the look of acrylic paint extended with a glossy gel medium, drag the Shine slider to 100%. To get a semi-matte finish, move the Shine slider to between 20% and 30%.

Painting with realistic Impasto. Impasto lets you go beyond showing the texture of paper as you paint. It gives you the power to show the texture of brushmark striations and the thickness of paint itself with realistic highlights and shadows—Impasto brings thick paint to the tip of your stylus! And with Painter 6, Impasto is now fully integrated into Painter. When you choose a variant of the Impasto brush (such as the Opaque Round), the Impasto effect is automatically enabled. You can use Impasto with the image canvas, or with multiple layers. You'll find new Impasto brushes in the Painter 6 Brushes palette.

Here's an Impasto primer: Create a new blank file (File, New). To activate Impasto, choose an Impasto brush (such as the Round Camelhair variant) from the Brushes palette. Make brushstrokes on the image canvas. To toggle the Impasto effect on and off, you can click the small paint splat icon in the upper right of Painter 6's scroll bar. To read more about painting with Impasto, turn to "Brushing Washes Over Live Canvas" and "Working With Thick Paint," later in this chapter.

> **BRUSHSTROKES WITH DEPTH**
>
> Using Impasto, you can add brushstrokes with 3D texture without altering color in the image. Select any Impasto variant and in the Draw To pop-up menu in the Impasto section of Brush Controls, select Depth.

Mixed media. You can create media combinations in Painter that would be impossible (or at least very messy!) in traditional media. Try adding strokes with a Water Color or Pencils variant atop oils, or use a Pens variant on a base of chalk and gouache. See how artists Phil Howe and Janet Martini combined media in the two paintings at the left.

Mixed media painting with a liquid feel. Painter 6 offers several new brushes that are reminiscent of wet paint on canvas, for instance the Sargent Brush, which can both lay down color and smear it, and the Palette Knife variant of the Brushes which can move large areas of color. Painting with these new brushes is a very tactile experience, as you learned if you experimented as described on page 49.

In the *Paths to Water 4* study, we sketched in color with the Square Chalk variant of Dry Media on top of Big Grain Rough. Then we switched to the Sargent Brush variant of the Artist's brushes to apply more painterly strokes. To blend areas of the foreground and mid-ground we used the Grainy Water variant of Liquid, then we used the Palette Knife variant of the Brushes to expressively pull color in the sky. To paint and blend using these brushes, choose the Sargent brush and a color, and begin painting.

Detail from study for Paths to Water 4. *The Palette Knife variant of the Brushes was used to pull and spread color in the clouds and sky.*

You can paint Impasto on layers and then set Composite Depth on each layer (in the Layers section of the Objects palette), to raise or excavate the paint, as described on page 151.

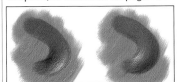

We painted each rust brushstroke on a separate layer with the Opaque Round variant of Impasto. Then we used Composite Depth controls, Subtract (left) and Add (right), to make the left stroke excavated and the right stroke raised.

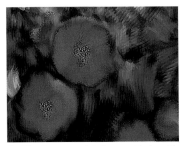

For Zinnias, *we painted over a photo with Dry Media variants, completely covering it with colored strokes. Then we used Liquid variants to distort the flowers, add texture and emphasize the focal point.*

When you are ready to pull and blend paint, switch to the Palette Knife. Try reducing its Opacity in the Controls:Brush palette for a more subdued effect.

Liquid variants are also helpful blending tools. To create *Zinnias*, shown at left, we used the Bulge variant of the Liquid brush to enlarge the pink flowers, and the Coarse Smear to pull pixels and add diffused texture to the edges. Then we used the Marbling Rake variant of Liquid to add linear texture and to pull pixels up and around the image to create a sense of movement.

Erasing techniques. Painter provides several ways to emulate traditional erasing techniques. Use the Scratchboard Tool variant of the Pens brush and a white or light color to *scratch out* pigment from a pastel or oil painting; to create strokes with a hint of texture, switch to Grainy Hard Cover for the subcategory in the General section of the Brush Controls palette. *Pull paint out* of an image but leave some pigment in the "valleys" of a paper grain by using one of the Bleach variants of the Eraser, lowering the Opacity slider in the Controls palette to 10%. (You can choose the grain that will be *revealed* by the Bleach variant by selecting from the Papers section of the Art Materials palette.)

Use the Wet Eraser variant of the Water Color brush to pull up pigment from a "wet" painting done with Water Color variants (similar to *sponging up* a traditional watercolor). For a more subtle result, lower the Opacity slider (in the Controls palette) to 40%.

Painting with texture. The Add Grain variant of the Photo brush is just as useful for painting as it is for photo manipulation, because it literally puts 3D texture on the end of your brush. You can switch textures at any time during the painting process. For

When you work with Impasto, the depth and lighting information is stored in a way that allows you to change it for the entire image—as many times as you like, for both past and future brushstrokes. To demonstrate this flexibility, select an Impasto variant (such as Texturizer-Heavy) and a color, and paint on your image. Next, choose Canvas, Impasto Lighting, and when the dialog box opens, increase the Shine (for more glossy paint); increase the Amount (to make the paint look thicker) and experiment with other settings in the Appearance of Depth and Light Controls sections. Also try toggling Impasto off and on using the Enable Impasto checkbox. To clear (delete) the effect entirely, choose Canvas, Clear Impasto. Clearing Impasto is useful if you want to completely start over with new Impasto. Also, if you decide not to keep the Impasto effects in your image, clearing can save memory use.

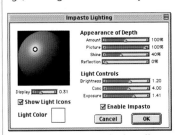

The Impasto Lighting dialog box allows you to dynamically set Appearance of Depth and Light Controls for Impasto brushstrokes in the entire image.

Brian Moose used the Glow brush variant of the F/X brush to make the brush tips burn in his painting, Creative Journey, *a detail of which is shown here. See his complete painting in the gallery at the end of Chapter 7, "Exploring Special Effects."*

best results, use very light pressure on the stylus. Make a few marks in the document to preview the effect. For a more subtle look, try lowering the Opacity and Grain penetration in the Controls:Brush palette.

Painting with special effects. Painter 6 introduces new special effects brushes that allow you to paint with fire, glows, fur, sparkly fairy dust, hair spray, piano keys and more! In the detail of *Creative Journey* (left), Brian Moose used the Glow variant of the F/X brush to make the paintbrush tips in his image smoulder with a fiery glow.

Painting with the Fire and Glow variants works best on a dark area of your image. To paint semi-transparent flames, choose the Fire brush variant of the F/X brush. For a subdued fire effect that you can build up gradually, with a light pressure on the stylus, choose a very dark orange color with a value (V) of 10–15% in the Colors section (Art Materials). Make short strokes in the direction you want the flames to go. For realism, vary the size of the brush-strokes. Change the size of the brush using the Size slider in the Controls:Brush palette, then paint more brushstrokes using a light pressure on the stylus.

We used the Fire brush variant of the F/X brush to paint semi-transparent flames on the bottom of these letters.

EASIER ACCESS TO CUSTOM CONTROLS

In Painter 6 you can add important brush modification commands to the Controls:Brush palette. That way all your important controls will be in one single palette and you won't have to work back and forth between the Controls:Brush palette and the various sections of the Brush Controls palette. From the Brushes palette's Control pull-down menu choose Custom Controls. The Custom Controls Palette dialog box will appear showing available settings for the current brush. To make it easy to customize our Broad Water

Brush (a Water Color variant) as we worked, we added two controls from the Customize Controls Palette dialog box. We selected Water from the Category menu and checked the Wet Fringe and Diffusion checkboxes and clicked OK. To save the brush variant with these custom controls added in the Controls:Brush palette, we chose Variant, Save Variant. If you want to delete the added controls, later you can choose Control, Custom Controls. Water, and uncheck the Wet Fringe and Diffusion checkboxes.

The Controls:Brush palette with added settings (Diffusion and Wet Fringe). These added settings made it easier to use our Broad Water Brush variant to paint the watercolor sketch shown above of Needle's Eye, Sunset Cliffs.

To paint the study, Cutting Back at Rincon, *we used the Pens, Brushes and Airbrushes variants to paint on transparent layers. After drawing the line sketch on its own layer, we created a second layer for the color work. Using low-opacity color, we painted on the "color" layer to build up brushstrokes without altering the image canvas or the layer with the line sketch. We finished by dragging the line sketch layer to the top of the Layers palette, placing it on top of the "color" layer.*

PAINTING ON LAYERS

Painter 6 lets you paint (and erase) not only on the program's canvas, but on transparent layers. A *transparent layer* is similar to a clear piece of acetate that hovers above the image canvas. When you paint on a transparent layer with a brush, you can see the canvas underneath, as well as color on other layers that you may have stacked up, and you can change the stacking order of the acetate sheets. If you work with Adobe Photoshop, you'll find Painter 6's transparent layers familiar.

To add a new layer to an existing file, open the Objects palette's Layers section (Windows, Show Objects) and click the left triangle on the Layers section bar to open it. Click the right triangle on the section bar to access the Layers palette's pop-up menu, and choose New Layer. To paint on the new layer, choose any brush except a Water Color variant, target the layer in the Layers section and begin painting.

Layers offer great flexibility to digital illustrators. Some artists prefer to draw each item in an image on its own layer, which isolates the item so that it can be repositioned, painted on, or composited as an individual element. Transparent layers are also useful when creating *glazes*—thin, clear layers of color applied over existing color. (Turn to Chapter 5, "Using Layers and Shapes" to read more about painting and compositing techniques.)

(Turn to Chapter 5, "Using Layers and Shapes" to read more about painting and compositing techniques.)

EASIER ERASING ON LAYERS

In Painter 6 it's possible to use an Eraser variant to erase a portion of a layer. There is no longer a need to edit the layer's visibility mask to erase information as was required in previous versions.

IMPASTO AND CLONING

Here's a speedy Impasto illustration method. If there's not time to paint from scratch, choose a photo you'd like to use for reference. Make a clone (File, Clone). In the Brushes palette, choose an Impasto brush, such as the Round Camelhair variant or the Smeary Flat. Apply color and depth to the Impasto image based on color in the clone source by choosing the Clone Color option in the Colors section of the Art Materials palette.

ORIGINAL PHOTO: CORBIS IMAGES

Painting with Impasto using the custom Round Camelhair variant on a cloned file

THE LOOKS YOU LIKE

If you like the look of a particular brush-and-paper combination (for instance, the Square Chalk variant of Dry Media on Ribbed Pastel paper), save the combo as a Brush Look so you can quickly call it up when you want to use it again: Select the texture from the Papers section of the Art Materials palette and the brush variant from the Brushes palette. Choose Brush, Brush Looks, Look Designer. Draw a stroke in the dialog box to preview your combination, and click the Save button. Naming your Brush Look saves it to the current Brush Look library, which is located in the Art Materials palette's Looks section. Open the section by clicking the left arrow on the Looks section bar. To paint with your new Brush Look, select from the Looks section's Look pop-up resource list.

Brush Looks are also useful with brushes that can paint with a source, such as the Graphic Paintbrush variant of the Brushes. You can save Brush Looks that include unique brush-and-pattern (or gradient) combinations. To try it out, choose the Graphic Paintbrush variant. In the Brush Controls:General section make sure the subcategory is set to Grainy Edge Flat Cover and the Source is set to Pattern as Opacity. In the Art Materials:Patterns section, choose the Filigree pattern. To save your new combo, choose Brush, Brush Looks Designer, and click the Save button.

A brushstroke painted with the Graphic Paintbrush using the Filigree pattern as the Source

Building Brushes

Overview *Creating these custom brushes will give you insight into the workings of the palette sections that control them.*

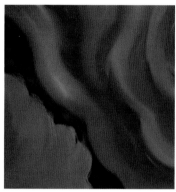

Mixing color on the image canvas using the custom Camelhair Blender brush described on page 58.

Brush Controls	
▶ General	Opacity 44%
▶ Size	Size 52.4
▶ Spacing	
▶ Angle	
▶ Bristle	
▶ Impasto	
▶ Expression	Direction 0°
▶ Well	Bleed 0%
▶ Airbrush	Flow 672
▶ Rake	
▶ Random	Jitter 0.80
▶ Water	
▶ Cloning	Clone Color Off
▶ Mouse	Pressure 100%

The Brush Controls palette contains most of the controls for customizing brushes. When closed, the palette displays important information about settings for the current brush—in this case, the Pixel Spray variant of the Airbrushes.

PAINTER 6 SHIPS WITH MANY NEW BRUSHES, and makes customizing them even easier than before. If you like trying new brushes but don't want to build them, check out the Brush libraries on the Wow! CD-ROM in the back of this book—you'll find the brushes shown on these pages and more. But if you enjoy creating your own brushes, read on. *Roses*, above, was painted with several of the custom brushes described here.

DAB TYPES

In Painter, brushstrokes are built from *dabs*. Painter 6 has 13 dab types, which fall into two general classifications: *Dab-based* brushes (such as the brushes in earlier versions of Painter) and brushes created with new *Rendered* dab types. The main difference lies in how brushstrokes are created from the dabs as described in "Dab-Based dab types (below) and "Rendered Dab Types" on page 55–56. You can switch dab types by using the pop-up menu in the General section of the Brush Controls palette, opened by choosing Window, Show Brush Controls (Ctrl/⌘-7).

Dab-Based Dab Types

For brushes that are *dab-based* you can think of the dab as the footprint for the brush—a cross-section of its shape. The brush lays down a series of dabs of color to make a stroke. If the spacing is set tight the stroke will appear to be a continuous mark. If the spacing is loose, the stroke will be a series of footprints with space between them.

Circular. Many of Painter's brushes use this round dab type. (Don't be fooled by the term *Circular*; even if you change a brush's Squeeze setting in the Angle section of the Brush Controls palette so that its footprint looks elliptical, it's still a Circular brush.)

Choosing the Camel Hair dab type in the General section of the Brush Controls palette

Single-Pixel. Just as it sounds, this is a 1-pixel-wide brush.

Static Bristle. Since Bristle brushes are made up of several "hairs," they have a rich potential. You can make adjustments in Bristle Thickness, Clumpiness and other settings in the Spacing and Bristle sections of the Brush Controls palette.

Captured. You can capture any area of a document to act as the footprint for a Captured brush. Use the Rectangular Selection tool and draw a marquee (press the Shift key if you want to constrain the selection to a perfect square) around a mark or group of markings. Go to the Brushes palette and choose Brush, Capture Brush; the brush footprint will appear in the Size section of the Brush Controls palette.

Rendered Dab Types

Brushes using new *rendered* dab types produce smoother-edged, more responsive brushstrokes because they are computed as continuous 1-pixel lines during the stroke. Each line represents an individual brush hair.

Camel Hair. With Camel Hair dabs, you can build brushes with circular-shaped dabs that paint brushstrokes with bristle marks. Brushes using the Camel Hair Dab Type (the Round Camelhair variant of Brushes, for example) are capable of painting very smoothly, and they can carry an individual color in each brush hair.

Flat. Like it sounds, a flat dab is used to create a flat-tipped brush with the dab always perpendicular to the stylus. With brushes using the Flat Dab Type, you can paint wide or narrow strokes, depending on the way you hold the stylus. The Opaque Flat variant of Brushes is an example.

Palette Knife. With Resat set low in the Well section of the Brush Controls palette, you can use brushes with Palette Knife dabs to scrape paint or move it around on the canvas. The Loaded Palette Knife and Palette Knife variants (Brushes) are examples.

Bristle Spray. Many brushes that use Bristle Spray dabs (such as the Opaque Bristle Spray variant of Brushes) paint like a cross between a real bristle brush and an airbrush. Use the controls in the Airbrush section to change the Spread and Flow of brushstrokes.

THINNING BRUSHES

For many brushes with certain rendered dab types (Camel Hair, Flat, Palette Knife and Bristle Spray) you can control how many bristles apply paint. Simply move the Feature slider in the Size section of the Brush Controls palette. High Feature settings have a thinning effect.

FINE OR COARSE SPRAY

For brushes with Airbrush dab types, you can use the Feature slider in the Size section of the Brush Controls palette to control the size of droplets. With a higher feature setting, Airbrush dabs spray larger droplets.

REDIRECTING THE SPRAY

When you paint a stoke with a brush that has an airbrush-like conical spray (Airbrush, Pixel Airbrush or Line Airbrush dab type), you can tilt the stylus to apply paint more densely along the edge closest to the stylus. To switch the direction of the spray without changing the tilt of the stylus, hold down the Alt/Option key as you paint.

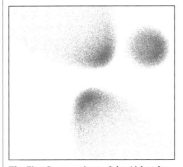

The Fine Spray variant of the Airbrushes is sensitive to tilt and bearing and sprays conic sections—similar to a beam of light projected onto the canvas—just like a traditional airbrush. Holding the stylus upright sprays a smaller area of color (top right). Tilting the stylus sprays color wider and farther (top left). And holding down Alt/Option redirects the spray (bottom).

Click on the brush footprint in the Size section's Preview window to switch the view between "hard" (showing the maximum and minimum sizes) and "soft" (showing bristles).

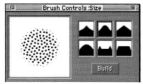

The Size section of the Brush Controls palette showing a "soft" view of a Static Bristle dab used to create the New Feathering Brush described on page 58.

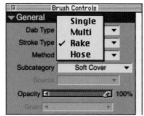

Choosing the Rake stroke type in the General section of the Brush Controls palette

Brush Loading enables a brush to carry a unique color in each brush hair. Many Painter 6 brushes have this capability already built into them—for instance, the Variable Round variant of the Brushes. (When Brush Loading is built into a brush, the Brush Loading checkbox is grayed out in the Brush Controls:Well palette.) To allow a static bristle brush (such as the Captured Bristle variant of the Brushes) or a dab-based brush from an earlier version of Painter to use Brush Loading, open the Well section of the Brush Controls palette and turn on Brush Loading.

Airbrush. Like Bristle Spray, Pixel Airbrush and Line Airbrush dab types, Airbrush dabs spray conic sections and "understand" Bearing (which direction the stylus is leaning) and Angle (amount of tilt). (See "Redirecting the Spray" on page 55.)

Pixel Airbrush. Brushes using this dab type work like brushes using the Airbrush dab type. With the Pixel Airbrush dab type, however, the individual droplets *cannot* be adjusted using the Feature slider.

Line Airbrush. Brushes using the Line Airbrush dab type (such as the Furry Brush variant of F/X) spray lines instead of droplets.

Projected. The Projected dab-type brushes spray conic sections, similar to the Airbrush dab type, but without the responsiveness. For now, MetaCreations recommends constructing brushes with the Airbrush and Pixel Airbrush dab types rather than a Projected dab type.

Rendered. (The naming scheme can be confusing here, because there is a *Rendered* dab type that's one of nine dab types within the larger *Rendered* category.) In addition to painting with color, brushes built using Rendered dabs can contain a pattern or gradation as a Source. The Graphic Paintbrush variant of Brushes is an example. To change the Source used by a Rendered dab brush, use the Source pop-up menu in the General section of the Brush Controls palette.

STROKE TYPES

The *stroke* is a dab applied over a distance. You can switch Stroke Types using the pop-up menu in the General section of the Brush Controls palette.

Single. Just as it sounds, Single stroke-type brushes have only one stroke path. Because of this, they're fast. If you use a Static Bristle, a Flat or Camel Hair dab type, you can create a fast Single stroke-type brush with a lot of complexity. Most Painter brushes incorporate the Single stroke type.

Multi. Painter's computation-intensive Multi stroke-type brushes can paint sensitive multicolored strokes, but are the least spontaneous of the programs's brushes. Painter 6 ships with only one Multi stroke-type brush because the new rendered dabs provide a much more responsive way to paint with multiple colors. Try drawing a line with the Gloopy variant of the Impasto. Instead of a stroke, you'll see a dotted "preview" line that shows its path; the stroke appears a moment later. Multi brushes are built from several randomly distributed dabs that may or may not overlap. The Gloopy variant of Impasto is the only example of a Multi stroke brush in the Painter 6 default brush library. But lovely, variable strokes can be made using custom Multi brushes. To spread the strokes of a Multi-stroke brush, increase the Jitter setting in the Random section of the Brush Controls palette.

When changing settings for a brush, sometimes typing numerals into the fields is easier than trying to hit a point on the slider.

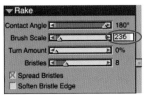

Most of the settings in the Brush Controls palette's sections can be typed in, as shown here in setting Brush Scale in the Rake section.

You can add settings to any brush that will allow it to paint with thick Impasto paint. To set up a brush for Impasto, begin by choosing a brush (such as the Dry Ink variant of the Brushes). We used these settings in the Well section of the Brush Controls palette to build a Dry Ink Impasto brush: Draw To: Color and Depth; Depth Method: Uniform; Height, 180%; Smoothing, 120% and Plow, 100%. To save your variant, from the Brushes palette's Variant menu choose Save Variant. To read more about Impasto turn to the beginning of this chapter and to "Working with Thick Paint," later in the chapter.

Painting thick Impasto brushstrokes with the new Dry Ink Impasto brush

Rake. The Rake stroke type is like a garden rake; each of the evenly spaced tines is a bristle of the brush. Painter gives you a lot of control over the bristles; for instance, you can make them overlap, letting you create wonderfully complex, functional brushes. And you can change the number of Bristles (keeping in mind that fewer bristles make faster brushes). You can also adjust the way the bristles interact in the Rake section of the Brush Controls palette. To try out an existing Rake brush, paint with the Broad Water Brush variant of the Water Color brush or the Van Gogh variant of the Artists brush.

Hose. The Hose stroke type sprays a variety of images when you paint each stroke. To read about painting with the Image Hose turn to "Creating a Tidepool" in Chapter 7 of this book and to Chapter 8, "The Image Hose," in the *Painter 6 User Guide*.

BUILDING CUSTOM BRUSHES

For the custom brushes that follow, we start with an existing Painter brush and radically modify its appearance by making adjustments that affect brush behavior. After you've created the brush (and perhaps made further modifications on your own), you will want to choose Variant, Save Variant from the Brushes palette menu to save it into your current palette. After saving your custom variant under a new name, restore the default settings for the Painter brush by selecting the variant you began with and choosing Variant, Restore Default Variant.

Try these brushes on images of 1000 pixels square or less. If you work with larger files, you'll want to proportionally increase the Size slider settings that we list here. When a Circular or Static Bristle dab type is used, you'll also want to optimize the Spacing and Min Spacing in the Brush Controls palette's Spacing section to accommodate the larger size. If you have trouble setting exact numbers with the

Do want a brush to pull and smear color? A low Resat and a high Bleed setting (in the Well section of the Brush Controls palette), works with Brush Loading to allow the brush to smear pigment while applying it. Choose the Variable Flat variant of the Brushes, and in the Well section, set Resat at 5% and Bleed at 80%. To see the colors mix, choose a new color in the Colors section and drag the brush through existing color on your image.

To make a brush that applies color when you use a light touch and scrubs underlying color when you use heavier pressure, in the Well section of Brush Controls, set Resat low and in the Expression section, turn on the Invert box for Resat.

sliders, try typing the number into the field to the right of the slider. Hit the Enter key to accept the number you've typed. And don't think your computer has crashed if nothing happens for a while when you try to paint: Painter is working away, building a very complex brush.

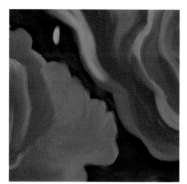

Roughing in the top right flower with the Fast Flat Wet Oils brush

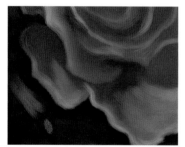

Modulating color on the background with the New Soft Oils brush

Using the New Feathering brush to layer color on the flower petals and background

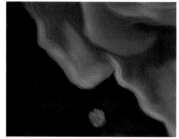

Using the Camelhair Blender brush to mix color on the petals and in the background

To make room for more brushes, we've shortened our descriptions of how to make the brushes. For instance, "*Well:* Resat, 80%" means, "From the Brush Controls palette's Well section set Resat to 80% but leave all other sliders where they are." The palette sections you will use are found in the Brush Controls palette. For a full description of the functions of the controls in each of the sections, you can refer to Painter's *User Guide*, although painting with the brush after you make each adjustment will teach you a lot, too. **Caution:** Before starting a brush recipe with a suggested brush, restore its default settings by choosing Variant, Restore Default Variant from the Brushes palette's menu.

Fast Flat Wet Oils. A Flat dab type and a Single stroke type make this a fast-painting brush, great for painting short dabs of color with a wet feel and a hint of transparency at the end of the stroke.

Start with the default Opaque Flat variant of the Brushes. *Size:* Size, 28; Min Size, 40%; Feature 2.1. *Well:* Resat, 70; Bleed, 40. *Expression:* Size/Pressure; Opacity/Pressure; Turn off Invert Bleed.

New Soft Oils Brush. This Single stroke-type brush was created to feel like a traditional soft, flat brush with long bristles.

Start with the default Opaque Flat variant of the Brushes. *Size:* Size, 31.2; Min Size 42%; Feature: 5.1. *General:* Opacity, 100. *Well:* Resat, 70; Bleed, 40. *Expression:* Size/Pressure; Opacity/Pressure. *Random,* Jitter .05. *Art Materials, Color Variability:* ±H, 1; ±V, 3.

New Feathering Brush. Created for feathering over existing color to add interest and texture, this Single stroke, Bristle brush paints tapered strokes quickly. Increase pressure to widen the stroke.

Start with the default Captured Bristle variant of the Brushes. *Size:* Size, 23.0; Min Size, 30%. *General:* Opacity, 9. *Spacing:* Spacing, 9. *Well:* Resat and Dryout, maximum; Bleed, 0; *Bristle:* Thickness, 40; Clumpiness, 0 (for smooth strokes), Hair Scale, 515. *Expression:* Size/Pressure; *Art Materials, Color Variability:* ±H, 1; ±V, 2.

Camelhair Blender Brush. The *Well* palette settings for this Single-stroke, Camel Hair brush let you pick up existing color and blend with it. The brush hairs spread with more pressure, because Feature is set to Pressure in the Expression section.

Start with the default Round Camelhair variant of the Brushes. *Size:* Size, 23; Min Size, 37%; Feature, 4.1. *General:* Opacity, 100. *Well:* Resat, 4%; Bleed, 96%. *Expression:* Feature/Pressure.

CONTINUOUS MEDIA FLOW

Thanks to Continuous Time Deposition, you can set up any brush to apply media at the first touch; if you continue to press the stylus, media will pool. Most of Painter 6's Airbrushes incorporate Continuous Time Deposition but you can also turn on this feature for a variant that does not. For example, select the Digital Airbrush variant of the Airbrushes, and in the Spacing section of the Brush Controls palette, turn on Continuous Time Deposition.

A footprint and brushstrokes made with the Flat Variable Water Color

A footprint and brushstrokes made with the Textured Water Color Wash

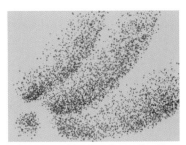

A footprint and brushstrokes made with the Tiny Spattery Airbrush

A footprint and brushstroke made with the Graduated Hairy brush

Footprints and brushstrokes made with the Random Leaves brush

Flat Variable Water Color. This flat Water Color brush paints washes with soft edges and subtle Color Variability.

Start with the default Broad Water Brush variant of Water Color. *Size:* Size: 23.6. *General:* Opacity, 85% Grain, 70%. *Spacing:* Spacing, 11%; Min Spacing, 2.7. *Angle:* Squeeze 25%. *Water:* Diffusion, 2; Wet Fringe, 0%. *Expression:* Size/Pressure; Grain/Pressure; Turn off Invert Bleed. Rake: Turn on Soften Bristle Edge. *Random:* Jitter 0.50. *Art Materials, Color Variability:* ±H, 3; ±S, 2.

Textured Water Color Wash. This Water Color brush paints transparent washes while revealing more of the current texture.

Start with the default Simple Water variant of Water Color. *Size:* Size: 34.1. *General:* Opacity, 20% and Grain, 92%. *Spacing:* Spacing, 12%; Min Spacing, 0.4; *Water:* Wet Fringe, 40%. *Expression:* Size/None; Grain/Pressure (turn on the Invert Grain).

Tiny Spattery Airbrush. This spatter brush with the Airbrush dab type sprays small droplets with subtle Color Variability.

Start with the default Variable Splatter variant of the Airbrushes. *Size:* Size, 34.5; Min Size, 0%; Feature, 2.9. *General:* Opacity, 75. *Expression:* Size/Pressure. *Random:* Jitter 0.50. *Art Materials, Color Variability:* ±H, 5; ±S, 5; ±V, 10.

Graduated Hairy Brush. With this special-effects brush you can paint fur or grass effects that have graduated color. First, choose a multicolor gradient (such as the Sunset gradient) in the Gradient section of the Art Materials palette. Start with the Furry Brush variant of the F/X brush. *Size:* Min Size, 33%. *General:* Source, Gradient. *Spacing:* Turn off Continuous Time Deposition. *Expression:* Opacity/None. *Random:* Jitter 3.00. *Art Materials, Color Variability:* ±V, 0.

New Random Leaves Brush. This Captured, Single-stroke brush with variable color and random size and direction is useful for texturizing—adding a natural look of random fallen leaves to a painting. It looks richest when used over a rough paper texture.

To create the brush dab, use the Fine Point variant of the Pens to make a few simple leaf shapes—similar to the footprint shown—then switch to the Flat Color variant and capture the brush (see "Captured," on page 55). *Size:* Size, 25.3; Min Size, 60%. *General:* Subcategory, Grainy Hard Cover; Opacity, 90%; Grain 14%. *Spacing:* Spacing, Maximum; Min Spacing, Maximum. *Expression:* Size/Random; Opacity/Random. *Art Materials, Color Variability:* ±H, 20; ±V, 7.

> **QUICKER CAPTURES**
>
> When you want to design and capture a brush, start by opening a variant that's close to the effect you want. That way you'll have fewer adjustments to make.

Painting an Expressive Color Study

Overview *Open a new file and sketch using the Pens; add color washes with Water Color brushes; finish the study with the Round Camelhair and Palette Knife brushes.*

We drew the loose sketch with the Fine Point and the Scratchboard Tool variants of the Pens.

Painting tints of color using the Broad Water Brush variant of Water Color

CHER THREINEN-PENDARVIS

SATISFYING TO USE WHEN CREATING expressive color studies, Painter 6's new brushes encourage spontaneity and quick gestural drawing because they make smoother, more continuous strokes and thus make possible a more tactile painting experience. For this color study of *Agave Shawii* (a threatened native in the California Maritime Succulent Scrub habitat) we sketched using Pens and Water Color variants. Then we painted with the Round Camelhair and Palette Knife variants of the Brushes, tools that can mix paint by dragging through existing pools of color on the image canvas.

1 Making a sketch. Open a new file (our file measured 1180 x 1741 pixels). Before you begin your sketch, open the Art Materials palette (Window, Art Materials). Open the Papers palette by clicking the left arrow on the Papers section bar, and click the push bar to open the paper drawer. Click on a paper texture to choose it. We chose Regular Fine from the default Paper Textures library. Click the left arrow on the Colors section bar to open the Colors section, and select a dark color to make your sketch. Open the Brushes palette (Window, Show Brushes), click on the Pens icon and from the variant menu choose the Scratchboard Tool variant. We chose the Scratchboard Tool because of the sensitivity of this tool when used with a stylus—with it you can make expressive, thick and thin strokes. Begin sketching. As you sketch, develop the darks and lights in your image.

3

Using the Bleach variant of the Eraser to remove areas of the sketch

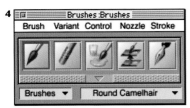

4

Brushes :Brushes				
Brush	Variant	Control	Nozzle	Stroke

Brushes ▼   Round Camelhair ▼

Choosing the Round Camelhair variant

5a

Painting soft afternoon light on the water

5b

Using a low-opacity Round Camelhair brush to modulate color in areas above the plants and develop atmosphere

5c

Mixing the paint on plant leaves by pulling the Round Camelhair brush through existing color on the study

6

Defining the edge of an agave leaf

2 Laying in water color over the sketch. We established a general color theme by laying in tints of color—blues and greens—using the Broad Water Brush and Simple Water variants of Water Color. When you paint with Painter's Water Color brushes, brushstrokes remain "wet" until you dry them by choosing Canvas, Dry. Your Water Color strokes will not disturb other "dry" media such as strokes applied with Pens or Pencils.

3 Selectively erasing the sketch. Because the Water Color strokes are separate, it's possible to selectively edit or erase marks made on the image canvas with tools such as the Pens or Pencils without disturbing the "wet" paint. To erase areas of your sketch (as we did), choose the Bleach variant of the Eraser and paint to remove areas. When you've completed the editing, dry the "wet" Water Color brushstrokes to merge then with the image canvas by choosing Canvas, Dry.

4 Developing the underpainting. We left some of the black from the sketch to retain a hand-drawn quality in the study. The brush we planned to use to complete the painting, the Round Camelhair, has unique qualities. By varying pressure on the stylus, you can add new color, or subtly mix color as you paint. To begin, choose the Round Camelhair variant of the Brushes and a color. Using your stylus, paint a few brushstrokes on your image using firm pressure, then select a new color and apply more brushstrokes over the original strokes using very light pressure. As you drag this brush through a pool of color, you'll notice the edges of the brush pick up a small amount of the existing color from the canvas. Resize the brush as you work using adjust the Size slider in the Controls:Brush palette.

5 Building atmosphere. After painting the sky, water and foreground, we created a sense of steamy afternoon light by building a subtle separation between the mid-ground plants and the water. We used a small low-opacity version of the Round Camelhair brush to modulate lighter blues, grays and yellows into the area. To lower the opacity of the brush, move the Opacity slider on the Controls:Brush palette to the left.

6 Adding details. To finish, we blended areas of the sky and water using the Round Camelhair and a low-opacity Palette Knife variant; we used a tiny Round Camelhair brush to define the edges of the plants and to brighten areas where sun was shining on the leaves; we built up more detailed, striated shadows. Finally, to spread paint and add more texture, we used a small, low-opacity Palette Knife. To build this knife, select the Palette Knife variant of the Brushes. Using the sliders in the Controls:Brush palette, make it smaller by moving the Size slider to 15 pixels, then reduce its Opacity by moving the Opacity slider to 40%. 🖌

Drawing with Colored Pencils

Overview *Create a sketch with the Colored Pencils variant; customize the brush to further develop the drawing; adjust Color Variability settings for a more active color effect.*

CHER THREINEN-PENDARVIS

The line sketch drawn with Colored Pencil

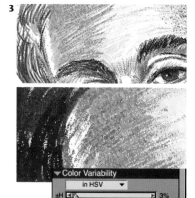

Developing values   *Adding color*

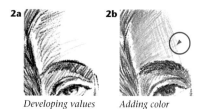

Building dimension using increased settings in the Art Materials:Color Variability section and strokes that follow the form

YOU CAN MODIFY THE COLORED PENCIL variant and get a broken color effect (where the color only partially covers the background or underdrawing) by brushing lightly across a textured surface.

1 Starting with a sketch. To work at the same size we did, open a new 883 pixel-wide file with a white background, then choose the Regular Fine texture from the Art Materials, Papers section. Choose a dark brown color in the Colors section, select the Colored Pencils variant of the Pencils and sketch the portrait.

2 Developing value and adding color. In the Brush Controls, General section, change the Colored Pencil's method to Cover and the subcategory to Grainy Edge Flat Cover. In the Size section, set Size to 3.4 and Min Size to 42%. Use this brush and a lighter brown to develop values throughout the sketch. Choose a skin color (we chose a tan for this portrait of Steve Pendarvis) and apply strokes with a light touch to partially cover some of the brown sketch. Follow the form with your strokes, switching colors and brush sizes as you draw.

3 Building dimension. To give a shimmery look to the color as it's applied, drag the Hue (± H) and Value (± V) sliders in the Art Materials, Color Variability section to 3%. Using a light touch to allow the under-painting to show through, apply a fresh layer of strokes in the areas of strongest color (in our drawing, the forehead and nose shadows and the hair). 🖌

COLORED PENCIL WASHES

If you're using Colored Pencils on rough paper, you can create a wash effect. Choose the Grainy Water variant of the Liquid brush, reducing Opacity and Grain penetration in the Controls:Brush palette to 40% or less. Stroke over your pencil work to blend colors while maintaining texture on the "peaks" of the paper grain.

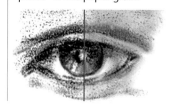

Blending and Feathering with Pastels

Overview Create and soften a sketch; build color and form; blend the painting; add feathered strokes to finish.

CHER THREINEN-PENDARVIS

Creating a loose sketch with Sharp Chalk

Smudging with the Grainy Water variant

Roughing in color and value with Chalk

Blending the underpainting with Water

Finishing with feathered Chalk strokes

FEATHERING—THIN, PARALLEL STROKES over a blended underpainting—is a traditional pastel technique that yields texture and freshness. Because the feathered finishing strokes remain unblended on the painting's surface, the viewer's eye must work to blend the colors. Here is an example of optical color blending.

1 Starting with a sketch. Open a new file with a white background—our file was 3 x 3.3 inches and 225 ppi. Select a rough paper texture from the Art Materials:Papers section such as Big Grain Rough, pick a neutral color (we chose a red-brown), and select the Sharp Chalk variant of Dry Media. To get a more sensitive response, in the Brush Controls:Expression section (Window, Show Brush Controls), we set Size to Velocity. Use this brush to create a sketch.

2 Softening the sketch. Select the Grainy Water variant of Liquid and blend your sketch, allowing your strokes to follow the direction of the form. To blend while revealing more paper texture, blend colors with the Smudge variant of Liquid.

3 Building the underpainting. Use the Artist Pastel Chalk variant of Dry Media and add color and value to your sketch. To blend your strokes, switch to the Grainy Water variant of Liquid; we lowered our variant's Opacity to 40% in the General section of the Brush Controls palette. Add layers to the underpainting with these two tools until you're pleased with the form.

4 Adding feathered strokes. To create thin, textured strokes on top of the blended form, decrease the Size of the Artist Pastel Chalk variant to 4.2 in the Brush Controls:Size section, and in the Expression section, set Size to Pressure. Stroke with this brush in the direction of the form. In our example, feathering is most noticeable in the upper portion of the apple. Finish the piece by using Grainy Water to soften the feathering in the shadow areas.

Painting with Pastels

Overview *Rough out a color composition; add layers of color with a custom Large Chalk; blend colors with Liquid brushes; add highlights and details with the Sharp Chalk; use "scrumbling" for texture to finish.*

CHER THREINEN-PENDARVIS

1a

Sketching in color with the Sharp Chalk variant of Dry Media

1b

Blending the hill and sky using the Smudge variant of the Liquid brush

2a

Adjusting the settings in the Controls: Brush palette

2b

Painting the sunlight shining over the ridge with a custom Large Chalk and yellow color

INSPIRED BY THE SPARKLING LIGHT on a moist, breezy morning, *Agave Meadow* was painted from memory using Painter's Dry Media, although we occasionally referred to pencil sketches made on location. To achieve the soft atmosphere, we painted layers of color with Chalk variants, blended color with Liquid brushes, and added details and broken color to finish the piece.

1 Starting with the drawing. Choose a photo or a sketch of a landscape to use as a reference and open a new file. We started with a 30 x 19.5-inch file at 120 ppi.

Choose a color from the Art Materials, Colors section (Window, Show Art Materials) and a paper from the Papers section. We chose Cold Press 1 (loaded from the Drawing Paper Textures library in the Paper Texture Libraries folder on the Painter 6 Application CD-ROM). Select Dry Media, choose the Sharp Chalk variant and begin sketching. To keep the freshness and energy of a sketch while you draw, don't get bogged down with details. We also used the Artist Pastel Chalk to add cross-hatching to the hills and the Smudge variant of Liquid to blend colors.

2 Building a custom Pastel variant. When you've finished sketching your composition and you're ready to layer color in the underpainting, create a midsized, soft Pastel variant: First choose the Large Chalk variant of Dry Media. In the Controls:Brush palette, set the Size to 12.0, and lower the Opacity to 30%. A lower opacity will allow you to build up color slowly with more sensitivity. To save this custom brush as a variant, from the Brushes palette choose Variant, Save Variant, name your variant and click OK. The new name will appear in the Brushes palette under the Dry Media category. Choose a color and begin painting. We adjusted our new variant's size and opacity as we worked, switching to a 50% opacity, for instance, when painting the sunrise light shining over the ridge of the hill.

Using the Grainy Water variant to "melt" the hill separation, and create a subtle line

Using the custom Large Chalk variant to paint "windy" hatching strokes on the hills

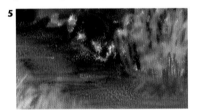

Scrumbling on the path with the Square Chalk variant

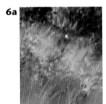 

Drawing the foreground grass blades and details on the acacia with the Sharp Chalk

Painting the highlights on the agave plants using the Artist Pastel Chalk variant

3 Blending colors. To achieve a smooth look with traditional pastels, you rub them with precise blending tools like a tortillion or a blending stump. Use the Just Add Water, Grainy Water, and Smudge variants of the Liquid brush to mimic these traditional tools. A few hints about these blenders: The Just Add Water uses Soft Cover subcategory, and blends smoothly without texture; Grainy Water use Grainy Flat Cover and blends showing a hint of texture; Smudge uses Grainy Hard Cover and reveals more texture as it blends color. Begin blending, and experiment with these brushes and various brush sizes while you work.

4 Achieving a feeling of movement. Select the Pastel variant you created in step 2. Imagine the wind blowing over your landscape, and apply light strokes over the hills in your painting, as if your strokes were blown by the wind. We switched to a rougher paper texture, (Big Canvas texture, loaded from the More Paper Textures library, in the Paper Texture Libraries folder), then added gold, rust-colored and blue strokes to the mid-ground hills and lighter blues to the sky. We covered most of the rolling coastal hills with soft, linear brushstrokes.

5 Scrumbling for more texture. Artists using traditional media will often finish a pastel drawing by brushing the side of the pastel lightly along the peaks of the rough art paper. This technique, called *scrumbling*, causes colors to blend optically and adds texture. To scrumble electronically, select the Large Chalk variant and adjust Opacity to 25% (Controls:Brush palette). Choose a rough paper (Big Canvas). In the Brush Controls, Size section, (opened by clicking the left triangle on the Size section bar) select the lower left brush tip profile. Apply strokes lightly using a color sampled from your image with the Dropper. We used scrumbling to complete the sky and clouds and to show subtle reflected light on the foreground path. To add a semi-transparent texture to the plant life in the foreground, we switched to the Grainy Soft Cover subcategory.

6 Finishing with fine details. After adding the scrumbling, we added fine details, such as the thin foreground grass blades and the planes of the agave leaves that were illuminated by full sunlight.

To draw grass blades we chose the Sharp Chalk variant and a light greenish-gold color in the Colors section. Before we began to paint, we opened the Color Variability section of the Art Materials palette and adjusted the Value (± V) to 4% so the color would vary slightly as we painted. We painted thin, slightly curved strokes (keeping the wind direction in mind). We made a few strokes overlap and adjusted the size of the strokes using the Size slider on the Controls:Brush palette.

To enhance the focal point of the painting, we painted bright highlights on the sides of the agave leaves that were catching the direct morning sun. For the highlights we chose a light golden yellow, and painted curved strokes with the Artist Pastel Chalk, using it at its full opacity.

Painting with Oils

Overview *Create a sketch with a Pencils variant; add color to the underpainting with the Artist Pastel Chalk; use a Liquid variant to create the look of oils.*

DENNIS ORLANDO

Sketching the canoes and shoreline

2a

Selecting the Artist Pastel Chalk and switching to Grainy Soft Cover

2b

Roughing in the beach with the Artist Pastel Chalk variant

3

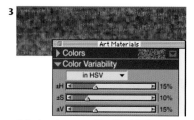

Painting the water (detail) with the Artist Pastel Chalk variant, using Orlando's Color Variability settings

ARTIST DENNIS ORLANDO CAPTURES an exquisite harmony between man-made and organic elements in his *Canoe Trip at Cedar Water*. A strong composition, deft modeling of shapes, sensitivity to light and shadow and his unique electronic oil painting technique all combine to give the piece its power. Orlando used a photograph taken on a camping trip in the New Jersey Pine Barrens as a reference for the painting.

1 Sketching the canoes. Orlando set up a new 8.25 x 3.5-inch document with a resolution of 150 ppi and a white Paper Color. He placed the reference photo under the clear plastic flap of his drawing tablet, then he modified a Pencils variant and used it to trace the four canoes and the shoreline. To create his custom variant, select the Thick & Thin Pencil variant of the Pencils. In the Brush Controls palette's General section, change to Cover method and Grainy Soft Cover subcategory. In the Size section, drag the Size slider to 2.0. Select Basic Paper in the Papers section of the Art Materials palette, choose a color in the Color section (Orlando started with a gray-blue) and begin sketching.

2 Beginning the underpainting. To help define the exterior shapes of the canoes, Orlando roughed in the beach with a Dry Media variant and a rough texture. To build Orlando's Chalk, select the Artist Pastel Chalk variant of Dry Media and in the Brush Controls:Size section set its Size to 10.1. In the General section, change the subcategory to Grainy Soft Cover—this gives softer brushstrokes than Grainy Hard Cover. From the Art Materials:Papers section's resource list, choose Load Library and load the More Paper Textures library found in the Paper Texture Libraries folder on the Painter 6 Application CD-ROM, and choose the Big Canvas paper texture (Orlando used this paper on the rest of the piece). He chose a creamy tan tint and quickly blocked in large areas of the beach around the edges of the canoes.

3 Using Color Variability in the water. One of Orlando's "electronic oil" trademarks is activity in the color. He achieves this by adjusting the Color Variability settings for certain brushes. To re-create the active color look he achieved in the water, start with the same Chalk variant that you set up in step 2. Choose a

Establishing values

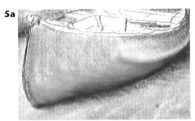

Pulling color along the canoe with the Smeary Bristle Spray Brush variant

Detail of canoe showing the sand reflection

Detail of the foreground sand painted with the Artist Pastel Chalk, Smeary Bristle Spray and Grainy Water variants

Painting crisp, final details on the boat with the Sharp Chalk variant

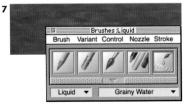

Using the Grainy Water variant to blend areas of the water

dark gray-green, then open the Color Variability section in the Art Materials palette and adjust the Color Variability sliders: set Hue (± H) to 10, Saturation (± S) to 5 and Value (± V) to 10. Name and save this variant (on the Brushes palette, choose Variant, Save Variant, enter a name and click OK). Begin painting. Using the Size slider in the Size section, Orlando changed to a smaller brush size when working close to the canoes in order to preserve their shapes.

4 Establishing values and adding details. Use a smaller version of the same Dry Media variant (Orlando resized his to 7.1) to rough in color and value details. Keep the same Color Variability settings. Orlando used a blue-gray color to paint the dark, recessed areas inside the canoes, then switched to a lighter value of the same color to paint the metallic hulls of the boats.

5 Simulating traditional oils. Several of Painter's new brushes let you smear existing "pixel paint" to get the same look that you would get by pushing conventional oils around a canvas. To apply paint while subtly blending it with existing color on the image, begin by selecting the Smeary Bristle Spray variant of the Brushes. In the Size section, move the Size slider to 18.5 (Orlando varied his brush size slightly as he painted.) With the Dropper tool, sample a color from the area you want to paint, or hold down the Ctrl/⌘ key while you're using the brush to temporarily switch to the Dropper. To maintain the modulated color of the underpainting, give this brush the same Color Variability settings used in step 3. Save this variant.

Use this brush and make short, crisp strokes to pull color from one area of your painting into another. Orlando switched between this brush and his Artist Pastel Chalk variant to work over the entire surface of the painting. He created the reflection of the sand on the canoes by sampling color from the sand and painting short, curved strokes on the canoes with the Smeary Bristle Spray variant. He also used the Grainy Water variant of Liquid to blend the highlights on the canoes.

6 Defining the details. Orlando used a small (approximately 5.1) Sharp Chalk variant of Dry Media, to define surface edges and to add color details on the sand and boats.

7 Blurring the water. The Grainy Water variant of Liquid is perfect for blending and softening areas, making them appear to recede. Orlando dabbed this brush on the water, using short strokes to preserve the modulated color.

Output. Orlando typically makes proofs of a painting on a Canon Color Laser Copier with an EFI Fiery RIP. He then picks a favorite to send out to be printed with an Iris inkjet using archival inks. This image was printed by Cone Editions Press on Somerset, a softly textured, handmade English paper. (To read how to contact Cone Editions Press turn to Appendix C in the back of this book.)

Watercolor: "Wet-into-Wet" and Glazing

Overview *Make a "pencil sketch;" apply layers of color to the sketch with Water Color brushes, drying the image between applications of color; add final highlight detail to the dried image with an Eraser.*

MARY ENVALL

TWO COMMON TRADITIONAL WATERCOLOR techniques that are easily emulated with Painter are *wet-into-wet* and *glazing*. Wet-into-wet creates a softer-edged look—the painting surface is kept wet as new color is applied, so new paint blends easily with old. Glazing involves applying transparent washes of watercolor, drying the painting between successive washes; colors are usually built up in layers from light to dark. Drying an image after applying each new layer of color allows crisper rendering than is possible with the wet-into-wet technique.

Mary Envall frequently paints a close-up view of her subject to emphasize subtle details. Before beginning *Cymbidium Orchids*, one of a series of watercolor flower studies, Envall shot photos to use for reference. She began this image with a tight pencil sketch in Painter and used transparent glazes to build layers of color and value, progressing from light to dark.

1 Starting with a sketch. Open a new file with a white background (Envall's file was 1580 pixels wide); then choose a texture from the Papers section of the Art Materials palette. Envall chose Basic paper because she felt its natural-looking grain would complement her watercolor rendering. Choose a neutral gray color, select the 2B Pencil variant of Pencils and draw your line sketch.

1

The line sketch made with the 2B Pencil

2 Adding the first washes. Using highlight colors for the first glaze layer, Envall added washes to her pencil sketch. Choose light colors and block in the large areas with the Simple Water variant of the Water Color. (Selecting a Water Color brush automatically activates Painter's Wet Layer.) With

2

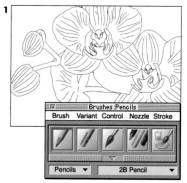

Light washes painted over the sketch with the Simple Water variant of Water Color

3a

Building up tones using slightly darker washes

3b

Building the bud forms and adding darker tones to the background and the flower

4a

Adding texture and detail with the Spatter Water and Simple Water brushes

4b

Using the Simple Water brush to paint washes, blending some of the painted spots on the petals

4c

Defining the edges of the petals and buds

conventional watercolor, you can't paint on areas that you ultimately want to keep white, but Painter lets you lighten or remove color: Use the Wet Eraser variant of the Water Color brush.

If you want to erase linework on the background without disturbing the wet paint, do so with a "dry" Erasers variant *before* you dry the Wet Layer, since drying the Wet Layer merges it permanently with the background. Envall kept the pencil lines she needed for emphasis and erased others with a small Eraser variant of Erasers.

To complete the first glaze, choose Canvas, Dry to dry the Wet Layer. Then start the next glaze by choosing a Water Color brush and continuing to paint. Select the Simple Water variant, for example, and add a slightly darker series of washes with more detail, as Envall did before developing the midtones in the next step.

3 Building form and midtone values. Choose medium-value colors and develop your midtones, applying lighter colors first, then darker ones to create form. Keep your light source in mind and let your strokes follow the direction of the forms.

Envall added the larger intermediate-value shapes and some of the shadows. She added deeper, more intense purple and fuchsia colors to the interior of the orchid, to enhance the focal point.

4 Adding texture, details and blending. Envall used the Spatter Water variant of Water Color to paint soft, speckled strokes from the interior of the orchid toward the tips of the petals, leaving the petal edges mostly white. To softly blend areas of the painted spots, she used a low-opacity Simple Water variant. After completing the blending, she dried her painting again, by choosing Canvas, Dry. Then she used a small Simple Water variant to brighten the fuchsia and gold details on the interior of the orchid. Using the same brush, she defined the linear details on the closed buds and added shadows, adjusting the Opacity and the Size of the brush in the Controls:Brush palette as she worked. If she needed to lighten an area while it was still "wet," she used the Wet Eraser variant of Water Color. She worked carefully to develop subtle layers of color and contrast.

To finish, Envall sharpened areas in the image that needed definition using a tiny Simple Water brush. After drying the image again, she defined highlights along the edges of the orchid petals with a tiny Eraser. 🖌

COMBINING WET AND DRY

You can easily switch between working with Wet Paint and painting on the "dry" background: Switch to a "non-wet" brush to add linework or erase lines on the background, then return to the Water Color brushes to continue your work in Wet Paint.

USING POST-DIFFUSE

To soften the edges of brushstrokes in the Wet Layer only, press Shift-D, Painter's Post-Diffuse command. Repeat the key combination to increase the effect.

Gouache and Opaque Watermedia

Overview Create a finely grained surface; build custom brushes; begin with a scanned sketch; sculpt highlights and details using the custom variants; blend colors with a Liquid brush.

NANCY STAHL

Scaling the Micro Grain texture to 25%

2a

Stahl's traditional pencil drawing

2b

Sketching with the Smooth Ink Pen variant

ARTIST NANCY STAHL HAS WORKED WITH TRADITIONAL gouache on illustration board since 1976. When she began to work with the computer, her clients would accept her digital art only if the quality matched her conventional style. After much experimentation with Painter's brushes and surfaces, she has been able to fully re-create the effect of traditional gouache, evident in the painting *Mercury,* above.

1 Emulating a traditional gouache surface. Stahl's favorite traditional gouache support is a Strathmore kid finish illustration board. The kid finish is soft and allows for a smooth application of paint. To create Stahl's surface for gouache, begin by choosing Load Library (it's located at the bottom of the pop-out list of papers in the Papers section of the Art Materials palette) to retrieve the Micro Grain paper texture from the More Wild Textures library (located in the Paper Texture Libraries folder on the Painter 6 Application CD-ROM). To make the surface even smoother, scale it to 25%. This finely textured surface is most noticeable when used with Stahl's Gouache brush in step 4.

2 Beginning with sketches. Stahl began by using traditional pencils and paper to draw a black-and-white study to establish the composition and work out values.

In Painter, she created a new file that measured approximately 1500 x 1200 pixels. Using the Flat Color variant of Pens, Stahl roughed a brown color into the background, then drew a russet-colored outline sketch with the Smooth Ink Pen (Pens). Begin creating a new file similar to the size of Stahl's, select the Smooth Ink Pen variant and set the Size to 2.0 in the Controls:Brush palette. Choose a russet color and begin sketching.

Using the Camelhair Medium to paint teardrop shapes suggesting the feathers

Painting textured highlights on the helmet

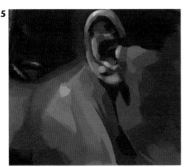

Wings painted with the Camelhair Medium and Gouache brushes

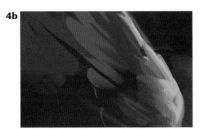

Using the Coarse Smear variant of Liquid to mix and pull color on the neck

Adding details to the eyes, lips and nose using the Smooth Ink Pen variant of the Pens and a russet color

3 Painting teardrop shapes. To paint smooth teardrop shapes suggesting feathers on the wings and to sculpt the facial features, Stahl created a new variant based on the Round Camelhair variant of the Brushes. All of the controls needed to build Stahl's brush are located in various sections of the Brush Controls palette.

In the Brushes palette, choose the Round Camelhair variant, and in the General section of Brush Controls, set Feature to 1.3. (Lowering the Feature setting "tightens" the bristles in the brush, giving the strokes a smoother, crisper edge with fewer bristle marks, similar to using a soft traditional brush loaded with paint on a smooth surface.) In the Size section of Brush Controls, set Size to 10 and Min Size to 29%. In the Well section set Resat to 65% and Bleed to 8% (increasing the Resat setting allows the brush to paint with more of the current color, with less mixing of colors on the image canvas.) In the Expression section, set Size to Pressure, and set Opacity, Resat and Bleed to None, making sure to turn off the Invert box for Bleed. From the Brushes palette's Variant menu, choose Save Variant, name your variant (Stahl named hers Camelhair Medium) and click OK. Stahl varied the size of her brush while she worked.

> **OPERATING BRUSH CONTROLS**
>
> The Brush Controls palette can be opened by choosing Window, Show Brush Controls. Then you can open one of its sections by clicking the left triangle on a section bar. Or press the Shift key and click one of the left triangles to open all of the sections at once.

4 Building a fast, grainy Gouache brush. Stahl wanted a fast, sensitive brush with grainy edges to use on the helmet, staff and background. To build a brush like Stahl's, start with the Graphic Paintbrush variant of the Brushes. In the Size section of Brush Controls, change Size to 25; set the Min Size slider at 40%. In the General section of Brush Controls, set Grain to 25%. Also in the General section, check to make sure that the Source is set to Pattern as Opacity and the Subcategory is set to Grainy Edge Flat Cover. In the Expression section, make sure that both Size and Opacity are set to Pressure and all others to None. Save the variant. To achieve Stahl's look—before painting with your new brush—make sure that Micro Grain is still chosen in the Papers section. When the stylus is used with light pressure, this grainy Gouache brush is sensitive to texture.

5 Pulling color. To blend colors in the background and on the shoulders, Stahl used varying sizes of the Coarse Smear variant of Liquid. Since this brush uses the Diffuse Motion Brush subcategory, she was able to soften color transitions while adding texture.

6 Finishing touches. Using a small Smooth Ink Pen (Pens), Stahl added linear accents on Mercury's eyes, lips and nose. She used a low-opacity version of the Dry Ink (Brushes) to paint a few brushstrokes with thick bristle marks on the background, shoulders and helmet. 🖌

Cloning
and Tracing

Overview *Open a reference
image; make a clone; delete the
contents of the clone; use tracing
paper to aid in tracing the
original image; add detail using
Cloning brushes.*

CHER THREINEN-PENDARVIS

PHOTO: CORBIS

The original photo

Sketching in the clone using Tracing Paper

Selecting the sky with the Magic Wand

WHEN THERE ISN'T TIME to draw from scratch—or if drawing from
life isn't your fancy—Painter's cloning and tracing paper features
make it easy to use a photo or other existing art as a reference for
a new illustration.

1 Selecting an image and making a clone. In Painter, start
by opening a reference image (such as a painting or photo). To
make a clone, choose File, Clone. The new clone will be linked to
the original file—its clone source. The cloning process maps the
clone (the destination image) directly to the original (the source
image), pixel-by-pixel. Leave the original image open.

2 Tracing and sketching. Working with Tracing Paper in Painter
is similar to using a conventional light table. In preparation for using
the Tracing Paper function, select all (Ctrl/⌘-A), and delete the
contents from the clone canvas (Backspace/Delete). Turn on Tracing Paper by clicking the Tracing Paper icon at the top of the scroll
bar or choose Canvas, Tracing Paper (Ctrl/⌘-T). The original image
will appear "screened back," ready to be traced with a brush.

Open the Art Materials palette (Window, Show Art Materials)
and click on the Papers section's name to open the Papers section.
Click on a paper texture or choose it from the pop-up list. We alternated between Basic Paper and Smooth textures. Open the Color
picker (by clicking the Colors section's name), click in the Hue
ring or Hue bar to choose a hue, and in the color triangle to select
a tint or shade of the color. We chose a warm gray for our sketch.

Open the Brushes drawer
(Window, Show Brushes), and
click on a brush to select it.
(You do not need to use a cloning method brush to sketch
using Tracing Paper.) Begin

USING CLONE COLOR

To paint with your own strokes in an
illustration with color from another
image, check the Clone Color
checkbox on the Color palette.

3b

Filling the sky with imagery from the source image

3c

Adding grainy strokes to the sky and foliage using the Chalk variants

4

To add crispness to the soft illustration we cloned in a few details from the original.

5

Cloning the border. Notice the crosshair denoting the sampled area.

painting using the clone source image as a guide. To toggle Tracing Paper on and off as you work press Ctrl/⌘-T. We drew a solid line to outline the building, using the Fine Point variant of Pens.

3 Making a selection and filling. Next, we selected the white sky above the solid line with the Magic Wand. (In the Controls: Magic Wand palette, we set the Tolerance to 1 and turned on Contiguous, so that only the white pixels would be selected in the sky area.) We saved the selection by choosing Select, Save Selection, New, to save it as a mask that we could use later. Then we chose Effects, Fill, Clone Source to bring the color from the original image into the selected sky. (For more information about selections, turn to Chapter 4.) With the selection still active, using shades of blue, we painted grainy strokes over the filled sky with the Large Chalk variant of Dry Media, and then dropped the selection (Ctrl/⌘-D).

4 Adding details with brushes. After painting the foreground foliage with the Smooth Ink Pen variant of Pens using greens and black, we switched to the Large Chalk to add loose curved strokes of white to denote highlights on the foliage. Then, changing the brush size in the Controls:Brush palette as we worked, we added more strokes to the foliage in various shades of green, some imported from the original image using Clone Color. To brush detail from the original image onto your illustration, choose a cloning brush variant. We used the Chalk Cloner variant of the Cloners to add detail to the door of the mission. You can change any Painter brush into a cloning brush by switching its method to Cloning. For a smoother look, try cloning using the Soft Cover Cloning subcategory available in the General section of the Brush Controls palette.

5 Cloning a border with a chalky edge. In preparation for adding a rough-edged border, we increased the canvas size of the file (Canvas, Canvas Size) by 20 pixels on all four sides. (When you change the size of your canvas, Tracing Paper will no longer be available unless you also change the source image to the same pixel size.) We added the border by sampling imagery and making rough strokes along the edge using the Chalk Cloner. To clone from one point to another within an image (much like using the Rubber Stamp in Photoshop), select a source point in your image (Shift-click, Windows/Control-click, Mac). Reposition the cloning brush in your document and stroke to bring the imagery into the area. Reload the cloning brush as necessary as you work around the edge.

CLONING FROM ONE UNRELATED IMAGE TO ANOTHER

To clone from one unrelated image to another (to map pixel for pixel, or to use the Tracing Paper function), the two images must have exactly the same pixel dimensions. Open two images that are the same size and choose one image for your destination image. Choose File, Clone Source, and designate the second image as the clone source. Use a Cloning brush to bring imagery into the destination image, in exactly the same position as in the source. To continue to clone or use Tracing Paper, the source image must be left open.

Coloring Pencil Illustrations

Overview *Scan a pencil sketch; clone it; tint it and add texture; restore from the original; add color with the Airbrush, Dry Media and Water Color brushes.*

PHILIP HOWE

The original pencil illustration, scanned

Adding a tint and a texture to the clone

Using a Cloning method brush to partially restore the gray tones of the original

MUCH OF THE BEAUTY of illustrator Philip Howe's work lies in his seamless, creative blending of the traditional with the digital. In a spread for *Trailblazer* magazine—a detail of which is shown here—Howe combined hand-drawn calligraphy, a photo of two slides, a photo of a watercolor block (for the background), and his own pencil sketches, colored to simulate traditional watercolor.

1 Starting with a sketch. Howe began by sketching the various birds in pencil on watercolor paper. He scanned the images on a flatbed scanner, saving them as grayscale files in TIFF format. Each bird image was 4 to 5 inches square and 300 ppi.

2 Modifying a clone. Open a grayscale scan in Painter. Choose File, Clone, to clone your scan, giving you an "original" and a clone. Keep the original open—you'll want to pull from it later. Howe added a color tint and a texture to the clone of the scanned bird. To add a tint, choose a color in the Art Materials:Colors section (Howe chose a reddish brown), then choose Effects, Surface Control, Color Overlay. Select Uniform Color from the pop-up menu, set Opacity to 30%, click the Dye Concentration button and click OK. To add texture, from Art Materials:Papers, select a paper texture (Howe chose Basic Paper) and choose Effects, Surface Control, Apply Surface Texture. Select Paper from the Using menu, set Amount to 50% and set Shine to 0%. Click OK.

3 Restoring from the original. Howe used Painter's cloning capabilities to replace most of the tint and texture in the bird's body with the light gray tones of the original. You could use a standard cloning brush to do this, but Howe chose the Digital Airbrush variant of the Airbrushes and made an Airbrush cloner. To make Howe's cloner, select the Digital Airbrush, open the General section of the Brush Controls palette and change the method to Cloning and the subcategory to Soft Cover Cloning. Also in the General section, try lowering this cloning brush's Opacity for more sensitivity. Once you've changed the brush, paint on the portion of your image that you want to restore. The original will automatically be revealed in the area covered by your strokes.

4

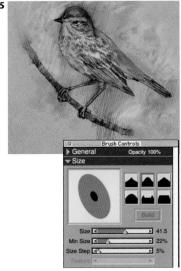

Applying color tints with the Fat Stroke Airbrush in Buildup method

5

Using a modified Large Chalk variant to add color to the background

6

Applying watercolor accents with the Spatter Water variant

Another spot illustration from the Trailblazer spread. Howe used the same brushes and technique for all illustrations.

4 Adding color tints with an Airbrush. To achieve the effect of traditional airbrushing with transparent dyes or watercolor pigments, Howe used two versions of the Digital Airbrush variant. In the Brush Controls:General section he switched back to Cover method, Soft Cover subcategory, and reduced the Opacity setting to between 5% and 10%. He used these settings to carefully lay in the golden brown tones on the bird's back. Next, he switched to the Buildup method, Soft Buildup subcategory, and added the more saturated yellow and rust hues. The Buildup method allowed him to use a slightly higher Opacity (between 10% and 20%) to achieve richer color while preserving the intensity of the pencil sketch.

5 Cloning again and brushing with Chalk. Howe uses the Clone feature like a flexible "Save As" command. When he's ready to move on to the next phase of an illustration, he often makes a clone and uses the original as "source material." Here, when he had colored the bird to his satisfaction, he chose File, Clone. If he over-worked an area in the new clone, he restored it by cloning in imagery from the previous version by opening that version and designating it as the "source" by choosing File, Clone Source. Then he painted with a cloning brush to restore the area.

Howe switched to the Large Chalk variant of Dry Media and began to paint loose, gestural strokes on the image background around the bird using two similar green hues. He changed the size of the brush as he worked by making adjustments in the Brush Controls:Size section. To make the brush elliptical, he set Angle to 116° and Squeeze to 60% in the Brush Controls:Angle section.

6 Adding a watercolor look. To add a finishing touch without muddying his existing color work, Howe used Water Color variants. He used the Simple Water variant to add more depth to the color on the bird's head and other areas. He switched to the Spatter Water variant to add a "water drop" effect on the background, sampling color from the bird and background using the Dropper tool. When he finished, he chose Canvas, Dry to combine the Water Color brushstrokes with the rest of the paint.

Merging the files. Using the Lasso, Howe drew a loose selection around the bird, then he chose Select, Feather and feathered it 30 pixels. Then he opened the 17 x 11-inch main image and used the Layer Adjuster tool to drag and drop the bird into the main image. To blend the bird layer with the background, he set its Composite Method in the Objects:Layers section to Multiply.

Spontaneous Pastels

Overview *Add texture to a new document; use variants of Dry Media to create a sketch; block in color; add detail.*

CHELSEA SAMMEL

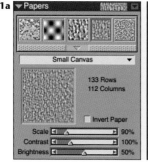

The Papers section of the Art Materials palette

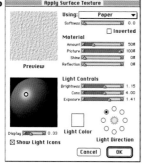

Sammel's Apply Surface Texture settings

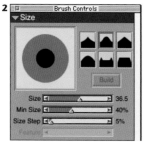

Adjusting the settings for Tapered Chalk

THE CHALK VARIANTS ARE AMONG PAINTER'S most responsive brushes, making them a natural match for artist Chelsea Sammel's spontaneous style. The Chalks are also grain-sensitive, another good match for Sammel, who worked for many years with traditional pastels on rough paper. She began *Poppies* at a Macworld demonstration and finished it in her studio.

1 Preparing the drawing surface. Sammel created a rough, textured surface across her entire canvas. To do this, create a new document with a tan paper color 750 pixels wide. Choose a rough paper texture in the Art Materials:Papers section. Drag the Scale slider to the left to make a finer grain. Sammel chose Small Canvas from the More Paper Textures library (from the Paper Texture Libraries folder on the Painter 6 Application CD-ROM) and scaled it to 90%. To apply the texture, choose Effects, Surface Control, Apply Surface Texture. Choose Paper from the pop-up menu and experiment with the settings. Click OK when you're done. Sammel set Amount to 50%, Picture to 100% and Shine to 0%.

2 Building brush variants. Sammel likes Painter's default Chalk variants (found under Dry Media in Painter 6) and makes only minor adjustments to their settings. She works quickly and spontaneously, creating a few variants on the fly and switching frequently among them. To create her Tapered Chalk, choose the Artist Pastel Chalk variant of Dry Media. On the Brushes palette, choose Control, Show Brush Controls; open the Size section by clicking the left triangle on the section bar; set Size to 36.5 and Min Size to 40%. On the Brush Controls palette, open the Expression section and set Size to Pressure. This setting, combined

THE VANISHING SURFACE

Applying Surface Texture to an empty canvas is a good way to give an entire surface a texture, but it will be covered as you paint if the brush you're using doesn't show grain (doesn't have the word "grainy" in its subcategory). Some artists apply Surface Texture before *and* after they paint.

3a

Drawing the poppy with the Conté variant over the ochre background

3b

The original finished poppy image, before the image canvas was extended to incorporate the second poppy

4a

The image canvas extended using the tan paper color, and the poppy duplicate in place to balance the composition

4b

Detail of the nearly completed image showing Sammel's dark green line work on the smaller poppy and the lighter complementary details added to the image

with a moderate Min Size setting, creates more taper at the end of each stroke. To save the variant, from the Brushes palette, choose Variant, Save Variant, then name your brush and click OK. To create Sammel's Conté Crayon, start with the Sharp Chalk variant. In the Size section, change Size to 9.4 and Min Size to 50%. In the Brush Controls:Expression section, set Size to Pressure. For a grainier stroke, drag the Grain slider in the Controls:Brush palette to 13%. Save the variant.

3 Sketching the first poppy. Sammel brushed a warm ochre onto the background using the Tapered Chalk, adding a few strokes of complementary blues and greens. She switched to her Conté variant, chose black, and sketched loose, dynamic shapes. She switched back to Tapered Chalk and began to block in areas of color, starting with the large poppy. She wanted an active, random look to the color, so she placed varying colors next to each other. Once she had blocked in the major areas, she chose the Grainy Water variant of Liquid and smudged her strokes into the background. She switched to the Smudge variant in areas where she wanted to preserve the textured look.

4 Adding the second poppy. To balance the composition, Sammel decided to add another poppy. If you need to make more room in an existing image, choose Canvas, Canvas Size, and enter the number of pixels you want to add to each edge of your image. Sammel first sampled a tan color from her image using the Dropper and chose Canvas, Set Paper Color, and then she added approximately 300 pixels. To give texture to the new image canvas, she selected it using the Rectangular Selection tool, and used Apply Surface Texture with the same settings described in step 1. Using the Tapered Chalk she added brushstrokes to match the color of the original background and to hide the vertical line where the addition was made.

Sammel created a duplicate poppy by carefully selecting the large poppy with the Lasso, switching to the Layer Adjuster tool, holding down the Alt/Option key (to copy) and clicking on the selected area. While the copy was floating, she scaled it smaller, flipped it horizontally, and rotated it slightly (all of these effects are found under Effects, Orientation). She combined the poppy and canvas by clicking the Drop button in the Layers section of the Objects palette.

Finalizing the image. Sammel extended the petals of the small poppy with the Tapered Chalk, blending and adding fresh color where needed. To further define the shapes, she added very dark green line work with her Conté variant. She finished the image by adding lighter complementary hues over the dark ones. 🖌

When creating custom variants, save the effort of building the brush each time by having Painter do the job for you. Turn on automatic brush building by checking Auto Build Brush (under the Brush Menu on the Brushes palette).

Applying Scanned Paper Textures

Overview *Scan a textured paper; open the file in Painter and capture the texture; use a grain-sensitive brush and Painter's special effects to apply the texture to your image.*

CORRINE OKADA

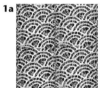

The scanned paper textures: rice paper (left) and maple leaf (right)

Increasing the contrast of the paper scan

Capturing a selected area of the paper scan

Saving and naming the new paper texture

WHILE PAINTER OFFERS A SEEMINGLY ENDLESS assortment of paper grains, many artists still choose to create their own surfaces. They draw from many sources: video grabs, scanned photos, texture collections on CD-ROM, scans of natural objects (leaves or richly grained wood), scans of papers or patterns and images drawn in Painter. They also generate their own seamless textures with Painter's Make Paper and Make Fractal Pattern features.

When Corrine Okada first began using Painter, she scanned her extensive paper collection, capturing the images in Painter and saving them into her own texture libraries. Her skill in applying these custom textures is evident in *Crane Maiden,* a CD-ROM cover commissioned by Silicon Graphics.

1 Scanning the papers. Okada scans her papers on a flatbed scanner in grayscale mode. She scans an 8 x 10-inch area at 300 ppi. If you're scanning a thin, light-colored sheet—like the piece of lacy rice paper that Okada scanned for this job—you may want to place a sheet of black paper behind it to create more contrast. Okada also scanned a sheet of Japanese maple leaf paper.

You'll have more flexibility when you apply the texture if the scan you apply has good contrast and a broad tonal range. So open your scanned texture and choose Effects, Tonal Control, Brightness/Contrast. Drag the top slider to the right to increase contrast. If necessary, adjust the lower slider (Brightness) and then click Apply.

2 Capturing the texture. Use the Rectangular Selection tool to isolate an area of your image. Start by selecting an area of about 200 x 200 pixels (read the Width and Height dimensions in the

3a

Detail of the Rice Paper texture brushed behind the head

3b

Detail of the Rice Paper texture brushed onto the kimono

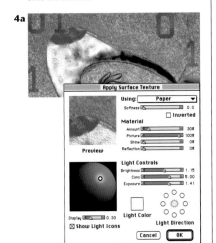

4a

Applying a Surface Texture using Painter's Rice Paper texture

4b

The Maple Leaf texture on the brushstroke (applied with Surface Control effects) and the computer monitor (applied with the Charcoal variant of Dry Media)

Controls:Selection palette). The repetition of your pattern may be too obvious if your selection is much smaller. In Art Materials, Papers section's pop-up menu (opened by clicking the triangle on the right side of the Papers section bar) choose Paper, Capture Paper. For the smoothest results, leave the Crossfade setting at 16. Name your paper and click OK. A picture of the texture will appear in your current Paper library.

3 Applying grain with brushes. Painter lets you apply textures in two ways: with a brush or as a special effect. Okada used both of these methods (within selections and on layers), in this piece. To brush the Rice Paper texture behind the woman's head, she first inverted the texture by checking the Invert Paper box in the Papers section. She selected the area behind the head, then brushed the texture into the selected area using the Charcoal variant of Dry Media and a white color. Okada selected a purple color to brush the same texture (with Invert Paper turned off) onto the woman's kimono. Near the end of the project, she used the same brush to apply the Maple Leaf texture onto the computer screen in blue, yellow and white.

4 Special effects with grain. To create a subtle woven look across the entire image, Okada selected the Rice Paper texture from the Wild Textures library found in the Paper Texture Libraries folder, on the Painter 6 CD-ROM. She selected Effects, Surface Control, Apply Surface Texture. In the Using menu she selected Paper, then she set the Amount at 30% and the Shine at 0 and clicked OK.

To add color, value and texture to the brushstroke that sweeps across the lower half of the image, Okada applied multiple special effects using the Maple Leaf texture. She selected, then floated the brushstroke, and used Color Overlay, Apply Lighting, and Apply Surface Texture (all under Effects, Surface Control) a few times each with various settings to get the effect she wanted. 🖌

Sculpting a Portrait

Overview *Make a sketch; block in color with Dry Media variants; sculpt the forms; refine the composition.*

RICHARD BIEVER

The sketch on a warm-toned paper color

Loosely blocking in mid-tone color

Sculpting the facial features

RICHARD BIEVER LOVES THE EXPRESSIVE FREEDOM he enjoys while working with Painter and a pressure-sensitive tablet and stylus— the natural brushstrokes, the sensitivity, the happy accidents of two colors blending together or a bit of canvas showing through. If he doesn't like a brushstroke, it's easy to "Undo" it by typing Ctrl/⌘-Z, or by simply using the chalk to draw over the area again. Biever's painting *The Parable,* a portrait of Jesus Christ, was painted using Painter's Dry Media and Liquid variants.

1 Sketching on a colored ground. To begin the portrait with a warm tone, Biever began a new file (about 3000 x 3500 pixels) with a sand-colored paper color. He chose the Sharp Chalk variant of Dry Media in the Brushes palette (Window, Show Brushes), a dark neutral color in the Colors section of the Art Materials palette (opened by clicking the left triangle on the Colors section bar) and Basic Paper in the Papers section. Using the Sharp Chalk, he sketched loosely, indicating the general position of the facial features and shape of the head.

2 Blocking in color and blending. Next, Biever blocked in the base tones using the Square Chalk variant (Dry Media). Using the Size slider on the Controls:Brush palette, he enlarged the Square Chalk to make thicker strokes. Using broad strokes of color, he established the planes of the face and set the general tone of the painting and the angle and color of light on the face. (Biever wanted the feeling of natural sunlight, outdoors.) He worked from dark to light, roughing in general shapes using mid-toned color to sculpt the facial structure, letting his brushstrokes follow the direction of the forms. (He planned to add the highlights last.) Using the Marbling Rake

4a

Roughing in the left hand

4b

The left hand and more canvas added

5

The completed face after the contrast was adjusted

variant of Liquid, he began to blend color and build up form.

3 Blending and sculpting.
Continuing to use the Marbling Rake, Biever began to develop the feeling of oil paint. To achieve a smoother stroke, in the Brush Controls palette, he reduced Size in the Size section, Opacity in the General section, lowered Resat in the Well section and reduced Brush Scale in the Rake section. The Marbling Rake gives an illusion of oil paint texture. You can lose the paper texture with the Rake, but through careful stroking Biever left bits and pieces of the canvas showing through. He continued to refine the face using the Large Chalk (Dry Media), while mixing and pulling color with the Marbling Rake.

4 Painting the hands and emphasizing the face. To emphasize the telling of a story, Biever roughed in the hand on the left. To balance the composition and give the picture more room, he added to the canvas using Canvas, Canvas Size. After he had rendered the right hand also, he selected them using the Lasso tool, floated them (Select, Float) and repositioned them using the Adjuster tool. Then, he dropped the layer by clicking the Drop button on the Layers section of the Objects palette. (To learn about using selections and layers, turn to Chapters 4 and 5.)

Using lighter colors, Biever brought out highlights in the face and hands using small Chalk variants (Dry Media). To emphasize the face even more, he painted over the tunic with the Large Chalk and lighter color, again blending with the Marbling Rake.

5 Adding final details and more texture. To enhance the highlights and shadows in the portrait, Biever increased the contrast using Effects, Tonal Control, Brightness/Contrast.

Then for *more* atmosphere, he added a papyrus texture from an Art Beats CD-ROM, copying and pasting the texture into the file as a layer. Using the pop-up menu in the Layers section of the Objects palette, he set the Compositing Method to Soft Light. He blended the texture into the hair and beard, creating a dusty feel. To blend a texture into your painting, target the texture layer in the Layers section, then click on its mask in the Masks section. Choose the Digital Airbrush (Airbrushes) and white color. Spray over the area of the mask that you want to remove. (To read more about working with masks and layers, see Chapters 4 and 5.)

Painter lets you specify Paper Color. You can set Paper Color in the New Picture dialog box (File, New) by clicking the Paper Color icon and choosing a color in the Select Paper Color dialog box, or you can change it midway through the painting process by selecting a color in the Color palette and choosing Canvas, Set Paper Color to apply the current color. The color of the existing background doesn't change, but if you make a selection and delete an area of the image or choose an Erasers variant (Bleaches don't work) and erase an area of the image, the new color appears.

Applying Rich Textures with Custom Brushes

Overview *Scan a traditional pencil sketch; modify brushes to include enhanced color and grain settings; paint rich color with varied textures using the custom brushes.*

DON SEEGMILLER

BY SKILLFULLY USING COLOR WHILE PAINTING with custom brushes and textures, Don Seegmiller created a dark and comically ominous atmosphere for *Strange High House*, painted from the imagination. He used somber colors in the highlight and shadow areas of the painting and developed a rich layering of multiple textures, applied with modified brushes that included increased color variability and enhanced grain settings.

Seegmiller, whose traditional oil paintings can be found in both private and public collections, is art director of Saffire Corporation, an innovative gaming development company. He also teaches illustration at Brigham Young University.

1 Sketching, scanning and equalizing. Seegmiller began by sketching with conventional pencil in his sketchbook. He scanned the pencil drawing at 300 ppi, a resolution suitable for offset printing. Because he likes working with a high-contrast version of the sketch, he removed the grays from the scan. To increase the contrast in your sketch, as Seegmiller did, choose Effects, Tonal

1a

The scanned pencil sketch

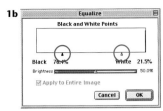

1b

Using Equalize to give the sketch more contrast

2

▼ Color Variability
in HSV
±H 8%
±S 8%
±V 11%

Painting the sky in the clone with a modified Simple Water Water Color brush, using these Color Variability settings. Tracing Paper if turned on to view the original scan of the pencil sketch

3

The study with soft watercolor background and the embellished sketch

Control, Equalize. When the Equalize dialog box appears, move the black point marker and the white point marker under the histogram closer together to eliminate the gray tones. Move them right or left to affect the line thickness and quality. You'll be able to preview the adjustment in your image before you click OK to accept.

2 Painting the background. Prior to painting with color, Seegmiller made a quick duplicate of his sketch to preserve the original, using Painter's cloning process. To make a clone, choose File, Clone.

Seegmiller planned to paint washes on the sky using a modified Water Color variant. He chose Pavement texture in the Papers section of the Art Materials palette because he likes its coarse, uneven look. Then he chose a soft blue in the Color picker and the Simple Water variant of Water Color in the Brushes palette. He added enhanced Color Variability and Grain settings to the Simple Water variant so that he could subtly paint the sky with varying colors of blue while revealing the texture.

To make his Water Color brush, choose the Simple Water variant of Water Color, then open the Color Variability section of the Art Materials palette by clicking on its section name. Adjust the sliders using Seegmiller's settings: ±H8 %, ±S8 %, and ±V11 %. In the General section of the Brush Controls palette move the Grain slider to 75%, to allow more grain to show as brushstrokes are applied. In the Size section increase the Size to 59.1. To avoid seeing circles (individual brush dabs as you paint) when using the larger brush size, decrease the spacing between the brush's dabs. In the Spacing section, move the Spacing slider to 14% and the Min Spacing slider to 0.5. To save your new Water Color brush (instead of leaving the new settings in the default Simple Water brush), choose Save Variant from the Variant menu on the Brushes palette. When the Save Variant dialog box appears, type in a name for your brush and click OK. To restore the Simple Water brush to its default settings, select the Simple Water variant and from the Brushes palette menu choose Variant, Restore Default Variant.

Using a soft touch on the stylus, Seegmiller painted brushstrokes over the sky. He changed color as he worked, choosing low-saturation blues, purples, browns and grays in the Colors section. (Water Color is kept separate from other painting on the image canvas. To read more about painting with Painter's Water Color brushes, turn to "Glazing with Water Color," earlier in this chapter.)

3 Strengthening the sketch. After establishing the sky, Seegmiller used a modified Pencils variant to embellish areas of the pencil sketch in his working study. (Drawing with the Pencils variants will not interrupt the wet Water Color brushstrokes.) His modified Pencil incorporates the Grainy Hard Buildup subcategory, and enhanced Grain settings, making it very sensitive to the Paper grain chosen in the Papers section. To build a Sketching Pencil similar to Seegmiller's, begin by choosing the 2B Pencil variant. In

Seegmiller switched between custom-made Cobblestones and Bark textures

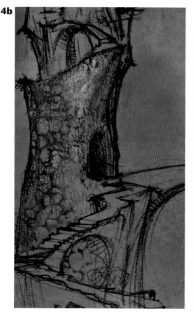

Using a modified Square Chalk variant to paint layers of custom-made Cobbles and Bark texture onto the cliff areas

Adding warmer, lighter tones to the top house and its windows

the General section of the Brush Controls palette, change its Dab Type to Single-Pixel, then set the Opacity slider at 69% and the Grain slider at 24%. Open the Random section of the palette and increase Jitter to 0.95 to make the brushstrokes uneven. Increasing Jitter also broadens the stroke slightly. Now choose a fine, even-textured paper (such as Regular Fine) in the Papers section of the Art Materials palette.

After drawing over certain areas, Seegmiller added more intensity to the pencil sketch by selecting the drawing in the original image, then choosing Select, All, and copying and pasting it into the working study. In the Layers section of the Objects palette, he set the Composite Method for the layer to Multiply, then he dropped it to the image canvas, by clicking the Drop button in the Layers section of the Objects palette. (Multiply mode makes the white areas of the image clear, while preserving the dark areas.) To read more about Layers and Composite Methods, turn to the beginning of Chapter 5, "Using Layers and Shapes."

4 Using a custom chalk to build up textures on the cliffs. Seegmiller used a modified Square Chalk to paint custom textures (primarily the Cobblestones and Bark textures) onto the cliffs. (Seegmiller creates custom textures from scans of his own photos or by painting in Painter, then capturing the elements as paper textures. To read more about paper textures, turn to "Applying Scanned Paper Textures," earlier in this chapter.) He built up layers of texture subtly. While painting with the custom Chalk, he occasionally switched to his modified Simple Water variant (described in step 2) to strengthen and lighten areas in both the sky and cliff areas. While he worked, he continually changed paper textures in the Papers section and applied the textures using slightly different colors.

To build Seegmiller's custom Chalk, begin by selecting the Square Chalk variant of Dry Media in the Brushes palette. In the Color Variability section of the Art Materials palette, move the sliders to these settings: ±H5 %, ±S7 %, and ±V10 %. Now set the Grain very low in the Controls:Brush palette: Move the Grain slider to 8%, to allow the Chalk to reveal more grain. To save your new custom Chalk without modifying settings for the default Square Chalk, choose Variant, Save Variant on the Brushes palette. Restore the Square Chalk variant to its default settings (select

USING GRAIN PENETRATION

Painter lets you control how much grain is visible as you paint with grain-sensitive brushes, such as the Dry Media variants. Choose the Square Chalk variant (Dry Media), and open the Controls:Brushes palette (Window, Show Controls) or access the Grain slider from the General section of the Brush Controls palette. With all brushes (except Water Color), moving the Grain slider to the left increases the grainy look because it decreases pigment penetration into the grain; moving the Grain slider to the right increases pigment penetration, and will cover more of the grain. Experiment with different Grain settings as you paint brushstrokes on your image.

5b

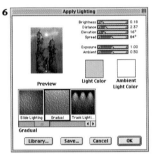

Using the custom Warm Fuzzy brush to add soft tones to the cliffs and path

6

Modifying the Gradual light

7a

The glow added to the window

7b

The highlights added to the roofs, and glows to the lights and the moon

the Square Chalk, and from the Brushes palette menu choose Variant, Restore Default Variant).

5 Adding lights and establishing the center of interest.
Seegmiller began to develop the feeling of light he envisioned for the house and high cliffs. He used another custom brush, the Warm Fuzzy, to achieve a softer feeling on the some of areas of the cliffs and edges of the path. Seegmiller's Warm Fuzzy brush paints with natural, "fuzzy-looking" strokes that made it a good choice for suggesting texture of vegetation on the cliffs. To build the Warm Fuzzy, begin by choosing the Opaque Round variant of the Brushes. In the Size section of the Brush Controls palette, change Size to 6.7, Min Size to 100% and Feature to 4.4 (to spread the Bristles). In the General section change Opacity to 68%. In the Expression section change Size and Jitter to None and Opacity to Pressure; set Resat, Bleed, and Feature to None. Finally, an important ingredient that adds a more natural look: In the Random section, increase Jitter to 0.43.

Using his Warm Fuzzy brush, Seegmiller added warm oranges and yellows to the two small windows to act as a balancing element against the purples, blue, grays and browns. He also added rusty-brown highlights to the roofs on the higher house to create the center of interest. He worked his way down the cliffs and added more subtle colors and texture to the houses and rocks.

6 Adding to the atmosphere and focal point. Seegmiller believes that Apply Lighting is one of the finest tools that Painter offers to change the complexion of an image without painting over underlying work. He used lighting to add atmosphere (for a more ominous feeling) and to create a soft vertical gradation from dark-to-light in the image (to strengthen the focal point). To create a custom light similar to Seegmiller's choose Effects, Surface Control, Apply Lighting and when the dialog box appears, choose the Gradual light. Make these changes to the light: Click on the Light Color square and in the Select Light Color dialog box, choose a light blue-gray. Reduce Brightness by moving its slider to 0.18. Leave other settings at their defaults. To save your light click the Save button, name your light and click OK. Then click OK to apply the light. To learn more about Apply Lighting, see the beginning of Chapter 7, "Exploring Special Effects."

7 Refining the painting. Seegmiller continued to add fine color detail over the entire image, particularly on the buildings, cliffs and path, while maintaining color harmony throughout the image. He added a small lamp outside the tunnel by the bridge, then embellished the lights in the windows and the lantern using the Glow variant of the F/X brush. He also used the Glow brush to lighten the moon. Using a tiny version of the Warm Fuzzy brush, he also added highlights along the roof edges of the buildings to give them a feeling of light from the moon. (For more about the F/X brushes see Chapter 7.)

Brushing Washes Over "Live" Canvas

Overview *Open a new file and use an Impasto brush to emboss texture into the image canvas; paint color washes over the canvas with brushes.*

STANLEY VEALÉ

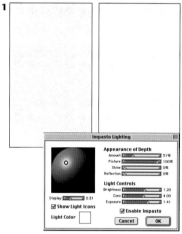

The canvas with the default Impasto Lighting settings (left) and with the reduced Amount and Shine (right), as set in the Impasto Lighting dialog box.

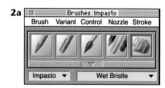

Choosing the Wet Bristle variant of Impasto in the Brushes palette

ON TRADITIONAL CANVAS YOU CAN USE OIL PAINT mixed with linseed oil and turpentine to brush washes over the surface without obliterating the canvas grain. With Painter's Impasto feature you can do something very similar, with the added advantage of being able to emphasize or de-emphasize the grain by changing the angle or intensity of lighting on the canvas. Using the Impasto feature to "emboss" the canvas will keep the grain "live" and changeable throughout the painting process. To paint *Ashanti,* a still-life study of an African wood carving, Stanley Vealé, an artist and designer at MetaCreations, used a unique method that allows the canvas texture to always show through the brushstrokes.

1 Embossing the canvas. Begin by creating a new file the size and resolution you need. (Vealé's file was 800 pixels square.) In the Papers section of the Art Materials palette, choose the Raw Silk texture. (Considering the 800-pixel file size, Vealé left the Scale of the Raw Silk texture at 100% in the Papers section.)

Vealé used the Grain Emboss variant of Impasto to "emboss" the Raw Silk texture values into the image canvas without adding color. Select the Grain Emboss variant of Impasto and paint wide strokes all over the image so that the paper texture is embossed into the image. You can reduce or increase the effect of the texture by choosing Canvas, Impasto Lighting, and adjusting the Amount slider to your liking. Because the default Impasto settings seemed too coarse and shiny, Vealé reduced the Amount to 51%, and for a matte finish on the canvas, he set the Shine at 0.

2 Customizing a brush. Vealé likes the Wet Bristle variant of Impasto because of its bristle marks and how it scrubs existing paint when you apply pressure on the stylus. However, if he used the

2b

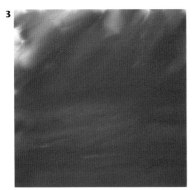
Changing the Impasto section settings for the Wet Bristle variant copy

3

Applying glazes to the image canvas

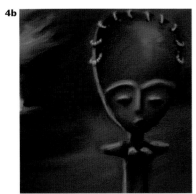
4a

The figure study in progress

4b

Vealé painted reflected light on the face of the Ashanti figure.

default Impasto Wet Bristle, the brush would paint with depth as well as color, eventually covering the embossed texture applied in step 1. So he modified a copy of the Wet Bristle so that it would apply only color to his image, as follows: Select the Wet Bristle variant of Impasto and copy it to the Brushes category by choosing Copy Variant from the Variant menu on the Brushes palette. When the Copy Variant dialog box appears, choose the Brushes category from the pop-up menu and click OK. Now choose the Wet Bristle copy from the Brushes category. In the Impasto section of the Brush Controls palette, change the Draw To pop-up menu to Color. Then choose Set Default Variant from the Variant menu in the Brushes palette to make the change permanent for the new Wet Bristle variant.

3 Painting colored washes. Using a light touch on the stylus, and the new Wet Bristle brush, Vealé freely brushed loose washes of color over the image canvas, suggesting a subtle horizon line and a glowing campfire in the background.

Choose your new Wet Bristle variant and paint brushstrokes on the image. The brush applies paint when you press lightly, but scrubs underlying paint when you press hard (because in the Expression section of the Brush Controls palette, Resat is set to vary inversely with Pressure and Bleed is set to vary with Pressure). These settings help the canvas texture to always show through the paint. (You can also achieve good washes with other brushes, such as the Smeary Round and the Variable Flat variants of the Brushes.)

4 Setting up a still life and painting the figure. Vealé set up a conventional light to shine from behind the figure that served as his model and another to reflect light onto its face. Then he carefully studied the Ashanti figure's form, and painted it directly on the image canvas with a smaller version of the Wet Bristle variant. He built up values slowly, gradually adding more saturated, darker tones to the still life study. Vealé brought out orange tones that were reminiscent of firelight in the background. He added deeper red and brown colors to the sky, and brighter colors and more detail to the bonfire in the background. Then he added stronger highlights and cast shadows to the foreground and to the carving. Finally, to relieve some of the rigidity of the centered composition, he repainted areas of the background to move the horizon up.

Variations. A slightly different effect (shown at right) can be achieved if you choose the new Wet Bristle, and in the General section of the Brush Controls palette, reduce the Opacity of the brush to between 20–40%. In the Expression section, set the Opacity menu to Pressure. 🖌

Figure study, by Stanley Vealé

Working with Thick Paint

Overview *Paint a color study; use Impasto brushes to add 3D brushwork to the study; use Impasto Lighting to adjust the appearance of the highlights and shadows on the thick paint.*

CHELSEA SAMMEL

Sammel's black-and-white pencil study

IMPASTO BRINGS THE TEXTURE OF THICK, LUSCIOUS PAINT to the tip of your stylus. When painting *Dying Orchids,* artist Chelsea Sammel used Painter 6's Impasto brushes to add the texture of brush marks with realistic highlights and shadows to a color study. Then she scraped back and added more expressive brush-work, bringing more texture and activity to the painting.

1 Designing the still life and making a sketch. Sammel envisioned a composition with strong side lighting in which the orchids appeared to be suspended in space. She designed an airy, asymmetrical flower arrangement with interesting negative space, set up in the natural light of a window.

To begin the sketch, she created a new file that measured 1200 x 1600 pixels. In the Brushes palette, she chose the Colored Pencil variant of the Pencils and in the Paper section of the Art Materials palette she clicked on Basic Paper. Then she drew a tight, black-and-white sketch. To sketch as Sammel did, choose the Color Pencil

2a

The color underpainting

2b

A detail showing scraped back canvas

3

Adding texture to the background with the
Loaded Palette Knife variant of Impasto

variant and check in the General section of the Brush Controls palette to make sure that the method for the Colored Pencil is set at Buildup and the subcategory at Grainy Hard Buildup.

2 Creating the color underpainting. She began to lay color in, directly over the sketch using Round Camelhair variant of the Brushes. She painted using warm autumn colors—browns, burnt sienna, golds—and other rich hues.

Traditional artists often add texture and complexity to the surface of their paintings by scraping areas of paint off the canvas. To scrape back areas Sammel chose the Loaded Palette Knife variant of the Brushes. To make a tiny version of the brush, she reduced its size using the Size slider in the Controls:Brushes palette. Switching between the Round Camelhair and Loaded Palette Knife variants of the Brushes, she painted and scraped back, pulled and blended colors, creating an expressive painting with a lot of movement.

3 Adding textured brushwork. Then Sammel added more interest and activity to the composition by adding textured brushstrokes that did not necessarily follow the lines of the colored paint. She modified the Loaded Palette Knife variant of Impasto, so that it would paint with negative depth, but not color, and she made it smaller. To make Sammel's custom palette knife, choose the Loaded Palette Knife variant of Impasto and set the Size slider in the Controls:Brush palette to 11.0. In the Brush Controls palette's Impasto section set the Draw To menu to Depth and the Depth slider to 35%, leaving other settings at their defaults: Smoothing, 77% and Plow, 100%. Save the variant by choosing Save Variant from the Brushes palette's Variant menu, giving it a new name. Then choose the original Loaded Palette Knife and restore its default settings by choosing Variant, Restore Default Variant.

When she wanted the new palette knife to paint with both color and depth, she modified it to pick up and smear underlying colors. To make this modification, select the new palette knife, and in the Impasto section of Brush Controls, set the Draw To menu back to Color and Depth. To pick up and mix underlying colors more—in the Brush Controls palette's Well section—set Resat to 20%. Save and name the new variant, then reselect the first modified palette knife.

Using warm creamy colors, Sammel painted loose, gestural brushstrokes over the background. At this point, she exaggerated the strong side lighting and enhanced the negative space in the painting by using

KNIVES THAT SOFTLY SMEAR

The Palette Knife and Loaded Palette Knife, by default, have blending capabilities controlled by pressure. In the Expression section of Brush Controls, Resat is set to Pressure. When light pressure is used on the stylus, both palette knives smear the current color with the underlying color while softly digging into the paint. Applying more pressure on the stylus covers more of the underlying paint and makes a harder-edged, deeper gouge.

4a

Painting details on the orchids

4b

Pulling and blending paint on the flowers with a small Variable Flat Opaque brush (Impasto)

5a

Adding more texture to the foreground using the Texturizer-Fine (Impasto)

the Variable Flat Opaque variant of Impasto with Draw To set to its default Color And Depth to apply more white brushwork to the right side of the image.

4 Painting details on the flowers, vase and table.

Once the background was painted in, Sammel painted over the orchids using the Variable Flat Opaque (Impasto). She added bright highlights to the right side of the orchids and deeper, richer colors to areas in shadow on the flowers, vase and table. As she worked, she frequently modified settings in the Impasto section of Brush Controls for the Variable Flat Opaque variant. To paint with color and texture, she left the Draw To menu set at Color And Depth; to add textured brushstrokes without adding color, she chose Draw To Depth setting. To paint brushstrokes with texture based on the current paper texture, she kept the Depth Method set to Paper.

5 Refining the painting. Sammel used a small Loaded Palette Knife (Impasto) to drag color through the image (especially in the vase), then she added more colored paint using the Dry Ink variant of the Brushes. To allow the Dry Ink to mix and pull colors on

5b

Painting final details on the vase and flowers using the Loaded Palette Knife (Impasto) and Dry Ink (Brushes) variants

the canvas, she made sure that Brush Loading was turned on in the Brush Controls palette's Well section. And to enhance the effect of pulling and mixing colored paint, she lowered the Resat (to about 20%) and raised the Bleed setting (to about 80%).

She added spattery Impasto texture to the image foreground with the Texturizer-Fine variant of Impasto. Then she brushed over areas that were too "impastoed" using the Depth Equalizer variant (Impasto) at a low Opacity (Controls:Brush). Finally, she reduced the overall effect of the Impasto by choosing Canvas, Impasto Lighting. For a more subtle Impasto look she reduced the Amount to 75%.

ERASING THICK BRUSHWORK

If you're not satisfied with the look of relief after you've applied Impasto brushwork, you can erase with one of these methods: To erase the entire depth effect, choose Canvas, Clear Impasto. To use a brush to smooth an area, choose the Depth Equalizer and brush over the area you want to smooth. Try experimenting with the Depth Eraser for more dramatic results.

Expressive Custom Brushes

Overview *Create black-and-white art and import it into Painter; build custom brushes; create a new brush library for the brushes; paint soft lines and fills with custom brushes; add more color and texture.*

AYSE ULAY

The black-and-white logotype

AYSE ULAY PREFERS TO NOT INTERRUPT the creative process by building variants as she works, so she prepares them in advance. Her *Harlequin*, painted from her imagination, was created for the California Institute of Technology's Beckman Auditorium for their seasonal program cover and promotional posters.

1 Beginning with black and white. Ulay's client requested two renditions of the illustration—a black-and-white logotype and a full-color illustration. Because the logotype would be used in several sizes, Ulay built it in Macromedia FreeHand so that she could scale it without degrading the artwork. She began by drawing a sketch using pencil and paper, then she scanned the sketch, saved it as a TIFF file and placed it in FreeHand to use as a template. Working in FreeHand, she used the Pen tool to draw black-and-white PostScript art using the sketch as a guide. She saved it as an EPS file so she could bring it into Painter.

You can import PostScript art directly into Painter by pasting through the clipboard while both applications are running or by using the File, Acquire, Adobe Illustrator file feature. To paste through the clipboard, begin by selecting the illustration elements in FreeHand (or Adobe Illustrator), copy the items to the

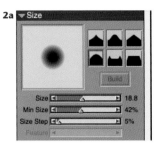

Ulay's settings in the Brush Controls:Size section showing a "soft view" of the Dull tip profile and brush dab

2b

Testing the Light Fills (upper left) and Grainy Light Fills (right) brushes on a sample image

3

Copying the Light Fills variant to the custom brush style

4a

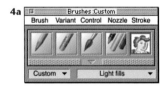

The custom brush style icon selected in the default Painter Brushes library

4b

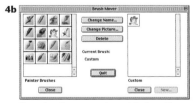

Dragging the new custom style from the Painter Brushes library into a new library

clipboard, switch to Painter and paste into an open Painter file. To use the Acquire method, choose File, Acquire, Adobe Illustrator File, navigate to the EPS file, select it and choose Open.

2 Creating variants. Using the Artist Pastel Chalk variant of Dry Media, Ulay created seven custom variants. The Light Fills, Medium Light Fills, Thick Lines and Thin Lines variants were built using the Soft Cover subcategory, and were intended to apply soft lines and graduated fills. The Grainy Light Fills, Grainy Thick Lines and Grainy Thin Lines variants were built to interact with the paper texture on the image canvas.

To build Ulay's Light Fills variant, start with the Artist Pastel Chalk variant. In the Brush Controls palette, open the Size section by clicking on its name. Set the Size to 18.8 and Min Size to 42%. Change the Brush Tip Profile from the default Medium profile (top center) to the Dull profile (bottom left). You can view the brush dab using the "soft" view by clicking in the brush dab window to toggle between the "hard" and "soft" views. In the Brush Controls:General section, set the Opacity at 14%. To create a brush that won't be grain-sensitive, in the General section switch the subcategory to Soft Cover. Save the variant by choosing Variant, Save Variant from the Brushes palette.

To create the Grainy Thick Lines brush, Ulay began with the new custom Light Fills variant. She changed these settings in the Brush Controls:Size section: Size: 15.4, Min Size, 40%. To allow interaction with grain on the image surface, she switched back to the Artist Pastel Chalk's default subcategory, Grainy Hard Cover, in Brush Controls:General, and she set Opacity at 68%, and Grain at 38%.

BRUSHES FROM SCRATCH

If you want to create custom brushes from scratch instead of basing them on pre-existing brushes, begin by making an icon for the brush. Select a square area of your image with the rectangular selection tool. Now, from the Brushes palette menu choose Brush, New Brush. Name your brush style and click OK. You'll see your selection appear in the Brush palette with no variants below it. You've just created an empty "variant holder," ready to be filled with custom variants.

3 Storing variants in a custom brush style. Besides creating variants, you can even create a new brush style. This is handy if you use certain brushes for specific jobs (as Ulay did here). And Painter 6 offers a variant mover (Variant, Copy Variant) that allows you to swap variants between brush styles.

You'll create an icon for your brush style in the process, so begin by using the Rectangular Selection tool with the Shift key to select a square area of an image that you want to represent your brush. On the Brushes palette choose Brush, New Brush. In the Save Brush Style dialog box, name the new style, and click OK. (Ulay named hers Custom). Having the selection ready on the image

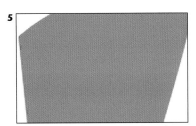

5

A flat color fill applied to a section of drapery

6a

Adding soft shadows and highlights to the drapery with the Light Fills variant

6b

Adding more colored elements and dimension to the illustration

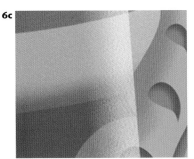

6c

Painting textured highlights onto the light beam with Grainy Light Fills variant

canvas will automatically give the new brush style an icon. To copy your custom variant from the Dry Media brush style to your new brush style, select it and choose Variant, Copy Variant. In the Copy Variant dialog box menu choose your new brush style, and click OK.

4 Making a new brush library. For optimal performance, it's a good idea to keep brush libraries small. Brushes will build more quickly and it will be easier to find a brush if the list is shorter. So it's better to create new libraries for your custom brushes rather than storing them in Painter's default library. To move your new brush style to a new library of its own, from the Brushes palette's menu choose Brush, Brush Mover. Click the New button to create a new brush library, and in the New Brush File dialog box, name the new library and click Save. On the left side of the mover select the new brush style that contains your new variants and drag and drop it into your new Brush library palette on the right side of the mover. To remove the original copy of your new brush style from your default Painter Brushes library (in the Painter 6 folder on your hard drive), select its icon on the left side of the Brush Mover dialog box and click the Delete button. Click Quit to exit the mover. Now—for housekeeping purposes—back in the Brushes palette, you can remove the custom variants you added to Dry Media. Select Dry Media and choose one of the custom variants. From the Brushes palette's Variant menu, choose Delete Variant. Repeat the process to remove the other added variants from the list of Dry Media.

To replace the current brush styles in the Brushes palette with the library you just created, choose Load Library from the brush style list. Navigate to your custom library. Select it in the directory and click Open to display it.

5 Adding flat color. Ulay had imported black-and-white Post-Script shapes from FreeHand in step 1. She chose each shape in the Objects:Layers section and converted it to a selection (Shapes, Convert to Selection). So she could recall each selection later as a mask for brushstrokes, she saved each selection as a mask in the Mask section by choosing Select, Save Selection. Then she chose Select, Load selection, and used the Paint Bucket to fill each area of her image with flat color. (For more information about using selections see Chapter 4, "Selections, Shapes and Masks.")

6 Adding more color, tone and texture. Ulay continued to lay down flat color within selected elements in her image. Next, she chose Basic Paper in the Art Materials:Papers section and used the Light Fills and Medium Fills brushes to add smooth dimension and contrast to the drapery, columns, foliage, harlequin and stage. She added smaller details with the Thin Lines and Thick Lines variants. Finally, she added touches of grainy texture to the highlighted and shadowed areas of the image using the Grainy Light Fills and Grainy Thin and Grainy Thick Lines variants.

■ **Cher Threinen-Pendarvis's**
experience with traditional style in pastel,
watercolor and acrylic translates easily to
digital pastel in Painter.

Paths to Water 1 (above), is one in a
series of paintings of Sunset Cliffs Natural
Park in San Diego, California. She began
the painting by making location studies
using a Powerbook laptop computer,
Painter and a Wacom pressure-sensitive
tablet. Sitting in the shade near the trees,
she began by creating a new file with a
beige background paper color. She chose
Sandy paper from the Drawing Paper
Textures library (located in the Paper
Texture Libraries folder on the Painter 6
Application CD-ROM), and sketched
using the Sharp Chalk variant of Dry

Media and a dark brown color. Observing
the afternoon light and shadows she
worked on location using the laptop until
she had established the composition,
general color theme and cast shadows in
the study. Later on her studio computer,
Pendarvis added more layers of color
using modified Square Chalk and Large
Chalk variants of Dry Media, working over
the entire piece. She blended areas with
the Grainy Water variant of Liquid and
added more textured, directional strokes
with the Chalk variants. As a last step, she
used Effects, Surface Control, Apply
Surface Texture to apply Sandy paper
texture to the entire painting, using
subtle settings.

■ **Richard Noble** has been an accomplished traditional painter and designer for many years. Today he paints most of his fine artwork in Painter, using techniques that emulate traditional acrylic painting. He typically begins a painting by shooting reference photos and making sketches on location.

For *Garden* (left) and *Coast* (below), two paintings from his Mendocino series, Noble roughed in vibrant, saturated color with the Sargent Brush variant of the Artists brush and the Round Camelhair variant of the Brushes. Both of these brushes allowed Noble to move paint around on the canvas. He also blended color using the Palette Knife variant of the Brushes and the Distorto variant of Liquid. Using a small Round Camelhair variant, he painted fine details in the shady areas of the foreground foliage as well as in the sunlit areas of the paintings. Noble usually prints his paintings on canvas with light-fast inks and finishes them with touches of acrylic paint. To see two other paintings from his Mendocino series, turn to the gallery at the end of Chapter 2.

■ **Cher Threinen-Pendarvis** often makes several color studies for a painting on location, carefully observing how light and atmosphere affect color in highlights and shadows.

An isolated, breathtaking view and unique plant life provided the inspiration for *Agaves on the Edge* (above). For this painting, Pendarvis began by making several colored pencil sketches—details of the agave plants, the cliffs and the overall seascape—in a traditional sketchbook that she'd carried in her backpack. Later, back at the studio she created a new file in Painter. Using the 2B Pencil variant of the

Pencils and Basic Paper texture, she sketched the composition. She loosely blocked in color directly over the sketch with a Round Camelhair brush, which she had modified to include a small amount of Color Variability which helped to modulate the color. To build up layers of color interest on the hills, cliffs and water, she dabbed small strokes of paint on top using a smaller Round Camelhair brush, then she blended areas of the cliffs, hills and water using the Grainy Water variant of Liquid. Pendarvis added softly colored clouds to the sky using the Square Chalk variant of Dry Media, then smoothed and blended

color using the Grainy Water. To add textured highlights to the beach and color interest to the cliffs, she used the Square Chalk and Artist Pastel Chalk (Dry Media). To balance the composition, she reworked some of the foreground plants and added soft brushstrokes to the path using the Round Camelhair variant. For the leaves, she also used the Artist Pastel Chalk to feather subtly colored strokes over the painted leaves, to further define their forms. The feathered strokes also helped add color complexity and movement. Finally, she added linear highlights to some of the leaves using the Artist Pastel Chalk.

■ When Heidi North, Art Director for Random House Publishing, commissioned **Marc Brown** to paint a cover illustration for *The New York Times Book Review*, Brown created an inviting image with comfortable emotional appeal. For *Woman Reading*, he painted a restful color scheme of predominantly blue and green with smoothly blended highlights and shadows.

Brown began the illustration in Adobe Illustrator and rasterized it by exporting it in Photoshop format. (Illustrator 8 files can be exported into Photoshop 5 format with layers intact.)

He opened the file in Painter and used Painter's brushes to render details on each layer, working from the background to the foreground. Using the Round Camelhair variant of the Brushes, he modeled the forms of the landscape and the figure. To smoothly pull and blend color, he used the Just Add Water variant of Liquid. He added more detailed highlights and shadows to the illustration by painting with a small version of the Round Camelhair variant, again blending areas with the Just Add Water variant. Finally, he sharpened a few highlights with the tiny Round Camelhair.

A versatile artist, designer and educator, **Kathy Blavatt** used free movement and flowing color to tie her vision of all of the arts—music, painting and dance—together in *Gestures,* which was juried into the 1999 MacWorld Digital Art Exhibition.

To begin the painting, Blavatt created a new file with a white background color. She sketched in black-and-white using the 2B Pencil variant of the Pencils, defining the figures in the composition. She added thicker strokes in black and gray over the dancers using the Artist Pastel Chalk and Sharp Chalk variants of Dry Media. Then she used the Sargent Brush variant of the Artists brush to paint vibrant color directly over her sketch. To add more movement to the dancers, she pulled the color around on the canvas using the Palette Knife variant of the Brushes. She painted transparent washes using the Broad Water Brush variant of Water Color, and to finish, she added a few watery splotches of color using the Spatter Water variant of Water Color.

Ray Blavatt is a creative artist and multimedia designer with roots in traditional fashion illustration. His conventional tools of choice are graphite pencil, charcoal and chalk.

Blavatt loves to paint from his imagination in Painter. To create *Fashion Statement,* he began by creating a new file with a tan paper color similar to newsprint paper. He chose Basic Paper in the Paper section of the Art Materials palette and the 2B Pencil variant of Pencils and black color. He drew a line sketch first with the Pencil variant, then he switched to a small Graphic Paintbrush variant (Brushes) to thicken the line work while revealing more texture on the edges of the strokes. Next, he made a mask for the black line work by choosing Auto Mask using Image Luminance from the pull-down menu on the Mask section of the Objects palette, so that he could paint freely while protecting the line work. Blavatt began to add color to the painting using the Digital Airbrush variant of Airbrushes. He added highlights using the Bleach variant of the Eraser, and shadows using the Darkener variant (Eraser). To finish, he strengthened the black line work. He loaded the line work mask as a selection, and painted over the active selection using the Graphic Paintbrush variant and black color.

One More and We're Outnumbered!

by Rick Kirkman & Jerry Scott

■ A freelance illustrator for over 15 years, **Rick Kirkman** divides his time between producing cartoons for commercial clients and creating the King Feature Syndicate comic strip *Baby Blues* (with partner Jerry Scott).

Kirkman began the cover illustration for ***One More and We're Outnumbered!*** (above) in Painter with black linework using the Colored Pencil variant of Pencils on Basic Paper texture. He switched to a rougher paper texture and added colored washes using the Simple Water variant of Water Color. To achieve the coarser texture on the green sweater and pink towel, he scaled the paper texture slightly larger using the Scale slider in the Papers section of the Art Materials palette. Then he used the Simple Water variant to paint

watercolor washes that revealed texture when he applied pressure on his stylus. (By default, the Simple Water variant of Water Color is set to the Grainy Wet Abrasive subcategory in the General section of the Brush Controls palette, a subcategory that preserves texture when new brushstrokes are applied over existing ones. In the Expressions section of Brush Controls, Grain is set to Pressure, which enhances the effect.)

After the Painter Illustration was complete, Kirkman saved it as a TIFF file and placed the TIFF file into Adobe Illustrator 8.0, where he added the green panel and type. (Illustrator 7.0 and 8.0 accept both RGB and CMYK TIFF files, which makes direct export from Painter possible.)

■ To create the vibrant look of oil paints, in *Tyler Path* (above) and *Martinique Beach* (opposite), **Dennis Orlando** layered color with the Artist Pastel Chalk (Dry Media) and the Smeary variants of the Brushes. Then he blended color with the Grainy Water and Distorto variants of Liquid. He modified the Artists Pastel Chalk and the Smeary brush variants by increasing their Color Variability settings (in the Color Variability section of the Art Materials palette), which allowed him to paint with modulated color.

To paint *Tyler Path,* Orlando began by making a loose color underpainting with the Art Pastel Chalk variant of Dry Media, establishing the color theme and working out values. He blended areas in the underpainting with the Grainy Water variant. When he was satisfied with the composition, he used the Smeary Flat and Smeary Bristle Spray variants of Brushes to add more color and to pull and blend colors into each other on the image canvas. First he used the Smeary brushes in large sizes, then as he began to do detail work, he resized the brush smaller to refine highlights and shadows in the painting. To pull color even more in certain highlights, for instance, the sunny glow in the high trees and the light areas of the path, he used the Distorto variant.

■ **Dennis Orlando** began *Martinique Beach* with the Chalk variants of Dry Media. Using saturated colors, he roughed out a study for the composition in Painter, then layered more color to build up an underpainting. He used the Sharp Chalk variant of Dry Media to define the edges of the sailboats and figure. Switching back and forth between the Artist Pastel Chalk (Dry Media) and the Grainy Water variant of Liquid, he continued to add color and smudge it. He painted the foreground sand by making short, curved strokes with a modified Smeary Flat variant of the Brushes. (To help to modulate color, Orlando increased Color Variability for the Smeary Flat variant, moving the Hue slider to about 15% in the Color Variability section of the Art Materials palette.) To pull and mix color in the water, sky and sand, he used a large Smeary Bristle Spray variant (Brushes). Then he added accents of more saturated color to the sails, the man's shorts and sunlit areas of the water using a small Smeary Bristle Spray variant. Finally, he used tiny Grainy Water and Distorto variants of Liquid to blend and finesse the highlights on the boat rails and on the shiny fabric of the sails.

■ Although fine artist and illustrator **Francois Guérin** still works with conventional media, most of his commercial illustrations are now created in Photoshop, Painter, or a combination of the two. Guérin painted *The Strawberries* using Painter's Water Color brushes exclusively. He used a modified Simple Water for most of the piece, adjusting the size of his brush as he painted. Guérin started with large areas of wash, then built volume and added detail. He liked the look of color pooled along the edges of his strokes, so as he blended the image with the Pure Water Brush variant, he left a few areas untouched. Guérin switched subcategories frequently as he worked: To pull color out of tones that had become too dark, he changed to Wet Remove Density. He switched to Grainy Wet Buildup to add crisp details.

■ Inspired by a concern for global ecology, **Pam Wells** painted *Angel for the New Millennium.* To begin, she collected several resource photos to look at while working on the illustration. Working in Painter, she made a detailed black-and-white line sketch with the 2B Pencil variant of the Pencils, making sure to create a solid lines around the exterior of the figure and the gown. Then she applied flat color fills to the areas using the Paint Bucket (Tools palette). To model the forms of the Angel's figure and the gown, she carefully painted over the entire illustration using a pressure-sensitive tablet and the Soft Charcoal variant of Dry Media, occasionally making slight modifications to the brush. To blend areas, Wells applied very light pressure on the stylus with the Soft Charcoal to lay subtly different colors over existing ones. To add texture to the fabric, she used more contrasting values and a tiny Soft Charcoal variant. To paint more texture in shaded areas of the wings, she changed the Soft Charcoal's Subcategory (in the General section of Brush Controls) from Grainy Soft Cover to Grainy Hard Cover.

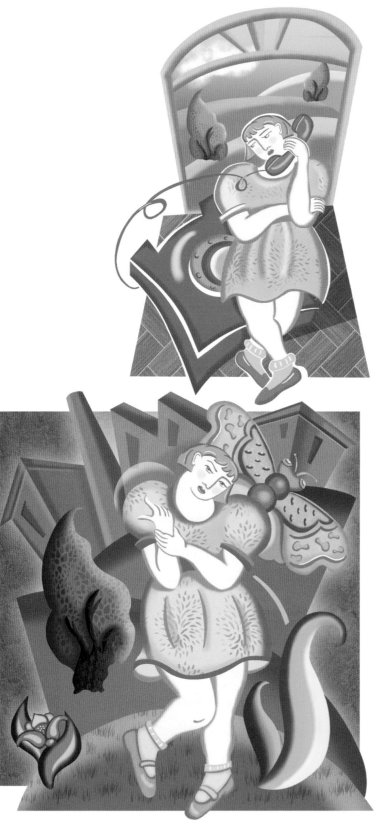

■ **Ayse Ulay** has been working in commercial illustration since 1985 and has used digital media since 1987. She loves Painter because she can achieve textural quality reminiscent of her favorite conventional medium: pastel. The two illustrations at left were created as part of a series of images to illustrate the children's book *The Magic Finger,* written by Roald Dahl.

Hello (top) began as a conventional pencil sketch. After scanning her sketch, Ulay opened it in Painter. Working on the scanned sketch, she made selections of major elements in her composition and saved the selections into the Masks section of the Objects palette. To begin the underpainting, she loaded each selection and filled it with a color using the Paint Bucket. To define highlights and shadows on top of the fills, she used a custom brush based on the Artist Pastel Chalk variant of Dry Media. Next, she added subtle colored textures to a few areas using Effects, Surface Control, Color Overlay using Paper and Dye Concentration. Ulay created the wood floor with the Parquet Floor texture from the Miles of Tiles library, chosen in the Papers section of the Art Materials palette and applied with Color Overlay using Paper. Finally, she added more texture using a custom Grainy Light Fills brush based on the Artist Pastel Chalk variant. Her brush incorporates a lower Opacity and lower Grain penetration setting in the Controls:Brush palette, which brings out the paper grain. To create soft light borders between colors, she used the Bleach variant of the Eraser.

The cover illustration for the book, *The Magic Finger* (bottom), was painted using the same techniques and brushes as *Hello* above. The tree in the front and the heroine's dress were further enhanced with the Leaf, Grass and Sprigs paper textures from the Trees and Leaves library (available from MetaCreations) applied with Color Overlay using Paper and Dye Concentration.

■ **Margaret Sweeney** is an accomplished traditional watercolorist. Today she paints most of her work in Painter directly on screen, without the use of photographic scanning. She usually prefers to paint on her own custom paper textures.

To begin *Nets* (above), she referred to sketches drawn on location. Sweeney used several favorite brushes from the Painter 5.5 Brushes library: To lay in color she used the Brushy and the Loaded Oils variants of the Brushes; she smoothly blended color in the image using the Sable Chisel Tip Water variant of the Brushes. She used a palette of low-saturation colors with subtle contrast to depict the soft light of an overcast day.

For *Sketchers*, Sweeney used Painter's Water Color brushes, including the Simple Water and Broad Water Brush variants. In contrast to *Nets*, above, she chose a palette of saturated reds, oranges and yellows with stark shadows for this painting. To create the look of dazzling light at mid-day, Sweeney applied color using short brushstrokes, without smoothly blended transitions between the colors, and she left some of the white paper color showing through.

SELECTIONS, SHAPES AND MASKS

Horsepower Heart. *Artist Chet Phillips began by making a drawing with the Scratchboard Tool variant. Then, working on top of the scratchboard drawing, he used the Pen tool to draw paths and converted each path to a selection. After making each selection, he saved it as a mask. Then Phillips turned the entire scratchboard drawing into a separate layer and set its Composite Method to Gel. Working on the image canvas, he loaded each of the masks he had made (Select, Load Selection), and applied colored tints to the selected areas using Effects, Fill. Then he painted colored details with the Airbrushes.*

IF YOU WANT TO GET THE MOST FROM PAINTER, you need to invest some time in understanding how the program isolates portions of images so that you can paint them, apply special effects or otherwise change them without affecting the rest of the image. Much of the program's power is tucked into the complex area of *selections*, *shapes*, which are also called *paths*, and *masks*.

A *selection* is an area of the image that has been isolated to allow changes to be made to the contents only, or to protect the area from change. There are two kinds of selections in Painter: outline-based and pixel-based. Like a cookie cutter, an *outline-based* selection (called a *shape* or *path*) defines the area inside an outline. But unlike cookie cutters in the real world, an outline-based selection in Painter can be freely scaled or reshaped. If Painter's shapes are like the outlines produced by cookie cutters, then *pixel-based* selections are more like painted resists. Pixel-based selections make the selected areas fully or partially available for change or copying, with the degree of availability determined by the nature and "thickness" of the "resist material."

The perimeter of a selection is indicated by an animated border, the selection marquee. There can be only one active selection at a time. Selections are temporary. If you choose Select, Deselect (Ctrl/⌘-D) or accidentally click outside the selection marquee, the selection will be lost, unless you have dragged it into the Selection Portfolio section of the Objects palette using the Selection Adjuster tool, or have saved it as a mask into the Masks section of the Objects palette by choosing Select, Save Selection

SELECTING THE CANVAS

Selections are typically used to isolate areas of the image canvas. However, in Painter 6 they can also be used in conjunction with layers. To learn about how to use selections with layers, turn to Chapter 5.

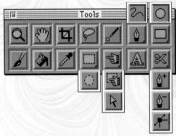

The selection and shape tools are located in the four right columns of the Tools palette. Some tools share a space in the palette with other tools, as shown here in pop-out view. In columns from left to right these tools are: Lasso, Rectangular Selection and Oval Selection; Magic Wand; Layer Adjuster, Selection Adjuster and Direct Selection; Quick Curve, Pen and Text tool; Oval Shape and Rectangular Shape; Scissors, Remove Point (or Delete Point) Add Point, and Convert Point.

USING THE OBJECTS PALETTE

In Painter 6, selections, masks and shapes are stored in three sections of the Objects palette: the Masks section, the Layers section and the Selection Portfolio. For instance, to open the Masks section, click the left triangle on the Masks section bar. To open all sections of the Objects palette at once, press the Shift key and click the left triangle on any closed section in the Objects palette.

To isolate areas of the canvas for filling, the Oval Selection tool was used to create an antialiased selection (left); the selection made by the Rectangular Selection tool needs no antialiasing (right).

(or by clicking the Save Selection button in the Masks section).

A *shape,* or *path,* is a mathematically described outline that can be stroked and filled. Shapes can be created with the Rectangular Shape, Oval Shape, Text, Pen or Quick Curve tool. Shapes are automatically stored in the Layers section of the Objects palette. They can be used as independent elements in an illustration, or they can be converted to selections and used to isolate areas of the image. When you convert a shape to a selection, (Shapes, Convert to Selection), its name disappears from the Layers section and an animated marquee appears on the image canvas. **Beware:** If you convert a shape to a selection using Painter 6.0, it will be permanently lost if you deselect it before you convert it back to a shape, save it as a mask, drag it into the Selection Portfolio with the Selection Adjuster tool, or choose Undo (Ctrl/⌘-Z). (This chapter tells about drawing shapes and their relationship to selections. The stroke and fill attributes of shapes, their layering capabilities and their relationship to layers, are covered in Chapter 5).

Unlike a shape, which is stored *outline* information, a *mask* is stored *pixel-based* information. Masks can store 8-bit grayscale information so that a painting, a photo, or a complex graphic can be saved and then loaded as a selection. Painter's 8-bit masks allow 256 levels of protection. When the mask is fully opaque it completely protects the pixels underneath from selection or change. When it is fully clear it fully selects them or exposes them to brushstrokes. Gray areas are partially protected. The protective mask can be thinned or even completely removed pixel by pixel. Painter 6 allows up to 32 masks in a single document stored in the Masks section. Besides allowing complex image information to be used as a selection, masks provide a way of converting selection information to "permanent" storage until you need to use it.

The Masks and Layers sections of the Objects palette not only store masks and shapes, but they also control operations such as turning them on and off so they can be used as selections. (The Masks section is described on page 116, and the Layers section is described in Chapter 5.) The Selection Portfolio (opened by clicking the left triangle on the Selection Portfolio bar in the Objects palette) is useful for storing path-based selections. (The Selection Portfolio is described on page 110.)

TWO KINDS OF SELECTIONS

The tool used to make a selection determines whether the selection is outline-based or pixel-based. Selections made with the Lasso, Rectangular, and Oval selection tools, as well as selections converted from shapes, are outline-based selections. (For more

HIDE THE MARQUEE

To enable the screen to more quickly redraw when illustrating, hide the active selection border while keeping the selection itself active: Choose Select, Hide Marquee; choose Show Marquee to display it again.

To vignette this photo, we began by making an Oval selection. We scaled the selection using the Selection Adjuster tool, then applied a feather of 15 pixels (Select, Feather) to soften the edge. Next, we reversed the selection by choosing Select, Invert. We chose Edit, Clear to delete the background, leaving the vignetted edge.

PHOTO: CORBIS IMAGES

MIDDLE OF THE ROAD

When you choose Select, Transform Selection and apply it to a soft-edged selection, Painter draws an outline-based selection at 50% transparency, but this doesn't necessarily return the selection back to its original border. For instance, if you make a hard-edged selection with the Rectangular Selection tool, then feather it (Select, Feather), fill it (Effects, Fill), and transform it (Select, Transform Selection), the result will be a hard-edged rectangle, but with rounded corners.

The original rectangular selection was filled with blue, then feathered 20 pixels and filled with a rose color (left). Then the selection was transformed and filled with yellow, revealing the new rounded hard edge (right).

information about outline-based selections, turn to "Creating Selections and Shapes," below.) Two procedures under the Select menu—Color Select and Auto Select—can be used to create pixel-based (or 8-bit) selections. Painter 6's Magic Wand tool also creates either a pixel-based selection or mask. (To read about the Magic Wand, turn to "Selecting and Masking by Color," on page 111.)

Using antialiasing. *Antialiasing* renders a smooth selection edge by making the pixels along the selection boundary semi-transparent. The semi-transparent edge is especially useful when making selections or masks for collaging images because the edge can blend with the image it's placed in, thus preventing jagged, pixelated edges. All of Painter's selection tools make smooth-edged selections. The Magic Wand is the one tool that gives you a choice—just uncheck the Antialiased checkbox on the Controls:Magic Wand palette if you want to make a jaggy-edged, aliased selection.

CREATING SELECTIONS AND SHAPES

You can make outline-based selections and shapes in a number of ways: Create them with the Lasso or the Oval or Rectangular Selection tool or with one of the shape design tools (Pen, Quick Curve, or Oval or Rectangular Shape tools) or with the Text tool. Or drag a stored selection from the Selection Portfolio section (Objects palette) into your image. You can also import EPS paths from a PostScript drawing program as shapes and convert them to selections. You can create a selection from a mask (Select, Load Selection) or change a mask-based selection to an outline-based selection (Select, Transform Selection). When a soft-edged selection is transformed, it loses its soft edge. For instance, if the selection has a 10-pixel feathered edge, the feather is built inward and outward from the border. When the selection is transformed, the new boundary will fall in the middle of the feathered edge.

Rectangular and Oval Selection tools. Drag to make selections with these tools. To constrain the Oval or Rectangular Selection tools so they select perfect squares or circles, hold down the Shift key and drag.

SAVE SELECTIONS!

If you've spent time making a careful selection, it's a good idea to store the selection for future use. To save an active selection as a mask, choose Select, Save Selection, or click the Save Selection button in the Masks section of the Objects palette. To save an outline-based selection to the Selection Portfolio section of the Objects palette (opened by clicking the left triangle on the Selection Portfolio bar), use the Selection Adjuster to drag the selection directly into the portfolio.

RESTORING A SELECTION

With Painter, you can re-activate the most recent selection. If you've made a selection and have deselected it to work outside of it—then want to use it again, choose Select, Reselect, or click on the Selection Adjuster tool in the Tools palette.

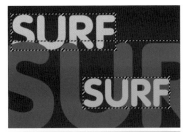

These type shapes were set with the Text tool and then selected with the Adjuster tool (top), converted to active selections (Shapes, Convert to Selection) and then used to fill areas of the image canvas (bottom).

PATH MANIPULATION

To manipulate a path while drawing it, press the Ctrl/⌘ key to switch from the Pen to the Direct Selection tool so you can adjust the anchor points and control handles.

These shapes were created with the Text tool. The type shapes, at the top, (with no fill or stroke and selected with the Direct Selection tool) show selected Bézier anchor points and curves. The lower letter shape, not selected, has been given a white fill using the Fill checkbox in the Shapes, Set Shape Attributes dialog box.

Lasso tool. The Lasso tool is good for making quick, freehand selections. Choose the Lasso and carefully drag around the area that you want to isolate.

Rectangular and Oval Shape tools. Drag with these tools to create rectangular and elliptical shape objects. Press the Shift key and drag with the tool to draw a perfect square or circle shape.

Text tool. As you type with the Text tool, each letter appears as a shape; the name of each letter also appears in the Layers section of the Objects palette. Make corrections as you type by using the Delete key, and press Return or Enter to start a new line of type.

Pen and Quick Curve tools. Choose the Pen tool for precise drawing using a combination of straight lines and curves. Click to create straight line segments; to draw curves, press and drag to pull out handles that control the curves; or drag with the Quick Curve tool to draw freehand shapes. To complete an outline drawn by the Pen or Quick Curve tool, close the shape by connecting to the origin point or by pressing the Close button on the Controls:Shape Design palette. To convert a shape drawn with the Pen or Quick Curve tool to a selection, click the Make Selection button on the Controls: Shape Design palette, or choose Shapes, Convert to Selection.

Selection Adjuster, Adjuster and Direct Selection tools. These tools share a space in the bottom row of the Tools palette. The Adjuster tool is useful for working with shapes and layers. Read more about it in the beginning of Chapter 5. Use the Selection Adjuster to move or transform selections. Read more about this tool in "Transforming Selections," on page 113.

The Direct Selection tool (hollow arrow) allows you to select and adjust individual anchor points and control handles to modify shapes. This tool works much like its counterpart in Adobe Illustrator.

Shape Edit tools. The Scissors, Add Point, Remove Point (or Delete Point) and Convert Point tools will also be familiar to Illustrator users. Like the Direct Selection tool, they are used for changing

PRECISION DRAWING SETUP

When you're drawing paths and you find that the default stroke and fill on the path make it hard to see your path outline so you can draw precisely, change the Shape Attributes to a skeletal line: Choose Edit, Preferences, Shapes; check the Big Handles drawing option and uncheck all the Fill and Stroke preferences. You'll be able to see the path outline with anchor points and handles so you can draw more precisely.

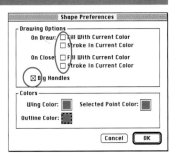

The Shape Preferences dialog box

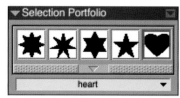

Choosing a heart-shaped path in Painter's Selection Portfolio section, located in the Objects palette.

When this bird, drawn in Adobe Illustrator, was copied and pasted into Painter, it came in as a compound shape. (To create a similar look, turn to "Dropping a Shadow," in Chapter 5.)

NOW YOU SEE 'EM

With Painter 6.0, when you paste PostScript outlines into Painter, or import them (using File, Acquire, Adobe Illustrator File), the outlines may not appear to be in the document but you'll notice their names in the Layers section of the Objects palette. To force the outlines to draw on-screen, click to open the eye icon to the left of the imported layer. (This behavior may be corrected in Painter 6.03 so that the outlines automatically appear in the image.)

shape paths. The Scissors tool allows you to cut a segment of a shape path selected with the Direct Selection tool. To add a new anchor point, select a path segment with the Direct Selection tool and click with the Add Point tool. To delete an anchor point, click on it with the Remove Point tool.

The Selection Portfolio. To use an outline selection, stored in the Selection Portfolio section of the Objects palette, drag it from the palette into your image. If you use a lot of custom paths in your work, use the Selection Mover (accessed by clicking the right triangle on the Selection Portfolio bar), to create custom libraries (see the "Libraries and Movers" section in Chapter 1).

Importing EPS outlines. Painter 6 supports two ways to reliably import shapes, such as type on a curve created in a PostScript drawing program, or preexisting EPS clip art. The first option (File, Acquire, Adobe Illustrator File) creates a new file, importing the EPS outlines—with their strokes and fills—into Painter as shapes. To add the shapes to an existing Painter file, copy and paste the shapes from the new file into your working composition.

The second option allows you to copy outlines with strokes and fills from a PostScript program to the clipboard and paste them into your Painter file. The outlines will be imported into your document as shapes and will appear in the Layers section of the Objects palette. Objects such as the letters "O" and "A" that have a *counter,* or hole, cut in them will come into Painter as compound shapes preserving the holes. Like other shapes, imported EPS shapes can be converted to selections (Shapes, Convert to Selection) so you can use the outlines to modify the image canvas.

EPS IMPORTING ALERT!

A word of warning: As of this writing, we encountered problems when importing some EPS files created in earlier versions of Freehand and Illustrator using both of the import methods. When importing compound objects, we obtained the best results with drawings completely created in Illustrator 5 or newer (simply resaving an older file created in the new format resulted in some compound objects not making the transition).

AUTOMATIC SELECTING AND MASKING

Two powerful functions—Auto Select and Auto Mask—create a selection or mask based on the criteria that you choose to sample, such as Paper, 3D Brushstrokes, Image Luminance, Current Color, Original Selection or Original Mask. The two dialog boxes are identical, with the exception that one creates a pixel-based selection whereas the other creates and stores a mask. Auto Select is located under the Select menu. To use Auto Mask, choose Auto Mask from the pulldown menu accessed by clicking the right triangle on the Masks section bar in the Objects palette or use the shortcut (Ctrl/⌘-Shift-M).

To generate a mask based on the brightness values in an image, try this: Create a new file with a white background. In the Colors

Susan LeVan used Painter's Auto Mask, Current Color feature to make rough-edged masks for brushstrokes shown in this detail of an illustration for a Boston Globe Book Review.

Killdeer *by Mary Envall. To create this wildlife illustration—featuring a black-and-white ink drawing floating on top of colored, textured paper—Envall began by making a black-and-white scratchboard drawing in Painter. To drop the white background out behind the drawing she made an automatic selection, choosing Select, Auto Select Using Image Luminance. She floated the active selection by clicking on it with the Adjuster and then deselected the layer. Next, she filled the background with a colored texture, using Effects, Surface Control, Color Overlay using Paper and Dye Concentration.*

section of the Art Materials palette, select black, and from the Brushes palette choose the Scratchboard Tool variant of the Pens. Make a sketch, and then generate a mask for your sketch by choosing Auto Mask (Ctrl/⌘-Shift-M) using Image Luminance. In the Masks section (Objects palette), click on the mask name to target the mask, and open the eye icon to the left of the mask name to view the mask as a red overlay. Highlighting the mask name will target the mask, allowing you to edit it by painting on it with a brush. For an example of Auto Mask using Current Color—the only one of these automated masking methods that produces an aliased, jagged-edged mask—turn to "Isolating Color with Auto Mask," later in this chapter.

SELECTING AND MASKING BY COLOR

Painter 6 offers useful tools and procedures with which you can make selections and masks based on color.

Magic Wand. Painter 6's Magic Wand is easier to use than before and is a real production time-saver. The Magic Wand lets you select an area of your image based on color similarities of contiguous or non-contiguous pixels. This is especially useful for selecting a uniformly colored element in an image, without having to draw around the area with the Lasso or Pen tool. You can choose to make a transient selection or store the selection as a mask using the Magic Wand by checking the appropriate button on the Controls:Magic Wand palette. To select a wider range of color, move the Tolerance slider to the right. To smooth the edge of the mask or selection, check the Antialias checkbox. To add soft partially transparent values to the mask, increase the Feather by moving the slider to the right.

To add areas of similar adjacent color to the selection or mask (like Select, Grow in Adobe Photoshop), Shift-click on the existing selection with

PHOTO: CORBIS IMAGES

We clicked the Magic Wand in the sky area and began with a Tolerance of 3 and Feather of 1. (Feather allows the selection to include intermediate values.) Changing the Tolerance to 6 and leaving the Feather set at 1 masked the entire sky. The mask was automatically updated when the sliders were moved.

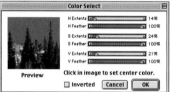

Our goal was to generate a selection based on color for the sky in this photo. Choose Select, Color Select and click in the image to sample the color you'd like to isolate. Adjust the H, S and V sliders until you see the red mask cover only the sampled color in the preview window. Alternatively, you can use Color Mask (accessed by clicking the right triangle on the Masks section bar) to accomplish the same thing, and the mask will automatically be stored in the Masks section of the Objects palette.

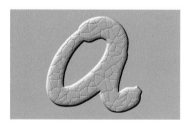

To create this letter "a" with textured highlights and shadows, we began by drawing the "a" with the Scratchboard Tool variant of Pens and black color on a white background. We made a luminosity mask for the letter using Auto Mask, Using Image Luminance. We filled the background with tan color (covering the letter), then we loaded the selection (Select, Load Selection), and used Effects, Surface Control, Apply Surface Texture, Using Paper and the Crackle texture, and a second time Using Mask, to add the bas relief effect. To create a similar look, turn to "Building a Bas Relief," in Chapter 8.

the Magic Wand. To remove colors, Ctrl/⌘-click on an area. To add areas of similar color that are not adjacent (like Select, Similar in Photoshop), turn off the Contiguous checkbox in the Controls:Magic Wand palette, and continue adding areas of non-contiguous color by pressing the Shift key as you click on the image. To turn off the non-adjacent mode, turn on Contiguous again in the Controls:Magic Wand palette.

ADJACENT AND NON-ADJACENT

Painter 6 improves the function of the Magic Wand by including a Contiguous checkbox in the Controls:Magic Wand palette. The selection or mask is dynamically updated when you turn Contiguous (adjacent) mode on or off.

Using Color Select and Color Mask. Painter 6 offers two closely related, automated features that are useful for isolating parts of images based on color. Use Select, Color Select to generate a pixel-based selection based on the color you sample from an image. Adjust the H (Hue), S (Saturation) and V (Value) extents sliders in the Color Select dialog box to control the amount of each of these properties sampled in the image. Experiment with adjusting the Feather sliders to improve the edge of the selection. Save the new selection as a mask to make it permanent. Color Select is closely related to Color Mask; both dialog boxes function essentially the same. Color Mask is found under the Mask pull-down menu in the Masks section. Masks generated using Color Mask are automatically saved into the Masks section. To learn more about Color Mask, turn to "Using Color Mask," later in this chapter.

Many artists begin the process of isolating complex areas of an image using Color Select or Color Mask, then finish a selection by editing it using the Lasso and the Ctrl/⌘ key to subtract from the selection and the Shift key to add to the selection. To convert a mask generated with Color Mask to a selection for editing, choose Select, Load Selection, and choose it from the menu in the Load Selection dialog box.

CONVERTING SELECTIONS, SHAPES AND MASKS

Outline-based and pixel-based selections have entirely different origins, but there is some degree of interchangeability. For instance, you can turn a *mask* into a *selection* (see the "Masks" section on page 116) and then into an *outline-based selection* using the Select, Transform Selection command, so you can move or modify the outline.

To convert a mask into an outline-based selection so you can transform the outline (scale, skew or rotate) using the Selection Adjuster tool, choose Select, Load Selection and from the Load From pop-up menu choose the appropriate mask, click the Replace Selection button and click OK. When the marquee is active, choose Select, Transform Selection.

To make a selection isolating the large dahlia in this photo, we used Select, Color Select, then used the Lasso to change the selection border—pressing the Ctrl/⌘ key to subtract from the selection—to exclude the smaller flower.

PHOTO: CORBIS IMAGES

To convert an active outline-based selection into a mask so you can save the selection permanently into the Masks section as pixel-based information instead of outline information, choose Select, Save Selection.

To convert a shape to an active selection so can you use it to isolate an area of the image canvas, select the shape by highlighting its name in the Layers section, and choose Shapes, Convert to Selection. An added bonus, the Pen and Quick Curve tools offer a Make Selection button on the Controls: Shape Design palette, allowing quick conversion of shapes made with one of these tools. **Beware:** If you convert a shape to a selection using Painter 6.0, it will be permanently lost if you then deselect it before you convert it back to a shape, save it as a mask, drag it into the Selection Portfolio or choose Undo (Ctrl/⌘-Z).

To convert an active selection into a shape so you can edit its outline (using anchor points and control handles), or fill and stroke it—choose Select, Convert to Shape. A word of warning: In Painter 6.0, counters in text selections (such as the hole in the letter "O") can be lost when converting from selections to shapes. Painter 6.03 should fix the problem.

TRANSFORMING SELECTIONS

Painter 6 offers great flexibility, allowing outline-based selection borders to be scaled, skewed or rotated without altering the image canvas. Selections made with the Lasso, Rectangular, and Oval selection tools, as well as selections converted from shapes, are automatically outline-based. Selections saved as masks must be converted to outline-based information before they can be scaled, skewed or rotated. To convert a selection stored in the Masks section to an outline-based selection, load the selection (Select, Load Selection), and when the selection marquee appears, choose Select, Transform Selection. (When a selection is loaded from a mask and transformed, the mask in the Masks section remains unmodified until it is replaced by another selection using the Save Selection, Replace Mask command.)

An important concept to understand when working with outline-based selections is that of *active* vs. *selected*. An *active* selection displays an animated marquee, sometimes referred to as "marching ants." As soon as you've drawn a complete boundary with a selection tool, dragged a selection into your image from the Selection Portfolio, loaded a mask as a selection or converted a shape to a selection, you will see a marquee,

We set this Adobe Woodtype Ornament shape using the Text tool—and Option-dragged with the Layer Adjuster tool to make a copy of the shape. We converted the copy into an active selection (Shapes, Convert to Selection) for treating the image canvas with Effects, Surface Control, Color Overlay Using Paper, Hiding Power with Pavement texture.

Use arrow keys to move selected selections or shapes one screen pixel at a time. Since the distance moved is a screen pixel and not a fixed width, zoom out from the selection or shape if you want to make coarse adjustments and zoom in for fine adjustments. Arrow-key nudging is especially useful for kerning type shapes.

WHERE'S THE PATH?

If you switch from the Pen to another tool (such as the Brush), and your paths seem to disappear, choose the Pen, the Quick Curve tool, the Direct Selection tool or a Shape Edit tool to see them again.

A TOOL FOR SELECTIONS ONLY

To move or transform a selection border without moving the image contents within the active selection, choose the Selection Adjuster. This tool operates on selection borders only.

An active selection (left) ready to accept brushstrokes within its boundary; a selected selection (right) ready to be moved by dragging with the Selection Adjuster tool. When the Selection Adjuster is chosen, an active selection becomes selected and displays eight square handles in addition to the marquee.

letting you know it's active. The image canvas within the marquee can now be painted into, filled or treated with an effect.

A *selected* selection displays eight bounding-box handles around its edges—the handles are visible only when a selection is active and the Selection Adjuster tool is chosen. You select selections in order to move them, or scale, skew, or rotate their outlines, or change them using commands under the Modify menu to widen, contract, smooth, or border them.

The distinction between "active" and "selected" gives you great flexibility: *You can move, scale, rotate and skew the selection outline without affecting the pixel information within it* by applying the Selection Adjuster tool to the interior or to the bounding box handles of a selected outline-based selection.

Working with the Selection Adjuster tool. Since outline-based selections are based on mathematical information, they can undergo all of the following transformations, carried out with the Selection Adjuster tool, with no loss of edge quality and without moving the pixels inside the selection boundary. To *move* a selection, position the Selection Adjuster over it; when you see the four-arrowed cursor, dragging will move the selection. To *duplicate*, hold down Alt/Option, drag and release. To *scale*, first select a selection by clicking on it once; position the tool over one of the corner handles; when the cursor changes, drag the handle. Use the Shift key to *resize proportionally*. If you want to *resize only horizontally or vertically*, drag on a center handle, on a side, top or bottom. To *rotate*, use a corner handle, adding the Ctrl/⌘ key as you position the cursor before dragging. To *skew*, press Ctrl/⌘ while positioning over a center handle on the side, top or bottom, and then drag.

SAVING SELECTION OUTLINES

Use the Selection Adjuster tool to drag outline-based selections to the Selection Portfolio to store them. If you want to save shapes into this library, first convert them to selections (Shapes, Convert to Selection) and then drag them to the Selection Portfolio. If you're very organized, you might create multiple selection libraries for different jobs. To swap outlines between libraries or to set up a new, empty palette, you can use the Selection Mover, accessed by clicking the right triangle in the Selection Portfolio section bar.

Use File, Export Adobe Illustrator File to export images to Post-Script drawing programs. We successfully exported simple shape objects and more complex objects that included blends and compounds, opening them in Illustrator 7 and 8.

SELECTIONS AT WORK

Once you've activated selections, you can choose to draw outside of them instead of inside, or use them to isolate areas of the image canvas when applying special-effects procedures found in the Effects menu.

Alt/Option-dragging a selection to make a copy

Dragging a side handle to scale horizontally

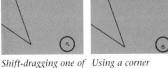

Shift-dragging one of the corner handles to scale proportionally

Using a corner handle and the Ctrl/⌘ key to rotate

PAINTER 6 TIMESAVERS

Use these Shift-key shortcuts to switch among the three Drawing icons (found at the bottom left of Painter's working window) to determine how the painting tools work with active selections:

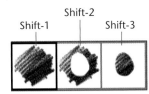

Shift-2

Shift-1   Shift-3

The Drawing icons are (from left to right): Draw Anywhere, Draw Outside and Draw Inside.

SELECT, INVERT—BEWARE!

Instead of using the Drawing icons, you can invert a mask by using the Select, Invert command. But *beware*, combining use of the Drawing icons and the Select, Invert command can be confusing. At least through the initial release of Painter 6.0, when Select, Invert is chosen, the Drawing icons do not change to reflect the new mask coverage.

Using the Drawing icons. The Drawing icons are found in the bottom left corner of an active document's window. Take the name "Drawing icons" literally; they affect drawing and painting actions only, not fills or other effects. A fill or effect is always constrained to the inside of an active selection, regardless of which drawing icon you choose. Several of the techniques in this chapter demonstrate how these icons work, and you can refer to "Drawing Modes" in Chapter 11 of Painter's *User Guide* for a detailed explanation.

Inverting a selection. If you want to apply a fill or effect to the *outside* of your active selection, use Select, Invert. This procedure reverses the current selection. It's often useful to save a selection as a mask in the Masks section, then save the inverse of it; for instance, save an element, then save the background, also as a mask.

Stroking a selection. In Painter, you can use any brush variant *to stroke a selection marquee*. Begin by making a selection using the Oval, Rectangle, Lasso or Quick Curve tool. The effect is more fun to observe if you choose one of Painter's grain-sensitive brushes. In the Brushes palette, choose the Large Chalk variant of Dry Media. Next, open the Papers section of the Art Materials palette and choose a texture from the default paper library. With the selection still active, use the Drawing icons (located at the extreme bottom-left of the image window) to choose whether you want your stroke inside (Draw Inside), outside (Draw Outside), or centered directly on top of the selection border (Draw Anywhere), then go to the Select menu and choose Stroke Selection.

A QUICK INVERT

When you want to *paint* inside or outside of a selection, you can use the Drawing icons to quickly invert the selection without forcing the whole image to redraw every time you switch. However, *to invert the selection if you are applying a special effect*, you must use Select, Invert which forces a complete screen redraw.

TRANSFORM FIRST. . .

If you'd like to stroke the outline of a pixel-based selection, use Select, Transform Selection to convert it to an outline-based selection before attempting to use the Select, Stroke Selection command.

EDITING SELECTIONS

Painter 6 offers methods for finessing outline-based and pixel-based selections that will be familiar to Photoshop users. To read about editing masks, turn to "Masks," on page 116.

Expanding a selection. To add to an existing selection marquee, press the Shift key and drag outside of the existing marquee with the Lasso or Rectangular or Oval Selection tool. The Add to Selection command is also useful—it is described on page 118.

Subtracting from a selection. To remove a portion of an active selection, press the Ctrl/⌘ key and drag inside of the selection

To create a light-valued border for an image, make a rectangular selection, and choose Select, Modify, Border and set the width for the border. (We used 30 pixels for this 750 pixel-wide image.) With the border selection active (as shown here), choose Effects, Tonal Control, Adjust Colors. Move the Value slider to the right to lighten the values within the selection.

Multiple applications of the Smooth function (Select, Modify, Smooth) can turn a perfectly good typeface (Stone Sans, left) into a trendy, avant-garde one. Set type shapes with the Text tool, convert them to selections (Shapes, Convert to Selection), apply the Smooth operation and fill them with a color.

marquee with the Lasso or Rectangular or Oval Selection tool. The Subtract from Selection and Intersect commands are also useful—they are described on page 118.

The Modify menu. Four commands under the Select, Modify menu—Widen, Contract, Smooth and Border—allow you to change active outline-based selections. Widen and Contract allow you change the size of a selection by a specified number of pixels. The Smooth command is useful for rounding corners and softening jagginess in a selection. The Border function adds a second selection marquee (based on a specified number of pixels), outside the existing marquee, selecting only the area between the two.

Feathering. Feathering a selection softens its edge. To see feathering at work, drag a selection from the Selection Portfolio into your image. Choose Select, Feather, and type 20 into the field to define the extent of the feather; click OK. Now choose Effects, Fill, select one of the options and click OK. Note the soft edges of the filled selection. The feather is always built both inward and outward from the selection boundary. The Select, Feather command changes an outline-based selection to a pixel-based selection.

MASKS

You can create masks in Painter in several ways: by making a selection and saving it as a mask, by painting directly onto a new blank mask with brushes, by generating masks with procedures such as Auto Mask or Color Mask, or by using Boolean operations to calculate new masks from existing ones.

Painting a resist using a mask. Instead of making masks by using Bézier curves to draw selections, artists with experience in drawing often feel more comfortable using brushes on the mask to paint the areas they want to isolate. One of the best ways to get acquainted with painting a mask is to paint a *resist*.

A traditional resist involves applying a protective substance to define an area and to prevent paint from being applied to it. To create a resist in Painter, begin with a new file and open the Masks section of the Objects palette. From the pull-down menu accessed by clicking the right arrow on the Masks section bar, choose New Mask. Target the new mask by clicking on its name in the Masks section to highlight it with blue. To see the red-tinted mask as you paint it, open the "eye"

MASK VIEWS

To view the mask and image canvas simultaneously (in the Masks section of the Objects palette), open both the eye icon for the mask and the eye icon for the RGB-Canvas. To view the mask alone in black-and-white, toggle the RGB-Canvas eye icon closed. To hide the mask, close its eye icon.

TARGETING A MASK

In the Masks section, make sure to click on the item's *name*—and not the eye icon—to target it.

Anderson Valley Apples. *To paint a resist for the trees with the Scratchboard Pen variant of Pens on the mask, the mask was set at 100% opacity in the Mask Attributes dialog box (top left); washes were painted on the background using the Simple Water Water Color brush (top right). The finished artwork included brushstrokes inside of the mask (above), made by reversing the mask after the other painting had been done.*

CHER THREINEN-PENDARVIS

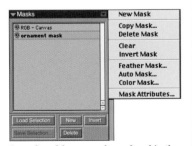

Several useful commands are found in the Masks section's pull-down menu.

icon next to its name. Choose black to paint a solid mask, white to erase your work, and any color in between if you want varying levels of mask transparency. When you're done, select the image background by clicking on the RGB-Canvas in the Masks section, and begin painting broad strokes across the image canvas. All red areas that you painted on the mask with black paint are protected from these strokes. To "reverse" the mask so you can paint with a brush on the areas covered by your mask, select the far right Drawing icon on the lower left corner of the image window. To view your work without the mask, choose the far left Drawing icon, or in the Masks section, target the mask and wink the eye icon shut.

USING THE MASKS SECTION

The Masks section lists all the masks in your file by name. A Painter file can contain a maximum of 32 masks. If you'll be doing a lot of work with masks, it's a good idea to get on friendly terms with this section of the Objects palette. Here are some basics:

To view a mask as an overlay on top of the RGB image canvas, open the eye icon to the far left of the mask's name.

To hide a mask, click its eye icon shut.

To view a mask alone in black-and-white, without the RGB-Canvas, open the mask's eye icon and close the RGB-Canvas eye icon.

To view a mask as an opaque overlay, choose Mask Attributes from the pull-down menu on the Masks section bar, and move the Opacity slider to 100%. Viewing a mask as an opaque overlay can often help you to see defects in the mask. Adjusting this slider changes the overlay appearance only, and does not affect the actual density of the mask.

To edit a mask, click the mask's name to select it (the mask's name will be highlighted in blue). Open the eye icon to the far left of the mask's name. You can edit the mask by painting on it with any brush except a Water Color brush.

To apply a paper grain to a mask, highlight the mask in the Masks section and use Effects, Surface Control, Express Texture, using Paper. Experiment with the Gray Threshold and Grain sliders.

PHOTO: CORBIS IMAGES

To change the mask overlay to a color easier to see while making a mask for an orange Garibaldi fish, we changed the overlay color from the default red to yellow using the Mask Attributes dialog box.

To copy mask information to another mask, select a mask and choose Copy Mask from the pull-down menu on the Masks section bar. From the Copy Mask To pop-up menu, select a destination mask, and click OK.

To blur a mask so that loading it as a selection will produce a feathered selection, select the mask and choose Feather Mask from the pull-down menu, type a number in the field and click OK.

CALCULATING AND OPERATING

Painter 6 offers Boolean operations, useful functions that help generate new masks that fit perfectly against existing ones. Skillful use of these techniques will save time and effort. To see these functions at work, turn to "Making Masks for Embossing," on page 119.

To edit a mask using a selection, create a selection marquee, and choose Select, Save Selection. In the Save Selection dialog box, choose the mask you wish to edit from the Save To pop-up menu, and the operation you wish to perform.

To replace a mask with the active selection, create a selection marquee and choose Select, Save Selection. In the dialog box, from the Save To menu, choose the mask you wish to replace, then click the Replace Mask button. This choice makes the original mask permanently unavailable.

To add a mask to a selection, create a selection marquee surrounding the area you want to add to. Choose Load Selection. In the Load Selection dialog box, choose the mask you want to add to the selection and click the Add To Selection button.

To subtract a mask from a selection, make a new marquee around the area from which you want to take away. Choose Load Selection, and in the Load Selection dialog box select the mask you want to subtract from the selection and click the Subtract From Selection button.

We used Intersect With Selection to create the filled half circle (above right). Begin by making a square selection with the Rectangular Selection tool and Shift key and save the selection by choosing Select, Save Selection, or choosing Save Selection from the Masks section's pull-down menu. View the mask as an overlay (above left) by clicking its eye icon open in the Masks section. Highlight the RGB-Canvas name again, and make a new selection partially overlapping the square, with the Oval Selection tool. With the oval selection active, click Load Selection on the Masks section. In the Load From pop-up menu choose the square mask, and click the Intersect With Selection button.

To create the intersection of a mask and a selection, creating a new selection that isolates only the overlapping area, begin with a selection marquee. Choose Load Selection. In the Load Selection dialog box, choose the mask you want to use to make the intersection and click the Intersect With Selection button.

PAINTER AND PHOTOSHOP

To save Painter selections into the Masks section and use them in Photoshop 5/5.5 as channels, save a Painter file in Photoshop 3.0 format. When you open the file in Photoshop, the named masks will automatically appear in the Channels palette. To learn more about using Painter masks and paths with Photoshop (and vice versa) turn to Chapter 9, "Using Painter with Photoshop."

Making Masks for Embossing

Overview *Open a new file with a colored background; set a type shape; convert the shape to a selection; save the selection as a mask; use the selection to build bevel and background masks; apply special effects to create three-dimensional looks.*

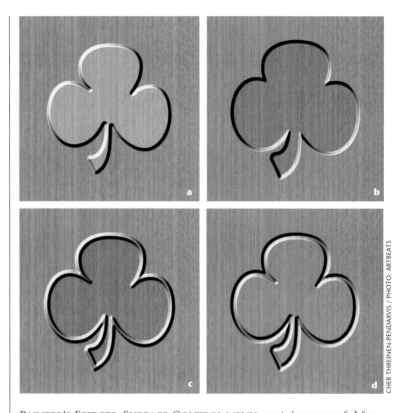

The shape before converting to a selection

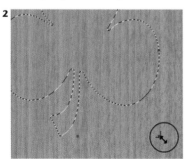

Using the Selection Adjuster to scale the selection

PAINTER'S EFFECTS, SURFACE CONTROL MENU contains powerful features for creating three dimensional artwork needed for an embossed look or for interactive buttons. These features are most effective when combined with a skillful use of selections and masks. To create these tooled wood reliefs, we began with a graphic shape for the face of the graphic. Then we created a series of masks based on the original graphic—a widened face, a bevel and a background—to isolate areas for special effects application. Preparing the masks up front allowed quick previewing of a variety of effects.

1 Setting a shape and converting it to a selection. Create a new file with a light background color, or open a textured background image (we chose Beechwood from the ArtBeats *Wood and Paper* CD-ROM). Choose black, click in the image with the Text tool and type a letter. (Using a 500-pixel-wide file, we set an ornament using the Adobe Wood Type Ornaments font.)

Before you can use the graphic shape to isolate areas of the image canvas, you'll need to convert it to a selection. Select the shape in the Layers section of the Objects palette, or click on it in the image with the Adjuster tool and choose Shapes, Convert to Selection.

2 Moving and scaling. Choose the Selection Adjuster tool (it shares a space in the Tools palette with the Adjuster). Press inside the active selection with the Selection Adjuster tool, and when you

3

Typing a descriptive name for the mask

4

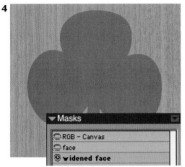

Viewing the widened face mask on top of the RGB-Canvas

5a

Loading the "widened face" mask

5b

Subtracting the "face" mask

5c

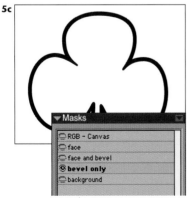

Viewing the bevel mask without the canvas

see the four-arrow cursor, you can safely move your selection without distorting it. To scale, drag on one of the selection handles; to scale proportionately, press Shift and drag one of the corner handles.

3 Saving and naming the selection. Saving a selection permanently stores it in the Masks section of the Objects palette as a mask. The first selection will be the top face of the bas relief, and we used it to create three masks. To save a selection, choose Select, Save Selection, or click the Save Selection button on the Masks section. When the Save Selection dialog box appears, accept the default in the pop-up menu—Save to New. Click OK. To rename the mask, double-click its name in the Masks section. We named ours "face."

4 Widening the selection. When you close the dialog Mask Attributes dialog box after renaming, the selection is converted from outline-based to mask information and the selection ceases to be active on the image canvas. Load the "face" selection (Select, Load Selection, Load From "face") and choose Select, Transform Selection. You can now transform the selection to create a wider boundary around the graphic. Choose Select, Modify, Widen and set the radius by typing a number in the field (we used 10 pixels). Save this new widened selection into the Masks section, naming it "widened face."

5 Creating new masks using calculations. Next, we created a bevel mask describing the thin area between the outside widened boundary and the original face boundary. Painter 6 offers Boolean operations, calculations in the Save Selection and Load Selection dialog boxes to make the job easier. To build a mask for the bevel, choose Select, Load Selection; from the Load From pop-up menu choose the "widened face" mask; choose the Replace Selection radio button, and click OK. When the marquee appears, choose Load Selection again, this time choosing "face" from the pop-up menu and under Operation, click the Subtract From Selection radio button to subtract the original face area from the widened face area, resulting in a mask for the bevel. Save and name the mask.

We also built a mask isolating the image area outside of the widened face mask. To do this, load a selection using the "widened face" mask, and then choose Select, Invert. We saved this selection as a mask, naming it "background."

QUICKER LOADING

To save a visit to the Select menu or Masks section when you'd like to load a selection—press Ctrl/⌘-Shift-E to display the Load Selection dialog box.

MODIFYING SELECTIONS

Only outline-based selections accept commands from the Modify menu such as Widen and Contract. To convert a mask-based selection to path-based information so you can modify it, choose Select, Transform Selection. For more information, turn to "Editing Selections," on page 115.

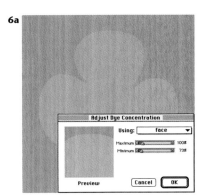

6a

Using Dye Concentration in conjunction with the "face" mask

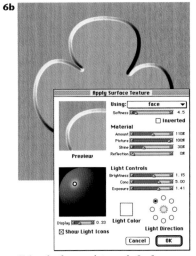

6b

Using the face mask to apply Surface Texture to create the embossed face

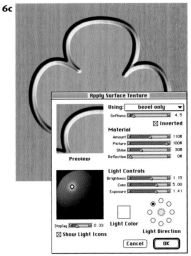

6c

Using the "bevel" mask to apply Surface Texture for the cut bevel effect

6 Putting the masks to work. Many operations available under the Effects menu in Painter 6—for instance, Tonal Control, Adjust Color; Surface Control, Apply Surface Texture; and Focus, Glass Distortion—offer a pop-up menu allowing you to apply the effect using any mask saved in the Masks section.

To **emboss** the face, creating the bas relief look in image "a" at the top of page 119, you can use the "face" mask to isolate an area of the image. Lightening the face of the graphic will enhance the illusion of relief. With no selection active and the RGB-Canvas active in the Masks section, choose Effects, Surface Control, Dye Concentration. In the Using pop-up menu, choose the "face" mask; to lighten the area, set the Minimum slider to 80%. Click OK. Now, for the relief effect: To "pop" the graphic face out (creating a convincing 3D effect), choose Effects, Surface Control, Apply Surface Texture. In the Using menu choose "face." Set Softness to 4.5, reduce the shine to 30%, click the top left Light Direction button and click OK.

To **deboss** the face, of the graphic in image "b" with no selection active and the RGB-Canvas active in the Masks section, choose Effects, Surface Control, Dye Concentration. In the Using pop-up menu choose the "face" mask. To darken the area, set the Minimum slider to 125%. Click OK. Then choose Effects, Surface Control, Apply Surface Texture. Click the Inverted checkbox to turn it on. In the Using menu choose "face." Set Softness to 4.5, reduce the shine to 30%, choose the top left Light Direction button and click OK.

To create the **beveled** look in image "c," begin by lightening the bevel area: With no selection active and the RGB-Canvas active in the Masks section, choose Effects, Surface Control, Dye Concentration. In the Using pop-up menu, choose the "bevel" mask. To lighten the area, set the Minimum slider to 80%. To emboss the bevel, making the face and background appear to recede, choose Effects, Surface Control, Apply Surface Texture. In the Using menu, choose "bevel." Set Softness to 4.5, reduce the shine to 30%, and click the top left Light Direction button. Be sure the Inverted box is not checked and click OK.

To **carve the beveled area *in*,** leaving the face and background flat (image "d"), begin by darkening the bevel area. With no selection active and the RGB-Canvas active in the Masks section, choose Effects, Surface Control, Dye Concentration. In the Using pop-up menu, choose the "bevel" mask. To darken the area, set the Minimum slider to 125%. To deboss the bevel, making the bevel appear to be carved into the wood, choose Effects, Surface Control, Apply Surface Texture. In the Using menu choose "bevel." Set Softness to 4.5, set the Shine at 30%, and click the top left Light Direction button. Click to turn on the Inverted feature and click OK.

Working with Bézier Paths and Selections

Overview *Use the Pen tool to create paths of straight and curved lines; convert the paths to selections; use a custom pencil to draw inside and outside of selections.*

JOHN FRETZ

TO DESIGN A LOGO FOR THE 100-YEAR-OLD Bethany Church in Seattle, John Fretz used a custom pencil to draw inside and outside of selections to create a hard-edged, graduated look similar to his conventional colored pencil illustration style.

The logo sketch, including a rough grid

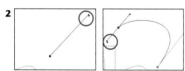

Pulling a handle from an anchor point to prepare for a curved path segment, then pressing and dragging to create the curve

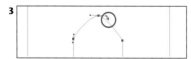

Dragging on a control handle to change the path's shape

1 Sketching the logo. Fretz created a 4 x 4-inch pencil drawing of the logo that included a rough grid aligning the roofs of the houses. He scanned the sketch at 300 ppi and opened it in Painter to use as a template.

2 Creating a path with Bézier curves. The most efficient way to create a combination of curve and straight-line path segments is with the Pen tool. Set up shape attributes (with no fill or stroke) to produce a skeletal line that will help you see precise lines and curves while you draw: Choose Edit, Preferences, Shapes to open the Shape Preferences dialog box. Under Drawing Options uncheck all the Fill and Stroke checkboxes. To make the anchor points and control handles easier to see and work with, check the Big Handles checkbox. Click OK. Now, choose the Pen tool and click to place anchor points for straight-line segments, and press, hold and drag to create anchor points with handles that control curve segments. When you want to close a path, place the cursor over the starting anchor point, and click when you see a small circle designating the origin point, or press the Close button in the Controls:Shape Design palette.

3 Changing the path shape. You can fine-tune a path during or after the drawing process with the Direct Selection tool. (While drawing with the Pen tool, press the Ctrl/⌘ key to temporarily change from the Pen to the Direct Selection tool.) Move the Direct Selection tool over an anchor point, a control handle, or a curve segment and drag to reposition it.

CHANGING DIRECTION

While drawing with the Pen, Alt/ Option-click on an anchor point to create a cusp and establish a new direction for the following curve. A cusp is a corner point between two curved line segments, such as the "dent" at the top of a heart shape.

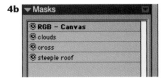

4a

Click on the Make Selection button to change the shape path into a selection.

4b

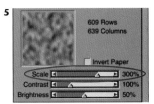

Selections stored as masks in the Masks section

5

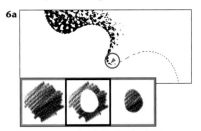

609 Rows
639 Columns

Scaling the Basic Paper texture

6a

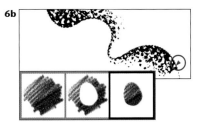

Painting outside of the cloud selection using the custom black pencil

6b

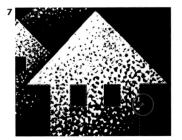

Painting inside of the cloud selection

7

When the house is filled with white, the subtracted selection around the windows protects the area, keeping them black. Fretz used his custom pencil to add black texture over the white fill.

4 Changing the path to a selection. Paths must be turned into selections before you can use them to control where paint is applied on the image. You can convert a path drawn with the Pen or Quick Curve tool to a selection immediately after drawing it by pressing the Make Selection button in the Controls: Shape Design palette. You can also change a path into a selection by selecting the shape in the Layers section of the Objects palette and choosing Shapes, Convert to Selection. In your image, the Bézier curves will turn into a black-and-white selection marquee. To save the selection as a mask in the Masks section for future use, choose Select, Save Selection. To name a selection, double-click on its name in the Masks sections to open the Mask Attributes dialog box. Type a new name in the field. Click OK. To return to the image canvas, click on RGB-Canvas in the Masks section.

5 Creating the pencil and surface. To re-create the graduated effect he gets with conventional colored pencils on rough illustration board, Fretz built a heavy, grainy pencil based on Painter's Colored Pencil variant. He modified the variant by switching to the Cover method and Grainy Hard Cover subcategory in the General section of the Brush Controls palette. He increased the Size to roughly 200 pixels using the Size slider on the Size section. (You might also experiment with a brush that uses Grainy Edge Flat Cover with a 10% Grain setting in the General section; it will give you an even coarser texture—black-and-white, with no grays.) Fretz chose Basic Paper because of its even texture, and scaled it to about 300% using the Scale slider in Papers section of the Art Materials palette.

6 Drawing in and out of selections. Fretz used the Drawing Modes, three icons located in the bottom left corner of the image window, to paint inside and outside of selections. Begin by loading a selection (Select, Load Selection). To protect the area inside an active selection, click on the middle Drawing button; to protect the area outside the selection, click on the far right Drawing button. Fretz switched back and forth between these two options as he rendered a graduated, even texture using his custom pencil. (You can also use the Select, Invert command to invert an active selection.)

7 Subtracting from a selection. To fill each house with white and leave the windows black, Fretz loaded each house selection and subtracted the window selection from it: Choose Load Selection again and in the Load Selection dialog box, choose a selection and click to subtract it from the original selected area. Fretz filled the resulting selection with white, then he added black texture to the house with his custom pencil. He continued to add textured, even tone with the black and white pencils until he completed the logo.

Fretz saved the finished image in TIFF format, and to eliminate all grayscale information, he opened the image in Photoshop and converted it from grayscale to a 600 ppi Bitmap image.

Using Selections to Limit Paint

Overview *Make a sketch on a colored ground; draw paths, convert them to selections and store them as masks; paint and apply effects within the selections.*

RAY BLAVATT

Sketching with the Flattened Pencil variant

Adding bolder lines to the sketch

RAY BLAVATT LOVES THE ENERGETIC, EXPRESSIVE line work of fashion illustrators (notably Carl Erickson and Rene Bouche) and political cartoonists (including Jim Borgman and Pat Oliphant). His background is in traditional illustration, but today most of Blavatt's work is in animation. His procedure involves drawing in Painter and then saving the illustrations for animation in Quick-Time format, importing them into Macromedia Flash and eventually exporting his work to VHS tape.

To create *Parisian,* Blavatt began by making a gestural drawing. Then he drew loose paths with the Pen tool directly on the sketch and converted the paths to selections so that he would have a boundary to limit paint when he painted fast. Artists familiar with drawing in a PostScript program (as Blavatt is) will like this method of drawing straight and curved line segments with the Pen, then converting the paths to selections. (To read more about different methods of making selections, turn to the beginning of this chapter.)

1 Sketching on a colored ground. Blavatt opened a new file measuring 1900 x 2100 pixels with a newsprint-colored background. He chose the Flattened Pencil variant of the Pencils, a gold color in the Colors section of the Art Materials palette and Pavement texture in the Papers section. Envisioning a young woman on a fictitious street in Paris, he sketched quick, gestural strokes to lay out the drawing. He changed the size of the pencil as he worked using the Size slider on the Controls:Brush palette. To sketch as Blavatt did, open a new file with a gold-colored background, choose the Flattened Pencil and make a sketch. The

Drawing the path around a building

The Controls:Shape Design palette showing the Make Selection button

The painting with textured chalk strokes added to the sky, street and figure

Pavement texture chosen in the Papers section of the Art Materials palette

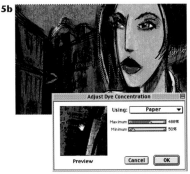
Using Dye Concentration to apply a darker tint to the selected background

Flattened Pencil incorporates the Buildup method, which allows color to be applied with transparency (overlapping strokes will darken); its Grainy Soft Buildup subcategory creates soft-edged strokes that are affected by the current paper texture.

2 Emphasizing the line work. Next, Blavatt added darker color and textured, thick and thin lines to the drawing using the Graphic Paintbrush variant of the Brushes. (The Graphic Paintbrush reminds Blavatt of the Rough Out brush, a favorite he liked using in earlier versions of Painter, although by default the Graphic Paintbrush reveals more of the paper texture.) To lay bold strokes over your pencil sketch, choose the Graphic Paintbrush and a dark color in the Color picker. For finer line work, Blavatt sized the brush smaller (to 7.3) using the Size slider on the Controls:Brush palette.

3 Drawing paths and converting to selections. So that he could isolate areas of the drawing while painting and applying special effects, he created selections. Because his subject included straight lines (buildings) and smooth curves (the figure and streetlight, for instance), Blavatt chose the Pen from the Tools palette to draw a path around each building and the figure of the young woman. To make it easier to see the path as he was drawing it, he applied a stroke without a fill. To set up Preferences to automatically stroke paths as you draw them, without filling: Choose Edit, Preferences, Shapes and under Drawing Options, for On Draw, turn on Stroke With Current Color, turning off Fill With Current Color; for On Close, turn on Stroke With Current Color, turning off Fill With Current Color. (To draw more precise paths, some artists prefer to draw the paths without a Stroke or Fill.) Choose the Pen tool and click and drag to draw a path. (For more information about drawing paths with the Pen tool, turn to "Working with Bézier Paths and Selections," on page 122.)

When the path was complete, Blavatt converted it to a selection. To make a soft selection edge that would help to make transparent color on the edges when he painted or filled, he feathered the selection 8 pixels by choosing Select, Feather. Then he saved the selection as a mask so he could use it later.

Convert the path you've drawn to a selection by clicking the Make Selection button on the Controls:Shape Design palette. When the active marquee appears, feather the selection (Select, Feather), then save it as a mask by choosing Select, Save Selection. When the Save Selection dialog box appears, choose New and click OK. The mask will be saved in the Masks section of the Objects palette.

4 Adding color and texture. Painting with blues and golds, Blavatt used the Square Chalk variant of Dry Media to quickly build up color over the entire image, using a light enough touch on his stylus, to preserve the texture.

6a

Drawing a path for the beam of light

6b

Airbrushing within the active selection

6c

The completed beam of light

7

The Flattened Pencil variant (Pencils) and the Graphic Paintbrush (Brushes) were used to add final details to the face.

5 Enhancing the figure as the focal point. Next, he added details to the blouse and more colored texture to the figure. He chose Select, Load Selection and chose the figure's mask from the Load From menu. When the selection was active, he added highlights to the woman's blouse using the Bleach variant (Erasers). To deepen color and build shadows, he used the Darkener variant (Erasers). Then he chose a creamy pink color in the Colors section, and with Pavement texture chosen in the Papers section, he used the Square Chalk to gently brush textured highlights over the figure's face, neck and arms. When he'd finished the figure and clothing, he reversed the selection by choosing Select, Invert so he could work on the background while protecting the figure.

To further strengthen the focal point, he added a dark burgundy "dye" to the background only, while leaving the focal point—the figure—in lighter colors. (The darkening also helped to enhance the mysterious atmosphere of the city street.) To add a "dye" to an area of your image, start by loading a selection. To re-create Blavatt's effect, make sure Pavement is the current texture in the Papers section. (When Paper is chosen in the Using menu, the luminance of the current texture chosen in the Papers section is used as the means to apply the transparent dye effect.) Then choose a deep red in the Colors section and choose Effects, Surface Control, Dye Concentration, Using Paper. (Blavatt set a Maximum of 488% and a Minimum of 50%.) Experiment with the settings. To scroll around your image in the Preview window, press in the Preview window to access the grabber hand. Click OK when you have an effect you like.

6 Airbrushing a beam of light. To balance the composition, Blavatt added a gold beam of light shining from a streetlight on the left side of the image. First he created a selection to limit the paint. Using the Pen tool from the Tools palette, he drew a path to define the beam of light; he converted the path to a selection by using the Make Selection button on the Controls:Shape Design palette. For a smooth edge, he feathered the selection to 8 pixels (Select, Feather), then he saved the selection as a mask by choosing Select, Save Selection. To ensure that the color of the light matched existing color in the illustration, he used the Dropper tool to sample a gold color from the image. Next, he chose the Fine Spray variant of the Airbrushes and used firmer pressure to spray denser color near the light source, then used lighter pressure to fade the spray of color as he painted lower within the selection.

7 Final details. To complete the painting, Blavatt went back over the image and added details: With the Flattened Pencil and a dark color he touched up the woman's eyes; with the Graphic Paintbrush he added more tiny strokes of white at the top of light beam and he strengthened highlights on the woman's hair and blouse collar. At last, he used the Bleach variant of the Erasers to brighten the highlight on the roof of the background building.

Selections and Airbrush

Overview *Create a pencil sketch; add PostScript outlines in a drawing program; import outlines and sketch into Painter; add texture and gradient fills within the selections; use the Airbrush to create a metallic look.*

JOHN DISMUKES, CAPSTONE STUDIOS

1a

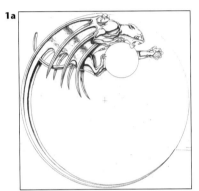

The original pencil sketch

1b

The selected and grouped panther outlines were copied to the clipboard in Illustrator.

2a

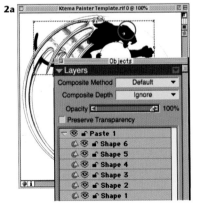

The pasted shapes selected with the Layer Adjuster tool on the image, showing their names in the Layers section

ARTISTS USING TRADITIONAL AIRBRUSH technique cut friskets out of paper, film or plastic to protect portions of their artwork as they paint. For complex jobs this can become quite a task. That's one of the reasons why John Dismukes of Capstone Studios traded in his traditional tools for electronic ones. For this logo for Ktema, a manufacturer of promotional clothing for the entertainment industry, he started with a pencil sketch, added PostScript paths and brought both into Painter. He turned the paths into selections and painted inside and outside of the selections as he would with traditional friskets.

1 Creating the EPS paths. Dismukes scanned his pencil sketch and used it as a template as he drew the elements to fit using Adobe Illustrator. He drew PostScript outlines for the panther, the wing ribs and membrane, the large and small globes, and the Ktema nameplate. Painter 6 can recognize fill and stroke attributes and groups when PostScript art is imported, so you may find it helpful to fill and group certain elements as you draw them. This will help you identify elements so you can move and scale them. To prepare a document for importing into Painter, save a version in Adobe Illustrator 5 (or later) or EPS format.

2 Importing, positioning and scaling. Dismukes opened the original pencil sketch in Painter and begin importing the paths into the document. There are two reliable ways to import Post-Script outlines into a Painter file: using File, Acquire, Adobe Illustrator file (which creates a new file) or copying from the PostScript program to the clipboard and then pasting into an open file in Painter. For the second method to work, both applications have to be running at the same time. Importing the outlines as shapes into a Painter file by pasting through the clipboard is fairly fast and always reliable. To do this, select the outlines in Illustrator

2b

The Layer Adjuster tool changes to an arrow cursor when scaling the panther shapes to fit the template.

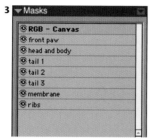

3 Masks

RGB – Canvas
front paw
head and body
tail 1
tail 2
tail 3
membrane
ribs

The named selections in the Masks section

4

Cloning texture into the membrane selection

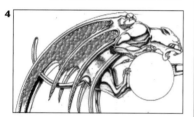

5

Airbrushing highlights on the panther

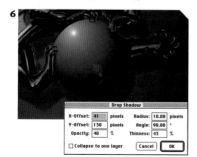

6

Drop Shadow

H-Offset: 41 pixels   Radius: 10.00 pixels
V-Offset: 130 pixels   Angle: 90.00 °
Opacity: 40 %   Thinness: 43 %

☐ Collapse to one layer   Cancel OK

Applying the shadow

and copy, then switch to Painter and paste. You'll see a closed group of shapes appear in the Layers section of the Objects palette. Move the shape group into position on the template using the Layer Adjuster tool or the arrow keys on your keyboard. To scale shapes proportionally, choose the Layer Adjuster tool, hold down the Shift key and drag on a corner handle.

3 Converting, saving and naming. If you have a complex graphic with overlapping shapes, you may want to ungroup the shapes before converting them to selections. This will enable you to save each selection as a user mask in the Masks section (Objects palette) that can be used individually, or added to or subtracted from the other selections. To ungroup, click the Ungroup button in the Layers section. To convert a shape to a selection so you can paint or fill it, select it in the Layers section and choose Shapes, Convert to Selection. The shape will disappear from the Layers section and will become an active marquee on the image canvas. Store the active selection in the Masks section as a user mask by choosing Select, Save Selection. To name it, double-click on its current name. Type a name for the mask in the Mask Attributes dialog box and click OK. Click RGB-Canvas in the Masks section to see the image again.

4 Filling selections. Dismukes created texture within the membrane selection using a Cloning brush and a modified paper texture from a second document. He filled the large globe with a maroon gradient and the small globe with a green gradient. To read more about cloning turn to "Cloning and Tracing" and "Coloring Pencil Illustrations," in Chapter 3.

5 Airbrushing. Dismukes's template showed good shadow and highlight detail. Using it as a guide, he began by laying down dark colors, gradually building forward to the white highlights. He used the Digital Airbrush variant of Airbrushes, adjusting only the Size and Min Size in the Size section of the Brush Controls palette.

6 Adding a shadow. Dismukes used a layer to create the panther's drop shadow on the maroon globe. Use the Create Drop Shadow command to do this: Load the selection by choosing Select, Load Selection. To load more than one user mask at a time as a single selection, load the first selection, then choose Select, Load Selection again and in the Load From menu, choose a second selection and Add To Selection. Continue to Load and Add to your selection until you have all of the elements active. Store this complex selection as a new user mask by choosing Select, Save Selection.

Turn the new selection into a layer by clicking on it in your image with the Layer Adjuster tool. Choose Effects, Objects, Create Drop Shadow. Use the default settings or experiment with other settings, then click OK to create the shadow.

As a final touch, Dismukes opened the image in Adobe Photoshop and applied the Lens Flare filter to the green globe. The 40 MB logo was output as a 4 x 5-inch color transparency at 762 ppi. 🐾

Working with Freehand Selections

Overview *Open a scanned drawing as a template; select areas of the image using the Lasso; use selections to constrain brushstrokes, fills and effects.*

STEVE CAMPBELL

The original pencil sketch

An active selection around the girl and hills

Adding to a selected area   *Subtracting from a selected area*

Paint applied within a selection

TO ISOLATE AREAS FOR PAINTING, FILLING AND LIGHTING effects in the whimsical *Ægypt*, artist Steve Campbell used the Lasso tool. He painted and applied special effects within each selection, then he unified the piece by applying effects across the entire image.

1 Sketching and scanning. Campbell started with a pencil sketch, which he scanned and opened in Painter.

2 Creating selections. Select the Lasso tool, and in your image, drag carefully around the area you want to select, dragging the Lasso precisely back to its origin point. You may find it helpful to zoom in on your image while making detailed freehand selections: Click with the Magnifier tool to zoom in, press Alt/Option and click to zoom out.

Painter 6's Lasso tool lets you add to or subtract from the currently active selection. To add to the currently selected area, hold down the Shift key and drag with the Lasso to reshape an area of the border to increase the selection. To subtract from the currently selected area, hold down the Ctrl/⌘ key and drag with the Lasso tool to cut part of the active selection away.

Saving the completed selection as a user mask will store it permanently with your image in the Masks section of the Objects palette. To save a selection, choose Select, Save Selection, or click the Save Selection button on the Masks section. Campbell created a selection for each element in the drawing.

3b

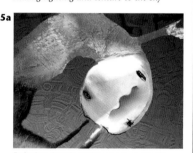

Painting brushstrokes using clone color

4

Adding lighting and texture to the sky

5a

Painting details within the face selection

5b

Adding paper grain texture to the face

5c

Applying lighting to the tumbler's back

3 Painting inside selections.
To paint within a selection, first make it active: Choose Select, Load Selection (or click the Load Selection button on the Masks section). Campbell loaded individual selections and used the Simple Water variant of Water Color to lay in color washes within each selection.

To begin painting the graduated sky, Campbell made a clone of his painting file (File, Clone), and filled the clone with the Night Sky gradient from the default Painter Gradient library (Effects, Fill, Gradient, with an angle of 90° in the Gradients section of the Art Materials palette). Then he selected the painting file and designated the filled clone as the clone source (File, Clone Source). In the painting file, he loaded the sky selection. He chose the Captured Bristle variant of Brushes and changed it into a cloning brush by switching its method to Cloning. To sample color from the graduated image—while painting in the destination file—he checked the Clone Color checkbox on the Colors section of the Art Materials palette. Using the new Captured Bristle "cloner," he painted angled and curved strokes into the sky selection.

4 Adding effects to the sky. To add a graduated golden tint within the sky selection, Campbell used Effects, Surface Control, Apply Lighting (using a custom version of the Splashy Colors light), then he used Surface Texture to build up "thick paint." To give your image realistic "thick paint" highlights and shadows based on dark and light values in the brushstrokes, choose Effects, Surface Control, Apply Surface Texture, Using Image Luminance.

5 Finalizing the image. To paint the central figure's face, Campbell used the Artist Pastel Chalk variant of Dry Media (on top of Basic Paper texture) to paint soft shading within the face selection. Then he blended areas using the Just Add Water variant of Liquid.

After painting the face, he changed its appearance dramatically by applying custom colored lighting and a paper grain effect within the active selection. To apply lighting within a selection, load a selection (Select, Load Selection) and choose Effects, Surface Control, Apply Lighting. Set up a light, and click OK. He used similar procedures to add rich textures and complexity to other elements in the image—including the foreground, table and tumbling figures on the horizon.

To apply a paper texture within a selection, load the selection, and choose Effects, Surface Control, Apply Surface Texture Using Paper. If you want, you can choose a different paper texture from the Papers palette with this dialog box still open.

Finally, to further unify the image, Campbell applied Surface Texture using Image Luminance to the entire image—this time using very low settings—moving the Amount slider to approximately 20 to 30%, and the Shine slider to about 20%.

A LASSO WITH A CLUE

As a reminder of how the existing selection will be edited, a plus sign (Shift key) or minus sign (Ctrl/⌘ key) appears next to the Lasso.

Using Color Mask

***Overview** Use Color Mask and brushes to mask an area of an image; convert the mask to a selection; use Adjust Color to shift the color of the selected area.*

CTP/PHOTO: PHOTODISC

1a

The original photo

1b

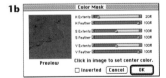

The default Color Mask dialog box

1c

Adjusting the sliders to isolate the leaf

COLOR MASK IS ONE OF PAINTER'S most powerful features, letting you create a mask based on a specific color in an image. In the example above, we used a combination of Color Mask and editing with brushes to create masks for individual leaves. We saved the masks in the Masks section, then used Adjust Color to change the hue and saturation of the individual leaves and the background.

1 Sampling color and adjusting the mask. Open an image and then open the Masks section in the Objects palette. Click the right triangle on the Masks section bar and choose Color Mask from the pull-down menu. When the dialog box appears, click in your image (*not* in the preview window) on the color you want to sample (the "center color" of the range of colors to be selected); the arrow will momentarily turn into a dropper as you do this. We selected a color on the tan leaf in the center of the image. To narrow the range of selected colors, drag the H (Hue) Extents slider to the left (we set ours to 10%). Press and drag to scroll the image in the Preview window so you can see how your settings are affecting selection in other parts of the image. Experiment with the S (Saturation) and V (Value) Extents sliders; we got the best results when we reduced the V Extents to 30% to isolate the leaf from darker tan colors in the background water. You may also want to adjust the three Feather sliders to create harder transitions in your mask. When you're satisfied with the preview of your mask, click OK. Painter will generate a mask based on the sampled color. The mask will automatically appear in the Masks section.

2 Cleaning up the mask. To view the mask as a red-tinted overlay on top of the image canvas, in the Masks section click the mask's name to select it, and open its eye icon. (Make sure the RGB-Canvas eye icon is also open.) To edit the mask, choose the Scratchboard Tool variant of Pens because it allows smooth painting with opaque "paint." Choose black and paint on the mask to add to your mask; paint with white to remove portions of the mask. The interior of your mask must be opaque to completely cover your subject, so unless you want some degree of transparency, use the brush to paint over any thin spots.

2a

Using the Scratchboard Tool and white paint to erase an area of the mask

2b

Using the Scratchboard Tool to erase the mask from an overlapping leaf. The mask is viewed at a reduced opacity, making both the mask and the image beneath it visible.

2c

The finished mask of the center leaf viewed at 100% opacity

2d

Replacing the original mask

3

Adjusting color within the center leaf selection

You'll need to view the mask at full opacity to identify areas where coverage is not complete. To adjust the opacity of the mask overlay, display the Mask Options dialog box by double-clicking the mask name in the Masks section. Move the Opacity slider to 100%. The Opacity slider has no effect on the actual density of the mask—it is for viewing only.

As a final check for your mask, turn the mask into a selection by choosing Select, Load Selection. You can use the Lasso to select any areas that you'd like to add to the selection: Press the Shift key, then use the Lasso to draw around the area you want to add. To remove an area of the selection, hold down the Ctrl/⌘ key and use the Lasso to draw around it. If you use this method, make sure you replace the original mask in the Masks section with the edited one: Choose Select, Save Selection; in the Save To menu choose the mask name and select the Replace Mask button.

3 Colorizing with Adjust Color. To make changes to the color within a selection, begin by loading a selection (Select, Load Selection). With the selection active, choose Effects, Tonal Control, Adjust Colors. Use this feature to change the hue, saturation or brightness in the selected area. If you prefer more radical changes, you can also paint within your selection or apply any of the commands under the Effects menu. To view your image without the mask, click the mask eye icon shut. 🐾

Isolating Color with Auto Mask

Overview *Use Auto Mask to generate a mask based on a selected color; load the mask as a selection; paint into the selection with various brushes.*

The black-and-white sketch

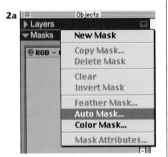

Choosing Auto Mask from the Masks section's pop-up menu

Viewing the new current color mask

WITH PAINTER'S AUTO MASK FEATURE you can isolate an area of an image with a mask. Once the mask has been created, you can use it to make a selection and fill the area with color or paint into it. When Susan LeVan of LeVan/Barbee Studio created *Man With Buildings,* she used brushes to paint within selections. She used Auto Mask's Current Color setting to create jaggy white "halos" around the background scratch marks, giving her piece texture, lightness and air. Repainting a printed, collaged and scanned version of the image produced the result above.

1 Establishing the composition. LeVan began a new document with a white paper color. She chose Basic Paper from the Papers section of the Art Materials palette, the Dry Ink variant of the Brushes and black color to sketch. Prior to drawing, she resized the brush smaller using the Size slider on the Controls:Brush palette.

2 Generating and viewing a mask. To create a mask for the black-and-white line drawing, LeVan used Auto Mask's Current Color option. To begin, first sample a color from your image with the Dropper tool, making that color your Current Color. (LeVan clicked the Dropper on a black area in her sketch.) To generate the mask, open the Objects palette (Window, Show Objects), on the Masks section bar click the left triangle to open the Masks section. Click the right triangle to access the command menu and choose Auto Mask (or press Ctrl/⌘-Shift-M), using Current Color and click OK. In your image, you'll see all instances of the current

The Mask List showing the mask name

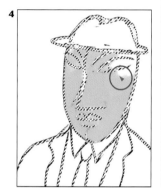
Painting within the selection with a brush

The Man 3 image   Scan of the collage

The image showing details painted on the face, tie, and eyes

color masked in orange. The mask name, by default, New Mask 1, will appear in the Masks section.

Since Auto Mask using Current Color lacks the feathering capabilities of Painter's Color Mask (see "Using Color Mask," earlier in this chapter), there will be rough, aliased areas around the unselected portions of your image. LeVan likes the white "halos" that result when she uses Auto Mask for color fills because they accentuate the texture on the background.

3 Viewing the mask as a selection. To work on a masked area, load an active selection from the mask: Target the mask name in the Masks section, click the Load Selection button and choose Replace Selection button. To view the RGB canvas and the active selection without the orange mask, click the eye icon to the left of the mask to shut the eye.

4 Painting and filling within the selection. With the selection active, LeVan changed the black line work to a textured white line by choosing Effects, Tonal Control, Negative. Then by inverting the same selection, she used it to protect the linework while she painted flat color areas on the image, as follows: Invert the selection by choosing Select, Invert. To paint within the selected area of the image canvas with a color, first choose RGB-Canvas in the Mask section to target the image canvas. Choose a color in the Color picker. Then select a brush and paint within the selected area. After painting and filling the large areas of color with the Opaque Flat and Dry Ink variants of the Brushes, LeVan inverted the selection again (to isolate the line work) and painted it green using the Square Chalk (Dry Media).

5 Printing, collaging and scanning. When LeVan had finished painting the flat color on her image, she printed the Man 3 image using a color inkjet printer, then she painted the print with acrylic paint and added other conventional media—tape and newspaper—to make a collage. When the collage was complete, she scanned it so she could rework it in Painter.

6 Adding rich color and texture. To add richness and complexity to her image, LeVan used the Auto Mask Current color again to mask areas in the face and then painted with the Square Chalk variant. To add more texture, she painted, then repeated painting with Auto Mask several times. First she painted in pale yellow, then masked the yellow; then she painted in tan, then masked the tan; and finally she painted in pink.

LeVan painted more detail using two Brushes variants: For the tie, eye and mouth she used the Opaque Flat; the magenta splotch outside the head and the ground line were done with the Smeary Flat. Then she drew over the background with the Square Chalk (Dry Media) and an orange color. Finally, she drew the buildings with a small Scratchboard Tool variant of Pens. Then to draw the even straight lines, she clicked the Straight Lines button on the Controls:Brush palette.

■ **Dewey Reid** began *City Day* (above), an image for Colossal Pictures, with traditional pencil sketches and photos shot for "scrap" by designer Cindy Reid. He scanned the final sketch and photos and assembled them using the sketch as a guide. He made selections for areas of the image such as the sky, buildings and car and saved them as masks. As he needed it, he loaded each selection and painted over the scanned imagery using the Grainy Water variant (Liquid), blurring and mixing the colors. He painted details (reflections on the buildings and grill of the car) using the Artist Pastel Chalk (Dry Media) and Digital Airbrush (Airbrushes) and blended the brushstrokes with Grainy Water. Finally, he painted the steam trailing behind the car with the Digital Airbrush and added highlights to the image using a small Eraser.

■ For *Basic Blues* (left), **Kerry Gavin** began with a pencil sketch drawn in Painter using the 2B Pencil variant (Pencils). He loosely selected areas of the image, the ashtray, the bass fiddle and the musician's shirt, with the Lasso. He also made selections for areas behind the figure. Gavin roughed color into the selected areas and the background with the Artists Pastel Chalk (Dry Media), then smudged the color with Grainy Water (Liquid) to give volume to the flat color shapes. Gavin used Effects, Surface Control, Dye Concentration to intensify color in the foreground elements and to deepen the shadows behind the bassist.

■ For *Love Connection* (above), **Kathleen Blavatt** used energetic line work, irregular, hard-edged selections and brightly colored fills to suggest an emotional interconnection between man and woman. To begin, she loosely sketched the figures in black-and-white using the Fine Point and Scratchboard variants of Pens. Then she made hard-edged selections with the Magic Wand, in aliased mode (set by turning off Anti-Alias in the Controls:Magic Wand palette). As she made a selection, Blavatt filled it with a bright color using the Paint Bucket. (To keep the painting fresh, she left small areas of white canvas showing through.) To finish, she added texture to the hair with the Scratchboard Rake variant (Pens) and pink color to the woman's lips with the Artist Pastel Chalk variant of Dry Media.

■ **James D'Avanzo** created *Deep Love* (right) using saturated, complementary colors to help communicate the powerful healing of love. To create the background, he used the Lasso, then feathered and painted into the selection to create the illusion of a horizon. He used the same technique for the hand and figure. D'Avanzo worked from background to foreground, painting into the selections with a low-opacity Digital Airbrush variant of the Airbrushes.

■ When **Susan LeVan** created these works, she used brushes to paint within selections. To build rough edges on line drawings and around shapes, and to give her work more texture, she repeatedly used Auto Mask's Current Color setting and then painted back into her image.

To begin the illustration for *Business Week* magazine (above), LeVan drew the main elements in black with the Scratchboard Tool and Smooth Ink Pen variants of Pens. She made rough-edged masks for areas of the image with Auto Mask Using Current Color. She used the Square Chalk variant of Dry Media and soft colors to paint grainy strokes within each selection. She added other details with the Digital Airbrush (Airbrushes) and Smooth Ink Pen.

■ For the *Boston Globe* magazine's Sunday Book Review (left), LeVan began by drawing in Painter with a modified Dry Ink variant (Brushes). Then she masked the line work using Auto Mask, Current Color and painted into it with the Square Chalk. For the shapes in the background, she made selections with the Rectangular Selection tool, painted into them with Digital Airbrush variant (Airbrushes), and added more brushstrokes with the Square Chalk variant. To build the richly textured background, she used the Sharp Chalk variant (Dry Media) to scribble graffiti and then repeatedly masked and drew over it with more layers of color.

■ A master illustrator skilled in the use of both traditional and electronic tools, **Mike Reed** takes an approach to digital illustration that avoids the sleek look often seen in art created on the computer. To re-create the traditional look of pastel on rough paper, in *Dancers* (above) and the illustration for *AARP (opposite),* Reed sensitively layered textured color with the Pastel and Chalk variants of Dry Media on top of Wood Shavings paper texture (loaded from Wow! Textures on the Painter 6 Wow! CD-ROM).

For *Dancers,* Reed began by making a gestural color study with the Square Chalk variant to establish the theme and general elements in the composition. So he could limit paint while working freely, he built selections, which he began by drawing shapes with the Pen tool. He drew shapes for the dancers and clothing and also added abstract, geometric shapes. He converted each shape to a selection (Shapes, Convert to Selection), feathered it (Select, Feather) and saved it as a mask in the Masks section (Select, Save Selection). Reed loaded and colored each selection, then he used the Square Chalk to paint within the selection of the red dress, for instance. Then he deselected the selection (Ctrl/⌘-D), loaded the mask for the woman's legs and used a complementary green to brush textured strokes on to the image. Using the Scratchboard Rake variant (Pens), he expressively added curved strokes of vivid blue and black to the dancers' arms and legs to enhance the feeling of movement. To finish, he added more texture to the background using the Square Chalk and blue color.

■ To begin the brochure illustration for *AARP* (above), Reed sketched the composition in saturated colors using the Square Chalk variant of Dry Media, painting free brushstrokes on top of Wood Shavings paper texture. So he could paint freely in some areas while protecting other areas of his composition, he created selections: He used the Pen tool to draw shapes on top of the colored drawing, then he converted each shape to a selection (Shapes, Convert to Selection). Because he wanted soft-edged selections, he feathered each one (Select, Feather) with a radius of 5 pixels, and

then saved it (Select, Save Selection) into the Masks section of the Objects palette so he could use the selection later as a mask. To add the texture to the background wall, he loaded a selection he'd made and used Effects, Surface Control, Dye Concentration using Paper (with a custom floral-motif paper texture) to apply the motif. Next, Reed brushed over the selected area with the Square Chalk and varying colors. To refine the tree and chair, he loaded selections and painted with the Oil Pastel and Artists Pastel Chalk variants of Dry Media on the Wood Shavings texture. To build the

abstract rectangular shapes for the walls and floor, he used the Rectangular Shape tool, then converted each shape to a selection and saved it as a mask. He loaded each wall selection and softly brushed inside it with the Square Chalk, suggesting subtle graduated light. To add to the look of light coming in the windows, he loaded each window selection and used the Square Chalk to hand-paint "gradations" with soft grainy strokes. To finish, he painted tighter highlight and shadow details on the rocking chair, tree and leaves with the Sharp Chalk variant of Dry Media.

USING
LAYERS AND
SHAPES

Emerald City. *Working in source files, we painted elements for the illustration, then we painted masks for the turtle, the fishes and the paint can with brushes. We loaded selections from the masks so we could float each illustration element and use the Layer Adjuster to drag and drop it into the final composite. After dragging the items in, we used the Layer Adjuster to position them. To create a transparent look on the bottom of the paint can, we used the Digital Airbrush variant of the Airbrushes and white paint to softly erase lower areas of the can's layer visibility mask.*

LAYERS AND SHAPES are elements that hover above Painter's image canvas, providing a great deal of flexibility in composing artwork. You can move, paint on, or apply a special effect to a layer without affecting other layers or the background canvas. So when building images you can try several possibilities by manipulating or repositioning the various elements. Then, when your layers are as you like them, you can drop them onto the canvas, blending them with the background.

The controls for compositing, naming, stacking, and grouping all five kinds of elements are found in the Layers section of the Objects palette, as described in "Organizing With the Layers Section" on page 149. Each of these elements has a Composite Method that affects how it interacts (or blends) with the background and with other layers. Painter 6 incorporates five types of hovering elements: *image* (or pixel-based) *layers, floating objects, reference layers, shapes* and *dynamic layers.*

You can preserve layers by saving your file in RIFF format. Saving in most other formats requires dropping or merging, the layers. However, if you'd like to open a Painter image in Photoshop

Recognizing items in the Layers section of the Objects palette: Image layers are designated by a stack of rectangles, a floating object by a star, a shape by a circle and triangle, a reference layer by a dotted rectangle and a dynamic layer by a plug icon. In the Layers section shown here, the document's Canvas is selected.

To create this poster comp we layered Helvetica Black Condensed type shapes, scaled to various sizes, over a colored background. To quickly view a variety of color combinations, we used Painter's interactive Shape Attributes dialog box. Select the Fill (or Stroke) color square in the dialog box. (Make sure the checkbox is checked.) When you click on a new color in the Colors section of the Art Materials palette, the color of the selected type shape will update in your image. Drag the Color Ring and watch the color of the shape change.

with layers intact, save the file in Photoshop 3 format. All layers and shapes will be converted to Photoshop layers, with their names and stacking order intact. To read more about working with Photoshop, turn to Chapter 9, "Using Painter With Photoshop."

To create an *image layer*, you can float any portion of the image canvas, including freehand selections made with the Lasso or Bézier paths drawn with the Pen tool and converted to selections, masks that are loaded as selections and so on. When you create a new layer by clicking the New button on the Layers section (or by choosing New Layer from the section's pull-down menu), it's completely transparent until you paint on it. Like the background layer, or Canvas, an image layer includes an 8-bit visibility mask that accompanies the 24-bit image. You can modify the mask to blend images with exciting transparency effects as described on page 150.

When you want to reposition portions of a layer, *floating objects* are essential. To create a floating object, make a selection and choose Select, Float, or click inside the selection on the layer with the Layer Adjuster tool. The floating object will appear below its parent layer in the Layers section. Each layer can have only one floating object at a time. Like the parent layer, a floating object includes its own 8-bit visibility mask.

You'll want to use *reference layers* if you regularly assemble large images from several separate source files. A reference layer is a 72 ppi screen proxy (or "stand-in"), for a pixel-based layer in the current image, or for a placed image that's linked to an image file outside of the document. Converting an image layer temporarily to "reference state" allows you to do rotation, skewing and other transformations much more quickly than if Painter had to manage the full-size original. (See "Using Reference Layers" on page 144.)

Shapes, including type characters set with the Text tool, are essentially a resolution-independent kind of layer. As described on page 109, shapes are outline-based elements with attributes such as stroke, fill and transparency. Shapes and their attributes are

LAYERS AND SELECTIONS

In Painter 6 there can be only one active selection at a time. You can use a selection to edit a portion of any *image layer* or *reference layer* listed in the Layers section. If you'd like to use a selection to isolate a portion of a *shape* or of a *dynamic layer,* you'll have to convert it to pixel information first. If you attempt to use a selection to edit a dynamic layer or shape by painting with a brush or applying an effect, Painter will display a Commit dialog box asking you if you'd like to commit the layer to an image layer.

In the Commit dialog box, we suggest not checking the "Commit and don't ask again" box. Otherwise, Painter can automatically convert a shape into an image layer without your realizing the conversion has happened.

To make a new layer from an active selection on Painter's image canvas (similar to choosing Layer, New, Layer Via Copy in Photoshop), make or load a selection in your image, then choose the Layer Adjuster tool, hold down the Alt/Option key and click or drag inside the selected area. To cut from the image canvas and turn the selected area into a new layer, click or drag with the Layer Adjuster without pressing the Alt/Option key. To make a new layer by copying the entire image canvas, click on Canvas in the Layers section and hold down the Alt/Option key as you choose Select, Float.

PHOTO: CORBIS IMAGES

If you don't hold down the Alt/Option key when you drag a selection with the Layer Adjuster, you'll leave a hole behind in the canvas if you then move the newly created layer. Occasionally this is desirable, but most of the time you'll want the Alt/Option!

Here's a quick way to copy a layer or shape into a composite file from a source image. Open both images. In the source image, select the layer or shape by clicking it with the Layer Adjuster tool. Now use the Layer Adjuster tool to drag the item into the composite image.

PostScript objects. But if you paint on a shape, adding pixel information, it stops being a shape and becomes an image layer.

Dynamic layers are special hovering devices that allow you to make adjustments to an existing image (such as an Equalize layer or Bevel World layer), or create entirely new effects (for instance a Liquid Metal layer), depending which kind of dynamic layer you use. You can choose dynamic layers from the Dynamic Layers section of the Objects palette (see page 147).

All of these hovering elements take up extra disk space and RAM (see Chapter 1). You can work around this, though. Float only what's necessary, and drop and combine layers when possible.

WORKING WITH IMAGE LAYERS

You can make an image layer by activating the Canvas layer and clicking on an active selection using the Layer Adjuster tool. This process cuts the selected area out of the canvas and floats it. Alt/Option-click to *copy* an active selection or to duplicate an entire layer. This leaves the original pixels in place as well as creating a copy. All elements pasted into a Painter document come in as image layers, and you can also drag a layer from the Image Portfolio section of the Objects palette into your image.

Here's how to work with image layers once you've created or imported one:

To select a layer, click its name in the Layers section of the Objects palette, or turn on Auto Select Layer in the Controls:Adjuster palette and click on a visible area of the layer with the Layer Adjuster tool.

To deselect a layer, click on another layer, or the blank area below the layers' names in the Layers section, or turn on Auto Select in the Controls:Adjuster palette and use the Layer Adjuster tool to click elsewhere in the image.

To apply an effect to an layer, make sure it's selected by clicking on it with the Layer Adjuster tool or by selecting its name in the Layers section. (If no layers are selected, your brushstrokes or effects will be applied to the Canvas.) Then choose a brush and paint strokes onto the layer.

To paint on a layer, make sure it's selected by highlighting its name in the Layers section. Choose any brush (except a Water Color variant) and paint brushstrokes onto the layer. (Water Color can paint only on the Canvas.) For more about painting on layers, turn to "Painting on Layers" on page 53, in Chapter 3.

To erase paint you have applied to a layer, making the area "clear" again, choose the Eraser variant of the Erasers (in the Brushes palette) with 100% Opacity set in the Controls:Brush palette, and paint on the layer to "erase." However, this method can yield unpredictable results on layers—at times it may not erase completely, but may leave a white or solid-colored patch on the

These type shapes were set in Painter using the Text tool. We specified color fills using Shapes, Set Shape Attributes, and used Saturation and Multiply Composite Methods (in Composite Methods pull-down menu in the Layers section) to blend colors where the shapes overlap.

DROP SELECTED LAYERS QUICKLY

You can merge more than one layer at once by Shift-selecting their names in the Layers section before clicking the Drop button or pressing Ctrl/⌘-Shift-D.

PHOTO: CORBIS IMAGES

To create a soft edge on this image layer, we feathered the layer's visibility mask.

LAYER OR FLOATING OBJECT?

New *image layers* can be made by selecting an area of the *Canvas* and cutting or copying. But if you select and cut or copy *on a layer other than the Canvas,* you produce a *floating object* associated with the layer you used to make it.

layer where the Eraser was used. If you get this result, choose Edit, Undo, and try "erasing" on the layer mask as described in "To erase a portion of the layer mask," below.

To erase a portion of the layer mask, making that area of the layer "clear" again, begin by choosing white in the Colors section of the Art Materials palette. Click on the layer in the Layers section of the Objects palette, then click on its mask in the Masks section. Click the eye icon open to view the mask in black-and-white, or click the eye icon closed to view the layer. Choose a brush (such as the Pens, Scratchboard Tool) with 100% Opacity set in the Controls:Brush palette, and paint on the mask with white to "erase."

To move a layer, choose the Layer Adjuster tool, turn on Auto Select Layer in the Controls:Adjuster palette, then click on it and drag. To adjust a layer's position a screen pixel at a time, click it with the Layer Adjuster and use the arrow keys on your keyboard.

To merge a layer with the canvas, select it in the Layers section and click the section's Drop button or press Ctrl/⌘-Shift-D. If you want to merge all of your layers—much like Photoshop's Flatten Image command—simply choose Drop All from the Layers section's menu. Another option is to choose File, Clone; a duplicate of the image will appear with all layers merged.

To scale, rotate, distort or flip a layer, click it with the Layer Adjuster and choose the appropriate command under Effects, Orientation.

To change the opacity of a layer, click its name in the Layers section and use the Layers section's Opacity slider.

To feather the edge of a layer, select the layer in the Layers section, then switch to the Masks section and target that layer's visibility mask. Now click the right triangle on the Masks section bar and choose Feather Mask.

WORKING WITH FLOATING OBJECTS

If you'd like to reposition a portion of a layer or edit an area on a layer, a *floating object* will be essential. A floating object is an area of a layer that has been isolated and lifted from the layer, to create a kind of sub-layer. A layer may have only one floating object at a time. Like the parent layer, a floating object includes its own 8-bit visibility mask.

To create a floating object, make a selection, click on a layer's name in the Layers section of the Objects palette and choose Select, Float, or click inside the selection with the Layer Adjuster tool. The floating object will be listed below its parent layer in the Layers section, indented to show the relationship. (If you turn off visibility for the floating object by clicking its eye icon, you'll see that it has been cut from the parent layer.)

PHOTO: CORBIS IMAGES

A selected reference layer, ready to have Free Transform applied, has a yellow-and-white striped bounding box with eight handles.

To make a floating object copy of information on the parent layer (without cutting out), make a selection, press the Alt/Option key, then choose Select, Float, or click with the Layer Adjuster tool. The floating object "copy" will be listed below its parent layer in the Layers section.

To recombine a floating object with its parent layer, click the Drop button in the Layers section. The floating object will also recombine with its parent layer if you do any of the following while the layer or its floating object is active (selected in the Layers section): make another selection, paint, edit the visibility mask, paste into the document or drag an item from the Image Portfolio.

USING REFERENCE LAYERS

If you work with large files and your computer slows to a crawl when you try to reposition a big image layer, consider converting it to a *reference layer*. Reference layers let you manipulate faster—moving 72 ppi proxy images in real time, instead of dragging huge 300 ppi images around your screen. Because you are working with a proxy—and not the original—you can perform multiple rotations, scaling, and skewing very quickly and without loss of quality. When you've finished all of manipulations, convert reference layers back to image layers.

To make a reference layer, select an image layer and choose Effects, Orientation, Free Transform. To get ready to operate on the layer, choose the Layer Adjuster.

To scale a reference layer proportionately, press the Shift key and drag on a corner handle with the Layer Adjuster tool to resize as many times as needed to get just the result you want.

To rotate a reference layer interactively, press the Ctrl/⌘ key and drag a corner handle with the Layer Adjuster.

To skew a reference layer interactively, press the Ctrl/⌘ key and drag one of the original four middle handles with the Layer Adjuster tool.

To scale, skew or rotate a reference layer numerically, choose Effects, Orientation, Set Transform, and type specifications into the fields.

To turn a reference layer back into an image-based layer, choose Effects, Orientation, Commit Transform, or paint or apply an effect to the reference layer, or drag it into the Image Portfolio.

Using the pyramid data structure. Painter's pyramid data structure is a way of getting the best possible speed and on-screen image quality from reference-layer technology. When you ask Painter to build a pyramid file by choosing File, Place and checking the Create Pyramid File box, Painter imports a reference layer that actually includes several sizes of the image. (If you're familiar with Kodak's Photo CD file format, you can think of a pyramid

If you're compositing large files, you may want to work with each component file separately, then make a reference layer by importing the image (with its mask, if you like) into your composite file using File, Place. When the positioning and transformations are complete, convert the reference layer to an image layer by choosing Effects, Orientation, Commit Transform.

file as a similar, but more flexible structure.) Painter uses the multiple versions stored in the pyramid file to calculate a new on-screen image when you scale an image (Canvas, Resize).

Another way to build a pyramid data structure is to save an existing file in Pyramid file format (File, Save As). We made a comparison, importing a large 300 ppi file as a reference layer into a composite image and also importing the same image that had been saved in Pyramid format. Because the pyramid file was saved with multiple resolutions already calculated, when we chose File, Place, it loaded faster. Also, as with reference layers, any rotations and scaling that were applied to the pyramid file were achieved with better quality.

WORKING WITH SHAPES

Shapes can be drawn using any of the Shape Design tools, or made from a selection (converted from a selection using the Select, Convert To Shape command), or imported from a PostScript drawing program such as Adobe Illustrator (this process is described in Chapter 4).

Before modifying a shape, you need to select it. There are three ways to select shapes: The first (using the Layer Adjuster) selects the entire shape and displays a bounding box with a black-and-yellow striped border with eight handles around its edges, as well as showing the shape's anchor points; this selection method allows you to duplicate, move or transform the shape. The second method (using the Direct Selection tool, which is the arrowhead that shares a palette space with the Layer Adjuster) displays the Bézier path with its anchor points and handles and permits manipulation of the path. The third method uses the Whole Shape Selection tool (solid arrow), made available by using the Direct Selection tool (hollow arrow) with the Ctrl/⌘ key held down. It selects the entire shape, displaying anchor points without a bounding box, and it allows you to move it as a unit without distorting it.

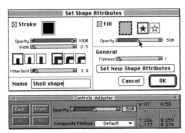

The opacity of a shape's fill can be set in the Set Shape Attributes dialog box (top), or in the corresponding Controls:Adjuster palette (bottom), which is visible when the Layer Adjuster tool is selected.

Painter offers useful tools for designers working with type. Resolution-independent shapes allow you to transform letterforms (rotate, skew or scale) without loss of quality. Kerning type is a snap—just select an individual letter in the Layers section and move it using the arrow keys on your keyboard. You can also use the Direct Selection tool to modify the Bézier outline of a letter by adjusting its anchor points and control handles. Turn to Chapter 8 "Working With Type in Painter," to see examples of type created with Painter.

To drag off a copy of a shape, select the shape with the Layer Adjuster tool, press Alt/Option and drag.

If you liked using the Whole Shape Selection tool (solid arrow) in Painter 4 to select an entire unfilled shape path, don't despair—it's available in Painter 6. Choose the Direct Selection tool (hollow arrow) and press the Ctrl/⌘ key to use it in Whole Shape Selection mode. You can now click on a shape path to select all of its anchor points at once, making it possible to move the path to a new location, undistorted, by dragging any anchor point.

You can Shift-select multiple shapes in the Layers section and convert them to *individual layers* all at once—as long as they are stroked and filled—using Shapes, Convert To Layer. To make a *single layer* from several shapes, first Shift-select the shapes and press the Group button on the Layers section. Then with the group closed (controlled by the arrow to the left of its name in the Layers section), choose Shapes, Convert To Layer.

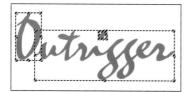

For this restaurant logo, we drew black calligraphy letters on the canvas using the Calligraphy variant of the Pens. We made a luminosity mask by choosing Auto Mask (Using Image Luminance), from the Masks section's pull-down menu, loaded the selection (Select, Load Selection, New Mask 1), then converted the selection to shapes (Select, Convert To Shape). The client planned to use the logo in a variety of ways, so it made sense to build the logo with compound shapes that could be layered easily over other images (or converted easily to selections). To make counters transparent in the letter "O," the two descending "g" shapes and the "e," we selected each individual counter and compounded it with its outer shape (Shapes, Make Compound). For best results, compound only one counter at a time. Seen here are the selected compounded filled shapes (top), and the logo applied onto Koa wood texture, from an Art Beats Wood and Paper CD-ROM (bottom). To read more about compound shapes turn to "Making a Compound," on the next page or to "Shapes," in Chapter 13 of The Painter 6 User Guide.

To duplicate, move or transform a group of shapes, select the group by clicking its name in the Layers section with the Layer Adjuster tool. (See "Organizing With the Layers Section" on page 149, to read more about groups.)

To move an individual shape within a group, choose the Direct Selection tool and press the Ctrl/⌘ key to switch to the Whole Shape Selection tool. Now click on the shape with the Whole Shape Selection tool and drag the shape; or move it using the arrow keys.

To move a shape within an open group, you can also click and drag it with the Layer Adjuster tool.

To scale a shape proportionately, click it with the Layer Adjuster, hold down the Shift key and drag a corner handle.

To rotate a shape, click it with the Layer Adjuster, press the Ctrl/⌘ key and drag a corner handle.

To skew a shape interactively, click it with the Layer Adjuster, press the Ctrl/⌘ key and drag a middle handle.

To scale, distort, rotate or flip a shape, select it in the Layers section of the Objects palette and use one of the choices found under Effects, Orientation.

To duplicate a shape and transform the copy, choose Shapes, Set Duplicate Transform. Set up specifications in the Set Duplicate Transform dialog box and click OK. Now when you choose Shapes, Duplicate, the transformation will be applied to the copy.

To modify the stroke and fill attributes of a shape, select it and choose Shapes, Set Shape Attributes, or double-click on the name of a shape in the Layers section (or highlight its name and press Enter) to open the Set Shape Attributes dialog box.

To change the fill or stroke of a shape to the current color, chosen while using the Shape Attributes dialog box, click once in the Stroke or Fill color field and choose a new color in the Color palette. (This method selects the current color without displaying the color wheel.) **A word of warning:** If you paint on, or apply an effect to, a shape—rather than simply changing its stroke and fill—it will be automatically converted into an image layer. When this happens, shape attributes (such as resolution independence, stroke and fill) are lost.

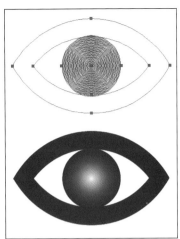

Viewing shape paths (top) and finished objects (bottom). For this filled compound outer object with blended interior object, we began by making a blend. To blend the interior blue circle with a very small white circle in its center, we selected both circles in the Layers section, then chose Shapes, Blend and specified 50 steps. To build the compound of the two outer shapes, we selected them both with the Shape Selection tool and chose Shapes, Make Compound. (Choose the Direct Selection tool and press the Ctrl/⌘ key to switch to Whole Shape Selection mode.) The compound cut a hole with the smaller eye shape, allowing only the outer fill to be visible.

SHAPES OF A CURRENT COLOR

To automatically fill or stroke a shape with the Current Color chosen in the Colors section as you draw it, set up your Shape preferences: Choose Edit, Preferences, Shapes, check the appropriate checkboxes and click OK.

Setting up the Shape Preferences to automatically fill with the Current Color

Blending between shapes.
To blend between two shapes, select both shapes in the Layers section and choose Shapes, Blend. Make choices in the dialog box and click OK. The *Painter 6 User Guide* contains a complete explanation of the Blend dialog box.

Here's a useful application for Painter's Blend command: If you've imported an image created in Illustrator that has blends and they don't make the transition successfully into Painter, zoom in and delete the interior objects inside the blend using the Direct Selection tool and Delete key. Shift-select the two outside objects with in the Layers section, choose Shapes, Blend and specify the number of steps to regenerate the blend.

Making a compound. To cut a hole in a shape and reveal the underlying image, make a compound using two shapes: Place a small shape on top of a large one, select both of them in the Layers section, and choose Shapes, Make Compound. The top shape will cut a hole in the bottom shape to reveal the underlying image. Compounds are made automatically to create counters in letters when the type is set or type outlines are imported.

USING DYNAMIC LAYERS

Dynamic layers are special devices that allow you to create a variety of effects. To keep dynamic layer "live" (allowing changes to be made and previewed on the image without becoming permanent), the file must be saved in RIFF format. Saving in Photoshop format preserves the dynamic layers as image layers, freezing the effects in their current state.

Dynamic layers, which are indicated by a plug icon in the Layers section, fall into three basic categories. The first kind is similar to an adjustment layer in Adobe Photoshop. It allows you to set up a procedure such as a brightness and contrast correction or a posterization of the underlying image, without changing your image surface. Image correction tools such as Equalize, Brightness and Contrast, and Posterize and special effects layers such as Glass Distortion, Kaleidoscope and Liquid Lens fall into this category.

AUTOMATIC DROP SHADOWS

To apply a drop shadow to a single shape, select the shape in the Layers section and choose Effects, Objects, Create Drop Shadow. Enter your own specifications, or just click OK to accept Painter's defaults. When the Commit dialog box appears, asking if you'd like to commit the shape to an image layer, click Commit. Selecting a closed group of shapes and choosing Effects, Objects, Create Drop Shadow will apply an automatic drop shadow to each of the individual shapes in the group and will convert the shapes to image layers as well! To convert a group of shapes to single image layer and make an automatic drop shadow for the new layer, begin by closing the group (click the eye icon to the left of it closed), then select the group's name in the Layers section and click the Collapse button. Then choose, Effects, Objects, Create Drop Shadow, and apply the shadow, as above.

Detail from Hot Beveled Metal. *Beginning with type shapes, we used the Bevel World dynamic layer to create a 3D type effect. Then we layered two more copies of the bevel—we painted on the first copy and we created the glow using the second copy. To learn more about type effects using Bevel World, turn to Chapter 8.*

PHOTO: CORBIS IMAGES

Cool Water Drops. *To add a water droplet effect to this photo (simulating water drops on a camera lens), we used the Liquid Metal dynamic layer. First we made a clone of the image (File, Clone). In the Dynamic Layers section of the Objects palette we chose Liquid Metal and clicked Apply, using the Clone Source Map type and a high Refraction setting to make the "water" translucent with a blue reflection. We clicked and dragged with the Circle tool from the Liquid Metal dialog box to place the drops. A drop can be extended simply by clicking with the Circle tool inside the edge of the existing drop.*

To generate a layer of this type (such as a Posterize layer), open the Dynamic Layers section of the Objects palette, choose Posterize from the pop-up menu and click the Apply button. The posterization will apply to all image layers, reference layers, shapes and dynamic layers listed below the Posterize dynamic layer in the Layers section. (To read more about Painter 6's image-correction layers, turn to Chapter 6. For more information about creating special effects with this series of dynamic layers, refer to Chapter 7.)

For the second kind of dynamic layer, you apply a special effect procedure to a selected image layer, the "source image layer," turning it into a dynamic layer. Because of the dynamic layer's "live" capability, you can preview changes and then return the source image layer to its original condition if you like. Bevel World, Burn and Tear dynamic layers require a source image layer to perform their magic. To make this kind of dynamic layer, select an area of your image with *any* selection tool, or select a layer in the Layers section of the Objects palette, and choose Bevel World, for instance, from the pop-up menu in the Dynamic Layers section, then click Apply. (If you make a selection on the image Canvas, clicking Apply will automatically generate a new dynamic layer from the selection.) Read more about these dynamic layers in Chapter 7.

The third type of dynamic layer allows you to build entirely new special-effects imagery. Liquid Metal falls into this category. To read about exciting techniques using Liquid Metal, turn to Chapter 7, "Exploring Special Effects," and to "Painting With Ice" in Chapter 8.

To change a dynamic layer's options, begin by opening the Dynamic Layers section of the Objects palette, and select the dynamic layer by clicking on its name in the Layers section. From the pull-down menu on the Dynamic Layers section bar choose Options to open the Options dialog box for the selected layer. Make changes in the dialog box and click OK.

To convert a dynamic layer to an image layer, so you can edit the layer's mask or convert the image layer into a reference layer (to scale it using Free Transform, for instance), from the Dynamic Layers section's

For the ultimate in management using the Layers section, see how Rick Kirkman did it in "Working With Shapes and Layers," on page 153.

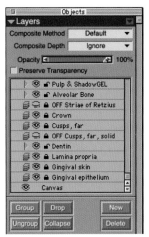

In the Layers section for David Purnell's Molar Cross Section (above), he organized some layers in groups and he locked other items so he wouldn't accidently select them with the layer Adjuster. Turn to page 173 to read about his illustration.

Create an empty Image Portfolio by opening the Image Portfolio section in the Objects palette and choosing Image Mover from the pull-down menu, opened by clicking the triangle on the right side of the Image Portfolio section bar.

IMAGES IN PORTFOLIO: PHOTODISC

pull-down menu, choose Commit. The following actions will also convert a dynamic layer to an image layer: transforming using Effects, Orientation (to scale, rotate or skew); applying an effect from the Effects menu (such as Effects, Surface Control, Apply Surface Texture); painting on the layer; applying a dynamic layer special effect (such as applying the Tear special-effect layer to an active Burn layer); or merging a group that includes a dynamic layer.

ORGANIZING WITH THE LAYERS SECTION

In the Layers section, Painter assigns sequential names to layers and shapes (such as Layer 1, Layer 2 and so on) in the order they were created. Rename them by double-clicking on a name (or select the name and press the Enter key) to bring up the appropriate Attributes dialog box. Enter the name and click OK. Grouping layers or shapes is an ideal way of connecting related elements—for instance, grouping a layer and its drop shadow. To group layers or shapes, Shift-select the elements in the Layers section and click the Group button or press Ctrl/⌘-G. To ungroup, click the Ungroup button or press Ctrl/⌘-U. If you want to apply effects (other than Scale and Create Drop Shadow) to a group of layers or shapes, you'll need to open the group, select individual items, then apply the effect.

You can hide layers or shapes by clicking to close the eye icons next to their names, so that you can more easily work with underlying items. Click the eye open to show an item again.

To lock an item or group (keeping it from being selected in the image window), click the lock icon to the left of its item name in the Layers section. To unlock, click to toggle the lock icon open.

Using the Image Portfolio. Open the Image Portfolio section of the Objects palette by clicking the left arrow on the Image Portfolio section bar. To remove layers from your image, but store them for later use or for use in another document, use the Layer Adjuster tool to drag them from the image into the Image Portfolio section. Hold down the Alt/Option key if you want to leave a copy of the layer in your document.

PRESERVE TRANSPARENCY

By turning on the Preserve Transparency checkbox in the Layers section, you can confine your painting and editing to those areas of an image layer that already contain pixels. Turn Preserve Transparency off if you'd like to paint with brushes or edit outside the existing pixels—for instance, to feather the edge by applying the Effects, Focus, Soften command, which would spread pixels outside of the original area.

MOVING LOCKED ITEMS

To lock a layer, preventing it from being accidently selected and dragged with the Layer Adjuster, click to close the Lock icon to the left of the layer's name. You can still select and move a locked item or group—just click on its name in the Layers section, then move it using the arrow keys on your keyboard.

You can use controls in the Layer Attributes box to determine which part of a layer is masked. To see how these controls work, open the Image Portfolio and drag one of the portfolio items onto a colored background. In the Layers section, double-click on the name of the new layer you just dragged in to open its Layer Attributes box. Since the items in the Image Portfolio are layers with masks already created for them, in the Layer Attributes dialog box the Normal button should be cho-

sen, meaning that everything in the layer outside of the mask is invisible. To reverse the effect, click the Inverted button, click OK and view the result. Clicking on the Disabled button in the Layer Attributes box will show both areas, inside and outside the mask, as if no mask existed. Keep in mind that these

Layer Visibility Mask: ○ Disabled
● Normal
○ Inverted

Layer Visibility Mask: ○ Disabled
○ Normal
● Inverted

Layer Visibility Mask: ● Disabled
○ Normal
○ Inverted

PHOTOS: IMAGE FARM

modes affect visibility only; any painting or effect applied to the layer will be applied to the entire layer, not just the visible areas. (To confine paint or effects, you can load the mask as a selection by choosing Select, Load Selection.)

LAYERS AND THEIR MASKS

Just as the background canvas uses 8-bit background masks (see Chapter 4's introduction), each image layer also has an 8-bit mask—the visibility mask—that allows for transparent effects. You can also edit layer masks using either brushes or special effect commands (such as Effects, Surface Control, Express Texture, with which you can apply a texture to a mask). View a mask on a selected layer by selecting it in the Masks section and opening its eye icon. For more information see the "Layer Mask Visibility" tip on this page.

Importing a source file with its mask. Because it's faster to work with small files than to manipulate large files, many artists assemble source files, then import them into a final composite file. Consider preparing a mask in a smaller

source file that you plan to import into a composite (using File, Place). In the Place dialog box, check the Retain Mask checkbox, and click OK to place the source as a reference layer in your document. To turn the reference layer into an image layer, select it in the Layers section and choose Effects, Orientation, Commit Transform. (For more information, see "Using Reference Layers" on page 144.)

In Painter 6 you can use the Eraser variant of the Erasers to remove information on an image layer. **Caution:** Using the Eraser permanently removes the information from the layer. Editing the layer's visibility mask using white paint is much more flexible, because you can restore the image on the layer by painting the visibility mask back in. Use *white* on the mask to *erase* the *layer*, use *black* on the mask to *restore* the *layer*.

If you've made a mask for a layer and want to use it on another layer or on the background canvas to constrain paint or effects there, here's a way to trade masks back and forth. To copy a mask and turn the copy into a layer visibility mask, begin by selecting the layer in the Layers section. Switch to the Masks section and select the mask you want. From the Masks section pull-down menu choose Copy Mask. In the Copy Mask dialog box menu, select the layer visibility mask as the destination and click OK. This action replaces the original layer visibility mask you selected with the mask. To copy a layer visibility mask to a mask in the Masks section, select the layer, switch to the Masks section and select the layer visibility mask. Choose Copy Mask from the Masks section pull-down menu. This time choose "New" to create a new mask for the image canvas based on the layer mask, or select an existing mask you want to replace from the menu as the destination and click OK.

If you want to merge the visible part of an image layer so it becomes part of the image canvas, choose "Drop and Select" from the Layers section pull-down menu. The selection made from the layer's visibility mask will be temporary, and will be lost unless you save it as a mask. To save the selection as a user mask in the Masks section, choose Select, Save Selection.

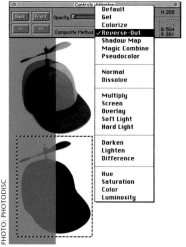

We applied two of Painter's Composite Methods to these beanies floating over a blue and white background. The top beanie uses Gel and the bottom one uses Reverse-Out.

COMPOSITE CONTROLS

Painter's composite controls can give you nifty special effects with very little effort. With a layer selected in the Layers section, choose from the Composite Method pull-down menu on the Layers section (or in the Controls:Adjuster palette when the Layer Adjuster is chosen). The scrolling list includes many of Photoshop's blending modes (exceptions are Color Dodge, Color Burn and Exclusion) listed below Painter's native ones. "A Visual Display of the Compositing Methods" below shows the Composite Methods in action.

LAYER COMPOSITE DEPTH

Painter 6's new Composite Depth controls work only on impasto paint (see "Painting With Realistic Impasto" on page 50 and "Working With Thick Paint" on page 88 for more information about Impasto). You'll find the Composite Depth pull-down menu on the Layers section of the Objects palette. The default Composite Depth method is *Add*. If you paint with an Impasto brush on a layer, *Add* raises the thick paint. *Ignore* turns off the thickness for the paint on the layer, *Subtract* inverts the paint thickness on the layer, making brushstrokes on this layer gouged or excavated, rather than raised on the surface. *Replace* changes the paint depth of Impasto on the underlying layer to the applied layer's depth where the layers overlap.

A VISUAL DISPLAY OF THE COMPOSITE METHODS

Painter's Composite Methods (from the Layers section of the Objects palette) change how a layer interacts with the image underneath. Here a leaf floats over a two-part background.

The Default and Normal methods give the same results, as do Shadow Map and Multiply. For complete descriptions of what the modes are doing, refer to Painter's *User Guide, The Photoshop 5/5.5 Wow! Book* or Photoshop's *User Guide.*

Default / Normal

Gel

Colorize

Reverse-out

Shadow Map / Multiply

Magic Combine

Pseudocolor

Dissolve

Screen

Overlay

Soft Light

Hard Light

Darken

Lighten

Difference

Hue

Saturation

Color

Luminosity

Dropping a Shadow

Overview *Convert a shape to a layer and fill the layer; make the shadow by copying the layer, moving the copy below the original, filling the copy, feathering it and reducing its opacity.*

CHER THREINEN-PENDARVIS

Background modified with Apply Surface Texture and Apply Lighting

Converting the pasted shapes into a layer

Filling the fish layer with a color

Filling the shadow layer

Selecting the layer shadow mask in the Masks section prior to feathering the mask

THERE ARE A NUMBER OF WAYS to create a drop shadow in Painter. Here's one that uses layers, feathering and transparency.

1 Preparing a background. Create a new document: Ours was 788 pixels wide with a tan Paper Color. To add a "cave wall" appearance, in the Papers section of the Art Materials palette choose Pavement texture. Select Effects, Surface Control, Apply Surface Texture Using Paper, and experiment with the settings until you get a look that you like in the Preview. Click OK. To create a spotlight effect, choose Effects, Surface Control, Apply Lighting. Choose Slide Lighting, lower the Distance and Spread settings, increase the Brightness and click OK.

2 Importing and converting. You can make a layer from any active selection or convert any shape to a layer. For this image, we imported fish drawn in Adobe Illustrator. With both Illustrator 8 and Painter 6 running, we copied the fish from Illustrator to the clipboard and pasted them into the cave wall image in Painter. Objects that have holes cut in them in Illustrator, such as the fish, or letters such as "O" or "A" converted to outlines, will import into Painter as compound shapes. Select the shape with the Layer Adjuster and choose Shapes, Convert To Layer.

3 Filling the layer. To apply a fill to the layer, choose a color from the Colors section of the Art Materials palette, turn Preserve Transparency on in the Layers section of the Objects palette, then select Effects, Fill, Current Color (100% Opacity) and click OK.

4 Creating the shadow. Use the Layer Adjuster to duplicate the layer to use for the shadow: Hold down the Alt/Option key and drag on the graphic in the direction you want the shadow. In the Layers section, double-click on the copy's name and rename it "shadow;" then drag its name below the original layer's name. Fill the shadow as you did in step 3, using black or a dark color sampled from the background image. To soften the shadow's edge by feathering it (with the layer still selected), switch to the Masks section (Objects palette) and select the mask for the shadow layer. From the pull-down menu on the Masks section choose Feather Mask and set the radius for the feather. To make the shadow more transparent, in the Layers section, target the layer and lower the Opacity.

Working with Shapes and Layers

Overview *Draw Bézier shapes in Painter; fill and name the shapes; convert the shapes to layers; paint details on the layers with brushes; edit a layer mask to achieve transparency; apply textured special effects with Color Overlay, Surface Texture and Glass Distortion.*

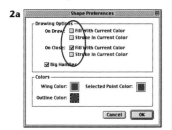

Kirkman's scanned pencil sketch

The Shape Preference dialog box

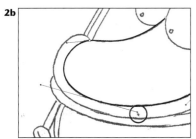

Dragging with the Direct Selection tool to adjust a control handle on a path

RICK KIRKMAN

SHAPES BRING POWER AND VERSATILITY to Painter, saving many illustrators a trip to a draw program to create Bézier paths for import. With Painter's Pen tool (now similar to Illustrator's) you can completely create and edit Bézier paths, add a stroke and fill, name them, and organize them in the Layers section. After you draw shapes, you can convert them to layers and add paint and special effects. Rick Kirkman created the illustration above—one in a series of editorial illustrations for *Professional Speaker* magazine—entirely within Painter.

1 Setting up a template. Kirkman began by scanning a pencil sketch, saving it as a TIFF file and opening the scan in Painter. The file measured 2374 x 3184 pixels.

2 Creating shapes. To create your outlines, you can work either in Painter or in a PostScript drawing program. If you plan to trace a template—as Kirkman did—set up shape attributes so that you can draw with a precise skeletal line. Choose Edit, Preferences, Shapes and choose these settings: Under "On Draw," uncheck the Fill and Stroke checkboxes; under "On Close," uncheck the Stroke checkbox and check the Fill checkbox. Using the Pen tool to draw Bézier shape paths, Kirkman carefully traced his sketch. To make adjustments on the fly while drawing a path with the Pen tool

3a

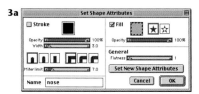

Preparing to fill the selected "nose" shape with a flesh color

3b

The selected nose shape showing the flat color fill applied

4

Painting the shadow on the fish's body using the Digital Airbrush variant

5

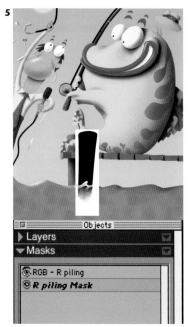

Clicking the "R piling" Mask eye open in the Masks section reveals a black-and-white representation of the mask.

(like adjusting a control handle or anchor point), press the Ctrl/⌘ key to temporarily switch to the Direct Selection tool.

3 Coloring, naming and converting.

Before he started drawing each shape, Kirkman selected a color in the Colors section of the Art Materials palette close to the color he would finally use, so the shape would fill with the color when he completed the path. By double-clicking the name of each shape in the Layers section of the Objects palette, he named each shape as soon as he had created it. As he worked, he adjusted the opacity of the shapes (using the Opacity slider in the Set Shape Attributes dialog box), so he could see the layers below more clearly. After he had filled the shapes with color, Kirkman Shift-selected them in the Layers section and chose Shapes, Convert To Layer.

4 Shading individual layers. To paint on an individual layer, target it in the Layers section. To create a nice grainy look (similar to colored pencil on kid-finish illustration board), Kirkman chose Basic Paper texture in the Papers section of the Art Materials palette and added shading to the clothing using the Fine Spray variant of the Airbrushes. For a smoother look on the man's skin and eyes, he added strokes with the Digital Airbrush variant. Overlapping elements on the layers helped Kirkman create the cast shadows. For example, to paint the shadow under the fish's lips, he deselected them and selected the underlying body layer and then airbrushed the shadow directly on it.

5 Editing layer masks. Kirkman edited the visibility mask on the layer he called "R piling" to achieve a transparent look. To achieve transparency—like Kirkman's—on your layer: Target the layer in the Layers section by clicking on its name and click the left triangle on the Masks section bar to open the section. (When a layer is selected in the Layers section, the Masks section lists the layer and its visibility mask.) Now click on the layer mask's name to select the mask. Click the Eye icon open if you'd like to view a black-and-white representation of the mask, but this is not necessary to edit the mask. Next choose white in the Colors section, choose a soft Airbrush variant (such as the Digital Airbrush) and carefully paint into the mask to make the layer partially transparent. (See "Melting Text Into Water" on page 159 for a more detailed description of this technique.)

(See "Melting Text Into Water" on page 159 for a more detailed description of this technique.)

NAMING AND FILLING SHAPES

To name and add a colored fill (or stroke) to a shape, double-click on the shape's name in the Layers section. Rename the shape in the Set Shape Attributes dialog box and check the Fill (or Stroke) checkbox. With the Fill (or Stroke) color swatch active (outlined by a black and gold box), click in the Colors section of the Art Materials palette, or click a color in your Color Set to update the color in the Fill field.

PRESERVING TRANSPARENCY

To constrain your painting to within the edge of the element on a layer, turn on Preserve Transparency in the Layers section.

6a

Kirkman targeted the "Fish body" layer in the Layers section before adding Apply Surface Texture to the fish's body.

6b

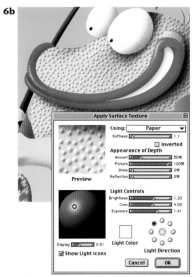

Using Apply Surface Texture to add the 3D texture to the fish

6c

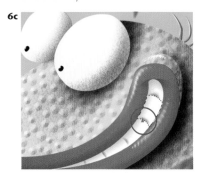

Adding dimension to the fish's teeth by airbrushing along a selection edge

6 Adding details and texture. Kirkman added the pattern to the tie using Effects, Surface Control, Color Overlay to apply the Op texture (from Crazy Textures, in Paper Texture Libraries on the Painter 6 CD-ROM). To add details to the water, he used Color Overlay to apply a colored texture using Globes from More Wild Textures (Painter 6 CD-ROM), scaling it larger using the Scale slider on the Papers section. To add more interest to the water, he added Effects, Focus, Glass Distortion using the Blobular texture from Molecular Textures (Painter 6 CD-ROM).

Using Effects, Surface Control, Apply Surface Texture, Using Paper, he added a 3D texture to the fish with Random Bubbles (Molecular Textures). He used these approximate settings: Softness, 1.1; Amount, 50%; Shine, 0; leaving other settings at their default values.

The final embellishments he added were the man's mouth, the fish's teeth and the separation of the man's pant legs. To paint these details, Kirkman drew on his many years of experience as a traditional airbrush artist using a technique very similar to traditional airbrush friskets. Using the Pen tool, he drew a shape for each element and converted each shape to a selection by choosing Shapes, Convert To Selection. To save each selection as a mask in the Masks section after he had converted it, he chose Select, Save Selection. When he wanted to use a selection as a frisket, he chose Select, Load Selection and then chose the appropriate mask from the Load From pop-up menu. When loaded, each active selection acted like a traditional airbrush frisket. For instance, to paint the fish's teeth, he selected the layer containing the teeth, loaded a selection and then airbrushed along the edges of the selection, letting the selection create the hard edge where he needed it. He let the spray from the Airbrush fade out across the selected area. This technique added more dimension and created a rounded, cushiony effect.

Adding an irregular edge. Finally, Kirkman created an irregular edge for the background. He used the Lasso to make a loose, freehand selection on the background canvas and turned it into a layer. (Drag with the Lasso and click with the Layer Adjuster). After the area was on its own layer, he reselected the canvas (click on the Canvas name in the Layers section) and deleted the unneeded background (Ctrl/⌘-A-Delete). Then he clicked on the layer and dragged it to the bottom of the layer hierarchy, to serve as a background element and renamed it Sky. To give the sky layer a smooth edge, he feathered the layer's mask 3 pixels by selecting it in the Masks section and choosing Feather Mask from the Masks section's pull-down menu (accessed by clicking the right triangle Masks section bar). After he had feathered the edge, he added a drop shadow based on the Sky layer by choosing Effects, Objects, Create Drop Shadow. To flatten the image, he dropped all layers (choose Drop All from the Layers sections's pull-down menu). The final result can be seen in the image at the top of page 153. 🖌

Illustrating With Layers

Overview *Begin with a blank image; or open a reference photo, clone it and make tracing paper; make new layers; paint on the layers, controlling the paint with masking if desired; and apply special effects.*

The optional reference photo with canvas added

The selected new layer in the Layers section of the Objects palette with Preserve Transparency turned off

Using Tracing Paper while sketching

PAINTER 6'S IMPROVED LAYERS bring more versatility to the program, allowing you to see and preserve underlying layers and the background canvas as you paint or apply effects. See "Painting On Layers" on page 51, in Chapter 3 and "Working With Image Layers" on page 142 for more information about image layers. To create *Diving Catch*, we painted onto several layers with Painter's brushes, then added a bit of texture.

1 Opening an image, extending the canvas and cloning. You can begin with a new blank file or start by tracing a reference photo, as we did. If you'd like to begin with a blank file, without tracing a reference, skip to step 2.

Our reference photo was 883 pixels wide. In our image, the player's feet were very close to the edge of the frame, so we added 50 pixels to the right side of the image to enhance the sense of speed in the flying jump (choose Canvas, Canvas Size).

To make a clone of your reference photo, choose File, Clone. Prepare for using tracing paper by deleting the contents of the clone: Select all (Ctrl/⌘-A) and press the Delete key, leaving the original clone source image open.

2 Making a new layer. Whether you've started with a blank file or a cloned reference photo, in the Objects palette, click the left triangle on the Layers section bar to open the Layers section. To make a new empty layer, click the right triangle on the Layers section bar and from the pull-down menu choose New Layer. You'll see the new layer appear in the Layers section. To name the layer, double-click its name in the Layers section, type a descriptive name in the Layer Attributes box and click OK.

3 Sketching on the layer. (If you're tracing a reference, with your new layer still selected, turn on Tracing paper by pressing Ctrl/⌘-T.) Make sure that Preserve Transparency is unchecked in the Layers palette. For the image above, we used the Sharp Pencil

4

The player selection saved as a mask. To see the mask in black-and-white, open the mask eye icon in the Masks section of the Objects palette and close the RGB-Canvas eye icon.

5

Targeting the "grass" layer in the Layers section of the Objects palette

6a

Click the right Drawing Mode to protect the area outside the selection and paint inside the selection.

6b

We painted colored brushstrokes inside the active ballplayer selection on the "player color" layer.

6c

Click the middle Drawing Mode to protect the area inside the selection and paint only outside it.

variant of Pencils to draw a sketch on the new layer. To sketch, choose a dark color in the Colors section of the Art Materials palette; choose the Sharp Pencil variant of the Pencils and draw or trace to create an expressive, line drawing.

4 Making a mask. When your sketch is complete, you can make a mask (or masks) to isolate any parts. Start by making a selection, and then convert it to a mask by choosing Select, Save Selection. (You'll use the mask in steps 5 and 6.) For more information about selections and masks, turn to Chapter 4 "Selections, Shapes and Masks." To isolate the player we made a selection with the Lasso and saved it as a mask in the Masks section by choosing Select, Save Selection.

5 Arranging the layers and painting. Add more layers as you need them using the process described in step 2. We created layers for the fence, grass, shadow and ballplayer and arranged them in the Layers section with the ballplayer elements and line drawing on top. (To change the layer stacking order, drag the layer names up or down in the Layers section.)

We used the Square Chalk variant of Dry Media (adjusting the size in the Controls:Brush palette) to paint the fence, grass, shadow and ballplayer. You can use the selection you made in step 4 in conjunction with the Drawing Modes to constrain your paint, as described in step 6. Or you can carefully paint up to the edge of the subject "by hand" without using a selection as described in step 7, and then correct the edge later by editing it with an eraser.

6 Drawing inside and outside of selections on a layer. Painter 6 allows you to use selections to constrain painting on any layer. To use the mask you made in step 4, which protects your subject while you paint around it, load a selection from the mask by choosing Select, Load Selection.

After loading the selection, you can use the Drawing Modes—three icons located in the bottom left corner of the image window—to paint inside or outside the selection. For instance, we painted inside the selection on the "player color" layer and outside it on the "fence" layer. (Keep in mind, the Drawing Modes are meant to constrain brushstrokes only; they do not work as described here to constrain effects.) To protect the area inside the active

6d

Painting brushstrokes outside the selection on the "background fence" layer

7

Erasing along the edge of the uniform on the "grass" layer

8

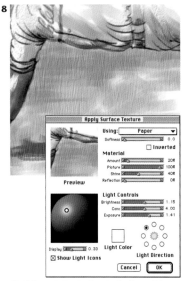

Applying a paper texture to the "grass" layer

9

The line drawing layer with the Default Composite Method (left) and Gel (right)

selection, click on the middle Drawing button. To protect the area outside the selection, click on the far right Drawing button. In the Layers section, click on the name of the layer you want to paint on, choose a brush and begin painting. To switch to another layer, click on its name in the Layers section, and continue to paint.

7 Hand-painting to clean up edges. If you use a selection to completely constrain all of the paint, you may create an undesirable hard edge. To preserve a fresh, hand-painted look, consider painting up to the edge without selecting, then use an eraser later to remove overlapping paint, if necessary. To use this method, begin by deselecting the selection (Select, None or Ctrl/⌘-D).

To erase some areas on our hand-painted "grass" layer that overlapped the ballplayer, we used a tiny Eraser variant (Erasers) to remove paint. To permanently remove paint from a layer, target the layer you'd like to correct by clicking on its name in the Layers section. Choose the Eraser variant of the Erasers, resize it smaller (using the Size slider on the Controls:Brush palette), and carefully remove the overlapping paint on the layer.

To erase any brushstrokes on the "background fence" layer that overlapped the ballplayer, we used the saved selection to edit it. We clicked on the "background fence" layer in the Layers section, chose Select, Load Selection to load a selection from the saved ballplayer mask and pressed the Delete key to remove all of the unwanted paint inside the selection on the "fence" layer.

8 Adding texture. By default, image layers have a smooth surface; unlike the Canvas, they do not interact with paper chosen in the Papers section of the Art Materials palette. But you can add texture using special effects such as Apply Surface Texture. When you apply an effect to an image layer, the effect is applied only to areas of the layer that already contain brushstrokes, a fill or other pixel information. To apply a paper texture to a layer, first select the layer in the Layers section, then choose Effects, Surface Control, Apply Surface Texture using Paper. To apply the texture to the "grass" layer we used a low Amount setting (about 20%), and we used Grass texture from the Wild Textures library (located in the Paper Texture Libraries folder on the Painter 6 CD-ROM).

9 Bringing out the line drawing. To enhance the loose, hand-drawn quality in our illustration by bringing out the sketch, we set the Composite Method of the "line drawing" layer to Gel. Gel is a transparent method that combines color on the layer with that on the underlying layers to create a darker color. Painter's Composite Methods are located in the Layers section under the Composite Method pull-down menu. (You can also find them in the Controls:Adjuster palette, when the Layer Adjuster is selected in the Tools palette. For a more complete description of the Composite Methods, turn to page 151 in the beginning of this chapter, or to Chapter 12 in the Painter 6 User Guide.)

Melting Text into Water

Overview *Use the Text tool to set type shapes over a background; convert the shapes to selections; float two copies of the type; use feathering and Dye Concentration to add dimension to the type; paint on the layer masks to "melt" the bottoms of the layers.*

CHER THREINEN-PENDARVIS

The selected text shapes appear in the Layers section of the Objects palette.

Alt/Option-clicking with the Layer Adjuster on the selection to make a layer

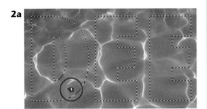

The Layers section after naming the layers

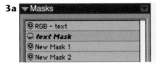

Selecting the text layer mask in the Masks section of the Objects palette

YOU CAN ACHIEVE A DRAMATIC TRANSLUCENT EFFECT using Painter's brushes to paint on the visibility mask of a layer. In the image above, we used the Digital Airbrush variant (Airbrushes) on the lower part of two layers—the type and the feathered shadow behind it—to create the illusion of type melting into water. You can get a similar result using other backgrounds such as clouds, stone or wood.

1 Setting type shapes and converting to selections. Open an image to use as a background; our photo was 3 inches wide and 225 pixels per inch. Choose the Text tool and select a font in the Controls:Text palette. Procedures (such as feathering) can erode a thin font, so we chose a font with thick strokes—90-point Futura Extra Bold Condensed. Open the Layers section of the Objects palette by clicking the left triangle on the Layers section bar. With the Layers section open, you'll be able to see each letter shape appear as you type. Click the Text tool in the image and begin typing. To kern the individual letters, click the shape's name in the Layers section with the Layer Adjuster tool, then use the arrow keys on your keyboard to tighten or loosen the spacing.

To achieve the result in the above image, using the text outlines to float portions of the background, it's necessary to convert the text shapes to selections. With the Layer Adjuster tool chosen and all the shapes selected in the Layers section, choose Shapes, Convert To Selection. The text shapes will disappear from your image and will reappear as animated marquees. To save your selection as a mask so you can use it later, choose Select, Save Selection. Open the Masks section bar to see the new mask (named New Mask 1).

With the marquee still active, (in preparation for making the soft shadow layer) choose Select, Feather and type 15 pixels. Click OK. Now save this selection as a mask by choosing Select, Save Selection. This mask (named New Mask 2) will appear in the Masks section.

2 Using selections to make layers. To make the two layers needed for this technique, begin with the active feathered shadow selection (if it's no longer active, load New Mask 2 by choosing Select, Load Selection). Choose the Layer Adjuster tool, press the

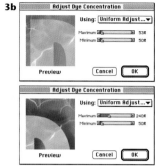

Using Dye Concentration to lighten the text (top) and create the shadow

Skewing the shadow to add a look of depth

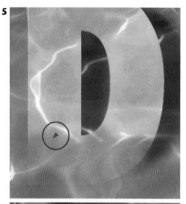

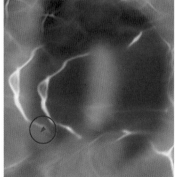

Using the Digital Airbrush variant on the text layer (top) and the shadow layer (with the text layer hidden) to reveal the underlying image

Alt/Option key and click on the active text selection. (Holding the Alt/Option key makes a copy of the selected area, leaving the background intact.) Click on the Canvas name to deselect Layer 1. Now load the text selection (New Mask 1), by choosing Select, Load Selection and when it appears, click on it with the Layer Adjuster. In the Layers section, you'll see two items named Layer, followed by a number. Double-click on the Layer 2 name (or select the name and press the Enter key) and rename it "text" in the Layer Attributes dialog box. Do the same for the Layer 1 below it, naming it "shadow."

3 Distinguishing the layers. Use Dye Concentration to make the layers stand out from the background and from each other. In the Layers section, click once on the text layer to make it active. Now, change the color of the layer by adding Dye Concentration. Choose Effects, Surface Control, Dye Concentration, using Uniform Adjustment and drag the Maximum slider to 53%. Click OK. To create a soft, saturated shadow, select the shadow layer in the Layers section and again choose Dye Concentration. This time experiment with a higher Maximum setting (we chose 240%). When you like the result you see in the Preview, click OK.

4 Offsetting the shadow. Give a greater illusion of depth to the type by nudging the shadow up and to the right using the arrow keys on your keyboard. To make the type appear to stand at an angle to the background, as we did, skew the shadow: With the shadow layer selected, choose Effects, Orientation, Distort. Drag the top center handle of the bounding box down and to the right, check the Better box and click OK. There's no preview of this effect, so it may take a few tries to get the look you want.

5 Painting into the layer masks. To "melt" the lower portions of the letterforms into the water, use a brush to partially erase the layer masks of both the text and shadow layers. Choose the Digital Airbrush variant of the Airbrushes. For more sensitivity, check to make sure the Opacity in the Controls:Brush palette is to set to 9%. Choose white in the Colors section of the Art Materials palette. Now select the text layer in the Layers section and select the text layer mask in the Masks section. To view the layer while editing its mask, keep the mask eye icon shut. Brush along the bottom of the letters to make the lower part of the text layer disappear. If you need to restore part of the text, switch to black paint. Painter won't restrict your restoration to the inside of the type, however, so you'll need to change to a smaller brush size. Then complete the effect by selecting the shadow layer in the Layers section and the shadow layer mask in the Masks section and brushing white along its bottom. You may find it easier to work on the shadow layer if you hide the text layer temporarily: Select it in the Layers section and click to shut its eye icon. When you're finished working on the shadow, click the text's eye icon open again. 🖌

■ **John Derry** designed and assembled the *Paint Can* image—an homage to the abstract expressionist artist Robert Rauschenberg—for the promotion of Painter 6, entirely within Painter. To begin, he opened several source files, including images from past promotional posters he'd designed (for instance, the Vermeer-inspired image in the lower left and the Statue of Liberty in the upper right), a scan of paisley fabric and several source photos—including a paint can photo, a candid portrait of himself with Rauschenberg, a 747 cockpit photo, a test pattern graphic and a space photo of the Eagle Nebula. To add interest to the paint can image, he applied a colored dot pattern to the source image by choosing Effects, Surface Control, Apply Screen. Then he used the Layer Adjuster tool to drag and drop each source image into his composite file. He temporarily turned each layer into a reference layer by choosing Effects, Orientation, Free Transform, and scaled and positioned the elements using

the Layer Adjuster tool. When the elements were in position and at the sizes he wanted, he changed each reference layer back into an image layer by choosing Effects, Orientation, Commit Transform.

Here's how Derry composited and added effects to some of the layers after bringing them into his composite file: To create transparency and unusual color in some of the elements, he used the Composite Method menu in the Layers section of the Objects palette. For instance, he set the "Statue of Liberty" layer to Hard Light. To achieve the transparency for the "747 Cockpit" layer, he lowered its Opacity to 67% in the Layers section of the Objects palette. To fill the "Test Pattern" layer with bright color, he turned on Preserve Transparency in the Layers section (to constrain the fill to the existing pixels on the layer), he chose a bright orange in the Colors section of the Art Materials palette and then chose Effects, Fill, Current Color. To create the textured number "6" in the

lower right, Derry chose the Text tool in the Tools palette, and set a font and size in the Controls:Text palette, then he typed a "6." To add texture to the number, he converted the shape to a layer by choosing Shapes, Convert to Layer, and with the layer selected in the Layers section, he clicked on its mask in the Masks section of the Objects palette. Alternating between black and white color, he subtly sprayed into the mask with a small Airbrush variant.

For the orange and yellow paint drips on the image, Derry added a new empty layer to the image and sprayed the drips on it using a custom Image Hose nozzle.

For the pink and aqua brushstrokes in the foreground, he created a blank, new layer, made sure Preserve Transparency was turned off in the Layers section, then painted on the layer with the Graphic Paintbrush and Smeary Bristle Spray variants of Brushes using bright colors.

■ For *Walking the Show Dog* (above), an image for self promotion, **Susan LeVan** began by scanning a ballpoint pen drawing. To put the line drawing on a layer, she chose Select All, then Select,

Float. To make the white in the line drawing layer transparent she set its Composite Method to Gel in the Layers section. Going back to the Canvas, LeVan painted under the line drawing with the Square Chalk variant of Dry Media (a grain-sensitive brush), drawing along the lines of the figure and the dog on top a rough paper texture. LeVan copied and pasted a digital photo (taken by studio-partner Ernest Barbee) into her image and brushed over it with the Square Chalk using bright color. For the photo's deckled bottom edge, she made a loose Lasso selection of the unwanted portion on the targeted layer, feathered the selection a few pixels (Select, Feather) and pressed the Delete key. Then LeVan gave the photo a drop shadow by choosing Effects, Objects, Create Drop Shadow.

Next she targeted the "Line Drawing" layer in the Layers section and used the Rectangular Selection tool to select the man and dog. She floated a copy of the area by pressing Alt/Option and clicking inside the selection with the Layer Adjuster. She made sure Preserve

Transparency was turned on in the Layers section before filling the new layer with orange color (Effects, Fill), and changed its Composite Method to Colorize to color the figures. Next, LeVan created an empty new layer by clicking the New button on the Layers section and (with Preserve Transparency turned off) painted a rough yellow form of the man and dog using the Square Chalk. She set this layer's Composite Method to Gel, lowered its Opacity to 60% in the Layers section and offset the layer by dragging it with the Layer Adjuster. She made another copy of the "Line Drawing" layer by selecting it in the Layers section and Alt/Option-clicking it with the Layer Adjuster, dragged it to the top of the Layers section's list and set its Composite Method to Gel. She duplicated the "Line Drawing" layer again, offset and filled it with blue, then set its Opacity to 60% in the Layers section. To complete the image, LeVan selected the Canvas in the Layers section and used the Simple Water variant of Water Color to paint saturated color on the figure's face, the ground and the photo.

Sharon Steuer began *August, Cosomo and Viola*—a painting commissioned by the child's parents, by drawing four pencil studies on paper—the baby August, drawings of the dogs and a study of the table. Then she scanned each of them into Photoshop. With each pencil study on a separate layer, she arranged the composition, which included some resizing of the dogs and reshaping of the foreground dog. Then she saved a flattened version of the image for import into Painter. In Painter, she clicked the New button on the Layers section of the

Objects palette to add an empty, new layer on top of the gray drawing. Steuer painted on the new layer with the Artist Pastel Chalk variant of Dry Media and the Round Camelhair variant of Brushes. Then, using the Composite Method menu on the Layers section, she set the painted layer to Multiply. To add richer, more complex color to the overall painting and to get color into the sketched lines, she duplicated the layer with colored brushstrokes by Alt/Option-clicking it with the Layer Adjuster tool. Then she set this layer's Composite Method to Overlay. As Steuer worked, she added more layers and painted on them with color. To remove a portion of a layer she didn't want, she used the Eraser variant of the Erasers. For instance, on the "Multiply mid-tones" layer, she erased the area covering the foreground, child and dogs, leaving the remainder to cover the background and trees. To strengthen the line work, she copied and pasted the gray line sketch into the working file and composited it using Multiply method. Steuer saved many versions of the image. When the painting

was near completion she opened favorite early versions and created flattened copies of the images by choosing File, Clone. Then she used File, Place to import the copies of the earlier versions into the final version of the file. (The Place command imported the images, with the file names listed in the Layers section.) She experimented with Composite Methods to get the look she wanted. To create an autumn-colored look in the foreground, Steuer created a new layer and painted using a custom Artist Pastel Chalk variant, and for a soft warmth she set this layer to Soft Light method. When the painting was nearly complete, she created a flattened copy of the image by choosing File, Clone and she lit the clone using Effects, Surface Control, Apply Lighting. She copied and pasted the lit image back into the layered file and erased any areas where she wanted to remove the lighting effect. Then she composited this layer using Hard Light to brighten its color. To finish, she added a last touch-up layer, where she painted details using the custom Artist Pastel Chalk.

Department of Art at New Mexico State University. He created *Summer Reading*, a cover for *Puerto del Sol*, the semi-annual international literary journal published by the English Department at New Mexico State University. Ocepek wanted *Summer Reading* to express the perpetual dream many readers have of catching up on their reading on a perfect summer day, sitting in the shade of a big tree.

To heighten the feeling of heat, he used very warm colors in the image. To add to the magical atmosphere, he made the tree very large. He camouflaged many abstract forms in the tree to represent the imaginary worlds of the reader and writer. And he separated the chair from the tree to reinforce the idea of a lone reader, reading peacefully.

After drawing the tree, Ocepek added interest with details from photos of trees he had shot and scanned. He opened the scans and copied and pasted portions of them into his working file, where he positioned them. Then he grouped the layered pieces with the tree drawing layer by Shift-selecting them in the Layers section of the Objects palette and pressing the Group button. Then he merged the grouped layers into a single tree layer by clicking the Collapse button.

When the tree was almost complete, Ocepek built the chair. He began the chair by drawing shapes with the Pen tool. Then he Shift-selected all the Shapes, grouped them by clicking the Group button and converted them to a single layer (Shapes, Convert to Layer). After turning on Preserve Transparency in the Layers section, he filled the chair layer with a dark purple color (Effects, Fill, Current Color). Then he painted over the chair with various brushes. Ocepek kept the tree and chair on their own layers to help control their colors and textures and to preserve the distinction between the two elements in the image.

For a rich, textured look, Ocepek switched paper textures as he painted. To enhance the textured look and to make sure the textures printed clearly in offset lithography, he painted with grain-sensitive brushes—such as the Chalk variants of Dry Media. While painting, he slowly built up subtle color, adjusting the Opacity slider on the Controls:Brush palette. To create the soft, light auras around the tree and the chair, he selected each layer in the Layers section and painted it using the Bleach variant of the Erasers. To protect the completed paint on the tree while he added the auras around it, Ocepek loaded a selection he'd saved for the tree (Select, Load Selection) then edited the tree layer. Then he loaded the selection for the chair and edited its layer. To keep the paint outside each selection on the tree and chair layers, he clicked the Draw Outside (middle) Drawing Mode icon located in the bottom left of Painter's image window.

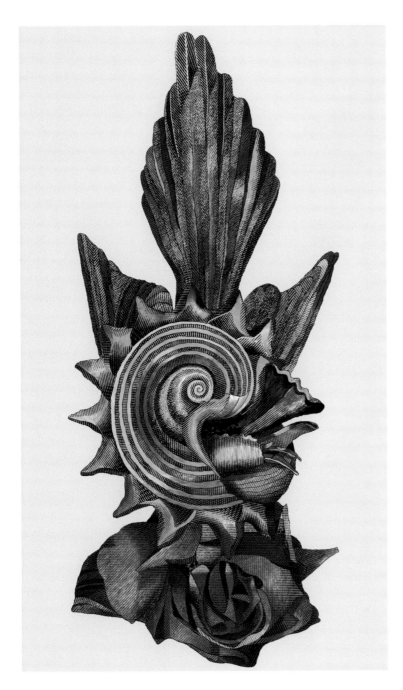

■ When creating *Puertoplasms Primavera*, also a cover for *Puerto del Sol*, **Louis Ocepek** was inspired by Ralph Waldo Emerson's essay, *Nature*, published in 1836. To begin the image, Ocepek assembled resource photos which he scanned and opened in Painter. He made a complete line drawing of each of the three components of the central creature and completely rendered each element in its own source file, then assembled them as layers in a single composite file.

To create an engraved look, Ocepek made several custom paper textures before he began painting: Each one consisted of lines drawn at a different angle.

As Ocepek painted with grain-sensitive brushes (for instance the Dry Media variants) he intuitively switched paper textures as he worked. After painting each element using the engraved line textures, he copied and pasted the three source elements into a final composite file, where he set each layer's Composite Method to Gel in the Layers section of the Objects palette.

The combination of painting on the various angled paper textures with grain-sensitive brushes and compositing the individual layered elements with the Gel method allowed Ocepek to achieve rich, transparent color and to imitate the look of a traditional 18th-century engraving.

Finally Ocepek selected the Canvas in the Layers section and filled the Canvas of the composite file with flat color (Effects, Fill, Current Color). He painted soft, transparent colors onto the Canvas using Water Color brushes and dried the wet paint by choosing Canvas, Dry.

■ Bear Canyon Creative commissioned illustrator **Cecil Rice** to paint *The Green Hornet*, one in a series of illustrations for a set of audio book covers entitled *The Golden Age of Radio,* published by Dove Audio. An expert draftsman, Rice painted the portrait in Painter from start to finish using traditional painting theory. He began by gathering references from movies done in the 1930s and 1940s. Then he did three portrait sketches in Painter and presented them to his client. The chosen sketch was based on a still from an old Alan Ladd movie. For the final artwork, Rice used Canvas, Resize to enlarge the sketch to the finished size plus bleed; then he made selections and clicked with the Layer Adjuster to put each element on a layer. While painting, he blended the color in the image with Liquid variants and added more color with the Brushes and Dry Media variants. Rice continued to refine the shapes of elements, for instance, the ascot and coat, by editing the masks for those layers. When he was pleased with the figure, he painted the background using the Artist Pastel Chalk variant (Dry Media). To blend the background, he used Effects, Focus, Soften.

■ For this illustration for Glidden Paint company, art directed by Terry Pacifico of the Arras Group, artist **Nancy Stahl** painted on layers using custom brushes she built to imitate her favorite traditional brushes.

Stahl started by photographing herself in the figure's position, then assembled the photo and a sign reference into a rough composition in Painter. She used the composite image as a reference when drawing a line drawing, which she sent to her client for approval.

Using custom brushes she had built to imitate her favorite gouache brushes, Stahl painted the figure and the Coca-Cola sign in two separate source files. She completed most of the painting in the source files because the complex brushes performed quicker than they would in a larger composite file. To learn about her painting techniques and custom brushes, turn to "Gouache and Opaque Watermedia," on page 70.

After the figure was complete, Stahl selected it with the Lasso tool and feathered the selection a few pixels by choosing Select, Feather (so the edge of the selection would be smooth). She saved the selection as a mask in the Masks section of the Objects palette by choosing Select, Save Selection. To bring the figure into the sign file, she loaded the selection by choosing Select, Load Selection, pressed Alt/Option (to float a copy) and used the Layer Adjuster to drag and drop the copy into the sign painting file. Keeping the sign and the figure on separate layers made it easier for Stahl to add the final details.

■ **Chet Phillips** expressively draws his illustrations with the Scratchboard Tool variant of Pens. Then he cuts the art to a layer which he composites using the Gel Composite Method, chosen from the Composite Method menu in the Layers section of the Objects palette. He uses Airbrushes in varying sizes to color the background (see page 27 for a step-by-step description of his technique). When the coloring is complete, he merges the layer with the Canvas using the Drop button on the Layers section. He often adds effects to complete the piece.

For *Bad to the Bone*, Phillips began by drawing a loose study with pencils on paper. He scanned the drawing and made a clone (File, Clone), deleted the contents of the clone file, and turned on Tracing Paper (Ctrl/⌘-T). Using the sketch as a guide, he drew in black-and-white using the Scratchboard Tool variant of the Pens. Then, working on top of the scratchboard drawing, he used the Pen and Lasso tools (from the Tools palette) to create shapes, then converted each shape to a selection (Shapes, Convert To Selection). After he converted each selection, he saved it as a mask in the Masks section of the Objects palette by choosing Select, Save Selection. Then Phillips made the entire scratchboard drawing into a layer by choosing Select, All and clicking inside the active selection with the Layer Adjuster tool. To make the white areas of the drawing transparent, he set the Composite Method in the Layers section to Gel. He deselected the layer by clicking on the Canvas layer in the Layers section, and began to add color to the image canvas. Working on the Canvas, he loaded each selection (Select, Load Selection) and applied colored tints to the selected areas using Effects, Fill, using various opacities. With the selection still active he painted color details with the Airbrushes.

■ For *Baseball Memories,* commissioned by The Dallas Morning News, **Chet Phillips** began by drawing with the Scratchboard Tool variant of Pens. Then he used the Pen and Lasso tools to create shapes. He converted each shape to a selection (Shapes, Convert To Selection) and saved the selection as a mask (Select, Save Selection). He floated the entire scratchboard drawing to a layer by choosing Select, All and clicking inside the active selection with the Layer Adjuster tool. Before deselecting the layer, in the Layers section of the Objects palette, he set the Composite Method to Gel.

Working on the image canvas, Phillips loaded each selection (Select, Load Selection) and applied colored tints to

the selected areas using Effects, Fill. To build the foreground shadows, he softly sprayed into the selections with the Digital Airbrush variant of Airbrushes, for a graduated effect.

To create the cast shadows for the older ballplayer, Phillips drew a shape with the Pen tool that was actually the taller shadow of a virile, young man. To convert the shape into a selection, he clicked the Make Selection button on the Controls:Shape Design palette and then he saved the selection as a mask in the Masks section of the Objects palette by choosing Select, Save Selection. He made a new, empty layer by clicking the New button in the Layers section; he loaded the selection for the shadow (Select, Load

Selection. Then for a soft edge, he feathered the selection several pixels (Select, Feather). Next he chose Effects, Fill and filled the selection with a custom black-to-white gradient (chosen in the Gradients section of the Art Materials palette. To stretch the shadow taller, he used Effects, Orientation, Distort (with Better quality), dragged the handles to shape the shadow the way he wanted it and clicked OK. To finish the image, Phillips made a shadow for the other figure, adjusted the Opacity of the cast shadow layers in the Layers section and added more color detail with the Airbrushes.

■ An award-winning fine artist and illustrator, **Carol Benioff** has illustrated for magazines such as *Atlantic Monthly* and *Parenting*—and her work appears in the *CA Illustration Annual*.

Speak Softly, Exuberance Checked, is a painted collage within Benioff's series *"The Twelve Covenants, or The Unspoken Rules of Growing Up Female."* The highly textured painting incorporates several components on layers, including a scanned traditional pencil sketch, an etching and expressive colored brushwork and washes added to Painter's canvas.

Benioff began the image by making a pencil sketch on paper. Then she used traditional copperplate methods to create an etching, which she printed on paper. She scanned the sketch and print and dragged and dropped them as new layers into a Painter composite file. She set the Composite Method for both the sketch and etching layers to Multiply in the Layers section of the Objects palette.

Working on the Canvas in Painter, she used the Nervous Pen variant of Pens and black color to add sketchy linework and texture to the image. Then she used

several Brushes (for instance, the Variable Round), as well as the Square Chalk and Oil Pastel variants of Dry Media to draw in color. She blended areas with the Just Add Water variant of Liquid. To finish, she painted soft transparent glazes using her own custom "glazing" brushes based on Painter's Water Color variants. Benioff's "glazing" brushes paint washes while revealing the current paper texture chosen in the Papers section of the Art Materials palette; this is accomplished with low Opacity and high Grain settings in the Controls:Brush palette.

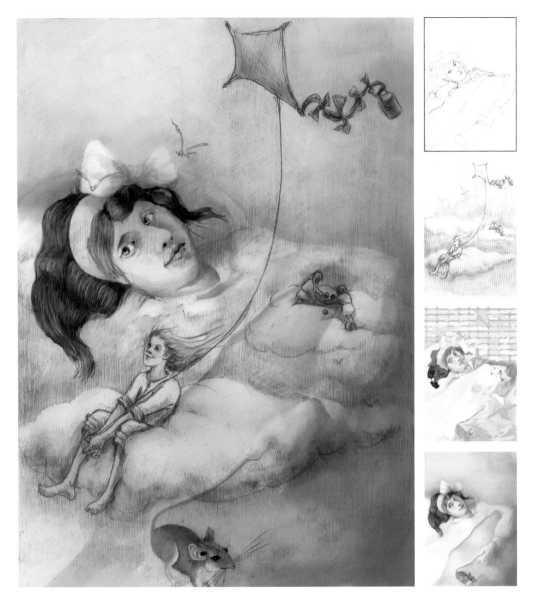

■ For *Air Travels*, **Carol Benioff** began by drawing two pencil sketches—the dreaming girl and the girl flying the kite. Then she scanned the sketches and dragged and dropped the kite flyer sketch into the dreaming girl file, which created a new layer for the kite flyer. She set the Composite Method for the layer to Multiply in the Layers section of the Objects palette.

Benioff used the drawings as a guide while she painted on the Canvas. To color the dreaming girl and background, Benioff painted over the sketch with Oil Pastel in a variety of sizes, and blended areas with the Just Add Water variant of Liquid, adjusting the Opacity of the brushes (Controls:Brush palette) as she worked. Using a custom "glazing" Water Color brush, she glazed over shadow areas to deepen them and to add more color. When the color in the dreaming girl was complete, she dried the Canvas, merging the Water Color "glazing" with the color applied with the Oil Pastel.

She wanted a watercolor look for the kite flyer, but Wet Paint cannot be used on a layer. Also, Benioff wanted to keep the watercoloring of the kite flyer separate from the painting on the main image canvas while she worked on it so she could see the detail more clearly. To create an image for the watercolor work that would be the same size as the composite, she saved a new version of the file and deleted the colored background from it (Select, All, then Backspace/Delete). Keeping the kite flyer sketch layer visible, in the Layers section but not active, Benioff used a modified Simple Water (Water Color) to tint the girl and kite. Then she merged this Wet Paint with the Canvas (Canvas, Dry). Next, she chose Select, All, and used the Layer Adjuster to drag the colored kite flyer Canvas into the composite file. She set its Composite Method to Multiply (Layers section), and moved the colored kite flyer below the black-and-white layer in the Layers section list.

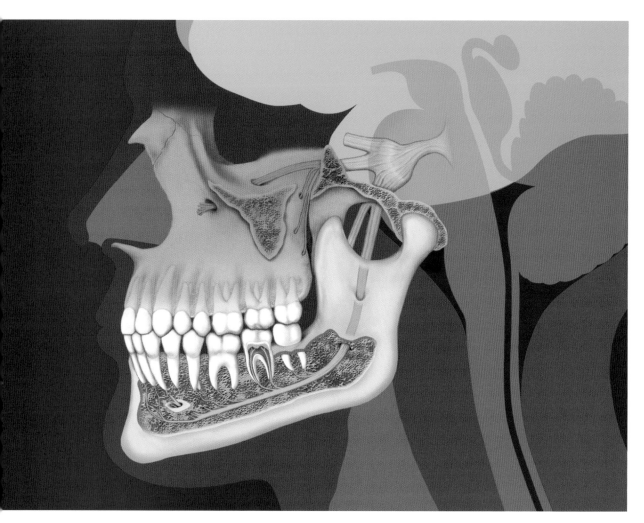

■ Medical illustrator **David Purnell** is proprietor of the New York West Medical Illustration Studio. When creating both of the illustrations on these pages for 3M Dental Products—for posting on the 3M Dental web site and for printed materials—Purnell used Painter's shapes and layers. The layers helped him to organize elements in his illustration and to keep items separate while he finished the details.

To create *Neural Pathway*, Purnell began by making a line drawing in Macromedia FreeHand and saving it in Adobe Illustrator EPS format. After client approval, he imported the vector line drawing into Painter as shapes, by choosing File, Acquire, Adobe Illustrator file. He converted the individual shapes

to image layers (Shapes, Convert To Layer) and filled them with flat color fills by choosing Effects, Fill With Current Color. One-by-one, he airbrushed the layers to sculpt the anatomy in the focal area of the illustration. He left the outer areas filled with simple flat color, to focus attention on the important neural pathway areas.

For the textured cross-section of bone, Purnell used a custom airbrush based on the Variable Splatter variant of Airbrushes. To build a brush that would spray narrower or wider splattery strokes depending on the pressure applied, he changed the Min Size in the Size section of the Brush Controls palette from the default 0% to 30%. To vary the size of the droplets, he also changed the Feature

size in the General section of the Brush Controls palette as he worked.

To make the bone look even more organic, he used the Distorto brush variant of Liquid to randomly push and pull areas of the splatter in order to vary its look. To constrain the paint within the element on the layer, he turned on Preserve Transparency in the Layers section of the Objects palette.

Purnell finished the illustration by applying effects: For instance, he targeted the jaw bone layer and applied realistic highlights and shadows based on the gray values in the spatter-airbrushed texture he had painted. He achieved this lighting with Effects, Surface Control, Apply Surface Texture Using Image Luminance, with subtle settings.

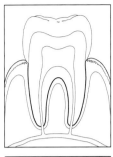

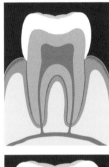

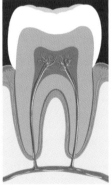

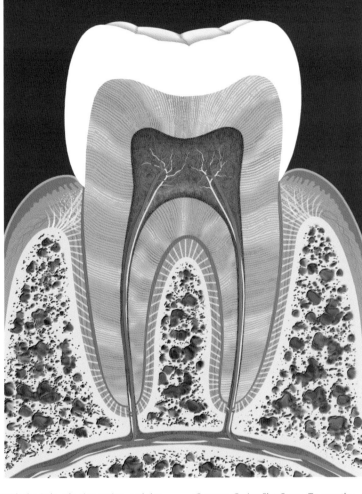

■ **David Purnell** created *Molar Cross-section* for 3M Dental Products to show the anatomy of an adult molar tooth. For a realistic look and to organize details, he decided to use "texture" layers for some of the elements which would sit on top of the flat color layers. To make masks that he could use to control the texture he duplicated each flat color layer (Alt/Option-click with the Layer Adjuster), and in the Layers section of the Objects palette he clicked the Layers menu triangle and chose Drop and Select. Then he saved the selection as a mask in the Masks section.

To create texture—for instance, the fibrous texture in the Pulp chamber—he loaded the selection he had saved (Select, Load Selection), clicked the New Layer button on the Layers section and turned off Preserve Transparency in the Layers section, so the layer could be painted on.

With the Pulp selection active, and the Pulp texture layer active, he was ready to begin applying the texture effect. When working with a selection, he used Painter's Drawing Modes to constrain brushstrokes to the inside or the outside of the loaded selection.

To achieve the cellular look of the odontoblasts on the edges of the pulp chamber, he used the paper texture Random Bubbles (from the Molecular Textures library located in the Paper Texture Libraries folder on the Painter 6 CD-ROM.) He varied the scaling of the texture as he worked from 100% to 30%. To apply the texture onto the layer, he used a custom grainy Airbrush that also incorporated variable Opacity and Size. So the brush would reveal grain as he painted, he changed the Subcategory in the General section of the Brush Controls palette from Soft

Cover to Grainy Flat Cover. To vary the Size and Opacity, in the Expression section of the Brush Controls palette he set Size and Opacity to be controlled by Pressure. Then he carefully airbrushed the Random Bubbles texture along the inner edge of the pulp chamber.

For the striations on the Dentin layer, Purnell chose a darker ochre color than the solid ochre on the original dentin layer. He made a new "texture" layer as described, then he used a custom Airbrush (which incorporated a Rake stroke type) to draw the striations, keeping in mind the subtle S-curves that are characteristic of the anatomy.

For the textured bone, he used much the same technique as in the *Neural Pathway* piece, painting with his custom Splatter airbrush and Distorto variant, then adding Apply Surface Texture.

6

ENHANCING PHOTOS, MONTAGE AND COLLAGE

Philip Howe created Police, *shown here in this detail. To see more of Howe's photo collage painting work, turn to page 200.*

PHOTO: CORBIS IMAGES

To enhance this portrait, we began by painting a mask to isolate the dancers. To create a shallow depth of field, we used Effects, Tonal Control, Adjust Colors to desaturate the background and Effects, Focus, Soften to blur it.

ALTHOUGH PAINTER BEGAN as a painting program, the features that have been added over the years have turned it into a powerful image processor as well. Many new tools designed *just* for photographers have been added—for instance, dynamic layers that allow you to adjust brightness and contrast, perform posterization, apply glass distortion effects and more! (For the basics of how to work with dynamic layers such as Glass Distortion, turn to page 147.) Painter 6 also includes brush variants specifically designed for photographers, such as the Scratch Remover and Saturation Add brushes found in the Photo brush category in the Brushes palette. And, of course, when it comes to achieving painterly effects with photographs, Painter has no peer. If you're a photographer, a photo-illustrator or a designer who works with photos and you want to get the most out of Painter, you'll want to pay attention to the following areas of the program.

The Effects menu. Most of Painter's image-altering special effects can be found in the Effects menu. The features under the subheads Tonal Control, Surface Control and Focus are loaded with creative promise for the adventurous digital photographer.

Selections and masks. To alter only a portion of an image, you'll need to become acquainted with Painter's shapes and its selection and masking capabilities. If you're not familiar with the Pen and Lasso tools, turn to "Working with Bézier Paths and Selections" and "Working with Freehand Selections" in Chapter 4.

Painter's powerful automatic masking features—located in the Masks section of the Objects palette—give you a big jump on the tedious process of creating masks to isolate parts of your image. And a bonus: All of Painter's brushes except Wet method brushes (such as Water Color) and Plug-in method brushes (such as the Add

To isolate the sky from the buildings in this photo we made a Color Mask for the sky. (In the Objects palette, on the Masks section bar, click the right triangle to access the menu and choose Color Mask.) Then we used the Scratchboard Tool variant of Pens and white paint to remove from the mask any areas in the photo's foreground that had also been selected with Color Mask.

PHOTO: PHOTODISC

PHOTO: CHER THREINEN-PENDARVIS

Correcting the tonal range in an overexposed image using Effects, Tonal Control, Equalize

Grain variant of the Photo brush) can be used to paint directly on a mask. (Wet and Plug-in brushes are designed to paint only on the Canvas.) For a detailed description of combining Painter's automatic and painterly masks, turn to "Using Color Mask," in Chapter 4.

Layers. Chapter 5 gave you an overall look at techniques using layers; this chapter focuses on using layers and masks for photo-compositing and other photo effects—for example, in "Simulating Motion," "Selective Coloring" and "Creating a Montage Using Masks and Layers," later in the chapter.

Dynamic layers. Painter offers dynamic layers that are useful for making adjustments to images: They are: Brightness and Contrast, Equalize, and Posterize. You'll find these versatile tools in the Dynamic Layers section of the Objects palette. Several of the techniques described later in this chapter use dynamic layers. To read more about dynamic layers and how they relate to other elements in Painter, turn to the beginning of Chapter 5.

Cloning. A very powerful and versatile feature, cloning (File, Clone) lets you make multiple copies of an image, alter each of them, then recombine them in various ways while preserving access to the original. Several of the techniques described in this chapter use this or another kind of cloning method.

IMAGE-PROCESSING BASICS

With its strong focus on *creative* image manipulation, Painter has left some *production*-oriented tasks such as color-correcting CMYK images to Adobe Photoshop. But there's no need to move an image from Painter to Photoshop to perform basic image-processing tasks such as sharpening and adjusting brightness and contrast, because Painter has tools that can be set to emulate many of Photoshop's.

Equalizing. Choosing Effects, Tonal Control, Equalize (Ctrl/⌘-E) produces a dialog box with a histogram similar to Photoshop's Levels dialog, which allows you to adjust the tonal range in an image—the difference is that in Painter the image is automatically equalized (an effect similar to clicking on the Auto button in Photoshop's Levels). Move the triangular sliders toward the ends of the histogram to decrease the effect.

Painter also features an Equalize dynamic layer that operates like Effects, Tonal Control, Equalize, but on a copy of your image so you can easily try out different tonal adjustments. To make an Equalize layer, open an image and choose Equalize from the resource list in the Dynamic Layers section of the Objects palette. With Equalize selected, click the Apply button to generate the dynamic layer. When the Equalize dialog box appears, set the controls as you would for Effects, Tonal Control, Equalize. Using an Equalize dynamic layer you can preview as many changes as you like: Click the Reset button to return your image to its original condition, then apply a new correction.

Using a feather setting of 15 pixels, we created a textured edge for this 500-pixel-wide photo. (To make a soft-edged vignette around an image, turn to page 108 in Chapter 4.)

To create a vignette with a textured edge, begin by making a selection with the Oval Selection tool. Use the Selection Adjuster (Tools palette) to position and scale the selection. Next, apply a feather (Select, Feather). Save the selection (Select, Save Selection). Now for the textured edge: In the Masks section of the Objects palette, select the mask, and open its eye icon and close the RGB-Canvas eye icon to view the mask in black-and-white. Select a rough paper texture in the Papers section of the Art Materials palette (we used Big Grain Rough), and choose Effects, Surface Control, Express Texture. Adjust the sliders to confine the texture to the soft edge. Click OK. (For more information about using Express Texture, turn to "Toning with Textures" on page 192.) In the Masks section, click the mask eye icon shut and select the RGB-Canvas. Load the selection (Select, Load Selection). Next, reverse the selection (to select the area outside the oval) by choosing Select, Invert. To clear the background, press the Backspace/Delete key.

Adjusting brightness and contrast. Painter offers two ways to change image brightness and contrast. The first—Effects, Tonal Control, Brightness/Contrast—applies a correction directly to an open image or selection. But if you'd like to preview several Brightness and Contrast options, consider making a Brightness-and-Contrast dynamic layer. In the Dynamic Layer section of the Objects palette, select Brightness and Contrast. Click the Apply button to generate the dynamic layer. When the Brightness-and-Contrast dialog box appears, continue to adjust the settings as you preview the corrections in your image. To read more about a Brightness-and-Contrast dynamic layer, see "Making a Selective Correction" on page 184.

Stripping color from an image. There are several ways to turn a color image into a grayscale one in Painter. The quickest way is to desaturate the image using the Adjust Color dialog box. Choose Effects, Tonal Control, Adjust Colors and drag the Saturation slider all the way to the left.

Changing color. While you're using the Adjust Color dialog box, experiment with the Hue Shift slider to change the hue of all of the colors in an image (or a layer or selection). You can get greater control in altering specific colors (turning blue eyes green, for instance) by using Effects, Tonal Control, Adjust Selected Colors. Click in the image to select a color, then drag the Hue Shift, Saturation and Value sliders at the bottom of the dialog box to make the changes. Fine-tune your color choice and the softness of its edge with the various Extents and Feather sliders.

To repair a white scratch on this photo we used a two-step process, beginning with Painter's useful Scratch Remover brush (located in the Photo category, in the Brushes palette). Open a photo you'd like to repair, choose the Scratch Remover variant and for the best results, use a small brush size (we used a 1.7 pixel brush on this 350-pixel-wide image) and a low Opacity setting in the Controls:Brush palette (we used 9%). Zoom in to a magnification where you can see the scratch in detail, and carefully paint to blend the scratch into the image. This first step is usually sufficient for images with even color. But the sky in our image was graduated and required more repair. Next, we used a Soft Cloner variant of the Cloners with a small brush size and a very low Opacity, set in the Controls:Brush palette. Shift/Control-click to set the clone source to a point near the repair, then gently paint over the repaired area to bring back appropriate colors.

The scratched image (left) and the repaired image (right)

Using the Saturation Add brush from the Photo brush library to "pop" the color on the red raincoat, umbrella and reflection

We applied Micro Grain (loaded from the More Wild Textures library in the Paper Texture Libraries folder on the Painter 6 CD-ROM), to this photo with Effects, Surface Control, Dye Concentration Using Paper with the Maximum slider set to 200%.

To "age" this photo, we painted with the Add Grain Brush using Crackle texture from the Painter Brushes library giving it a crackled texture.

The image above was sharpened to produce the result on the right using these settings: Radius, 2.15; Highlight, 90%; Shadow, 80%. A larger image can accept a higher radius setting.

Painting saturation with brushes. To "pop" the color in a specific area, use Painter's Saturation Add brush, located in the Photo brush category in the Brushes palette. For a more subtle look, lower the Opacity to about 10%.

Adding film grain. Photoshop's Noise filter is a good way to emulate film grain. To get a similar effect in Painter, choose a fine Paper grain in the Papers section of the Art Materials palette, like Regular Fine (or choose Micro Grain or Synthetic Super Fine loaded from the More Paper Textures library, located in the Paper Texture Libraries folder on the Painter 6 Application CD-ROM). Then select Effects, Surface Control, Dye Concentration. Scale the texture in the Papers section until the grain in the Preview window is barely visible—try 50% as a starting point. Try minor adjustments to the Maximum and Minimum sliders in the Adjust Dye Concentration dialog box.

Adding grain with a brush. Painter offers an exciting pressure-sensitive brush—the Add Grain Brush—that allows you to paint grain onto your images. To begin, choose the Photo brushes icon in the Brushes palette and select the Add Grain Brush variant. Choose a texture in the Papers section of the Art Materials palette, scale it if necessary and brush lightly onto your image. For a more subtle effect, reduce the Opacity of the brush in the Controls:Brush palette.

Creating a shallow depth of field. By softening the background of an image, you can simulate the shallow depth of field that you'd get by setting your camera at a low *f*-stop. Select the area you want to soften and feather the selection by choosing Select, Feather to avoid an artificial-looking edge. Then choose Effects, Focus, Soften.

Smearing, smudging and blurring. To smoothly smear pixels in the image, choose the Just Add Water variant of Liquid, varying Opacity (in the Controls:Brush palette) between 70% and 100%. To smudge the image, while bringing out texture chosen in the Papers section of the Art Materials palette, choose the Smudge variant of Liquid. For a "wet oil" effect, try the Distorto variant of Liquid. To softly blur an area of the image, use the Blur variant of the Photo brushes set to a low Opacity (about 20%).

Sharpening. Painter's Sharpen feature (Effect, Focus, Sharpen) gives you control equivalent to unsharp masking on a drum scanner. (Unsharp masking sharpens the edges of elements in an image.) Use it to give definition to a selected area of interest, or to an entire image as a final step in preparing for output. To sharpen an area in an image using a brush, choose the Sharpen variant of the Photo brush. This brush puts sharpening (very similar to the Effects, Focus, Sharpen command) on the tip of a brush.

Retouching. The Straight Cloner and Soft Cloner variants of the Cloners brush work like Photoshop's Rubber Stamp tool in Clone

To add a mysterious gold spotlight to this woman's portrait, we used Effects, Surface Control, Apply Lighting. We modified the Center Spotlight by changing the Light Color from white to gold. To make the spotlight softer, we decreased the Exposure from 1.00 to .85.

Aligned mode to reproduce imagery; use the Shift/Control key as you would Photoshop's Alt/Option key to sample an area (even in another image), then reproduce that image (centered at the point of sampling) wherever you paint. The Straight Cloner variant reproduces imagery without changing it; to clone imagery with a soft edge and low opacity (like an Airbrush) use the Soft Cloner variant of Cloners.

ADVANCED TECHNIQUES

It often takes a lot of time and trial-and-error to get cool effects in-camera or in the darkroom. Some third-party plug-in filters do an adequate job of replicating these effects, but Painter gives you more control than you can get with filters alone.

Here's a short guide on how to use Painter to re-create traditional photographic techniques, starting with simpler, in-camera ones and progressing to more complex darkroom procedures.

Motion blur. You can use the camera to blur a moving subject by using a slower shutter speed or jittering (shaking) your hands while you hold the camera, or you can blur the background by panning with the subject. (See "Simulating Motion" on page 182 to read about a versatile motion-blur technique that involves using an additional layer.)

To create the look of "camera jitter," just as if you had moved the camera while taking a picture, choose Effects, Focus, Camera Motion Blur. When the dialog box appears, drag in the image (not the Preview), to specify the camera's direction and distance of movement. Dragging farther in the image will create a wider blur. To move the origin of the movement along the path of motion, adjust the Bias slider.

Lens filters and special film. To re-create in-camera tinting effects achieved with special films or colored filters, use Effects, Surface Control, Color Overlay. If you want to mimic the effect of a graduated or spot lens attachment (partially colored filters), choose a gradation and fill your image (Effects, Fill) with the gradation at a reduced opacity. (You may need to add contrast to your image afterwards with Effects, Tonal Control, Equalize.)

Shooting through glass. With Painter's Glass Distortion effect or Glass Distortion dynamic layer you can superimpose glass relief effects (using a paper texture or any other image) on your photo. A small amount of this feature adds texture to an image; larger amounts can make an image unrecognizable! To apply the effect directly to your image choose Effects, Focus, Glass Distortion. To make a Glass Distortion dynamic layer for your image, in the Objects palette click the left triangle on the Dynamic Layers section bar to open the section, then choose Glass Distortion from the list and click the Apply button. (See Phil Howe's work with Glass Distortion in the gallery at the end of this chapter.)

This classic solarization was created by merging positive and negative clones of the same image using Effects, Fill, Fill With Clone Source. The purple tone was added with Effects, Tonal Control, Color Overlay.

Using Effects, Surface Control, Express Texture to get the effect of a line conversion using a straight-line screen. We used Line 40 from Simple Textures in the Paper Texture Libraries folder on the Painter 6 Application CD-ROM.

PHOTO: PHOTODISC

We posterized this Craig McClain photo using a Color Set of "desert" colors and Effects, Tonal Control, Posterize Using Color Set.

PHOTO: CRAIG MCCLAIN

The original photo of a kelp frond had strong contrast, contributing good detail for this embossed image.

PHOTO: PHOTODISC

Lighting effects. Use Painter's Apply Lighting feature (under Effects, Surface Control) to add subtle or dramatic lighting to a scene.

Multiple exposures. Whether created in camera (by underexposing and shooting twice before advancing the film) or in the darkroom (by "sandwiching" negatives or exposing two images on a single sheet of paper), it's easy to reproduce the effect of multiple exposures by using layers or clones in Painter.

Solarization. Painter's Express Texture (Effects, Surface Control) command is a great way to re-create darkroom solarization. Read about a Painter version of a "classic" solarization on page 190.

Line screen. Instead of developing your image in the darkroom onto high-contrast "line" or "lith" paper, try getting a similar effect in Painter. Choose a lined paper texture from the Simple Textures library (in the Paper Texture Libraries folder on the Painter 6 Application CD-ROM), or make your own using the Make Paper dialog box found in the menu accessed from the Papers section bar in the Art Materials palette. (Read more about the Make Paper feature in Chapter 7's introduction.) Next, choose Effects, Surface Control, Apply Screen, Using Paper to get a two- or three-color effect with rough (aliased) lines. Or try Effects, Surface Control, Express Texture, Using Paper to get a broader range of color, more subtle control and smoother, anti-aliased lines. Turn to "Toning with Textures," on page 191 to read about using Express Texture to apply colored, textured effects to an image.

Posterizing an image. Painter lets you limit the number of colors in your image via posterization. To apply a posterization directly to your image choose Effects, Tonal Control, Posterize and enter the number of levels (usually 8 or fewer for best results). You can also perform a posterization using the Posterize dynamic layer. In the Objects palette, click the left triangle on the Dynamic Layers section to open it. Then select Posterize from the resource list. Click Apply and enter the number of levels. Because the Posterize plug-in layer is dynamic, you can experiment and preview the effect on your image until it's the way you like it.

You can get creative posterization effects by making a Color Set (see "Capturing a Color Set" in Chapter 2) and selecting Effects, Tonal Control, Posterize Using Color Set. This is a great way to unify photos shot under a variety of conditions.

Embossing and debossing. To emboss an image, raising its light areas, choose File, Clone; then Select All and delete, leaving a blank cloned image. Now choose Effects, Surface Control, Apply Surface Texture, and choose 3D Brush Strokes from the Using pop-up menu. To raise the dark areas instead of the light, click the Invert box *or* change the Using menu choice to Original Luminance. Images with a lot of contrast give the best results, and busy images work better if less important areas are first selected and softened using Effects, Focus, Soften.

Creating a Sepia-Tone Photo

Overview *Use gradient features to tint a color or black-and-white image; adjust the image's contrast and saturation.*

1a

The original photo

1b

Choosing the Sepia Tones gradation

2a

Applying the Sepia gradient

2b

Adjusting the contrast

2c

Neutralizing the browns

CHER THREINEN-PENDARVIS / PHOTO: CORBIS IMAGES

TYPICALLY FOUND IN IMAGES CREATED at the turn of the century, sepia-tones get their reddish-brown color cast in the darkroom when the photographer immerses a developed photo in a special toner bath. You can use Painter's gradation and tonal control features to quickly turn color or grayscale images into sepia-tones.

1 Tinting the image. Open a grayscale or color photo. In the Gradients section of the Art Materials palette, select the Sepia gradient from the resource list. Choose Express In Image from the pull-down menu at the right end of the Gradients section bar. (Read more about gradients in Chapter 2.) Click OK in the dialog box to tint your image with shades of brown. (You can also use a similar procedure to turn a color image into shades of gray, but make sure the back and front Color rectangles in the Colors section of the Art Materials palette are black and white, respectively, and choose Two-Point in the Gradients section.)

2 Adjusting the white and black points. If you're working with an image that has poor contrast, you can adjust the white and black points by choosing Effects, Tonal Control, Equalize (Ctrl/⌘-E). When the dialog box appears, the image will be automatically adjusted so that its lightest tones are pure white and its darkest ones are pure black. The automated contrast was too dramatic for our taste, so we decreased contrast by dragging the white point slider to the right to 14.9 and the black point slider to the left to 96.0.

3 Desaturating the image. We wanted to emulate the mild tinting effect usually used for traditional sepia-tones, so we desaturated the image using Effects, Tonal Control, Adjust Colors, dragging the Saturation slider to the left to –44. Set the Hue Shift at 0% and experiment with the Saturation slider until you see the effect you want in the Preview window and click OK. 🖊

180   CHAPTER 6: ENHANCING PHOTOS, MONTAGE AND COLLAGE

Selective Coloring

Overview *Open a color photo and copy it to a layer; desaturate the layer; paint with a brush to erase areas of the layer mask and reveal the underlying color photo.*

CHER THREINEN-PENDARVIS / PHOTO: PHOTODISC

The original color image

Using the Adjust Colors dialog box to desaturate the floater to black-and-white

Painting on the layer's mask to reveal the color image underneath

IF YOU WANT TO FOCUS ATTENTION on a particular element in a color photo, you can turn the photo into a black-and-white image and then selectively add color back into it for emphasis. Here's a way to use Painter's layers and brushes to "paint" color on an image.

1 Copying the image. Open a color photo and choose Select, All (Ctrl/⌘-A). Choose the Layer Adjuster tool, hold down the Alt/Option key and click on the image. This creates a layer with an exact copy of the original image.

2 Desaturating the layer. Now use the layer to make the image appear black-and-white: Choose Effects, Tonal Control, Adjust Colors, drag the Saturation slider all the way to the left, and click OK.

3 Revealing color in the underlying image. To allow parts of the color image to show through, use a brush to erase portions of the "black-and-white" layer's mask. In the Brushes palette, choose the Digital Airbrush variant of the Airbrushes and choose white in the Colors section (Art Materials palette). In the Masks section of the Objects palette, select the layer mask. (To view the layer in color while editing its mask, keep the layer mask eye icon shut.) As you paint with white to erase the mask in the area you wish to colorize, the color will appear. If you want to turn a color area back to grayscale, choose black from the Colors section and paint on the area. 🖌

FINE-TUNING YOUR MASK

It's difficult to tell if you've completely covered (or erased) areas when working on a mask with a brush. To view a layer mask in black-and-white, select the layer in the Layers section, and in the Masks section, open the Mask eye icon. Choose the Digital Airbrush (Airbrushes) or the Scratchboard Tool (Pens), and paint directly on the mask to clean it up. (Black creates an opaque mask that hides the layers below; pure white creates no mask, allowing the layers below to show through; shades of gray create a semi-transparent mask.) To switch back to color view, click the layer mask eye icon shut.

Painting on the layer mask using the Digital Airbrush variant of Airbrushes

Simulating Motion

Overview *Open a color photo and copy to a layer; apply Motion Blur to the copy; paint with a brush to erase areas of the layer mask and reveal the original photo.*

CREATING A SENSE OF MOVEMENT for a subject *after* the film is out of the camera is easy with Painter's layers and Motion Blur command. We blurred a layer, then erased some areas to reveal the untouched image underneath. The benefits of this method over applying effects to selections are that you can control the amount of the effect by adjusting opacity of the layers, you can simultaneously add effects other than a blur (such as lighting and texture) and you are altering a copy leaving the original intact, and this makes it easy to correct errors.

The original photo

1 Copying the image. Open a color photo and choose Select, All (Ctrl/⌘-A). Using the Layer Adjuster tool, Alt/Option-click on the image. This creates a layer that's an exact copy of the original image.

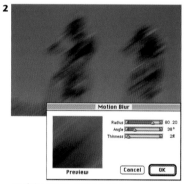

Applying Motion Blur to the layer

2 Blurring the layer. Select the layer by clicking on its name in the Layers section of the Objects palette and choose Effects, Focus, Motion Blur. To get a dramatic blur on our 1500-pixel-wide image, we set Radius to about 80, Angle to 31° (to complement the direction the bikers were moving) and Thinness to 2%. Experiment with different Angle settings for your particular image.

Erasing the layer mask on the face and arm

3 Painting on the mask. To allow parts of the original image to show through, use a brush to erase portions of the layer's mask. In the Brushes palette, choose the Digital Airbrush (Airbrushes) and choose white in the Colors section of the Art Materials palette. Select the layers in the Layers section and in the Masks section and select the layer mask. As you paint the layer mask in the area you wish to erase, the underlying image will appear. If you want to restore an area of the blurred layer, choose black in the Colors section and paint on that area of the layer mask. To give the leading rider an illusion of more speed we erased the frontal blur, leaving long trails of motion blur behind her. We erased most of the blur on the second rider to give the illusion of slower speed.

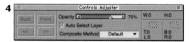

Adjusting the opacity of the blurred layer

4 Adjusting the opacity. To reduce the blur we made the layer slightly transparent by lowering the Opacity of the layer in the Layers section to 75%.

Zooming and Solarizing

Overview *Float a copy of the image, use Painter's Zoom Blur feature to zoom in on an area of the layer; paint the layer mask to accentuate the focal point; make a solarization by changing the Composite Method.*

1

The original photo of the volleyball players

The Zoom Blur dialog box after clicking in the image

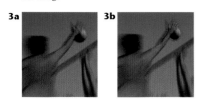

The zoom-blurred layer (left) and the mask retouched to reveal the sharp underlying image of the hand and ball (right)

The Opacity and Composite Method settings for the solarization

CHER THREINEN-PENDARVIS / PHOTO: CORBIS IMAGES

WITH PAINTER'S ZOOM BLUR feature you can create zoom and pan effects that rival results you can achieve when shooting with a zoom lens. Here we used Zoom Blur to elongate the subjects, adding to the excitement and illusion of speed during a volley. Afterwards, to add more drama we changed the photo into a mysterious "night scene."

1 Copying the image. Open a color photo and choose Select, All (Ctrl/⌘-A). Choose the Layer Adjuster tool and Option-click on the image. This creates a layer with an exact copy of the original image.

2 Blurring the layer. Select the layer by clicking on its name in the Layers section of the Objects palette and choose Effects, Focus, Zoom Blur. To get a moderate blur on our 600-pixel-wide image, we set the Amount to 31%. Set the focal point of the zoom by clicking in the image (not in the Preview). To create the elongated, distorted effect of zooming in, check the Zoom In box. Click OK.

3 Painting on the mask. To enhance the focal point of the image, we erased areas of the layer mask to reveal the underlying image, for instance, the ball and hands. To allow parts of the original image to show through, use a brush to erase portions of the layer's mask. Choose white in the Colors section of the Art Materials palette and in the Brushes palette, choose the Digital Airbrush (Airbrushes). Select the layer in the Layers section of the Objects palette, switch to the Masks section and select the layer mask. As you paint the layer mask, the underlying image will appear.

4 Making a solarization. Next, we created a solarized "night scene" from the image by selecting the layer in the Layers section, choosing the Layer Adjuster tool and changing the Composite Method to Difference in the Layers section. To make the layer slightly transparent, allowing the original colored image to show through, we also lowered the Opacity of the layer to 85%.

Making a Selective Correction

Overview *Use a dynamic layer to adjust the brightness and contrast of an image; convert the dynamic layer to an image layer; make a selection; use the selection to remove a portion of the layer.*

CHER THREINEN-PENDARVIS / PHOTO: CORBIS IMAGES

1a

PHOTO: CORBIS IMAGES

The original photograph

1b

Making a Brightness and Contrast dynamic layer

1c

Increasing the Brightness by moving the lower slider to the right

HERE'S A USEFUL IMAGE-EDITING TECHNIQUE that combines a dynamic layer Brightness-and-Contrast adjustment and a selection. Using a dynamic layer has the advantage of being able to make a correction and dynamically preview the changes on the image without harming the image. To enhance the focal point of this image—shining more light onto the faces—we selectively lightened the shaded window area.

1 Editing brightness and contrast with a dynamic layer.
Open a grayscale or color photo. To make a Brightness and Contrast dynamic layer for your image, begin by clicking the left triangle on the Dynamic Layers section in the Objects palette and when the section opens, choose Brightness and Contrast from the resource list. Click the Apply button on the Dynamic Layers section to generate a dynamic layer covering your entire image. (Turn to "Using Dynamic Layers" on page 147 on Chapter 5, to read about the basics of using dynamic layers.)

When the dialog box appears, adjust the sliders and preview the correction in your image. To see more detail on the faces, we moved the Brightness (lower) slider to the right, making the image lighter. We also slightly increased the contrast by moving the Contrast slider (upper) to the right.

We only wanted the Brightness-and-Contrast adjustment to affect the shaded area within the window, so we planned to make a mask and load a selection that we could use to isolate a portion of the layer. To use a selection on a dynamic layer, the layer must first be converted to an image layer. When you've finished making adjustments, convert the dynamic layer to an image layer as follows: Click the right triangle on the Dynamic Layers section bar to open the menu and choose Commit. Next, hide the layer temporarily: In the Layers section of the Objects palette, click the layer's eye icon shut, then click on the Canvas layer's name.

2

The active selection around the window

3a

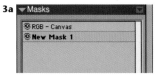

Selecting the mask to view it as a red overlay

3b

Viewing the mask as a red overlay before editing and feathering

3c

The completed mask

4b

Detail from the final corrected image with more detail in the shaded areas

2 Making a selection and saving it as a mask. In our example, when we were satisfied with Brightness-and-Contrast adjustment in the window area, the blue wall was too light and flat. In preparation for using only the window area of the adjusted layer, we made a selection of the window area on the image canvas and saved it as a mask. In the Tools palette, choose the Pen tool or Lasso and make a selection. (We drew a shape with the Pen tool and converted it to a selection using Shapes, Convert to Selection.) When you've completed the selection, choose Select, Save Selection to save it into the Masks section of the Objects palette.

3 Editing and feathering the mask. To get a clear view of the mask as we edited and feathered it, we worked back and forth between viewing it as a red overlay (on the image) and as a black-and-white mask. We used the Digital Airbrush variant of the Airbrushes and white paint to spray soft edges along the top of the window and added a 3-pixel feather to the entire mask to give it a soft transparent edge. If your mask needs editing, select the mask name in the Masks section. To view your mask as a red overlay, click both the mask eye icon and the RGB-Canvas eye icon open. To view the mask in black-and-white, click the RGB-Canvas eye icon closed. With the mask active you can give it a soft edge by applying feathering as follows: Click the right triangle on the Masks section bar to open the menu and choose Feather Mask. Type a feather width in the field and click OK. Now shut the mask eye icon and click on the RGB-Canvas in the Masks section to prepare for the next step.

4 Using the selection to edit the layer. In our example, we used the selection to remove the area on the Brightness-and-Contrast layer outside the window. Now that your mask is complete, load the selection from the mask, as follows: In the Layers section, click on the Brightness-and-Contrast layer name to select it, and also open its eye icon to display the layer. Choose Select, Load Selection and choose the mask that you saved (New Mask 1) to isolate the area on the layer. To reverse the selection (so that the area outside of the window is selected) and to remove the unwanted portion of the layer, choose Select, Invert and press the Backspace/Delete key. 🖌

USING SELECTIONS WITH LAYERS

You can have several masks saved in the Masks section of the Objects palette and choose any one of them to load as a selection to then isolate paint or effects on any image layer. Choose Select, Load Selection and pick the selection you need from the menu. In the Layers section of the Objects palette, click on the name of the layer with which you want to work.

Hand-Tinting a Photo

Overview *Retouch a black-and-white photo; use selection and masking tools to isolate areas of the photo; tint the image using Water Color brushes.*

Using Equalize to adjust the tonal range of the black-and-white photo

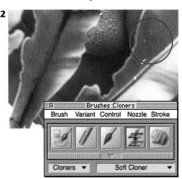

Repairing scratches with the Soft Cover variant of the Cloners brush

Image with the background mask visible

CHER THREINEN-PENDARVIS

HAND-TINTING IS A GREAT WAY to give an old-fashioned look to a black-and-white print. It also gives the sensitive artist plenty of opportunities to add depth to an image using hues, tints and shades. To create *Rell with Bird's Nest Fern,* we hand-dyed a portrait of Hawaiian friend Rell Sunn using Painter's Water Color brushes, applying transparent color without disturbing the existing photo.

1 Equalizing the image. To preserve shadow detail during tinting, choose a light image without solid shadows or correct the tonal range after scanning as described below. We scanned our 8 x 10-inch print at 100%, 150 pixels per inch. The print was slightly overexposed, so we darkened it, taking care to preserve detail in the shadows. If your image needs tonal correction, select Effects, Tonal Control, Equalize (Ctrl/⌘-E). Your image will be automatically adjusted when the dialog box appears. To obtain a more subtle result, experiment with spreading the triangular sliders on the histogram; or move them closer together for a stronger effect. Use the Brightness slider to make the gray tones brighter or darker overall. The adjustments will be reflected in your image.

STARTING WITH SEPIA

Before tinting an image, try giving it a sepia-tone: Select the Sepia gradient in the Gradients section of the Art Materials palette, click the right triangle on the Gradients section bar and choose Express in Image before equalizing. Use Edit, Fade for a subtle look (try 50–75%).

3b

The Masks section, showing mask
visibility settings for Figure 3a

4a

Tinting the background with the Large
Simple Water variant. The mask (green
marquee) protected the foreground.

4b

Flat transparent washes on the foreground

5

Adding color and highlights to the shirt

2 Retouching scratches. To touch up scratches, use the Magnifier tool to enlarge the area that needs retouching. Choose the Soft Cloner variant of Cloners. Establish a clone source by Control-clicking (Shift-clicking in Windows) on your image near the area that needs touch-up, then begin painting. A crosshair cursor shows the origin of your sampling. If necessary, re-establish a clone source as you work.

3 Making selections and a mask. Before beginning the tinting process, make several selections to isolate areas of the image that you want to tint with different colors. Choose the Pen tool and draw a shape path around an area you want to isolate. When you've finished drawing the path, click the Make Selection button in the Controls:Shape Design palette. To smooth the edges of the selection, choose Select, Feather and set a 1-pixel feather. As you make each selection, it's a good idea to store it in the Masks section of the Objects palette for future use: Choose Select, Save Selection.

To isolate larger areas you may want to paint a mask with a brush; to do this, in the Masks section, click the New button. To view the new mask as a red overlay on top of your image—as you paint it—select the mask in the Masks section and open its eye icon. Now choose black in the Colors section of the Art Materials palette and select a brush. We used the Scratchboard Tool variant of Pens to isolate the background from the figure. When you're finished painting the mask, feather it 1 pixel to smooth its edge, as follows: click the right triangle on the Masks section bar to open the menu, choose Feather Mask and set the amount of Feather. Click OK.

4 Applying transparent color. Turn off the mask eye icon and select the RGB-Canvas by clicking on its name. Choose a color and the Simple Water variant of Water Color. (The Simple Water variant is the fastest Water Color brush.) Choose Select, Load Selection to activate a selection, then apply strokes to your image. The strokes are Wet Paint, which is separate from other media such as the Pens and Pencils variants. Wet Paint is turned on whenever you use a Water Color brush.

5 Emphasizing the area of interest. After you've painted color washes, look at the overall balance and color density of your image. Add more or brighter color to the areas that you want to emphasize and apply darker or less saturated colors to make other areas appear to recede. For detail work, make the Simple Water smaller using the Size slider on the Controls:Brush palette. To remove color from over-saturated areas, use the Wet Eraser variant of Water Color, adjusting its Opacity setting in the Controls:Brush palette as you work.

If your coloring extends for more than one work session, save your image in RIFF format to keep the Wet Paint "wet." Choosing Canvas, Dry merges the Wet Paint with the Canvas, so do this when you're finished tinting. If you dry your image and then want to add more color, you can add more Water Color brushstrokes and chose Canvas, Dry again. For a complete example of this *glazing* technique, turn to "Glazing with Watercolor" in Chapter 3.

Blending a Photo

Overview *Open a photo and clone it; use the Just Add Water variant of Liquid to smear pixels in the image; restore a portion of the original with the Soft Cloner variant of Cloners.*

Hathaway's original photo of the dogs

Choosing the Just Add Water variant of the Liquid brush

Making loose strokes with the Just Add Water variant at 40% opacity

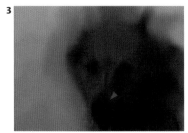

Partially restoring the dog's face using a low-opacity Soft Cloner variant of Cloners

TO CREATE THE EXPRESSIONISTIC *DOGS OF THE SURF*, Andrew Hathaway used Painter's Just Add Water brush to paint directly onto a clone of one of his photographs, transforming it into an intense, emotionally charged abstract painting. He gave the piece a touch of realism with a Cloners brush, using it to restore a hint of the original photo to the clone.

1 Choosing a subject and making a clone. Open your photo in Painter, then choose File, Clone to make a copy of your image to alter. Hathaway chose one of his own photos—an image of two dogs running toward him on the beach—then cloned it.

2 Blending with a Water brush. Hathaway used the Just Add Water variant of Liquid; since it uses the Soft Cover submethod and doesn't show paper texture, it's the smoothest of the blending brushes. For a more subtle smearing effect, you may want to reduce the Opacity in the Controls:Brush palette. To make more expressive strokes, with the brush size changing as you vary pressure on the stylus, in the Size section of the Brush Controls palette, move the Min Size slider to about 15%. Now, make some strokes on your clone. Hathaway painted energetic, angled, smeary strokes on the clone to emphasize the focal point and perspective in the foreground; then he smeared the background into more abstract shapes. He modified his brush as he worked, varying Size between 10 and 30 pixels, and lowering the Opacity to 30–40%.

3 Partially restoring from the original. As a last step, Hathaway used the Soft Cloner variant of the Cloners brush with a very low opacity (5%) to subtly restore the foreground dog's face. Try this on your clone. Use the Soft Cloner brush to bring the original back into the blurred areas of your image. Experiment with the Opacity slider in the Controls:Brush palette until you find a setting that suits your drawing style and pressure.

Cloning a Portrait

Overview *Retouch a photo and soften background detail; clone the image with brushes; paint details by hand; add texture.*

1a

The original photograph

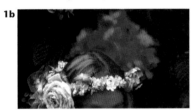

1b

Using darker colors to paint over the busy flowers in the background

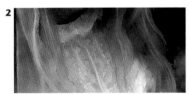

2

Adding hand-painted details to the hair

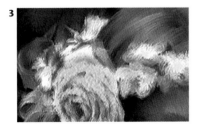

3

Adding relief to the brushwork with Apply Surface Texture Using Image Luminance

LAUREL BECKER

PAINTERLY CLONING IS A GREAT WAY to add natural atmosphere to photos. To create *Flower Girl*, Laurel Becker began by retouching a photo. Then she enhanced a clone of the photo by painting expressive brushstrokes and adding texture. When cloning, after blocking in the image, add hand-painted details, highlights and shadows.

1 Scanning, adjusting and retouching. Becker scanned an 8 x 10-inch photo at 100% and 150 ppi. Then she bumped up the image contrast using Effects, Tonal Control, Brightness /Contrast. To focus attention on the girl, she selected the background and "played down" the busy foliage details. If your background is busy, consider making a selection and using Effects, Focus, Soften to blur details or paint over areas with darker colored brushstrokes, as Becker did. (For information about making selections, turn to Chapter 4.)

2 Cloning and painting. Next, Becker cloned the photo (File, Clone). For this portrait, she chose Basic Paper in the Papers section of the Art Materials palette and the Captured Bristle variant of Brushes. Before beginning to paint, she checked the Clone Color box in the Colors section (Art Materials), to sample color from the original image. Then she painted over the entire clone. As she worked, she sized the brush using the Size slider on the Controls:Brush palette. She used a larger brush while painting loose strokes behind the girl and a tiny brush to paint the details on the face, dress and hair. She turned off Clone Color, then painted brighter highlights on the cheeks, nose, eyes, chin and lips, her brush following the contours of the forms.

3 Adding texture. After she was finished painting, Becker added relief and texture to her brushwork using two applications of Effects, Surface Control, Apply Surface Texture: The first, Using Image Luminance, Amount 20% and Shine 0%; the second, Using Paper, Amount 20% and Shine 0%. She left other settings at their defaults.

Making a Custom Solarization

Overview *Use Express Texture on positive and negative clones of an image; merge the images by filling with a Clone Source.*

1

The original image after equalizing (left), and the negative clone

2

Creating black-and-white positive (left) and negative versions of the clones using Express Texture

3

Merging the positive and negative images

4

Adjusting the image's brightness and contrast

IN THE DARKROOM, SOLARIZATION OCCURS when a negative is exposed to a flash of light during the development process, partially reversing the photo's tonal range. To achieve this effect digitally, we tested other image-processing programs and filters, and found that we got the most control and detail using Painter's Express Texture feature. This technique gives you a lot of control over the image's value contrast and it frequently creates a glowing edge-line effect where contrasting elements meet.

1 Making positive and negative clones. Open an image with good value contrast, then choose Effects, Tonal Control, Equalize (Ctrl/⌘-E) to increase its tonal range. Choose File, Clone twice. Make one of the clones into a color negative by selecting Effects, Tonal Control, Negative.

2 Making black-and-white separations. Use Painter's Express Texture feature to convert both clones to black-and-white: Choose Effects, Surface Control, Express Texture, and select Image Luminance from the pop-up menu. Experiment with the sliders and click OK. Repeat the process for the second clone. We set Gray Threshold to 72%, Grain to 72% and Contrast to 160%. These settings helped emphasize the gradient effect in the sky.

3 Merging the two exposures. Choose File, Clone Source and choose the positive clone. Now fill the negative image with a percentage of the positive (the "flash of light"): With the negative window active, choose Effects, Fill, Clone Source. Set the Opacity slider between 40% and 60%.

4 Pumping up the tonal range. To achieve a broader tonal range while maintaining a silvery solarized look, we selected Effects, Tonal Control, Brightness/Contrast. We increased the contrast (the top slider) and decreased the brightness. 🐛

Solarizing Color

Overview *Use Correct Colors, Color Correction to make positive and negative tones; enhance the solarization by compositing a desaturated layer.*

EARLY DARKROOM SOLARIZATIONS were black-and-white, but today they include color as well. Classic color solarizations have solid areas of color and glowing gradations with elements often separated by edge-line effects. To achieve the effect of a color solarization digitally, we used Painter's Color Correction, Freehand Curve function.

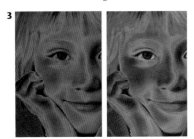

The color photograph from Corbis Images

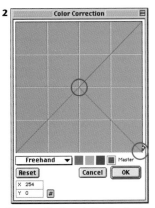

Setting the curve for the solarization in the Color Correction dialog box

The color image on the Canvas (left) and the desaturated layer (right)

1 Choosing an image. For the best results, open an image with good value contrast and color.

2 Solarizing the image. Choose Tonal Control, Correct Colors. When the Color Correction dialog box appears, from the pull-down menu choose Freehand. As you'll notice in the Color Correction dialog box, the standard curve is a diagonal line from lower left to upper right. Making an inverted "V" shaped curve will create both positive and negative tones in an image. Press the Shift key and click in the center, then in the lower right corner to snap the line into an inverted "V." If you have trouble making the "V" shape, click the Reset button and begin again. To achieve a broader tonal range in the solarization, we selected Effects, Tonal Control, Brightness/Contrast and subtly increased the contrast (top slider).

3 Enhancing the solarization. We wanted to achieve more dramatic tone and color in our image, so we copied the solarized image to a layer that we could use to intensify the effect. Open the Layers section of the Objects palette by clicking the left arrow on the section bar. Choose Select, All (Ctrl/⌘-A), press the Alt/Option key then choose Select, Float.

Now, to make the image on the layer gray, while preserving its tonality, choose Effects, Tonal Control, Adjust Colors and move the Saturation slider all the way to the left. (Leave the Hue and Value sliders at 0.) To give the solarization richer colors and tones, we composited the gray layer with the colored image on the Canvas using the Luminosity Composite Method in the Layers section. For different color effects, experiment with other Composite Methods such as Pseudocolor and Darken.

Toning with Textures

Overview *Use Painter's Express Texture feature to make two line conversions of a color image; colorize the two images and merge them into a single file.*

CHER THREINEN-PENDARVIS / PHOTO: PHOTODISC

The original photo

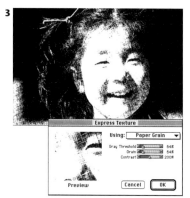

Scaling down the Angle Weave texture

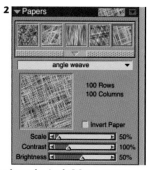

Express Texture settings for Light Exposure

CONVERTING CONTINUOUS-TONE PHOTOGRAPHS into custom line art effects—like mezzotints, etch tones and straight-line screens—can be accomplished either in the darkroom or with a graphic-arts camera using a screen made of film printed with a textured pattern. There are digital plug-in filters that give similar results, although they often eliminate much of the original's fine detail. By using Painter's Express Texture feature on two separate, textured exposures and then "sandwiching" them, you can retain more highlight and shadow detail during the conversion process than through any other digital means.

1 Selecting an image and cloning. Open a file with good tonal balance and contrast. Make two clones of this file—by choosing File, Clone twice. Save and name one clone "Light Exposure," and the other "Dark Exposure."

2 Choosing a texture. Select a paper texture that resembles the screen effect you wish to achieve. To get a random line effect, we chose Angle Weave loaded from the Wild Textures library (located in the Paper Texture Libraries folder, on the Painter 6 CD-ROM); to preserve detail in our 738-pixel-wide image, we scaled the texture to 50%.

3 Making a light exposure. To create a light, "overexposed" image that brings out shadow detail, click on the Light Exposure clone to make it active. Choose Effects, Surface Control, Express Texture, Using Paper. Drag all three sliders to the left and experiment to see which settings bring out the most shadow detail: We got the best results in our image by setting Gray Threshold to 64%, Grain to 64% and Contrast to 200%.

4 Making a dark exposure. Next, create an "underexposed" image—dark, with texture visible in the midtones and highlights. Select the Dark Exposure clone and again choose Effects, Surface Control, Express Texture. Drag all three sliders farther to the right,

4

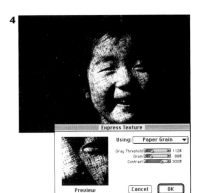

Express Texture settings for Dark Exposure

5

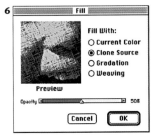

Applying a brown-to-white gradation to Dark Exposure (left) and a brown-to-tan gradation to Light Exposure

6

Filling Dark Exposure with Light Exposure

near their original (default) settings of 110%, 80%, 300%. We got good results by setting Gray Threshold to 112%, Grain to 88% and Contrast to 300%.

5 Coloring the clones. Tinting the two clones before merging them gives richer tonal depth to the final image, than coloring it after merging the images. Start by selecting the Two-Point gradation in the Gradients section of the Art Materials palette and choose colors for the front and back Color rectangles in the Colors section. Next, choose Express in Image from the Gradient section's menu, and click OK. We applied a brown-to-white gradation to Dark Exposure, and a brown-to-tan gradation to Light Exposure.

6 Combining the images. Painter offers many ways to blend images; we got the best results on our example by filling with a Clone Source. Begin by making Light Exposure the Clone Source by choosing File, Clone Source, Light Exposure. Now fill Dark Exposure with Light Exposure: With the Dark Exposure window active, select Effects, Fill. Click the Clone Source button and experiment with a 40–60% Opacity setting (we chose 50%). Click OK.

As a final step to increase the color and tonal range, we selected Effects, Tonal Control, Equalize (Ctrl/⌘-E). The effect was too strong, so we selected Edit, Fade at a 50% setting.

EXPRESSING TEXTURE

Painter's Express Texture dialog box gives you a lot of control over how to express a texture in an image. The Gray Threshold slider (which controls the overall brightness of the image) works interactively with the Grain Penetration slider (which controls the intensity of the grain in the image). These two sliders work best when kept relatively close together. The Contrast slider can give you a completely gray image (all the way to the left) or a black-and-white image (far right); the middle area is a good place to begin.

COLOR CHOICES

When you create a Two-Point gradation (for use with the Express in Image command), consider using analogous colors—those near each other on the color wheel. A gradation of complementary colors can result in muddy tones. For a wild effect, try choosing bright, saturated colors for the highlights.

TRADITIONAL LINE CONVERSION EFFECTS

Here's our best guess at the Painter textures required to emulate the look of a few traditional line conversions, using Express Texture on a single 553-pixel-wide color image. Use these examples as inspiration for your own experimentation. To give your image a greater tonal range before using Express Texture, you may want to use Effects, Tonal Control, Equalize.

Mezzotint: *Fine Grain (More Paper Textures library, from the Painter 6 CD-ROM), scaled to 50%*

Dry brush: *Wheat String (More Wild Textures library, from the Painter 6 CD-ROM), scaled to 65%*

Halftone: *Halftone 1 (More Paper Textures library, from the Painter 6 CD-ROM), scaled to 40%*

PHOTO: PHOTODISC

Creating a Montage Using Masks and Layers

Overview *Create masks for the component photos in Photoshop or Painter; copy them into a single document; use a brush to edit the layer masks when compositing them; paint on the final image.*

JOHN DISMUKES / CAPSTONE STUDIOS

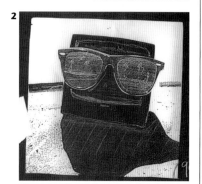

The original photos

The cut-and-pasted comp ready to be scanned and used as a template

WHEN CONTINENTAL CABLEVISION asked John Dismukes of Capstone Studios to illustrate a direct-mail piece, he and his team turned to Painter. He combined photographs and splashy color with loose airbrush and chalk brushstrokes to illustrate the theme "Can Summer in California Get Any Better?"

1 Gathering illustration elements. Begin by collecting all of the individual elements that you'll need for your illustration. Dismukes and his associates photographed separate images of clouds, a pair of sunglasses, ocean foam, palm trees, and a television on the sand. The photo negatives were scanned in Kodak Photo CD format.

2 Making a template from laser prints. Dismukes' team created a traditional comp by printing the individual elements, then photocopying them at different scales and assembling them using scissors and adhesive. They turned the completed comp into a template by scanning it at 72 ppi, opening it in Painter and sizing it to the final image size of 4 x 5 inches at 762 ppi, using Canvas, Resize. The template would act as a guide for Dismukes to accurately scale and position the various elements. If you choose to include this step, don't be concerned about the "bitmapping" that occurs when scanning the comp at a low resolution; when the composition is finished, the template will be completely covered by the source images.

3 Masking unwanted portions of the source images. Working in Photoshop, Dismukes used the Pen tool to cut masks for the sunglasses, ocean foam, palm trees and television on the

3

Three of Dismukes' Photoshop masks

4a

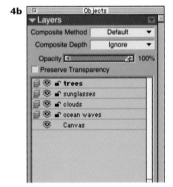

The glasses source file with active selection, ready to copy and paste or drag and drop into the background image

4b

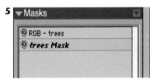

Bringing the layers into the composite file

5

Selecting the layer mask in the Masks section of the Objects palette

6a

Using the Digital Airbrush variant to erase the portion of the cloud layers's mask that covers the TV

beach. He converted each path to a selection, saved the selection as an Alpha Channel, then saved each image as an RGB TIFF file, including the alpha channel. You can accomplish the same result in Painter. Open one of your source photos and use the Pen or Quick Curve tool (Tools palette) to draw a shape around the desired portion of the image. When you're done, choose Shapes, Convert To Selection; then to save the selection as a mask, choose Select, Save Selection. View the selection as a mask by opening its eye icon in the Masks section of the Objects palette. You should see your image covered by a red overlay—the default color for the mask. To view only the mask in black-and-white, click the RGB-Canvas eye icon shut in the Masks section.

PHOTOSHOP MASKS

When you open a file in Painter that contains a mask created in Photoshop, the area that was masked in Photoshop now seems to be exposed in Painter. Don't despair: Although the mask appears inverted, it's functionally the same as it is in Photoshop. If you need to reverse the mask, highlight its name in the Masks section of the Objects palette, click the right triangle on the Masks section bar and choose Invert Mask.

FEATHERING A MASK

To add softness around a hard-edged mask, select it by clicking on its name in the Masks section (Objects palette). Click the right triangle on the Masks section bar and choose Feather Mask. Type in the amount of feather in pixels and click OK.

4 Compiling the source files. When you've finished masking the images, bring them into a single document. Open the template if you have one, or the photo that will become your background image. Choose the Layer Adjuster tool and in the Objects palette, click the left triangle on the Layers section bar to open the Layers section. Then open each of the source images and choose Select, Load Selection and Alt/Option-click on each selection to make a layer. Loading the selection and making a layer prepares Painter to export the item from the source image with its mask.

There are three ways to import source images into a composite file: Copying and pasting through the clipboard, performing a drag-and-drop, or using the File, Place command to bring the source image in as a reference layer. To paste using the clipboard, select the layer in the source image with the Layer Adjuster tool, choose Edit, Copy, then make the background image active and choose Edit, Paste. If your component images are approximately the right size, the easiest way is probably to drag-and-drop: Select the layer in the source image with the Layer Adjuster. Now use the Layer Adjuster to drag the masked item to the background image.

If you're working with large files, positioning and scaling can be accomplished much more quickly using reference layers. To import an image as a reference layer with a mask, save the source file in RIFF format (to preserve its mask), then choose File, Place, navigate to the source image and choose Open. In the Place dialog

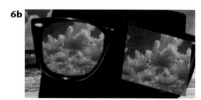

Compositing the clouds inside the glasses

Revealing the cloud layer around the tree

7

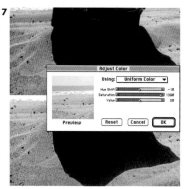

Using Adjust Colors to increase saturation in the image

8

Adding squiggles and lens glare (top) and smudges and blurs

box check the Retain Alpha checkbox and click in the image to place the layer. (For more information about reference layers, see "Using Reference Layers" on page 144 in Chapter 5.)

5 Putting the masks to work. To view the mask on a layer, select the layer in the Layers section, and in the Masks section open the layer mask's eye icon. To switch back to Color View, shut the layer mask's eye icon.

6 Positioning the layer and painting on its mask. First scale, rotate and position one layer on top of another and make sure that the top layer is selected in the Layers section. Now, fit the top element inside the element below it by using a brush to erase a portion of the top layer's mask, as follows: Begin by selecting the layer name in the Layers section, then click on the layer mask's name in the Masks section. Choose the Digital Airbrush variant of Airbrushes and choose white in the Colors section of the Art Materials palette. Begin painting around the edge of the top layer to erase part of its mask, making it appear "inside" of the layer beneath it. Paint with black to restore the mask.

When you've completed all compositing, turn off visibility for the template layer in your file by selecting its name in the Layers section and shutting its eye icon. Then make a copy of your image with the layers merged with the background by choosing File, Clone. This step gives you a lot of flexibility—you have an "original" with layers intact, and a "working image" (the clone) on which you can paint and make other adjustments.

7 Shifting colors. To make the image "pop" a bit more, Dismukes increased the color saturation. Choose Effects, Tonal Control, Adjust Colors, and experiment with the Hue Shift, Saturation and Value sliders to modify the colors in your image.

8 Painting on the photo montage. To transform the television into a lively caricature in vivid color, Dismukes first used the Digital Airbrush variant to add details such as glare on the glasses. He switched to the Impressionist variant of the Artists brush to paint on the sand and water, and then painted spontaneous, textured squiggles around the TV and on the sand and water with the Artist Pastel Chalk variant of Dry Media using the Big Canvas paper (loaded from the More Paper Textures library, in the Paper Texture Libraries folder, on the Painter 6 CD-ROM). As a final touch, Dismukes switched to the Grainy Water variant of Liquid. To smear while revealing texture, he changed the subcategory to Grainy Hard Cover in the General section of the Brush Controls palette and added the smudges and blurs on the sand and television.

Finishing the job. Using the same style, technique, tools and colors, Dismukes created similar illustrations on a smaller scale that were used throughout the brochure, as well as a border around the edge of the piece.

■ **Jeff Burke** and **Lorraine Triolo** of Burke/Triolo Productions created *Painted Sunflower* (left), as a promotional piece. The partners styled the still life, photographed it and scanned it. Then Burke opened the scanned photo in Painter. He used the Grainy Water variant of Liquid (on top of Basic Paper texture) to smear and blend edges of the flower and its shadow. To add hand-painted detail and texture, he used the Dry Media variants to paint subtle streaks and small dabs of color behind the stem and along the edge of the flower and shadow.

■ A national news report of a white buffalo born in the Plains of the Midwest was the inspiration for *White Buffalo* (bottom), by **Gary Clark**. Clark shot the buffalo, figures and tree photographs with a digital camera. Then he assembled two more source files: a landscape generated in Vista Pro and a sky built in Bryce. He copied and pasted all four source files into a large composite file as layers and made silhouette masks for the buffalo, tree and figures. Clark positioned the sky and landscape layers, then merged them with the Canvas using the Drop button in the Layers section of the Objects palette. To add interest to the landscape and sky, he cloned texture from a photo of grass into the image using a low-opacity Straight Cloner variant of Cloners. To add color to the tree, Clark cloned color from a scan of brightly colored paint swatches.

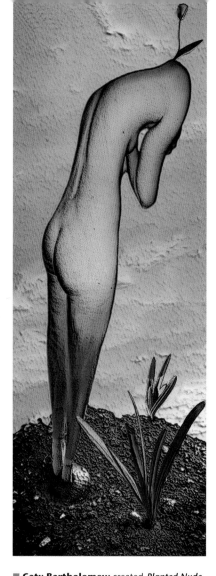

■ For this double-page illustration for IBM's *AS/400* magazine, **Jean Francois Podevin** began with conventional pencil sketches based on his own photographs. Podevin then collaborated with colleague **Larry Scher** on the computer. The team scanned Podevin's sketch and used it as a guide to position Podevin's Photo CD images. The image was composed and filter effects added in the DOS programs RIO and VIP, and then it was imported into Painter. Podevin retouched and painted on the image using the Airbrushes, Liquid and Dry Media brushes. To create the drop shadow of the final composite, the team selected the image, then copied it to a layer. The shadow layer was feathered, filled and moved behind the composite.

■ **Caty Bartholomew** created *Planted Nude* as a vivid symbol of personal growth. She envisioned a distorted nude that would express "growing pains" and incorporated a tulip as a symbol of hope. She began with some initial photo-compositing work in Photoshop. To avoid a slick, photographic look, she imported the nude into Painter and retouched the legs and bulb with Airbrushes variants, then stretched the figure disproportionately using Effects, Orientation, Scale. She cut and pasted the nude and other plants onto the dirt. To give texture and dimension to the piece, she used Effects, Surface Control, Apply Surface Texture twice: first using Image Luminance; then using Paper and a medium-rough paper texture.

■ Inspired by the beautiful, clear expression of love between two young people in this black-and-white photo, **Jeremy Sutton** created the colorful portrait *Love.* He began by scanning the photograph shot in the 1950s of a friend's parents. Then he made a clone (File, Clone). After deleting the contents from the clone, (Select, All, then Backspace/Delete), he filled the background of the clone with a dark color. Then he turned on Tracing Paper (Ctrl/⌘-T). Using saturated color, he freely painted with custom bristle brushes and airbrushes to develop the composition. To expressively blend and smear color, he used Liquid variants. Sutton continued to work back and forth, painting loosely, then blending brush strokes in the image. When the work was nearly complete, he added a few details from the original photo to the facial features of the subjects (for instance, their eyes), by switching to the Soft Cloner variant of the Cloners brush and carefully brushing over those areas.

■ **Philip Howe** was commissioned by Harry Hansen to create *Police,* a photo collage painting to promote positive aspects of law enforcement. The final piece—printed on canvas and enhanced with oil paints—is part of a traveling show of police art touring the United States. To build the image, Howe began with two source photos: a horizontal photo of a brick wall with a cast shadow of a motorcycle rider, and a vertical photo of a policeman standing against a brick wall. Beginning in Photoshop, Howe copied the rider image and pasted it into a copy of the vertical wall image as a layer. He worked back and forth between Photoshop and Painter as he retouched the brick areas above the standing figure's head to match the bricks of the top image. When the retouching was complete, Howe began the process of building relief on the background wall image in Painter. He applied Effects, Focus, Glass Distortion Using Image Luminance and the Refraction Map Type, using strong settings. Next, he opened the original vertical brick wall image and again applied Effects, Focus, Glass Distortion, Using Image Luminance and the Refraction Map type, this time using subtle settings. Finally, he selected the composite file and defined the subtly distorted image as the clone source (File, Clone Source.) Using an Airbrush Cloner variant, he cloned the subtle distortion onto areas of the image canvas to softly smooth out areas of the relief.

When Microsoft commissioned **Philip Howe** to illustrate their *Encarta CD-ROM Interactive Encyclopedia* packaging, he created a photo montage that included a transparent glass effect. Howe began by building two source files of the same size: the first a montage that incorporated an illustrated background, a time line and several photos; and a second image, a retouched cloud photo. To begin the crystal effect, he opened both the cloud image and the montage and made the montage the clone source (File, Clone Source). Working in the cloud image, he applied Effects, Focus, Glass Distortion, Using Original Luminance and the Refraction Map type to create the crystal. (The crystal effect appeared only where there were dark-and-light values in the montage clone source.) To combine both images, he cloned the montage into the crystal image, taking great care to preserve the crystal effect around the edges of the image. To further define the head against the clouds, he used white paint and an Airbrushes variant to paint a glow around the inside edge of the back of the head. Finally, to increase the glass effect, Howe used Effects, Surface Control, Dye Concentration, Using Original Luminance, keeping the montage as the clone source.

■ The work of **Laurence Gartel,** a pioneer of computer art and digital photography, has been exhibited in museums and galleries worldwide for over two decades. *Millenium Girl* is one in a series of images he created for a European exhibition. Gartel scanned each of the source photos into Photoshop and made selections to isolate a few of the subjects from their backgrounds. He opened a large new blank file, copied each source image and pasted it onto its own layer in the composite. Next, he opened the layered image in Painter and repositioned the layers with the Layer Adjuster tool until the piece felt balanced. Gartel painted on many of the layers. To emboss a few of the layers, he applied Effects, Surface Control, Apply Surface Texture, Using the Layer Mask (for instance, the painted areas in the lower middle of the work). Then he changed the Opacity and Composite Method in the Layers section of the Objects palette for a few of the layers (for instance, the seashells in the top of the work). Gartel feels that by combining images using different composite methods and opacities, an artist is sharing critical information—the image is in a translucent state, giving the viewer the opportunity to see each layer of imagery without losing the overall message. "Naturally, as a collagist, I like to pack an image with lots of pictures that add up to a full story. It's then up to the viewer to interpret," says Gartel.

■ **Ellie Dickson** began each of these
photo illustrations by scanning a black-
and-white photo in RGB-mode. In
Photoshop, she made loose freehand
selections with the Lasso and filled the
selections with tints of color (using Color
mode). Dickson opened the tinted image
in Painter and applied strokes with a low-
opacity Artist Pastel Chalk variant of Dry
Media, using the Soft Cover subcategory
for a smooth look. She softened the
Pastel strokes using the Just Add Water
variant of Liquid and intensified the
image's watery look with the Distorto
variant of Liquid. Finally, to emphasize
details in the images, she modified the 2B
Pencil variant of Pencils, changing its
method to Cover in the General section
of the Brush Controls palette, so she
could paint light over dark.

Dickson created *Sprawlers* (top), beginning
with a treasured family photo. For this
image, she used warm, saturated color and
painted loosely over the image with
modified Dry Media and Pencils variants.

For *Warren* (bottom), Dickson's client
requested a portrait print with a painterly
look. She began by scanning the aged and
torn photo: She opened the scan in
Photoshop, retouched it using the Rubber
Stamp tool and applied color tints. In
Painter, she painted over the image using a
custom Artist Pastel Chalk. Facial details
were important, so Dickson completed the
faces of the subjects using a very small
custom 2B Pencil variant. The final piece
was output to an Iris 3047 ink jet printer as
a 24 x 36-inch print on soft rag paper.

■ "Although the program is called Painter," says renowned photographer **Pedro Meyer**, "it's important not to exclude photography from its repertoire, given that the program can also be used effectively in that medium."

Both of the images on this page (taken with a Nikon D1 digital camera) reflect Meyer's observations in the year 2000, when he made many flights to and from Los Angeles and Mexico City. After making the montages, he adjusted their coloring, making each one look as much as possible like a real, single photo.

Meyer's photographic eye captures a moment at sunrise, in *Firstbird at Century City*. Intrigued by the scale of the buildings in the photo, he added the bird to it to distort scale and proportions.

Apocalypse LAX is a photo montage, that Meyer created to communicate the accelerated pace of modern life. "When we play with the proportions of photographic images, we add to the confusion about what is and what could be. Before digital photography it was very hard to make credible images which had these traits. It was quite complicated and time-consuming. These days, almost all it takes is the imagination to use the tools in ways which are more about the ideas than in showing off the virtues of the tools themselves," says Meyer.

■ An internationally acclaimed studio portraitist, **Phillip Stewart Charris** has created elegant and timeless likenesses of celebrities, individuals and families for over three decades. Known for his life-size portraits, which are printed, and then mounted on canvas, Charris has drawn inspiration from artists such as John Singer Sargent, Raphael and Rembrandt. The portrait *Pretty Little Girl* was photographed in his studio in Southern California. Then a transparency was scanned, saved as an RGB TIFF file and opened in Painter. To protect the figure while he worked on the background, Charris made a mask. Then, using expressive brushwork, he painted over the image background with the Sable Chisel Tip Water variant of Brushes (loaded from the Painter 5.5 Brushes library). To smooth some areas, he painted finer strokes with a low-opacity Just Add Water variant of Liquid. He used the brushes not to apply color, but to blend and smear pixels in the image in a painterly way. For the figure and clothing, Charris used smaller versions of the same two brushes. When brushing over the face and hair, he carefully painted with a small brush to preserve the important details. "The photographer must seek out the personality of the sitter, which lies beneath a veil that subtly alters the surface of the face. Piercing that veil to reveal the subject's character is something that, after the posing is taken care of, can only be done for a fraction of a second," says Charris.

■ *Napoleon's Keepers* began as a photographic idea for a poster about the famous cannon, but **Donal Jolley** wanted to create an image with more of a painterly feeling. He took the original photograph on the top of Kennesaw Mountain, Georgia in the fall after the leaves had fallen. The sky in the photo was a bright blue and the lighting was from a direct afternoon sun. The strong contrasts caused by the intense sunlight allowed him to see the forms in the photograph clearly.

Jolley made a mask for the blue color in the sky using the Color Mask command and saved it into the Masks section of the Objects palette. (For information about Color Mask, turn to "Using Color Mask" on page 131.) He loaded the sky selection (Select, Load Selection) and he pressed the Backspace/Delete key to remove the original sky. Then, working in

a source file, he created a new sky; he pasted in several photos of clouds he had taken. After positioning them, he removed unwanted areas on the layers by editing the masks on the layers with white paint. (For more information, turn to "Layers and Their Masks" on page 150.) Then he merged the layers and added more color to the clouds by painting over them with low-opacity Dry Media and Brushes variants. For a more painterly look, he blended areas of the clouds with the Just Add Water variant of the Liquid brush.

Working in the final composite file, Jolley pasted in the finished sky as a new layer in the Layers section of the Objects palette. Then he selected the Canvas in the Layers section and made it into a layer by clicking it with the Layer Adjuster tool. He painted over the image using several brushes, such as the Round Camelhair and Smeary Round variants of Brushes.

Jolley repainted the cannon with brass color, so it would look newer. Also, he painted over the landscape, eliminating many of the trees and replacing them with hand-painted trees.

For the smoke, he began by adding a new layer, then airbrushing using a low opacity Variable Spatter variant of the Airbrushes. For more a realistic smoke-like effect, he smeared it with the Just Add Water variant of Liquid. To complete the hazy look on the smoke, he set the layer's Composite Method to Magic Combine and reduced its Opacity to about 50% in the Layers section.

Once the basic composition was complete, he painted over the entire image with brushes to brighten color and add more contrast and texture. To finish, he added a few more details to the people.

7

EXPLORING
SPECIAL
EFFECTS

An innovative artist, Laurence Gartel combines digital photography with painting and special effects, as shown here in this detail of Coney Island Baby. *He used Liquid Metal layers, Apply Surface Texture and transparent Composite Methods to add depth and excitement to the piece. To view the complete painting, turn to page 235 in the gallery.*

PAINTER'S SPECIAL EFFECTS ARE SO NUMEROUS and complex that an entire book could be written about them alone. Because they're so powerful, there's much less need for third-party filters than with Photoshop or other image processors. But with that power comes complexity; some of these effects have evolved into "programs within the program." This chapter focuses on five of Painter's most frequently used "mini-programs"—Apply Surface Texture, Apply Lighting, Patterns, Glass Distortion and Mosaics plus several special effect dynamic layers—including Bevel World, Burn, Tear and Liquid Metal—along with a handful of other exciting effects.

ADDING EFFECTS WITH SURFACE TEXTURE

One of the most frequent "haunts" of Painter artists is the Effects, Surface Control, Apply Surface Texture dialog box. You'll find it used in a number of places throughout this book. The Surface Texture dialog box contains intricate, powerful controls, allowing you to apply paper textures to images, build realistic highlights and shadows for masked elements, and more. First, the Softness slider (located under the Using pop-up menu) allows you to create soft transitions, such as smoothing the edge of a mask or softening a texture application. Adding Softness can also increase the 3D effect produced when you apply Surface Texture Using Mask. And with the Reflection slider (bottom Material slider), you can create a reflection in your artwork based on another image or the current pattern.

Another very important Surface Texture control is the preview sphere, located below the image Preview. Think of the sphere displayed as a dome supporting lights above your image. Although the preview sphere seems to show a spotlight effect, any lights you set are applied evenly across the surface of your image.

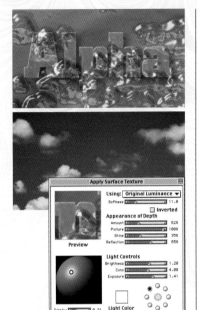

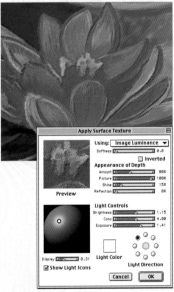

Creating the illusion of type under water (top), with Apply Surface Texture using Original Luminance and a reflection map. We applied the reflection using a clone source image of a cloudy sky (tinted red using Effects, Tonal Control, Adjust Colors to match the color in the type).

Creating textured, dimensional brush strokes with Apply Surface Texture using Image Luminance

Experiment with adding more lights to the preview sphere by clicking on the sphere. Adjust an individual light by selecting it, changing its color, and adjusting its Brightness and Conc (Concentration). Use the Exposure slider to control ambient light in the environment.

You can get some interesting effects by changing your color choices for the lights. For instance, if the area to be lit contains a lot of blue, you can add more color complexity by lighting with its complement, an orange-hued light.

Applying a reflection map. Reflections can add interest to shiny type and to other surfaces like glass or metal objects in your illustrations. The Reflection slider allows you to apply an image that you designate as a clone source to your illustration as a reflection. Open an image and make a selection or mask for the area where you'll apply the reflection. You can use a pattern as a source for a reflection map or you can open an image the same size as your working file (the current Pattern is applied automatically if you don't choose another image as clone source). (Turn to "Making an Environment Map" and "Applying a Environment Map," later in this chapter to read about how Michelle Lill builds custommade maps and applies them to her images. And for more inspiration, check out Michelle Lill's E-Maps folder on the Painter 6 Wow! CD-ROM, and the Painter Pattern libraries in the Pattern Libraries folder on the Painter 6 CD-ROM.)

Creating 3D effects. You can use Apply Surface Texture to enhance the surface of your image and give dimension to your brushstrokes. Image Luminance, in the Using pop-up menu, adds depth to brushstrokes by making the light areas appear to recede or "deboss" slightly. If you want to bring the light areas forward, check the Invert box. Experiment with the sliders to get the effect you desire. You can get a stronger 3D effect by clicking to add a second light (a bounce or a fill light) to the preview sphere with a lower Brightness or a higher Concentration (Conc) setting.

While painting Still Life, *Chelsea Sammel created drama in her image using Effects, Surface Control, Apply Lighting. Then she painted over some areas with Brushes variants. She finished the image with an application of Apply Surface Texture Using Paper and a rough paper texture.*

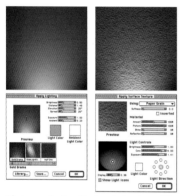

If you use Surface Texture in tandem with Apply Lighting, you'll get more dramatic results if you choose similar lighting directions for both commands.

SOFT LIGHTING TRANSITIONS

If you're using Apply Lighting on a selection, you'll get a softer transition between selected and unselected areas if you use Select, Feather (with a high feather setting) on your selections before you apply the light.

MOVING LIGHTS

To access the Lighting Mover in Painter 6, so you can move lights from the Painter Settings file into a new custom library, press Ctrl/⌘-Shift-L. To load the new library, click the Library button in the Apply Lighting dialog box.

Combining Surface Texture with other effects. Apply Surface Texture works especially well when combined with other Painter tools. "Creating an Impressionist Look," on page 215 uses a Glass Distortion dynamic layer and Surface Texture to add paint-like texture to a photo; John Derry used a combination of Glass Distortion and Surface Texture to give the illusion of refracted water in "Creating a Tidepool," on page 222; "Draping a Weave," on page 224, uses a powerful Glass Distortion displacement in combination with Surface Texture to achieve the look of draped fabric. And Steve Campbell used Surface Texture and Apply Lighting together to add gradations to textured areas while creating the illustration "Clouds I Never Saw in Kansas" on page 234 in the gallery.

ADDING DIMENSION WITH LIGHTING

Painter's *User Guide* gives a good description of how to adjust the controls under Effects, Surface Control, Apply Lighting. Here are some tips and practical uses for the tool.

Applying Lighting to unify an image. Like most of the Surface Control effects, applying lighting across an entire image can help to unify the piece. (If the lighting effect is too dramatic, try using Edit, Fade immediately afterwards to reduce it.)

Preventing hot spots. You can avoid "burnout" of lit areas by increasing the Elevation of the light, reducing the light's Exposure or Brightness, or giving the light a pastel or gray color.

Lighting within selections or layers. Add instant dimension to a selection or a layer by applying lighting within it.

Creating subtle gradient effects. To achieve colored gradient effects in an image, some artists prefer lighting with colored lights instead of filling with a gradient; they prefer the lighting command's smooth luminosity shifts over the more "mechanical" result usually achieved when using gradations.

Painting back into lit areas. For fine artists who want to achieve a more painterly effect, the Apply Lighting command can look a bit artificial. Chelsea Sammel (left) and Sharon Steuer (see Chapter 5's gallery) use Apply Lighting and then break up the lit area with brushstrokes, sampling color from the image as they work.

Creating softly lit backgrounds. On a white background, start with the Splashy Colors light effect. Increase the Brightness and Elevation on both colored lights until they form very soft-edged tinted circles on the background. Click in the Preview to add another light or two and change their colors. Move the lights around until the color, value and composition are working. Save and name your settings and click OK to apply the effect. Repeat this process two or three times, returning each time to your saved effect and making minor adjustments in light color, light position and other settings.

Painter's F/X brush variants are capable of creating many subtle or dramatic effects such as fire, glows and shattering, to name a few. See the gallery at the end of this chapter for other examples.

For Caterpillar, *Matt Dineen used the Furry Brush variant of the F/X brush to paint the caterpillar's colorful hair.*

Grunion Run *is an illustration for a calendar designed and illustrated by Kathleen Blavatt. She used several special effects brushes to paint the image. Beginning with a black-and-white pen drawing, she modeled the hills using the Pixel Dust variant of Pens (loaded from the Painter 5.5 Brushes library). She added sparkling texture to the sky using the Fairy Dust variant of the F/X brush (from Painter 6's default brush library). Blavatt painted the water with the Piano Keys variant of the Artists brush. She added textured brushstrokes to the sun's head using the Grain Emboss variant of the Impasto brush. To finish, she applied a colored KPT texture filter to the fish.*

EXPLORING PATTERNS

On the Patterns section bar in the Art Materials palette, there are commands that let you make seamless wrap-around pattern tiles. (To access the menu, click the right triangle on the Patterns section bar.) Once a pattern has been defined and is in the Patterns section, it becomes the default Clone Source when no other clone source is designated. You can apply a pattern to an existing image, selection or layer with Cloning brushes, with the Paint Bucket tool (by choosing Fill With: Clone Source in the Controls: Paint Bucket palette), with any of the special effects features that use a clone source (such as Original Luminance or 3D Brushstrokes), or by choosing to fill with a pattern or clone source (Ctrl/⌘-F). (The Fill dialog box shows a Pattern button if no clone source image is designated; if a clone source *is* available, a Clone Source button appears.) Use the pattern feature to create screen design backgrounds, textile design, wallpaper—anywhere you need repeating images.

To turn off a clone source so you can fill an image with the current pattern (if the clone source is another image), close the clone source image. If you've cloned from one place to another in the *same* image, click on a pattern in the Patterns section of the Art Materials palette to clear the clone source.

Defining a Pattern. When you choose Define Pattern, Painter creates a wrap-around for the pattern tile you create. Here's a great way to see it work. Make a new document that will become your pattern tile, click the right triangle on the Patterns section bar and choose Define Pattern from the menu. To create the pattern, choose the Image Hose icon in the Brushes palette (or use any brush). Select an Image Hose nozzle as follows: In the Art Materials palette's Nozzles section, click on a nozzle. Begin spraying across your image and beyond its edge. Notice how the hose images "wrap around" the edges of the pattern tile you've defined (so that when an area is filled with these pattern tiles, the edges match seamlessly).

Capturing a Pattern. To make and store a pattern image in the Patterns section, select an area of your document with the Rectangular Selection tool (or press Ctrl/⌘-A to select the entire image) and on the Patterns section bar, click the right triangle and choose Capture Pattern. To offset your pattern use the Horizontal and Vertical Shift options and the Bias slider to control the amount of the offset. Experiment with these settings to get nonaligned patterns—for example, to create a brick wall look, wallpaper or fabric.

Making a Fractal Pattern. You don't need an open document to use Make Fractal Pattern because choosing Make Fractal Pattern from the Patterns section bar menu automatically creates a pattern as a new file when you click OK. If you have a lot of memory

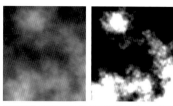

The evolution of a fractal pattern. The original pattern, made by choosing Make Fractal Pattern from the Patterns section menu (top left); a hard edge added with Effects, Surface Control, Express Texture Using Image Luminance (top right); the Earthen gradient applied via Express in Image (chosen by clicking the right triangle on the Gradients section bar (lower left); adjusting the Bias to 46% in the Express in Image dialog box (lower right).

allotted to Painter, you'll be able to create large tiles; if not, the larger size options will be grayed out. Some of the textures you can create with Make Fractal Pattern make very cool paper textures: Select the area of the fractal pattern that you want for your texture (or choose Select, All) and on the Papers section bar, click the right triangle and choose Capture Paper.

Enhancing fractal patterns. You can add any special effect to fractal (or regular) patterns and they still remain patterns. Here are two creative applications of fractal pattern.

To create a hard-edged fractal pattern with wild color, make a Fractal Pattern, setting Power to –150, Feature Size to 75 (for a relatively coarse pattern), and Softness to 0. Click OK. Select Effects, Surface Control, Express Texture Using Image Luminance. Adjust the Gray Threshold and Grain sliders to about 80, and set the Contrast slider at 200 for a contrasty effect. Click OK. Now color the pattern by choosing the Bright gradation, from the Gradients section of the Art Materials palette, click the right triangle of the Gradients section bar and choose Express in Image. Experiment with shifting the image's hue by dragging the Bias slider.

To make an abstract topographical map image with color and relief, create a new pattern using Fractal Pattern's default settings: Power, -150%; Feature Size, 100%; Softness, 0%; Angle, 0°; Thinness, 100; and Channel, Height as Luminance. Give the image a "topographical" look by choosing Effects, Surface Control, Apply Surface Texture, Using Image Luminance (Amount, 200%; Picture, 100%; and Shine, 0% and Reflection, 0%). Tint the image with Express in Image and the Earthen gradation. Now, add a little relief by applying a second pass of Apply Surface Texture, Using Image Luminance (Amount, 100%; Picture, 100%; and Shine, 0%).

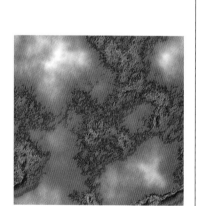

After creating this topographic map using Make Fractal Pattern, we added clouds for more atmosphere by copying our original Fractal pattern file and pasting it into the map image as a layer. We changed the Composite Method in the Layers section of the Objects palette to Screen to apply it in only the dark areas of the original topographic map image. Then we adjusted the Opacity slider to 90%.

CREATING REPEATING TEXTURES WITH MAKE PAPER

Using the Make Paper dialog box, accessed by clicking the right triangle on the Papers section bar (Art Materials palette), you can make seamless repeating textures to apply to your images. For the image below, Corinne Okada created her own repeating texture that resembled a grid of pixels to represent the digital output process. She created the grid of beveled squares with Make Paper using the Square Pattern, then chose her new paper from the list on the papers section and applied the texture to the central portion of her image using Effects, Surface Control, Color Overlay.

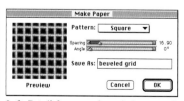

Left: Detail from a package design created by Corinne Okada for The Digital Pond. Above: Okada's settings for the grid of beveled squares.

To change the hue of an image, use Effects, Tonal Control, Adjust Colors, then drag the Hue Shift slider. Use Uniform Color to shift the hue of the entire image, or use Image Luminance to change color properties only in the lighter (but not white) areas.

Highpass (under Effects, Esoterica) acts like a color filter. It looks for smooth transitions in dark areas (as in a sky or shadowed background) and replaces them with abrupt edges or halo effects. Keep the Radius slider to the left for a more pronounced halo effect. To further enhance Highpass, try using Effects, Tonal Control, Equalize.

The initial, unaltered photograph

PHOTO: CHER THREINEN-PENDARVIS

Adjust Colors, Uniform Color: Hue Shift, -44%; Value, 25%

Adjust Colors, Image Luminance: Hue Shift, 20%; Value, 25%

Highpass: Radius, 26.05

Conventional diffuser screens attach to the camera lens, breaking up or softening the image as it refracts through the screen. Painter's Glass Distortion layer works the same way but with more variety. To make a Glass Distortion layer for your image, in the Objects palette, select Glass Distortion in the Dynamic Layers section and click the Apply button. From the Using menu, choose Paper and experiment with refracting your image through different textures chosen in the Papers section. On this photo, we used Diagonal 1 from the More Paper Textures library (in the Paper Texture Libraries folder on the Painter 6 CD-ROM).

To add a swirl to your "map" choose Effects, Surface Control, Quick Warp and click the Swirl button. Experiment with different Angle Factor settings in the dialog box.

CREATING EFFECTS WITH GLASS DISTORTION

Try using another image as a "refractor" for your main image. With Painter's Glass Distortion features you can superimpose glass bas relief effects (using a paper texture or another image). You can apply the procedure directly to your image choose Effects, Focus, Glass Distortion. A benefit of the Glass Distortion layer is that you can preview the effects on a copy of your image without changing the original image; however, the Effects, Focus, Glass Distortion command features a dialog box with more controls. (To learn more about using Effects, Glass Distortion turn to "Diving into Distortion" and "Draping a Weave" later in this chapter. To read about using a Glass Distortion layer, turn to "Creating an Impressionist Look.")

WORKING WITH MOSAICS

Tile mosaics became a popular medium at about 200–300 BC in the Roman Empire, Greece, Africa and Asia; floors and walls of many buildings were decorated with mosaics made of small pieces of glass, stones or shells. They were most often built to celebrate a historic event or for religious purposes.

Inspiration for mosaics. You can build mosaics using Painter's Mosaic brush and dialog box in any of three ways: by drawing them from scratch, by basing them on a line drawing that you've scanned, or by creating a clone-based mosaic using an existing piece of art or a photo. Keep in mind that because of the nature of

To create Pencil and Brush, artist John Derry built a mosaic in Painter beginning with white grout.

Using a colored pen-and-ink sketch as reference for a mosaic. Top: The cloned sketch (with tracing paper turned on) shows the mosaic in progress with recently applied tiles. Bottom: The same stage with tracing paper turned off. Click tracing paper on and off without closing the Make Mosaic dialog box by using the checkbox.

The default grout color is white, shown here (left) in the Select Grout Color dialog box, which uses the Apple color picker. Dragging the Lightness slider to the left darkens the color of the grout.

the Mosaic tool, your decorative design or photo reference should have a strong compositional focal point. If you want to use a photo that has a busy background, consider simplifying it first by desaturating or blurring. (For tips on neutralizing busy backgrounds, see the beginning of Chapter 6.)

Laying down tiles. Here's a way to try out Painter's Mosaics. Open a new blank file, or a reference on which to base your mosaic. Visualize the forms in your design before you begin laying down the tiles, and rotate your page by dragging with the Rotate Page tool (nested with the Grabber tool in the Tools palette) to accommodate your drawing style so you'll be able to make smooth, controlled strokes to describe the forms.

Choose Canvas, Make Mosaic to open the Make Mosaic dialog box. Opening the dialog box will turn the background of the currently active image white, the default grout color. To change the grout color using the Apple color picker in the Select Grout Color dialog box, click in the Grout box, and choose a new color in the color picker. Then choose a contrasting color in the Colors section of the Art Materials palette to paint some tiles. Switch colors again and continue to make tiles. Once you have tiles in place, you can sample color from an existing tile by pressing the Ctrl/⌘ key as you click on it. You can undo an action without closing the Mosaic dialog box by pressing Ctrl/⌘-Z. To erase a tile, press the Ctrl-Shift/⌘-Control keys and stroke with the Mosaic brush over the tile. While working on a mosaic, save it in RIFF format to preserve the resolution-independent nature of the mosaic. (Because mosaic tiles are mathematically described, a mosaic can be resized without loss of quality.) For an in-depth explanation of Painter's mosaic-building tools check out Chapter 10 of the *Painter 6 User Guide*. And to read about using a photo-reference for a mosaic, turn to "Building a Clone-Based Mosaic," on page 220.

SPECIAL EFFECTS USING DYNAMIC LAYERS

Painter features seven kinds dynamic layers (plug-ins) that allow you to create exciting special effects quickly. They are Glass Distortion, Kaleidoscope, Liquid Lens, Burn, Tear, Bevel World and Liquid Metal. In the paragraphs below, we focus on special-effects applications for several of these plug-ins. (To read more about working with plug-in layers turn to the introduction of Chapter 5; see Chapter 6 to see how dynamic layers apply to image correction and photography. Turn to "Creating an Impressionist Look" later in this chapter to read about using the Glass Distortion dynamic layer in combination with Apply Surface Texture. And the *Painter 6 User Guide* contains good descriptions of each of these dynamic layers.)

Painting with metal and water. Painter's versatile Liquid Metal dynamic layer allows you to paint with bas relief and give it the look of chrome, steel, ice, water and other materials. The Liquid Metal layer works in an existing file to make a layer on which you

Hiroshi Yoshi painted Bird *with Painter's Liquid Metal. He used colored environment maps and multiple Liquid Metal layers to sculpt the bird's outline and body. See Yoshi's work in the gallery on page 228 for a more complete description of his Liquid Metal technique.*

To create the title T3, Jack Davis began by with a scanned image that he colored in Photoshop. He opened the image in Painter and made a Liquid Metal plug-in layer. In the Liquid Metal dialog box, he chose the Standard Metal Map type and the Brush tool, and these settings for the 800-pixel-wide file: Smooth 100%; Size, 10; Volume, 83; leaving other settings at their defaults. Then he painted on the layer to hand-letter the logo. To carve into areas of the metal he held down the Alt/Option key and painted with the Brush.

We used the Kaleidoscope plug-in to make a seamless tile from a Corbis Images photo. To read a step-by-step description of the technique, turn to "Making a Seamless Tile" in Chapter 11, "Using Painter For Web Graphics."

BURNED AND TEXTURED

By checking the Use Paper Texture box in the Burn Options dialog box you can apply the current Paper texture to the burned edge of a layer.

create the metal. To make a dynamic layer, open an image, choose Liquid Metal from the list on the Dynamic Layers section in the Objects palette and click the Apply button. To paint with chrome, select the Brush in the Liquid Metal dialog box and choose Chrome 1 or Chrome 2 from the Map menu. Drag in the image with the Brush. For thin lines, try a Size of 8.0 and a Volume of 25%. For thick lines, increase Size to 50 and set Volume over 100%.

If you'd like to paint with bubbles or water drops that reflect your image, begin by making a clone of the image (File, Clone). On the clone, make a Liquid Metal layer. From the Map menu choose Clone Source, choose the Circle or Brush and drag to paint on the layer. For fairly flat drops use an Amount of 0.5 –1.5. For the look of 3D water drops on a camera lens, move the Amount slider to between 3.0 and 4.0. For bubbles use an Amount of 5.0.

You can color the objects on a Liquid Metal layer based on a clone source (as above) or on the current pattern. Begin by making a Liquid Metal layer. In the Liquid Metal dialog box, choose Clone Source from the Map menu. Select a pattern in the Patterns section of the Art Materials palette or open an image and define it as the clone source (File, Clone Source). Now use the Circle or Brush tool to apply metal to the layer.

Tearing, burning and beveling. The Tear, Burn and Bevel World layers require a selected "source image layer" to perform their effects. To **Tear** or **Burn** an image's edges, begin by opening a file. You can select a layer in the image and apply the plug-in to it or you can reduce the image canvas to accommodate the torn or burned edge to come: Choose Effects, Orientation, Scale—we scaled our image at 80%. The Scale command will automatically create a "source layer." With the layer still selected, open the Dynamic Layers section, choose the Tear or Burn plug-in from the list and click the Apply button. To change the color of the torn (or burned) edge, click in the Color box and choose a new color from the color picker. **Bevel World** allows you to create complex bevels quickly. You can apply a

A striking beveled button designed by Michelle Lill. She captured a custom-made environment map as a pattern, and applied it to the button graphic using the Reflection slider in the Bevel World dialog box. To learn more about reflection maps, turn to "Making an Environment Map" and "Applying an Environment Map," later in this chapter.

bevel to a "source layer" in an image or make a unique beveled frame for an image. Open an image you'd like to frame, choose Select, All, and choose the Bevel World plug-in from the Dynamic Layers section's list and click the Apply button. Choose your settings and click OK. To read more about using the Bevel World plug-in layer, turn to "Creating Beveled Chrome," in Chapter 8 on page 248.

Diving into Distortion

Overview *Use Glass Distortion to displace an image using a clone source; then combine a dramatic distortion with a subtle one to create a water-stained effect.*

CHER THREINEN-PENDARVIS / PHOTO: CORBIS IMAGES

The original photograph

The water image displacement map

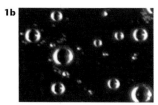

Settings for the subtle distortion

The Extreme clone (left), and the Subtle clone (right)

Cloning in a dramatic water drop

PAINTER'S GLASS DISTORTION can move pixels in an image based on the luminosity of another image. We used it here to simulate water drops on a camera lens.

1 Choosing images and making clones. Choose an image for a displacement map (the water drops in this case) that has good contrast; both crisp and soft-focus images can give good results. Because you'll be applying the displacement map image to the original image as a clone source, you'll need to size the map image to the same pixel dimensions as the image you want to distort. (Our images were 883 x 589 pixels.) Make two clones of the image you want to distort by choosing File, Clone, twice. Save the clones, naming them Extreme and Subtle, then size and position them on your screen so that you can see both of them.

2 Applying the distortion. Open the displacement map image. Now, click on the Extreme clone, and designate the displacement image as the clone source (File, Clone Source). With the Extreme clone active, choose Effects, Focus, Glass Distortion, Using Original Luminance, and choose the Refraction Map model. (Refraction works well for glass effects; it creates an effect similar to an optical lens bending light.) Our settings were Softness, 2.3 (to smooth the distortion); Amount, 1.35; Variance, 6.00. We left Direction at 0, because it has no effect when using a Refraction map, and clicked OK. Click on the Subtle clone, and apply Glass Distortion with subtler settings. (Our settings were Softness 15.0; Amount, 0.06; and Variance, 1.00.) We wanted the diving board to curve, while preserving smoothness in the image.

3 Restoring from the Extreme clone. We added several dramatic water drops from the Extreme clone to enhance the composition of the Subtle image. Click on the Subtle clone to make it active and choose the Extreme clone as clone source. Use the Soft Cloner variant of the Cloners brush to clone dramatic effects from the Extreme clone into your Subtle image. 🖌

Creating an Impressionist Look

Overview *Combine Glass Distortion and Surface Texture special effects to transform a photo into a painting, creating brush-strokes and building up paint.*

The original photograph

Applying Glass Distortion to the photo

Adding highlights and shadows to the distorted image with Surface Texture

BY COMBINING TWO POWERFUL EFFECTS, Glass Distortion and Apply Surface Texture, you can create an Impressionist look with textured highlights and shadows—turning a photo into a painting. This effect can be applied to an entire image, a selection or a layer, giving you much more flexibility than you would have in the darkroom working with diffuser screens and masks.

1 Choosing an image and making a selection. Choose an image with a strong focal point and good highlights and shadows. You can achieve good results with either crisp or soft-focus images. In preparation for generating a Glass Distortion plug-in dynamic layer for the image in the next step, choose Select, All.

2 Initiating strokes. Choose a coarse paper texture—woven textures with a broad tonal range help to emulate the look of paint on canvas. We chose Raw Silk from the default Painter Textures library, and scaled it down to 88% to complement our 883-pixel-wide image. To diffuse or break up the image into paint-like strokes on paper, apply the Glass Distortion dynamic layer: In the Dynamic Layers section of the Objects palette, choose Glass Distortion from the pop-up menu and click the Apply button. In the Using menu select Paper. Choose subtle settings—our settings were Amount, 0.71; Variance, 2.06; and Softness, 0. Click OK to apply your settings.

3 Adding texture and shadows. To add realistic relief to complete the painted effect choose Effects, Surface Control, Apply Surface Texture. (If the Commit dialog box appears asking you if you'd like to convert the dynamic layer to an image layer, choose Commit.) In the Using menu choose Paper. Use subtle-to-moderate Surface Texture settings to avoid a harsh look and to preserve the original image. We used Amount, 90%; Picture, 100%; Shine, 10%; Softness, 0 and Reflection, 0; (to raise the highlights, we turned on Inverted). Choose a light direction that complements the light in your photograph, and click OK. 🎨

Making an Environment Map

Overview *Choose a file and resize it; make a selection; use Quick Warp to bend the image into an environment; capture it as a pattern.*

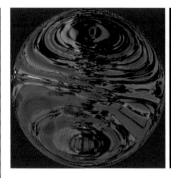

MICHELLE LILL

Michelle Lill's original photo

Making a square selection on the image

Applying the Quick Warp Sphere option

Naming the water map in the Capture Pattern dialog box

YOU CAN USE PAINTER'S QUICK WARP FEATURE to bend any image into a useful environment map, an image that shows an environment as if it were seen through a fish-eye lens or reflected in a shiny metal sphere. Multimedia designer Michelle Lill creates her own environment maps—like the one above on the left, and uses the maps to enhance images by applying them as she did in the image on the right.

1. Opening an image and making a selection. Open the image that you want to use as the basis for your reflection map. To conserve disk space and optimize performance, Lill recommends that a reflection map image be a square that is 256 pixels or less. Using the Rectangle Selection tool, make a 256 pixel square selection (holding down the Shift key as you drag to constrain the selection to a square), as you check the Width in the Controls:Selection palette. If you need to move or scale the selection, use the Selection Adjuster tool. (Turn to "Transforming Selections" in Chapter 4 for more about manipulating selections.) Copy the selected area (Edit, Copy), and paste it into a new file by choosing Edit, Paste Into New Image.

2 Bending the image. To get the "fisheye lens" effect that adds realism to the map (since most surfaces that reflect their environment are not flat), Lill chose Effects, Surface, Control, Quick Warp and selected the Sphere option. She used the default settings of Power 2.0 and Angle Factor 2.0. The effect was applied to the entire canvas.

3 Saving the image as a pattern. To save the map into the current Pattern library, capture it as a pattern: With the environment map image open, select all, click the right triangle on the Patterns section bar and choose Capture Pattern from the menu. Name the map when prompted and click OK. The environment map is now a permanent member of the library. Now you can use the map to enhance special effects—as Lill did in her water illustration above. To read a step-by-step description of how Lill used a custom environment map to enhance an image, turn to "Applying an Environment Map," on the next page. 🖌

Applying an Environment Map

Overview *Open a file and set type shapes; convert the shapes into a layer; add an environment map, dimension and a soft drop shadow to the type; add a border to the image.*

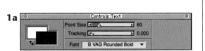

Choosing a font and size in the Controls:Text palette

Selected type shapes on the image

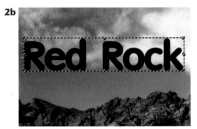

The selected type shapes in the Layers section of the Objects palette

Grouping the type shapes

TO CREATE THE TITLE DESIGN *RED ROCK*, multimedia designer Michelle Lill used a custom-made environment map in combination with one of Painter's most powerful and versatile tools, Apply Surface Texture.

1 Opening an image and setting the type. For this example, Lill began by setting 60-point VAG Rounded Bold type shapes on top of a photo. Begin by opening a background image (Lill's image was 889 pixels wide). Select the Text tool and choose a font in the Controls:Text palette. For the best results, choose a bold font with a broad stroke and rounded corners. Position the cursor in your image and type the text.

When you're finished setting the text shapes, select the Layer Adjuster tool and kern the type by repositioning the letters to your taste. To select an individual letter, click on its name in the Layers section of the Objects palette. Move it using the arrow keys on your keyboard. (To read more about manipulating shapes, turn to "Working with Shapes," in the beginning of Chapter 5.)

2 Converting the shapes to a layer. If you'll be applying a series of effects to an entire word or block of text, it's most efficient to make the type into a single image layer. To do this, select all of the type shapes by Shift-clicking on their names in the Layers section. Group them by clicking the Group button, or type Ctrl/⌘-G. To turn the grouped shapes into one layer, click the Collapse button on the Layers section and if the Commit dialog box appears, click the Commit All button.

3 Selecting the reflection map. Open the Patterns section of the Art Materials palette and choose the Exterior Reflection Map pattern from the list. Lill used her own pattern, made from the

3

Choosing Lill's custom-made environment map in the Patterns section

4a

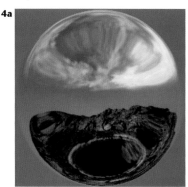

Michele Lill's Red Rock environment map

4b

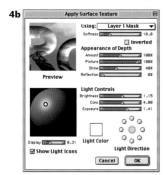

Settings for the second Surface Texture application showing dimension on the type

5a

Setting up an automatic drop shadow

5b

The Red Rock image with the drop shadow applied to the text layer

same Red Rock photo she used for the background. (To read about how to make your own environment map, check out Michelle Lill's method in "Making an Environment Map," on page 216.

4 Adding reflection and dimension to the type. To achieve a strong reflection in the type and a realistic 3D look, Lill used two applications of Apply Surface Texture. Begin by selecting the text layer with the Layer Adjuster tool, then choose Effects, Surface Control, Apply Surface Texture. To reflect the environment map onto your type, use these settings: In the Using menu choose the text mask to restrict the reflection to the type. Move the Reflection slider to 100% (so the environment map shows up) and move the Softness slider to the right (to scale the reflection map). Adjust the other settings to suit your image. The Surface Texture dialog box is interactive, so you can size your pattern while viewing the reflection map in the Preview window. When the reflection looks good, click OK in the Apply Surface Texture dialog box. Lill's Apply Surface Texture settings for the Red Rock image at the beginning of this story are as follows: Softness 40.0; Amount 200%; Picture 100%; Shine 40%; and Reflection 100%.

Now add a realistic 3D look to the text by choosing Apply Surface Texture a second time. This time, check the Inverted box (to add a second light source); decrease the Reflection slider to 0% by moving it all the way to the left; and decrease the Softness to about 10. Lill's second Surface Texture application settings are as follows: Softness 10.0, Amount 100%, Picture 100%, Shine 40% and Reflection 0%. Click OK.

5 Adding a shadow and a soft black border. Next, Lill added a black drop shadow to her text, adding to the 3D look and giving her image more contrast. To generate the shadow, she chose Effects, Objects, Create Drop Shadow. In the dialog box, she specified settings for the X and Y coordinates to fit her image, and she increased the Opacity of the shadow to 80%, left the other settings at their defaults, and she checked the Collapse To One Layer box to combine the text and shadow.

Then, to finish the image with a more graphic look that would complement the shadow, Lill added a softly feathered black border to her image. To create her border effect, begin by choosing Select, All. Then from the Select menu choose Select, Modify, Contract. In the Contract Selection dialog box, type in 12 pixels. Now choose Select, Feather and set the feather to 24 pixels. Finally, Lill filled the selected, feathered edge with black. Begin by choosing black in the Colors section of the Art Materials palette. Choose the Paint Bucket, in the Controls:Paint Bucket palette make these choices: From the What To Fill menu choose Image, and from the Fill With menu choose Current Color. Click inside the active selection with the Paint Bucket tool. 🖌️

Building a Terrain Map

Overview Create a terrain map from elevation data; make a custom gradient; color the map; use Apply Surface Texture to give it realistic dimension.

Olympic National Park

MT. OLYMPUS   Mt. Mathias
West Peak   East Peak
Hoh Peak   Mt. Tom   Middle Peak

STEVEN GORDON / CARTAGRAM

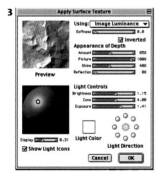

The grayscale image representing elevation

2a

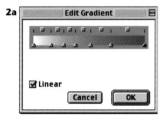

Building a custom gradient for the map

2b

The map with the custom gradient applied using Express in Image

3

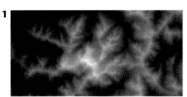

Gordon's settings in Apply Surface Texture, used to produce the terrain map

TO CREATE THIS REALISTIC MAP of Mount Olympus, Washington, Steven Gordon built a color terrain background from real data. As principal cartographer and owner of Cartagram, Gordon produces custom maps for electronic and print publication, specializing in tourism maps with relief renderings of the terrain.

1 Making a grayscale-to-height image. To begin the map, Gordon downloaded a digital elevation model (DEM) file from the USGS (www.usgs.gov). He processed it using a shareware DEM reader he found by searching for the keyword "DEM" in an internet search engine. The resulting PICT image contained grayscale values mapped to elevation values, which Gordon could then use in building the image.

2 Coloring the image. Gordon opened the grayscale PICT file in Painter and built a custom gradient to color the map. To make your own gradation, open the Colors and the Gradients sections of the Art Materials palette; in the Gradients section choose the Two-Point gradation. Now open the Edit Gradient dialog box by clicking the right triangle on the Gradients section bar and choosing Edit Gradient. Using the dialog box, you can create a new gradation with color control points representing elevation zones (as Gordon did). Add control points to the center of the gradient by clicking in the Gradient bar. Click each control point and then click in the Colors section to choose a color for that point. Gordon's gradation progressed from dark blue-green valleys to white mountain crests. When the gradient looks good, click OK and then save it by choosing Save Gradient from the Gradients section's menu. Apply the gradient to your image by choosing Express in Image from the Gradients section's menu.

3 Building Terrain. To add realistic relief to your map, choose Effects, Surface Control, Apply Surface Texture, Using Image Luminance. Click the Inverted box to make the light areas in the map "pop-up." To blur undesirable detail, move the Softness slider to the right. Adjust the Amount to build dimension and shadow. Gordon decreased the Amount to 85% to keep the shadows from being too dark and prominent. He used the default 11:00 light direction setting and left the Shine at the default 40%.

Building a Clone-Based Mosaic

Overview *Choose a photo reference and retouch it if needed; make a clone of the retouched photo; use the Make Mosaic dialog box to design and lay down colored tiles in the clone.*

1

The original photograph

2a

Increasing the contrast in the source image

2b

Detail of the retouched source image

MOSAICS HAVE BEEN USED AS A NARRATIVE and decorative art form since Hellenistic and Roman times. Because of its graphic nature the mosaic is a medium that can be used to express strong emotion. S. Swaminathan created the digital mosaic *Soul of Homelessness*, based on his photograph of a homeless man. His vision was to create an abstracted mosaic portrait of the man that would portray the dignity he projected.

1 Selecting a source image. Choose a photo with a strong focal point and meaningful content, so the mosaic technique does not overpower the image. The photo should also have a broad tonal range and good color detail to help build value and color complexity into the tiles. Swaminathan began with a 675 x 920-pixel photo.

2 Retouching and cloning. To separate the subject from the background, Swaminathan used a modified Digital Airbrush variant of Airbrushes to simplify the background of the photo, adding soft blue and white strokes. He also increased the contrast in the image using Effects, Tonal Control, Brightness/Contrast.

When he was satisfied with the retouching, he cloned the image. Choose File, Clone to make a clone of your source image. In preparation for laying down colored tiles in the clone based on the color of the clone source image, check the Clone Color checkbox in the Colors section of the Art Materials palette.

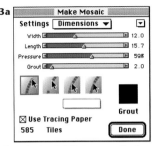

3a

Designing a horizontal tile to use on the face

3b

Using Tracing Paper to view the clone source while positioning tiles on the clone

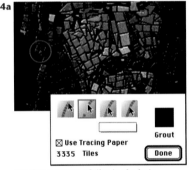

4a

Erasing a course of tiles in the hair

4b

Adding new irregular tiles in the hair

3 Laying tiles. With the clone active, open the Make Mosaic dialog box (Canvas, Make Mosaic), and check the Use Tracing Paper checkbox so you can see the source image while laying down the tiles. To design a custom tile, begin by setting Dimensions for the tile; choose a Width, Length and Grout size. Make a stroke on your image to test the settings. Press Ctrl/⌘-Z to Undo a test stroke without closing the Make Mosaic dialog box. Experiment with the settings until you get just the look you want.

Swaminathan began with the face, which would become the focal point of the mosaic portrait. As he worked, he varied the size of the tiles, using larger tiles for the broader areas of the face (the forehead and cheeks), and smaller tiles to render detailed areas (the shadowed right side of the man's nose, eyes and eyebrows).

Generally, he worked from the center out, beginning with the face and hair and then rendering the shirt, shoes and background. To depict the long hair (and to contrast with the more uniform shapes of tiles on the subject's jacket) he designed narrow, irregularly shaped tiles. To vary the tile shapes and grout (as Swaminathan did), choose Randomness from the Settings pop-up menu to access the sliders. Begin by moving the Cut slider to the right to increase Randomness in the shape of the tile ends. To vary the spacing between tiles, move the Grout slider to the right. Experiment with each of the sliders individually until you arrive at the look you want.

4 Completing the image. To refine the tile design, Swaminathan sampled color from existing tiles and applied the color to new tiles. (Before sampling color from a tile, turn off Clone Color in the Colors section then press the Ctrl/⌘ key and click on a tile). To erase tiles, click the Remove Tiles icon and drag the cursor over the tiles that you want to remove. Click back on the Apply Tiles icon and drag to add new tiles.

SAMPLE WITH A CLICK

To sample color from an existing tile in your mosaic (with Clone Color turned off in the Colors section of the Art Materials palette), press the Ctrl/⌘ key and click on a tile. You won't see the Mosaic brush's crosshair cursor change to the Dropper when you're working with the open Make Mosaic dialog box, but you *will* be able to sample the color.

CORRECTION SHORTCUT

To remove tiles without clicking the Remove Tiles icon, press the Ctrl-Shift/⌘-Control keys and drag the Mosaic brush over the tiles that you want to remove.

Adding highlights and shadows. Finally, Swaminathan used Apply Surface Texture to add realistic highlights and shadows like those you would see on the slightly uneven surface of handmade tiles. Choose Effects, Surface Control, Apply Surface Texture Using Image Luminance. Try these subtle settings: Softness, 0; Amount, 20; Picture 100; Shine, 25; and Reflection, 0. Click OK.

Creating a Tidepool

Overview *Create a sandy background; spray plants onto the ocean floor using the Image Hose; light the scene; combine special effects to "ripple the water."*

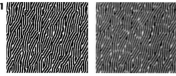

Wheat Stalks texture applied to the blank image (left), then Super Softened

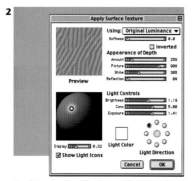

Applying Surface Texture with Original Luminance to the sand-colored clone

The Pressure Plant nozzle file with images from small to large size

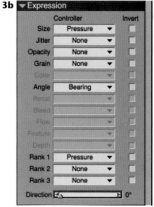

The Expression section with Size and Rank 1 set to Pressure

JOHN DERRY

THE ILLUSION OF LIGHT REFRACTING through water is essential to creating a realistic underwater scene. In *Tidepool*, after using a variety of Image Hose nozzles to paint undersea plant life, John Derry engineered the look of rippling water by applying Lighting, Glass Distortion and Surface Texture to the image.

1 Creating a soft sandy bottom. To begin as Derry did, open a new 1200-pixel-wide image with a white background. Select black in the Colors section of the Art Materials palette, choose Wheat Stalks paper texture from the Textures 1 library (in Paper Texture Libraries, on the Painter 6 CD-ROM) in the Papers section of the Art Materials palette and scale it to 400% using the Size slider. Apply the black texture to your file with Effects, Surface Control, Color Overlay, Using Paper and Hiding Power at 100% Opacity. Derry liked the Wheat Stalks texture but felt it needed softening to look like rippled sand. Soften the background by choosing Effects, Focus, Super Soften; enter 12 when the dialog box appears. Click OK.

2 Giving the rippled sand color and texture. To make the background look like sand, you can combine a sand-colored file with the gray rippled image. First, clone the gray image (File, Clone), choose a sand color and fill the clone with color (Ctrl/⌘-F, Current Color, 100% Opacity). Next, combine the sand-colored clone with the gray image. Go to Effects, Surface Control, Apply Surface Texture and choose Original Luminance. For a subtle effect use these settings: Amount, 25; Picture, 90; Shine, 30. Set the Light Direction at 11 o'clock, Brightness at 1.19, increase Concentration (Conc) to 5.00 (to decrease the spread of the light) and Exposure at 1.41.

3 Loading a nozzle and spraying images. Most of the Image Hose nozzles that Derry used in this piece can be found in the Tidepool Nozzles library on the Painter 6 Wow! CD-ROM, in the John Derry's Nozzles folder. To choose an Image Hose nozzle from the current library in the Nozzles section of the Art Materials palette, open the Nozzles section and click on a nozzle. To paint with a

3c

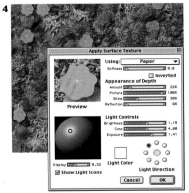

Using short spiral strokes to Spray plants and pebbles onto the sandy ocean floor

4

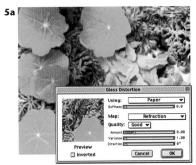

Creating a soft, diffused custom light

5a

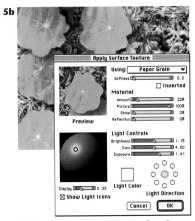

Applying Glass Distortion to initiate the ripple effect

5b

Adding Surface Texture to complete the illusion of rippling water

nozzle, select the Image Hose icon in the Brushes palette and begin painting. To make a nozzle spray in a specific way, change the hose variant in the Brushes palette or use the controls in the Expression section of the Brush Controls palette.

Load the Tidepool library from the Painter 6 Wow! CD-ROM by choosing Load Library from the bottom of the nozzle list on the Nozzles section. For the undersea image, choose the Pressure Plants nozzle, select the Image Hose icon and paint with short, spiral strokes in your image. Derry added strokes to the piece using a number of nozzles: Shadowed Coral, Pastel Coral, Shiny Coral, Pointed Plant, Nasturtium, Pressure Plants and Pebbles. See Chapter 8 in the *Painter 6 User Guide* to learn how to create your own Image Hose nozzle.

4 Applying Lighting. To create a diffused lighting effect with soft pockets of light and dark areas, Derry modified an existing light, copied it four times, then modified the individual lights. To create a look similar to the one he achieved, choose Effects, Surface Control, Apply Lighting, Slide Lighting. Reduce the Brightness, Distance and Spread settings, then click on two new locations in the Preview window to create two more lights with settings identical to the original. To reposition a light, drag on the large circle, and to aim the light in a new direction, drag on the small circle. Make further modifications to one of the three lights, then click in the Preview window two more times to create two more lights with those new settings, making a total of five lights. To create a softer effect on the whole scene, drag the Exposure slider to the left and the Ambient slider to the right. Store your custom light in the library by clicking the Save button, then click OK to apply the lighting to the image.

5 Creating a water ripple effect. Derry used a powerful but subtle combination of Glass Distortion and Apply Surface Texture to create a realistic water ripple effect. To ripple your image, in the Papers section choose the Seismic texture loaded from the Wild Textures library (in the Paper Texture libraries folder on the Painter 6 CD-ROM) and scale it to 400%. Now select Effects, Focus, Glass Distortion using Paper and accept the default settings of Amount, 0 and Variance, 1.00, with the Refraction Map type. To add a subtle bump to the transparent water ripple, choose Effects, Surface Control, Apply Surface Texture using Paper: Amount, 22%; Picture, 100%; and Shine, 0%. Click the 11 o'clock Light Direction button to set a general light direction.

Draping a Weave

Overview *Paint a grayscale file that will be your source image; fill a clone of that file with a weave; use a combination of Glass Distortion and Surface Texture to wrap the weave around the source image.*

CHER THREINEN-PENDARVIS

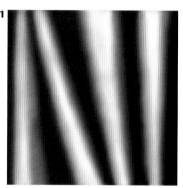

The grayscale form file with strong values

2a

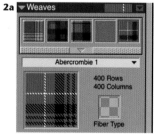

Choosing a weave in the Weaves section

2b

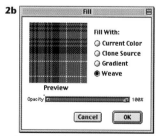

Filling the clone with the weave

YOU CAN USE PAINTER'S WEAVES, located in the Weaves section of the Art Materials palette, to fill any selection or document, using either the Fill command or the Paint Bucket tool. Weaves can be used in fashion design, and they make good backgrounds for scenes, but their flat look can be a drawback. To create the appearance of fabric—to hang behind a still life, for instance—we added dimension to a weave by "draping" it over a painted form using a powerful Glass Distortion displacement effect along with Surface Texture.

1 Making the form file. Think of the form file as a kind of mold—or fashion designer's dress form—over which you'll drape your fabric. Create a grayscale form file that has strong value contrast and smooth dark-to-light transitions. As a reference for our 500-pixel-square form file, we draped fabric over a chair and sketched it in Painter, then cleaned up the sketch with the Digital Airbrush variant of Airbrushes. Since any hard edges in the form file would make a noticeable break in the weave's pattern, we softened the image with Effects, Focus, Super Soften. We used a 7-pixel Super Soften setting on our file.

If you don't want to paint the form file, here's a fast, but less "organic" way to create it. Open the Make Paper dialog box by clicking the right triangle on the Papers section of the Art Materials palette. Choose Line from the pop-up menu, use a high spacing setting and to make vertical lines, set Angle at 90°. In the Save As field, type a name for the new paper. Choose it in the Papers section and choose black in the Colors section. Then select Effects, Surface Control, Color Overlay, Using Paper and Hiding Power at 100% Opacity. Use Super Soften as described above.

2 Making a clone and filling it with a weave. Choose File, Clone to make a duplicate of the form file with identical dimensions. Now choose a weave from the Weaves section of the Art

3

Applying Glass Distortion to the weave

4

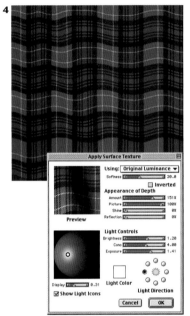

Adding highlights and shadows to the distorted image using Surface Texture

Materials palette, and fill the clone with your weave (Ctrl/⌘-F, Weaving, 100%). We used the Abercrombie 1 weave from the Scottish Tartans library (in the Weaves folder on the Painter 6 CD-ROM).

3 Initiating the distortion. Here's where the movement begins. Choose Effects, Focus, Glass Distortion, Using Original Luminance. Now let Painter know the direction that you want the fabric to go when it overlies the form file. When a clone image is displaced by Glass Distortion using Original Luminance, the distance each pixel moves is based on the luminance of each pixel in the source file. We chose Vector Displacement to move pixels in a specific direction, and used the Amount slider to get a moderate "ripple" effect in the Preview (we chose 1.54), leaving Variance at 1.00. To establish the direction (and make the light areas move up and to the right, dark areas move down and to the left—based on the form file), we moved the Direction slider to 80°. We added a Softness of 15.2 to smooth any rough edges that might be caused by the distortion of the weave. Experiment with your settings; the Softness, Amount and Direction may change based on the size of your file.

4 Adding highlights and shadows. Using Apply Surface Texture adds to the illusion of folded fabric by contributing highlights and shadows based on the form file. Choose Effects, Surface Control, Apply Surface Texture, Using Original Luminance. Experiment with your settings—paying special attention to how the lighting controls affect the look—and click OK. We set Softness to 20.0 (to smooth the image and slightly increase the depth of the folds), Amount to 151%, Picture to 100% (to make the image lighter while maintaining weaving detail), and Shine to 0%, then chose the 9 o'clock Light Direction button. 🐾

MOLDING A WEAVE OVER TYPOGRAPHIC FORMS

Try wrapping a weave (or other image) around type or a logo. Follow the same steps as in "Draping a Weave," and remember to use the Super Soften command on the type. For the "Wow!" image we chose Angle Displacement Map in the Effects, Focus, Glass Distortion dialog box (it makes the angle of the distortions vary based on luminance information in the form file), and we used a high Softness setting to compensate for the extreme wrap applied to the weave. This helped to smooth out the threads. In Effects, Surface Control, Apply Surface Texture, we set Softness at 2.2, Amount at 171%, Picture at 100%, Shine at 40%, and chose the 9:00 Light Direction with a Brightness of 1.19.

Type set in Adobe Reporter 2 (left), then given a Super Soften setting of 7 pixels.

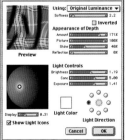

Using Glass Distortion and Apply Surface Texture to complete the "wrapped type" effect

■ Inspired by a photo of a DeHaviland Beaver seaplane in flight, **Brent Houston** created *Seaplane.* He painted the plane taxiing out from a dock on a mountain lake with a loose style, using a variety of brushes.

To begin, Houston sketched the plane, the dock and the outline of the mountains. He cloned this first image and deleted the clone contents, and pressed Ctrl/⌘-T to turn on Tracing Paper. He filled the clone with a blue–to–gray gradient to make the background. Then he added a new layer by clicking the New button on the Layers section of the Objects palette, and then roughed in the airplane with Dry Media and Airbrushes variants using white color on the new

layer. Next, he targeted the Canvas and loosely painted the dock and shadows. Houston envisioned the trees and mountains mostly obscured by clouds. For the trees, he used the Small Trees image hose nozzle and painted a few trees onto the Canvas. He covered most of the trees by painting with the Clouds nozzle, using various sizes and opacities. To bring some of the trees back in, he retouched some areas by painting with the Trees nozzle, using low opacities.

To add more depth and contrast to his composition, Houston painted the darker silhouetted trees (which are closer to the foreground) with the Dry Media variants. To bring the cloudy atmosphere into the foreground trees, he painted over the

trees with the Clouds Image Hose nozzle using low opacities.

Houston completed the coloring and detailing of the plane with various media (the Oil Pastel variant of Dry Media, the Airbrushes, the Scratchboard Tool variant of Pens and the 2B Pencil variant of Pencils for details). He merged the layer with the Canvas by clicking the Drop button on the Layers section and then worked over the docks, adding more grainy strokes and detail. Finally, he painted transparent washes with Water Color variants on the dock and water. To complete the overcast look, he subtly adjusted the color using Effects, Tonal Control, Adjust Color.

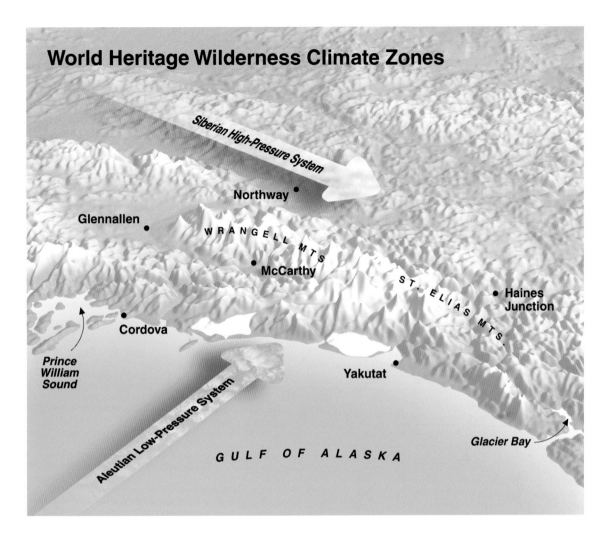

World Heritage Wilderness Climate Zones

Siberian High-Pressure System

Northway

Glennallen

WRANGELL MTS

McCarthy

ST-ELIAS MTS.

Haines Junction

Cordova

Prince William Sound

Aleutian Low-Pressure System

Yakutat

Glacier Bay

GULF OF ALASKA

■ Alaska Geographic commissioned **Steven Gordon** to create this weather map of south-central Alaska for their publication the *World Heritage Wilderness,* published in 1999. Using the process described on page 219, Gordon created a grayscale PICT of the terrain and colored it with Painter's Express in Image command from the Gradients section of the Art Materials palette. In Bryce 3, Gordon used a copy of the original grayscale terrain PICT to create the perspective landscape. Next, he imported the color PICT and wrapped the landscape with it. Back in Painter, Gordon imported the landscape, and created a coastline vignette with the masking tool.

To begin the three-dimensional arrows, Gordon drew shapes in FreeHand 8, and saved the file as a PICT. He used Bryce to help visualize the three-dimensional arrows, as follows: He opened the file in

Bryce, where the arrows became 3D objects and part of an overall scene. When he had positioned the arrows the way he wanted them and the scene's view and lighting were set, he saved the scene as a Photoshop file, and then opened it in Painter. Gordon wanted to use the Bryce file as a guide for tracing, so he cloned it (File, Clone), deleted the contents of the clone (Ctrl/⌘-A and Backspace/Delete), and turned on Tracing Paper (Ctrl/⌘-T). Then he used Painter's Pen tool to trace the two arrow shapes and he used the shapes to make selections (Shapes, Convert To Selection).

For the clouds in the arrows, he dragged and dropped an image of clouds (taken with a digital camera on a warm spring morning) into the composite file. He used the arrow selections to capture the imagery from the cloud layer by activating the layer, loading the selection (Select, Load

Selection), and Alt/Option clicking to copy the area of the clouds image to a new layer.

To differentiate the two kinds of cloud masses represented by the arrows, he used the Effects, Tonal Control, Adjust Color feature to make the moisture-laden Aleutian Low grayer, and the dryer Siberian High bluer. To complete the illusion of depth, Gordon added drop shadows to the arrows.

Next, he used the Digital Airbrush variant of Airbrushes to spray the two white glacier fields with light blue color. To finish, he flattened the layers in his file by choosing Drop All from the Layers command menu (accessed by clicking the right arrow on the Layers section bar). Gordon saved the Painter image as a TIFF file and placed it in FreeHand, where he added the rivers, the type and the leader arrows.

■ **Hiroshi Yoshi** is an award-winning Japanese illustrator, known for his fantastic characters and animals and his unique illustration style.

Yoshi created *Yokogao (Profile)* using Painter's Liquid Metal dynamic layers and custom environment maps. To design his character, Yoshi opened a new file in Painter that measured 1181 x 1181-pixels and used a Pencils variant to draw a sketch over a white background.

He wanted to make most of his character red, so to prepare for the Liquid Metal to come, he loaded a custom Pattern library into the Patterns section of the Art Materials palette and chose a red environment map. When no image is defined as a clone source (File, Clone Source), Painter uses the current Pattern in the Patterns section as the Clone Source in the Liquid Metal dialog box.

Next, Yoshi chose Liquid Metal from the plug-ins menu in the Dynamic Layers section of the Objects palette and to generate the first layer, he clicked the Apply button. He set the controls in the Liquid Metal dialog box so that he could draw a very fine outline of metal around the edge of the head and around sections inside the head. He knew that with

Surface Tension turned on in the dialog box, the Liquid Metal outline would constrain the larger amounts of metal he planned to add later. He used these settings for the outlines: Amount: 4.4; Smooth, 183%; Size, 7.8; Volume, 447%; Spacing, 0.808; Map, Clone Source; Surface tension turned on; and Refraction set to 0%. Using his sketch on the Canvas as a reference, he used the Liquid Metal Brush tool to carefully draw the red outlines of metal. His settings produced a fine outline with a peaked ridge. Then he deselected the outline by clicking on a blank area of the layer with the Liquid Metal Selector (arrow).

To add Liquid Metal to fill the areas of the head, Yoshi used these settings: Amount, 5.0; Smooth, 198%; Size, 33.1; Volume, 100%; Spacing, 0.808; Map, Clone Source, (the same red environment map); Surface Tension turned on; and Refraction, 0%.

When the red outlines and volume were complete, he generated new Liquid Metal layers for each of the colors in the image, and applied metal and color to each layer (using different colored environment maps) as described above with the outlines and fills. To make the

chrome areas on the eye, ear and chin, Yoshi used the Liquid Metal Brush tool to paint lines and pools of Liquid Metal on a new layer. He chose a different environment map in the Patterns section, and this time he used a metallic reflection map, similar to the Reflection Map pattern in the default Painter Patterns library. When the Liquid Metal was complete, he merged the layers by grouping them (Ctrl/⌘-G), and clicking the Collapse button on the Layers section of the Objects palette.

Next, to add depth to his composition, Yoshi added a subtle drop shadow behind the character. With the character layer selected in the Layers section, he chose Effects, Objects, Create Drop Shadow.

To complete the scene, Yoshi used Effects, Surface Control, Apply Surface Texture, Using Paper, to add a woven texture to the image Canvas. Then he merged the layers with the Canvas by choosing Drop All from the menu on the Layers section, accessed by clicking the right triangle on the Layers section bar. Finally, to add a gradient over the entire image, he used Effects, Surface Control, Apply Lighting and a custom spotlight.

■ *Creative Journey,* conceived by **Brian Moose,** is a narrative illustration built for the packaging of Painter 6. The narrative begins on the left of the image with a pencil sketch of a night sky and the moon over a sea of creativity. Then it evolves through many areas of Painter, Pastel, Pen-and Ink, Airbrush, Oil, and Impasto, and Mosaic tiles and finally culminates with a stained glass effect and the "creative destination."

Moose used many of Painter's brushes and special effects to realize his concept: He used Painter's Airbrushes when painting the auroras in the starry sky. And by defining the Airbrush's Source in the General section of the Brush Controls palette so it would paint with the current pattern in the Patterns section of the Art Materials palette, he airbrushed the snake-like patterns next to the can boat and the string patterns in the water.

Moose used the Fire and Glow variants of the F/X brush to paint highlights and glows around the tips of the brushes.

For the liquid flowing out of the can, he drew a filled shape with the Pen tool and converted it to a layer (Shapes, Convert To Layer). To give the liquid dimension, he manipulated the layer's mask, as follows: He clicked on the mask's name (Shape 1 Mask) in the Masks section of the Objects palette and using the Digital Airbrush variant of Airbrushes, he painted soft white and black strokes to represent high and low areas. He deselected the mask by clicking on the Layer's name (RGB-Shape 1) in the Masks section, and with the layer still selected in the Layers section, he added relief to the liquid flowing from the can. He used the mask to apply texture by choosing Effects, Surface Control, Apply Surface Texture, choosing Shape 1 Mask from the Using pop-up menu.

■ **Chet Phillips** expressively draws his illustrations with the Scratchboard Tool variant of Pens. Then he cuts the art to a separate layer, which he composites using the Gel Composite Method, chosen from the Composite Method menu in the Layers section of the Objects palette and he uses Airbrushes in varying sizes to color the background. (See page 27 for a step-by-step description of his technique.) When the coloring is complete, he merges the layers using the Drop button on the Layers section. He often adds special effects to complete the piece.

Once the coloring for *Mercury* (above) was complete, Phillips used the Pen tool to draw curved shapes, and he converted each shape to a selection by clicking the Make Selection button on the Controls: Shape Design palette. He saved each selection as a mask in the Masks section of the Objects palette, so he could use it again later. Next he activated each selection by choosing Select, Load Selection, and copied and pasted the selected portions into a new, blank image with the same dimensions as the original. Once all of these layers were in the image area, he

moved some forward and others back, merged several of them and used the Digital Airbrush variant of the Airbrushes along the outside of the remaining layers to give the image a greater feeling of depth. To add interest to the foreground, Phillips created smaller triangular layers one at a time, and used Effects, Tonal Control, Brightness/Contrast to adjust the value of one, and then dropped it, then he created, adjusted and dropped the next, and so on.

■ Master illustrator **Mike Reed** created the illustrations for the charming children's book *Catching the Wild Waiyuuzee*, (one of which is shown above), written by Rita Williams-Garcia, and published by Simon and Schuster. Reed began the illustration by roughing out the composition using the Square Chalk variant of Dry Media and saturated colors. With Wood Shavings paper texture (from the Painter 6 Wow! Book CD-ROM) chosen in the Papers section of the Art Materials palette, he sketched freely. Then to refine the illustration, he created selections so he could protect areas of his image: He used the Pen tool to draw shapes for elements (such as the hand, bird, leaves, berries and flowers)

on top of the colored drawing. Then he converted each shape to a selection (Shapes, Convert To Selection). Because he wanted soft-edged selections, he feathered each one (Select, Feather) with a radius of about 5 pixels and then saved it (Select, Save Selection) into the Masks section of the Objects palette so he could use the selection later as a mask. Next, using saturated colors, Reed painted over the selected areas. Working over the entire image, he slowly built up textures using several Dry Media variants: Sharp Chalk, Artist Pastel Chalk, Square Chalk and Oil Pastel, with Wood Shavings texture chosen in the Papers section. To refine the birds, for instance, he loaded selections and

painted with a small Artist Pastel Chalk variant over the Wood Shavings texture. To refine the details more, he used a tiny Sharp Chalk variant and painted tighter highlight and shadow details on the leaves, berries and birds.

He felt that the illustration needed more texture, so he added a transparent overlay of the Wood Shavings texture to the entire image using Dye Concentration. He chose Effects, Surface Control, Dye Concentration, Using Paper (and the Wood Shavings texture) and applied subtle settings.

■ "Discontinuity, wars that I did not partici-
pate in, but was affected by," provided inspiration for *Vietnam* (above), by fine artist and
multimedia designer **Patrick Litchy**. He
began the work with four source photos—a
rifleman, a boy and skull, a blindfolded pris-
oner and a photo of the Vietnam War Memorial in Washington, DC. Litchy applied custom
color gradations to the small source images by
choosing Express in Image from the Gradient
section bar. He used Convolver to filter the
War Memorial background image, spiraling
the type. Then he copied and pasted the three
photos into the background file. For a subtle
transition with the background, he feathered
the edges of the layer masks to make them
transparent. He used Effects, Surface Control,
Apply Surface Texture, Using Image Luminance to add highlights and shadows to the
layer. To finish, he used Apply Surface Texture
on the background using more subtle settings.

■ **Bill Niffenegger's** illustration *AIDS* (left) for
Dentistry magazine was honored with the APEX
award for magazine covers. The piece reflects
the devastating, yet sensitive, nature of the subject. Author of the book *Photoshop Filter Finesse*,
Niffenegger painted the piece in Painter using a
wide variety of brushes, custom paper textures
and Apply Lighting as well as Texture Explorer
and Gradient Designer.

■ **Lorenzo Paolini** created *Giordano Bruno* as a tribute to the great 16th-Century Italian monk and philosopher, jailed for many years for advocating personal and intellectual freedom and finally burned (with his mouth wired shut) in Rome at Piazza di Campo de' Fiori. To begin the painting, Paolini drew sketches with pencil and paper. Then he used Strata Studio Pro to create several elements in source files—for instance, the foreground desk still life. He copied and pasted the source files into Painter as layers, using the Layer Adjuster tool to reposition the elements and Effects, Orientation, Scale to resize them. For the embossed calligraphy background, Paolini began by opening a black-and-white scan of calligraphy and cloned it (File, Clone); then he deleted the contents of the clone, leaving a blank clone image. To carve out the dark areas in the calligraphy, he chose Effects, Surface Control, Apply Surface Texture, Using Original Luminance, checking the Inverted box. When the relief was established, he copied and pasted the calligraphy into the composite file and merged it with the background (Drop button, Layers section of the Objects palette). Then he used custom-made brushes to paint shadows on the background behind the layered figure of Bruno and to paint final details on the figure and still-life elements.

Clouds I Never Saw in   *Kansas*

■ Inspired by the inscription on a Polaroid photo of clouds taken by his mother, and a sketch he made of an old man reading tattered papers and books filled with scrawled handwriting, **Steve Campbell** created *Clouds I Never Saw in Kansas*. The central figure—whom Campbell calls the Prophet—sits in the middle of a maelstrom. "The piece is, quite simply, about where we expect our lives to take us and where we actually end up," Campbell says.

He began by scanning his pencil sketch. Then he opened it in Painter and roughed in basic colors to create an underpainting.

The piece is built of many layers, and combined they build a rich texture.

Campbell scanned old photos, fabrics, leaves, pieces of rusted metal, money, schematics of various kinds, printed material and old drawings. Then he dragged and dropped the elements from their source files into the composite image.

To layer many of the elements so that nothing was completely covered or buried in the image, Campbell set the Opacity and Composite Method in the Layers section of the Objects palette to make sure the layers were transparent overlays, revealing, rather than hiding, the underlying layers (he used Composite Methods such as Gel, Pseudo Color, Overlay, Soft Light, Screen and Multiply). He used Apply Surface Texture Using Paper to add many of his own paper textures to the layers in

the image (for instance, the printed text in the sky).

For the mummy wrap, Campbell drew letters by hand on a new layer and added three-dimensional texture to it with Apply Surface Texture Using Image Luminance. To add more contrast and depth to some areas of the layer, he painted over it with the Dodge and Burn variants of the Photo brush.

To create the title at the top of the painting, Campbell set type shapes with the Texas Hero font from Three Islands Press in Maryland. The font is based on the handwriting of a Union officer located in Texas during the mid 1800s.

■ The surreal photo-collage *Coney Island Baby* is one in a series of images **Laurence Gartel** created for an art exhibition. (To see more of Gartel's work, turn to the galleries in Chapters 6 and 12.) Gartel began the image by scanning each of the source photos into Photoshop. Working in Photoshop, he made selections to isolate the subjects from their backgrounds. He opened a large new blank file, copied each component image and pasted it onto its own layer in the composite. Next he opened the layered image in Painter and used the Layer Adjuster tool to position elements until the composition seemed balanced.

To build a flashy surreal look, Gartel made several Liquid Metal layers. He used the Brush tool in the Liquid Metal dialog box to paint chrome brushstrokes of different thicknesses on the woman's face, neck and hair and to outline the ice cream cone. To reposition droplets of the chrome, he used the Liquid Metal Selection tool (arrow). He applied Standard Metal and Chrome Map Types using the pop-up menu in the dialog box. For some of the layers, he increased the Refraction setting to create the look of clear glass. The live capability of the Liquid Metal dynamic layers allowed Gartel to finesse the Liquid Metal on each layer until he was satisfied with the effect. When these elements were complete, he converted the dynamic layers into image layers by choosing Commit from the menu accessed by clicking the right triangle on the Dynamic Layers section bar.

To create the granular texture in the lower right of the image, Gartel made a new layer and painted the area with dark gray. With a rough texture chosen in the Papers section of the Art Materials palette, he increased its size using the Scale slider. Then he chose Effects, Surface Control, Apply Surface Texture, Using Paper, with strong settings to apply the texture with highlights, shadows and shine. To complete the image, Gartel changed the Opacity and Composite Method in the Layers section of the Objects palette for a few of the layers (for instance, the purple Liquid Metal droplets in the middle area of the work).

WORKING
WITH TYPE
IN PAINTER

Diablo Publishing commissioned Susan LeVan to create this illustration for an article in Sutter Health magazine about head injuries. LeVan used type shapes and Dynamic Text to build elements for her illustration.

PAINTER IS A POWERFUL TOOL FOR DESIGNING creative display type and for special effects. With Painter you can set type and put an image inside it; add texture to type; rotate type, stretch it and paint on it; fill and stroke type for a neon look; add type with special effects to your illustration (for a book cover design, for example); and create three-dimensional chrome type for a logo. You can set text on a path, fill the type with a color, add a shadow and much more. This typography primer will help you get the most out Painter's type tools.

TYPOGRAPHY BASICS

Painter is not recommended for setting large amounts of text—it's a good idea to leave this task to your favorite page layout program, for instance QuarkXPress or PageMaker. Instead, we'll focus on type as a design element using display type, because this is where Painter's tools shine. Display type is generally set in sizes 14-point or larger; it's usually used for feature headlines in magazines, for book covers, for posters and billboards and for Web page headers, to name a few applications.

Fonts and font families. A *font* is a complete set of characters in one size and one typeface. The characters usually include upper-case and lowercase letters, numbers, punctuation and special characters. A *font family* is all of the sizes and style variations of a typeface (for instance, roman and italic styles in light, medium and bold weights).

Serif and sans serif. One way typefaces differ from one another is in the presence or absence of *serifs,* the small cross-strokes on the ends of the strokes that make up the letters. Serif faces were the first typefaces designed for printing. The serifs help our eyes to recognize the shape of a letter sooner and to track horizontally

The letter "E," showing the City font family which includes upper and lowercase City Light and City Light Italic, City Medium and City Medium Italic and City Bold and City Bold Italic.

Serif fonts have small cross-strokes at the ends of the letters. The letter "G" is shown here in a serif font, Goudy (left) and a sans serif font, Stone Sans Semibold (right)

The letter "T," demonstrating examples of several type classes. From left to right, top row: Black Letter, Fette Fraktur; Roman, Century Old Style; Slab Serif, City Bold; Bottom row: Script, Reporter Two; Sans Serif, Stone Sans; and Novelty, Arnold Boecklin.

from one letter to the next across a page, which makes these faces typically easier to read than Sans Serif faces.

The term *sans serif* refers to type without serifs. Usually sans serif fonts have a consistent stroke weight. Because of this quality, they can be ideal for display type because they look good in larger sizes and are good candidates for graphic treatments such as beveling and edge texture application. A sans serif font with very broad strokes has plenty of room to work with when you apply special effects!

Classes of fonts. Fonts can be further grouped into several classes: Black Letter, Roman, Slab Serif, Sans Serif, Script and Decorative. *Black Letter* type resembles the style of hand-lettering that was popular during the time of Gutenberg's first printing press in 1436; Fette Fraktur is an example. These faces are usually used for an old-fashioned, formal look. Many typefaces fall into the *Roman* classification, including Old Style (for instance, Caslon and Century Old Style), Transitionals (Times Roman), and Modern (Palatino). The Old Style fonts have angled serifs, while the modern Roman faces have straight vertical or horizontal serifs. *Slab Serifs* are also known as Egyptians, and they are characterized by even stroke weights and square serifs (examples are City Bold and Stymie). *Sans Serif*, mentioned earlier, is also considered a classification of type. Examples are Helvetica, Franklin Gothic, Futura and Stone Sans.

Designs for *Script* type were originally inspired by penmanship. Script fonts with dramatic thick-and thin strokes (such as Linoscript) are often not good

HELPFUL FONT UTILITIES

Painter reads all of the open fonts when it starts up. If you're a designer with hundreds of fonts on your computer, consider organizing your fonts with a utility (such as Suitcase or MasterJuggler) that enables you to turn them on and off, for a faster startup.

USE EVEN STROKE WEIGHT

Many serif and script fonts have interesting thick and thin strokes. But for type manipulation, choose a font that has strokes with even thickness, rather than dramatic differences in stroke weight, unless your goal is to have the thin strokes disappear when softened or textured.

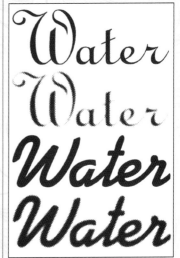

We set type using two script fonts, Linoscript (above) and Monoline Script (below). Our example shows the original typeset word on top of the type with textured edges. As you can see, the Monoline type kept its integrity of design through the special-effects application because of its even stroke weight, while the thick-and-thin Linoscript did not. (For a step-by-step description of how to use texture to erode type, turn to "Edges With Texture," on page 244.)

John Dismukes employed Painter's air-brushes, selections and layers while hand-lettering The 1800 Grand Margarita *logo, shown here in this detail. To view the entire image and more of Dismukes's exceptional work, turn to page 256 in the gallery.*

For this storyboard for The Crossing Guard, *shown here in this detail, Geoff Hull used Painter. To see more of Hull's innovative typography work, turn to the gallery at the end of Chapter 10.*

Each typeface has its own aesthetic and emotional feel, as shown in this example. With Painter's type shapes you can easily set type in different faces and colors. Shown here, from left to right are Fenice Ultra, Brush Script, Vag Rounded Black and City Medium.

candidates for special effects because many techniques involve blurring of the edges or beveling, which can destroy the thin strokes. If you'd like to try special effects and still preserve the script typeface, find a font with thick strokes, such as Kaufman Bold, Monoline Script or Reporter Two. For an example of a logo created using Kaufman Bold type, then treated with effects that include Apply Surface Texture, turn to "Setting a Logo in Stone," on page 252.

Finally, the *Novelty* category is diverse and graphic. These faces are often used to communicate emotion in special projects like poster designs (Arnold Boecklin and Stencil are examples).

Legibility. Have you ever driven past two billboards and noticed that one was easy to read as you drove by, and the other was not? The easier-to-read one was more *legible* than the other. When it's easy to recognize the words so you can absorb their meaning quickly, the type is legible. Legibility was important when you drove by the billboard, or when you were able to efficiently scan the headlines on the front page of a newspaper this morning.

When you set type in Painter, choose fonts carefully if you intend to manipulate them with special effects. Are you using the typeface simply as an element in a collage, where the letters are employed for graphic purposes only and content is not as important? Or do you plan to set an important, legible headline and enhance it with beveling? If the latter is the case, make sure to choose a font with strong enough strokes to withstand the bevel effects, such as a bold Sans Serif face. Turn to "Creating Beveled Chrome" on page 248 for a step-by-step example of a three-dimensional chrome effect applied to sans serif type with Painter's Bevel World plug-in.

DESIGNING WITH PAINTER'S TYPE TOOLS

Each type element that you design has its own purpose: a Web page header, a food advertisement in a magazine, a billboard, the headline for a feature story in a magazine or a signage design. Know your client and research the style aesthetics needed for the design. This knowledge will help you choose the tools to use for the project.

GO FOR CONSISTENT-LOOKING LETTER SPACING

Kerning is the process of removing (or adding) space between pairs of letters so that the spacing is *visually* consistent. To kern type visually, train your eye to see the negative spaces *between* the letters. After adjusting the spacing, the look should appear balanced. To kern in Painter, select each type shape in the Layers section of the Objects palette and move it using the arrow keys on your keyboard.

These type shapes were set in Meta Bold. The original type shapes with visually "uneven" letterspacing (top), were kerned to make the spacing appear consistent (bottom).

To put a photo inside the type, we opened the image and set type shapes in a font with thick strokes, Futura Extra Bold Condensed (top). Then we converted the shapes to a selection (Shapes, Convert To Selection), reversed the selection (Select, Invert), and deleted the background (Backspace/Delete).

We created this clear, embossed look by setting Painter's type shapes in the Machine Bold font, then using Apply Surface Texture and Composite methods.

To make the type break up into sharp ice shards, we set type on a Dynamic Text layer using Futura Extra Bold, then painted on the type with the Shattered variant of the F/X brush.

Working with Type Shapes

When you set type with Painter's Text tool from the Tools palette, each letter that you set is an individual vector object on its own layer. Type shapes have editable Bézier curve outlines and unique transparency capabilities. You can stroke and fill them, then change fill and stroke, or scale or rotate them without loss of quality. Because each letter is a separate element, it's easy to do custom kerning of the individual letterforms.

When to use type shapes.

Use type shapes when setting small amounts of type, when you want to pay special attention to spacing between individual letters, or when you want to edit the outline shape of the letters. Also, type shapes are useful when you want to make a quick selection or mask from type (Shapes, Convert To Selection)—for instance, when you want to put an image inside of the type. (For more information about working with shapes, turn to "Working With Shapes," in Chapter 5, page 145.)

Setting type shapes. With Painter, setting type shapes is simple. From the Tools palette, choose the Text tool, then select a font from the pop-up menu in the Controls:Text palette. Click in the image and you'll see a cursor flashing. If the cursor doesn't look the right size, you can adjust the point size using the Size slider in the Controls:Text palette, or click your cursor on the Size readout to the right of the slider, and type in a new size. Then click the cursor in the image and begin typing. To type a second line, press the Return key (without moving the cursor), and Painter will begin a new line of type. To remove the last letter you typed, leave the cursor where it is and press the Backspace/Delete key.

Using Dynamic Text

If you need to keep the content of type editable (so you can correct or change the spelling) and you don't need to hand-kern it, consider creating the type using a Dynamic Text layer. Dynamic Text is editable, which means you can easily change the size, color,

Mike Reed used Dynamic Text to set type for bumper stickers and a license plate in an Utne Reader *cover illustration, as shown in this detail. Turn to page 255 to see the entire illustration.*

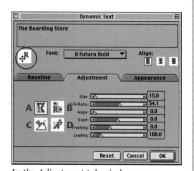

In the Adjustment tab window you can choose settings numerically, or you can click the icon for Size (A), and drag on the type in the image to resize it; V/H Ratio (B), to adjust the text's vertical or horizontal size; Angle (C), to change the degree of orientation; Skew (D), to slant the type. Use the Position icon (in the top section of the dialog box to move your type).

PHOTO: CORBIS IMAGES

With Dynamic Text, you can set type on a curve. We created a wavy baseline curve that included several anchor points and applied the Baseline Curve Style.

font or content of the text, until you decide to convert the dynamic layer into an image layer so you can paint on it or add special effects.

Setting Dynamic Text in your image. Begin by opening the Objects palette (Window, Show Objects) and click the left arrow on the Dynamic Layers section bar to open the section. From the plug-in list choose Dynamic Text and click the Apply button. When the dialog box appears, enter your text into the field at the top of the dialog box. The type will be displayed on a new layer in your image. To specify a type size numerically, in the Dynamic Text dialog box, click the Adjustment tab and set the Size. You can also adjust the V/H Ratio (the relative ratio of the text's vertical and horizontal size), Angle (the degree of orientation), Skew (the slant of the type from the left or right of center), Tracking (the spacing between the letters) and Leading (the spacing between the lines of type).

Scaling, stretching and slanting. If you'd prefer to proportionally scale your type by eye, use the Size tool to drag on the image to make the type larger or smaller. To scale the type by eye, without keeping it in proportion, choose the Stretch tool and drag in the image to scale the type horizontally or vertically. To slant type, drag on it in the image with the Skew tool. You can specify all of these settings numerically using the settings in the Adjustment tab.

Rotating and repositioning. Use the Rotate tool on the image, dragging the type in the direction you want to rotate it. To move your type, use the Position icon, located in the main part of the Dynamic Text dialog box, above the three tabs.

Applying a fill. When you're ready to color the type, click the Appearance tab in the Dynamic Text dialog box and choose the Text button. Under Fill With, select the Color, Grad, Pattern or Weave button. Click the Apply Fill button to update to a new fill. Or turn on Auto Apply so Painter will automatically update as you try out solutions.

Adding a shadow. When you'd like to add a shadow to your type, click the Outside Shadow or Inside Shadow icon in the Appearance tab. By default, a black shadow will be

A GOOD MEMORY

Painter remembers the last font you chose and other specifications you entered in the Dynamic Text dialog box. To clear settings in the dialog box tabs and start over, see "Restoring Dynamic Text Defaults" on page 241.

MOVING A SHADOW

After adding a shadow to type, if you'd like to move the shadow, click the Shadow button to select it, and then drag in the image.

We dragged the shadow slightly down and to the right.

For a snowboarding theme, we set this type on a steep curve using the Vertical Curve Style in the Baseline tab. We added a fill and colored shadow using the controls in the Appearance section, and we used the Skew tool in the Adjustment tab to make the text lean to the right and slant on the baseline.

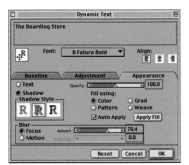

The settings in the Appearance tab for a soft shadow outside the letters in the snowboarding theme type above

The Baseline tab in the Dynamic text dialog box, with the Reshape tool selected. Below it are the Add point and Delete Point tools. Under Curve Styles, from left to right are: the Straight style, the Vertical style (selected), the Baseline style and the Transform style.

applied. To adjust the softness of a shadow, use the Focus or Motion Blur sliders. For a colored shadow, choose a color in the Colors section and click the Apply Fill button.

Setting type on a curve. Painter's Dynamic Text controls include the capability to automatically create a path for the type baseline right in the Baseline tab of the Dynamic Text dialog box. Then you can use the tools in the dialog box to reshape the curve. To begin, select the Dynamic Text plug-in from the list in the Dynamic Layers section. Click the Apply button and when the dialog box appears, enter your type in the field at the top of the dialog box. To place type on a curve in your image, open the Baseline tab in the Dynamic Text dialog box. Painter allows you to fit the type to the curve created in the dialog box using three methods. You can choose the Vertical style (keeps the letters upright), the Baseline style (the base of the letters sit on the curve) or the Transform style (distorts the shape of the letters to fill in the space in the bend of a curve). Use the Center slider in the Baseline tab to center the type on the baseline curve. You can also use the slider to set where the type begins on the baseline.

For a sample similar to the "Under the Sea" type at left, set your type, choose the Baseline curve option in the Baseline tab and you'll see the text curving around the baseline of a newly generated path in your image. To change the shape of the curve, choose the Reshape tool, click on an end (anchor) point and drag a control handle in the direction that you want the curve to go. To add more anchor points (for instance to make a wavy line, like we did), click the baseline curve with the Add Point tool. To remove a point, click the anchor point with the Delete Point tool. Use the control handles on each anchor point to finesse the curve. For more information about other features included in the Dynamic Text dialog box, refer to Chapter 15 of the *Painter 6 User Guide.*

Putting Type Over a Photo

Overview *Set headline type shapes and adjust their opacity; draw a rectangular shape and use it to lighten an area of your image to make the body copy on top of it more readable.*

The East Cape of Baja California Sur offers crystal clear waters, white sand beaches and a lush tropical desert along the tranquil Sea of Cortez.

1a

The settings in the Set Shape Attributes dialog box

1b

Scaling a shape group proportionally by Shift-dragging on a corner handle

2

Positioning the text box using the Layer Adjuster tool

3

The Controls:Adjuster palette showing the reduced opacity of the shapes

PAINTER OFFERS MANY TECHNIQUES to make text and other objects stand out against a background. Here's one of our favorite (and fastest) methods, applied to a comp for a magazine layout.

1 Preparing the type. Open your photo and select the Text tool. Choose a typeface and size from the pop-up menu in the Controls: Text palette (we chose Futura Condensed Extra Bold). To fill the type shapes with white as you set them, select white in the Colors section of the Art Materials palette and choose Shapes, Set Shape Attributes. In the dialog box, check the Fill checkbox and make sure that the Stroke checkbox is unchecked. Then click in your image and type your headline. Kern individual letter pairs by selecting a letter in the Layers section of the Objects palette and using the arrow keys to move it. After you've kerned the letters, group the letters in each word to make them easy to select and reposition as a unit, as follows: Shift-select the letters in the Layers section and Group them (Ctrl/⌘-G.) When you're finished, use the Layer Adjuster to move or scale the type shape groups. (To learn more about transforming shapes, see "Working With Shapes" in Chapter 5 on page 145.)

2 Adding the text bar. We wanted to be able to reposition the text box to try out different layout options, so we drew a white-filled rectangle with the Rectangular Shape tool. After drawing your rectangular shape, use the Layer Adjuster tool to move or resize it.

3 Adjusting the opacity. Finally, get the "screened-back" look by Shift-selecting the items in the Layers section of the Objects palette and lowering the Opacity slider in the Layers section. We set ours to 70%. 🖐

SEE-THROUGH LAYERS

You can use the keyboard to change a layer's opacity. Select the layer in the Layers section (Objects palette), choose the Layer Adjuster tool and press 1 for 10% opacity, 2 for 20%, and so on. Lowering a layer's opacity temporarily can help you position it over a background template.

A Spattery Graffiti Glow

Overview *Use the Text tool to set text shapes over a background; convert the shapes to selections; stroke the selections using the Draw Outside mode, to spatter the background outside the type.*

CHER THREINEN-PENDARVIS / PHOTO: IMAGE FARM

Selected text shapes on the background

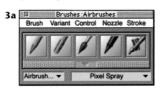

Converting the shapes to a selection

Choosing the Pixel Spray variant of the Airbrushes

Selecting the Draw Outside mode and stroking outside the active selection

WITH THE HELP OF PAINTER'S TYPE SHAPES, selections and Draw modes you can stroke around the edges of type with an Airbrush to create this fast, fun title solution. (It's more efficient to use type shapes rather than the Dynamic Text plug-in for this technique, because in step 2 we'll convert the type to selections.)

1 Choosing an image and setting type shapes. Open an image to use as a background; our photo was 864 x 612 pixels. Choose the Text tool in the Tools palette, then select a font in the Controls:Text palette. (We chose 200-point City Bold Italic.) Click in the image and begin typing. If the Layers section of the Objects palette is open, you'll see each letter shape appear as you type. To kern the type, select individual letters in the Layers section and use the arrow keys on your keyboard to adjust the space between individual letterforms.

2 Converting the shapes to selections. To achieve the result at the top of this page, it's necessary to convert the shapes to selections. Shift-select all of the shapes in the Layers section and choose Shapes, Convert To Selection. The text shapes will disappear from your image and will reappear as animated marquees.

3 Stroking outside of the selection. With the help of Painter's nifty Draw icons in the bottom left of the image window, we used a brush to stroke around the edge of the selection. The Draw icons allow you to use a selection, just like a traditional airbrush frisket, to paint inside or outside of a selection. From the pop-up in the bottom left corner of the image window, choose the Draw Outside (center) icon. In the Brushes palette choose the Pixel Spray variant of the Airbrushes. (We increased the size of the brush to 60 pixels, using Size slider on the Controls:Brush palette.) Now, choose Select, Stroke Selection and watch as Painter gives your type a fine grained, spattery glow. Try stroking your selection with other Airbrushes such as the Coarse Spray or the Variable Spatter variant.

Edges with Texture

Overview *Set type using Dynamic Text; soften the edge of the type; give the type edges texture; adjust the opacity and Composite Method to make the type transparent.*

YOU CAN USE PAINTER'S EXPRESS TEXTURE command to give the smooth edges of a typeface texture. For the image above, we set type over a photo on two Dynamic Text layers. Then we applied a texture to the edges of the word love and adjusted the opacity and Composite Method for both layers. A similar process might be used to texturize the edges of photos when making a collage.

The original photo from Corbis Images

1 Choosing a photo. We began by selecting a photo to use as a background. The photo measured 883 x 450 pixels.

2 Sampling color for the text. Painter's Dynamic Text layer has the capability to update color fills in live text automatically. For the type and photo to work as a cohesive unit, we sampled colors from the image so we could apply these colors to the text layers. To set the current color in the Colors section of the Art Materials palette for the "Love" text to come, we sampled a color from the image's sky using the Dropper.

Using the Dropper to sample a color

3 Setting the type. We used Painter's Dynamic Text to set our type because of its capability to preview many type choices quickly, right on the image. And we set type in two separate Dynamic Text layers because we wanted to be able to scale and position the elements individually in our design.

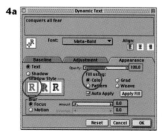

Setting the "live" type and scaling it using the Adjustment section

To make a Dynamic Text layer, open the Dynamic Layers section of the Objects palette and choose Dynamic Text from the resource list menu. Click the Apply button on the front of the palette (or choose Apply from the Dynamic Text section bar's menu). When the dialog box appears, select a typeface from the Font pop-up menu (we chose Meta Bold). Type your text into the field at the top of the dialog box.

Applying a solid color fill in a contrasting color using the Appearance section

To reposition the type, click the Position icon to the left of the Font menu and drag the cursor. To interactively resize the type, click on the Size icon in the Adjustment section and drag on

TYPE AND TEXTURED EDGES

Textured edge treatments work best on type or logos that have a large point-size and broad stroke widths. Special effects can obliterate type with thin strokes.

4b

The Dynamic Text applied over the image

5a

Choosing Commit to convert the Dynamic Text to an image layer

5b

The feathered mask, with visibility turned on in the Masks section

6a

Trying out Express Texture settings

6b

The "Love" type with textured edges

7

The layers with lower opacities and Screen Composite Method applied

a corner of the type in your image. Or specify a numeric size for the type by typing a number in the Size field or adjust the Size slider.

4 Experimenting with color. We colored each Dynamic Text layer with two subtle colors sampled from the image. To experiment with the color of your type, in the Appearance section of the Dynamic Text dialog box, choose the Text style icon on the far left and under "Fill using," choose Color. If you'd like to try out more colors, turn on Auto Apply, choose a new color in the Colors section and click the Apply Fill button. (If you'd like to sample another color from your image and apply it to a Dynamic Text layer, you'll need to temporarily close the Dynamic Text dialog box by clicking OK to accept. Then click on a new color in your image with the Dropper. To open the Dynamic Text dialog box again, double-click the name of the layer in the Layers section. Click the Apply Fill button and the color of your text will be updated.)

5 Converting the layer and feathering its mask. Before you can add a textured edge to your type, you'll need to convert the Dynamic Text layer to an image layer so you can manipulate the layer mask. To convert the dynamic layer, select its name in the Layers section of the Objects palette. On the Dynamic Layers section bar, click the right triangle to access the menu and choose Commit.

To "texture" the edges of the type, we applied texture to the layer's mask. With the layer still selected in the Layers section, click on its mask in the Masks section. To view the mask in black-and-white, turn on the layer mask eye icon. To prepare the type layer for the texture to come, we gave the type mask a soft 10-pixel feather. Click the right triangle on the Masks section bar to open the menu and choose Feather Mask. Type a number in the field and click OK.

6 Adding texture to the edges. In our image, we textured the edges of only the "Love" type. Choose Effects, Surface Control, Express Texture Using Paper. The Express Texture dialog box is interactive, so you can test different paper textures or even switch to a new paper library without needing to close the dialog box. For the "Love" type, we used the Streaks texture loaded from the Wild Textures library (in the Paper Texture Libraries folder on the Painter 6 CD-ROM). With Express Texture, you can apply texture to only the shades of gray in the feathered edge. Change the shape of the type and the quality of the edge by moving the Gray Threshold, Grain and Contrast sliders. The Gray Threshold slider controls the overall brightness and works interactively with the Grain slider, which controls the intensity of the grain in the image. These two sliders work best when kept relatively close together. We used settings of Gray Threshold, 69%; Grain, 80%; and Contrast, 300%.

7 Giving the type transparency. For a more subtle look, we blended the type into the photo by setting the Composite Method of both layers to Screen in the Layers section. We set the "Love" type layer to 60% Opacity and the "conquers all fear" layer to 50%.

Stroked and Glowing

Overview *Create a dark, textured background; use the Text tool to set type shapes; kern the letters; apply a fill and stroke; convert the type shapes to a layer; copy the layer; feather the layer masks to make soft glows; fill each glow layer with a color.*

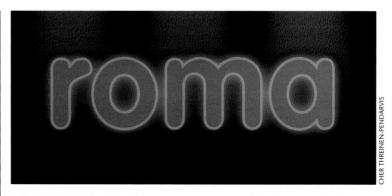

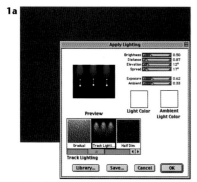

Choosing Track Lighting in the Apply Lighting dialog box

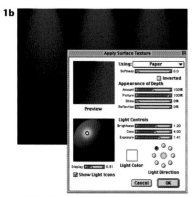

Adding Surface Texture to the background

The grouped cherry red type shapes on the completed background

PAINTER IS THE IDEAL TOOL FOR CREATING quick design solutions. When building these color comprehensives for a new restaurant's signage, we created a variety of solutions using Painter's type shapes that included strokes and glows. Here are two of them.

1 Making the background. Open a new file (ours was 883 x 675 pixels) and fill the image canvas with a dark color by choosing Effects, Fill. (Neon glows best at night!) When the dialog box appears, choose the Current Color button.

We added atmosphere to the background—simulating track lighting on a stucco wall—by applying two effects that Painter is famous for: Apply Lighting and Surface Texture. First we turned on the lights by choosing Effects, Surface Control, Apply Lighting. We chose Track Lighting, accepted the default settings for the light and clicked OK. To suggest the stucco wall behind the lights, we selected Basic Paper in the Papers section of the Art Materials palette prior to adding the 3D texture effect. To apply the 3D texture we chose Effects, Surface Control, Apply Surface Texture, Using Paper. We turned Shine down to 0 (for a matte look) and left the other settings at their defaults.

2 Setting type shapes. For these solutions we used type shapes rather than Painter's Dynamic Text, because in step 3 it would be easier to add a stroke to the type. Our objective was to create a variety of neon looks for our client.

To suggest the look of a neon tube, we chose a bold typeface with thick, even strokes and smooth curves (170-point Vag Rounded Bold), that would work well with the stroking we planned to add. Choose the Text tool in the Tools palette, select a font in the Controls:Text palette and choose a bright, neon-like color in the Colors section of the Art Materials palette. Open the Layers section of the Objects palette (so you can see the letters appear as you type). To set your type, click in the image and begin typing. To kern the type, click on a letter's name in the Layers section and use the arrow keys on your keyboard to adjust the space between the letters.

After you've finished kerning the type, group it so you can efficiently move it around as one unit: With all the type shapes selected, click the Group button on the Layers section (Ctrl/⌘-G).

3a
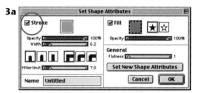

Applying a stroke to the type shapes

3b

The type shapes with gold stroke applied

4

Choosing Feather Mask on the Masks section of the Objects palette to add a feather to the layer mask for the glow

3 Stroking the type. Our concept was a sign made out of solid, brightly colored material, backlit with a neon glow. With shapes you can add a colored stroke to enhance your design. Click on the shape group in the Layer section to select it, choose Shapes, Set Shape Attributes and click the Stroke checkbox to apply a stroke. Change the stroke's color by clicking the Stroke's color swatch and then by clicking on a new color in the Colors section. (We chose a golden orange.) After applying the stroke, we increased the stroke width to 6.2 using the Width slider and clicked OK. To rename the shape group, double-click on its name in the Layers section and when the Layer Attributes dialog box appears, name it "Stroked/Filled Type."

4 Adding colored glows. To give the title a multicolor glow, we made two copies of the shape group (Alt/Option-click on the shapes in the image with the Layer Adjuster) and converted each duplicate to a single layer (choose Shapes, Convert to Layer). Rename the first layer "Yellow Glow." Drag the "Yellow Glow" layer below the "stroked/filled" layer in the Layers section so you'll be able to see the glow effect when it's applied. Rename the second layer "Red Glow." Position it below "Yellow Glow" in the Layers section. For soft glowing edges, we feathered both layer masks. To feather the "Yellow Glow," click on its mask in the Masks section (Objects palette), click the right triangle on the section bar and choose Feather Mask using a feather of 20 pixels. To select the Layer again, click back on RGB-Yellow Glow in the Masks section. Next, in the Layers section, turn on Preserve Transparency and fill the "Yellow Glow" layer with a gold color that complements the stroke and fill (Effects, Fill with Current Color). To make the Red Glow, select it in the Layers section and repeat the process above, but this time use a feather of 50 pixels in the Feather Mask dialog box. The final image with the fill, stroke and glows can be see at the top of the facing page.

A variation. With Painter's shapes it's easy to change the inside of the letters to transparent for the look of neon tubes, rather than a cut-out sign. Within the group of shapes selected in the Layers section, choose Shapes, Set Shape Attributes and uncheck the Fill box. The transparent neon variation is shown below.

The multicolored glow shows through the type shapes when the Fill attribute is turned off.

Creating
Beveled
Chrome

Overview *Open a file and apply*
lighting to build a background; set
type shapes; convert the shapes to
a layer; bevel the forms and apply
a reflection; add a drop shadow.

CHER THREINEN-PENDARVIS

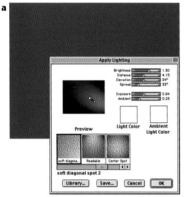

Creating a new soft diagonal spotlight
based on the Slide Lighting light.

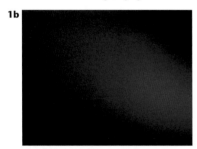

The softly lit background, ready for the type

The selected, ungrouped type shapes and
the background with lighting

PAINTER'S BEVEL WORLD DYNAMIC LAYER allows you to try an endless variety of custom bevels on a selected layer quickly, without
time-consuming masks and channels. To create this three-
dimensional chrome title, we applied effects that included custom
lighting, a rounded bevel with a reflection map and a shadow.

1 Creating a background with custom lighting. Begin by
creating a new file with a deep blue-green background (our file
was 883 pixels wide). To add depth to the background we applied
soft diagonal lighting that would complement the bright, shiny
chrome to come. To open the Lighting dialog box, choose Effects,
Surface Control, Apply Lighting. When the dialog box appears,
click on the Slide Lighting choice. In the Lighting Preview, drag
the large end of the light up a little higher in the Preview. Turn
the light around by dragging its small end to point in the opposite direction—to the lower right of the image canvas. Now
increase the Brightness of your light: move the Brightness slider
to 1.30 and adjust the Distance to 4.15 to add to the distance
between the light and the image canvas and thus make the light
softer. To save your new light, click the Save button and name it
when the Save Lighting dialog box appears.

2 Setting the type. Now that the backdrop is finished, you're
ready to create the type. Choose a contrasting color in the Colors
section of the Art Materials palette to automatically fill the text
with color as you type. The contrasting color will make it easier
for you to see your type as you adjust the space between individual letters. Select the Text tool, choose a font and size in the
Controls:Text palette and set the type. We set 120-point type using
Vag Rounded Bold. (If you don't have the typeface we used,
choose a bold font with broad strokes to accommodate the beveling
effect to come.) Group the shapes (so you can work with the type
shapes as a unit) by Shift-selecting them in the Layers section of
the Objects palette and clicking the Group button, or press Ctrl/⌘-G.

3a

The rough bevel generated by the Bevel World layer default settings

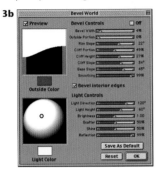
3b

Our settings in the Bevel World dialog box

4

We used "emap 27" from the "emaps 2" library on the Painter 6 CD-ROM.

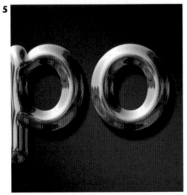
5

We moved the shadow down and to the right of the chrome type.

3 Beveling the type. In preparation for using the Bevel World dynamic layer, merge the shapes group to a single image layer by selecting the group in the Layers section and choosing Shapes, Convert To Layer. With the layer still selected, open the Dynamic Layers section of the Objects palette by clicking on the left arrow on the Dynamic Layers section bar; choose Bevel World from the resource list and click the Apply button. To build a 3D effect with a smooth rounded shape that would show off the reflection map we planned to add, we used these settings: Bevel Width slider to 4% (for narrower sides and a broader top); Outside Portion, 0% (for no bevel outside the original pixels on the layer); Rim Slope, 22° (for a rounder top); Cliff Portion, 29% (for a smaller vertical distance between the base and rim); Cliff Height, 27% (to reduce the height of the sides); Cliff Slope, 34° (to decrease the angle for the middle of the bevel); Base Slope, 45° (leaving the angle of the outermost portion at its default); Smoothing, 99% (to add roundness to the base, cliff and rim of the bevel).

4 Achieving the chrome effect. The secret to achieving this chrome effect is choosing a bright shiny environment map in the Patterns section of the Art Materials palette and using the Reflections slider in the lower part of the Bevel World dialog box. We chose an environment map that included shiny metal reflections and bright red colors. To apply the reflection map we used, you'll need to load the "emap 2" library. To load this library, choose Load Library from the resource list on the Patterns section and navigate to the "emap 2" library on the Painter 6 CD-ROM. Select "emaps 2" and click Open. Back in the Patterns section, choose "emap 27" from the resource list menu. Now move the Reflection slider in the Bevel World dialog box to the far right (we used 99%). Your type will magically change to bright shiny chrome!

5 Adding a shadow. To increase the depth of our image, we added a drop shadow. To build your shadow, Alt/Option-click with the Layer Adjuster to make a copy of the selected layer and convert the lower of the two layers to an image layer so you can fill and feather it: Choose Commit from the Dynamic Layers menu (accessed by clicking the right triangle on the Dynamic Layers section bar). In preparation for filling the shadow, turn on the Preserve Transparency checkbox in the Layers section, so the fill will stay within the type. Next, choose black in the Colors section of the Art Materials palette and fill the layer by choosing Effects, Fill, Current Color. To build the soft edge for the shadow, give the layer mask a soft feather: Begin by selecting the layer mask in the Masks section of the Objects palette, then click the right triangle on the Masks section bar and choose Feather Mask. Type a number in the field (we used 25-pixels) and click OK. After feathering, position the selected shadow using the arrow keys on your keyboard. We moved our shadow 10 pixels down and 6 pixels to the right of the chrome type layer.

Painting With Ice

Overview *Set Dynamic Text to use as a template for "hand-lettering"; paint icy script on a Liquid Metal plug-in floater; composite a copy of the floater to enhance the design.*

CHER THREINEN-PENDARVIS

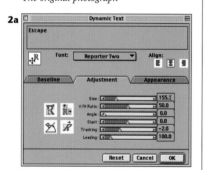

PHOTO: CORBIS IMAGES

The original photograph

The Dynamic Text dialog box with settings for our title

The image with the Dynamic Text applied

YOU CAN CREATE TEXT EFFECTS QUICKLY with dynamic layers. To begin this cover comp for an online travel agency catalog, we set type using a Dynamic Text layer. Using this text as a template, we "hand-painted" new 3D letters onto a Liquid Metal dynamic layer using a tablet and stylus. Then we applied special settings to give the liquid letters a clear, frozen look.

1 Choosing an image. We began by selecting a photo that measured 768 x 512 pixels. Although the final art used online would be smaller, we preferred to work at a larger size so we could zoom in and finesse the details. We chose a photo with a Mediterranean theme and refreshing colors that would complement the Liquid Metal title.

2 Setting Dynamic Text. To make a Dynamic Text layer, open the Dynamic Layers section of the Objects palette and choose Dynamic Text from the resource list. Click the Apply button on the front of the palette (or choose Apply from the Dynamic Text section bar's menu). When the dialog box appears, select a typeface from the Font pop-up menu (we chose Reporter Two). Type your text into the field at the top of the dialog box. Click on the Adjustment tab. To interactively resize the type, click on the Size icon and drag on the live text in your image. You can repeatedly rescale the type without loss of quality. Use the Position icon (near the top of the box) to move the text block. When you've finished making adjustments to your image, click OK. (If you want more control over the spacing of the individual letterforms, you can use Painter's Text tool, instead of Dynamic Text, to set type for your title template. To read about using the Text tool and type shapes, turn to Chapter 5, "Using Layers and Shapes.")

3 Drawing the liquid metal type. To make a Liquid Metal dynamic layer, choose Liquid Metal from the Dynamic Layers section's resource menu, and click the Apply button. Painter will

3

Beginning to hand-letter the Liquid Metal type using the dynamic text as a template

4a

Increasing the Refraction setting in the Liquid Metal dialog box for the icy look

4b

The Liquid Metal type changed to ice. The underlying template layer is visible.

4c

The icy type with underlying layer removed

5

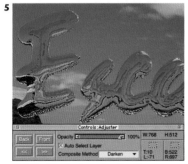

Detail of the icy type showing the underlying layer's Composite Method set to Darken

generate an empty, transparent Liquid Metal dynamic layer, and the Liquid Metal dialog box will appear.

With the Dynamic Text title as an underlay, we used a stylus to trace the text with the Liquid Metal brush tool. To begin, choose the Brush tool in the Liquid Metal dialog box and carefully paint your title. Adjust the Amount, Smooth, Size and Volume settings to your liking. To select all of the Liquid Metal so that you can apply new settings, choose the Liquid Metal Selector (arrow) and drag a marquee around the metal. Our settings were Amount, 5.0; Smooth, 90; Size, 17.0; Volume, 97; Spacing, .001; Map, Standard Metal, with Surface Tension checked.

A Liquid Metal dynamic layer is *live*, which means you can continue to finesse the dialog box settings. To keep a layer dynamic, do not "commit" the layer (change it into an image layer), and make sure to save the file in RIFF format. For more information about dynamic layers, turn to Chapter 5, "Using Layers and Shapes."

4 Changing the metal to crystal-clear ice. Giving the title an icy look is easy! To make the Liquid Metal crystal clear, move the Refraction slider all the way to the right. We set our slider to 90%, because it helped the type stand out from the photo. After completing your letters, delete the Dynamic Text layer you used as a template: Select its name in the Layers section of the Objects palette and click the Delete button.

5 Compositing a second layer. As you can see in your image, Painter's Liquid Metal dynamic layer "refracts" an underlying image. To give the ice more texture and make it look shinier, we set up another layer between our ice layer and the image beneath. To begin, make a copy of the Liquid Metal layer (Alt/Option-click with the Layer Adjuster), then drag the copy below it in the Layers section of the Objects palette. To enhance the copy of the Liquid Metal layer using tonal effects, choose Effects, Tonal Control, Brightness/Contrast and slightly increase the contrast. To add more texture and bring out the highlights in the icy type, we changed the underlying layers' Composite Method in the Layers section to Darken. 🖌

So many options! When you have the underlying layer in place, experiment with changing the Composite Method in the Layers section to different settings. We chose Gel (left), and Pseudocolor (right). Control the effect with the layer's Opacity slider.

Setting a Logo in Stone

Overview *Open a background image; enhance its texture; set type for the logo and make a border; convert the shapes to a selection and copy the selection to a layer; use Apply Surface Texture to create a three-dimensional look.*

CHER THREINEN-PENDARVIS / ARTBEATS

1a

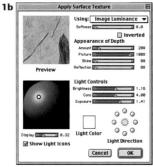

The background image from ArtBeats

1b

Applying texture to the background image based on luminosity in the image

2a

Tightening the space between the letters

YOU CAN CREATE THE ILLUSION of a logo carved out of sandstone with Painter's Apply Surface Texture. By selecting part of a background image, you can use Apply Surface Texture to emboss type, logos and other graphics, while preserving the image texture and striations, as in the image above. For this surfboard designer's classic style, we used a "retro" script typeface (Kaufman Bold) and Painter's type shapes to build the logo. Kaufman's even stroke weight and its clean, flowing lines help to make the logo easy to read from a distance. (If your logo was created in a PostScript program such as Adobe Illustrator turn to page 110 in Chapter 4 for information about importing vector artwork.)

1 Preparing the background. Open an image to use as a background. We chose Sandstone from the ArtBeats Marble and Granite 2 collection, then we resized the image to 883-pixels-wide. (The point size of the type described in step 2 and the Surface Texture settings described in step 7 reflect the size of the file we used.) To give the sandstone a realistic texture based on its light-to-dark values, we chose Effects, Surface Control, Apply Surface Texture Using Image Luminance. We used a subtle Amount setting of 22%; for a matte effect, we reduced Shine to 0, leaving the other Material settings at their defaults. Under Light Controls, we chose the top left Light Direction button (to complement the natural lighting in the image), increased Brightness to 1.23, and left the other settings at their defaults.

2 Setting the logo type. Next, open the Layers section of the Objects palette (Window, Show Objects, Layers) so that you can see the type shapes appear in the list as you type. Click in the image with the Text tool, choose a font and size in the Controls:Text palette and begin typing. (We chose 80-point Kaufman Bold.) To connect the script letters to one another, we selected the letters in turn using the Layer Adjuster tool and moved them closer together using the arrow keys on the keyboard. After kerning your type, it's a good idea to group each word so you can reposition it easily. To

3a

The selected, grouped type shapes for the logo in final position

4a

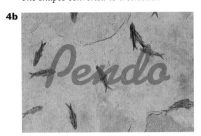

The shapes converted to a selection

4b

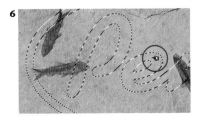

Viewing the mask as a red overlay

5

Load Selection

Load From: [New Mask 1 ▼]

Operation
- ○ Replace Selection
- ● Add To Selection
- ○ Subtract From Selection
- ○ Intersect With Selection

[Cancel] [OK]

Loading a selection from the type (New Mask 1) and adding it to the border selection

6

The Layer Adjuster tool positioned over selected area, ready to copy

group, Shift-select the letters in the Layers section and click the Group button. To scale the group proportionately, press Shift and drag one of the corner handles. To move the group, drag with the Layer Adjuster tool.

4 Converting the type to a selection and storing it as a mask. Before you can use the type shapes to apply effects to the image, you'll need to convert them to a selection. Using the Layer Adjuster tool, select the type shape group in the Layers section and choose Shapes, Convert To Selection. The shape group will disappear and the selection (a black-and-white animated marquee) will appear. To store the selection as a mask, choose Select, Save Selection. The mask will be listed in the Masks section of the Objects palette as New Mask 1.

So you have a guide when you make the oval section for the border in the following step, view the mask as a red overlay on your image by opening its eye icon in the Masks section of the Objects palette.

5 Adding a border selection to the type. Next, we made an oval selection for the border. Choose the Oval Selection tool in the Tools palette and drag to make an oval, set up where you want the inside of the border to be. To reposition or scale your selection, choose the Selection Adjuster. (It shares a space with the Layer Adjuster in the Tools palette.) For more information about working with selections, turn to "Transforming Selections" on page 113, and "Editing Selections" on page 115 in Chapter 4.

To give the selection a border, choose Select, Modify, Border and specify a width (we used 18 pixels). A second marquee (the border), will be added outside the current selection marquee.

Now combine the border selection with the type: Load the type selection by choosing Select, Load Selection, choose New Mask 1 from the Load From menu, and under Operation choose Add To Selection. (This command will build a new selection based on the type and the border.) Save this new selection as a mask by choosing Select, Save Selection. For more variations on using masks to emboss a graphic, turn to Chapter 4, "Making Masks for Embossing" on page 119.

6 Making two layers. We made two layers in preparation for the Surface Texture applications that are to follow in step 7. To copy the contents of the selection and make two layers, position the Layer Adjuster tool inside of the marquee and Alt/Option-click two times. (After the first click the marquee will disappear, but the second click will still work to make a second layer.) In the Layers section, to name the top layer, double-click on its name to access the Layer Attributes dialog box. Name the layer "Logo 1" and click OK. Click on the layer below it in the Layers section and name this second layer "Logo 2."

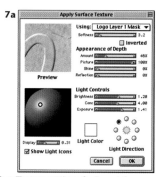

7a

Surface Texture settings for Logo 1 layer

7b

Surface Texture applied to Logo layer 1

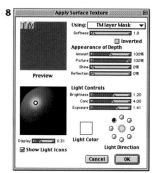

7c

Surface Texture applied to Logo 2 layer

8

Applying Surface Texture to the TM symbol

7 Giving the logo dimension. We wanted a realistic 3D look in which the letters and logo would be raised above the sandstone surface. To avoid burning out the highlights on the logo, we applied Surface Texture to both logo layers, using subtle settings on the top layer and stronger settings on the bottom layer. To begin, select the "Logo 1" layer by clicking on its name in the Layers section and choose Effects, Surface Control, Apply Surface Texture. When the dialog box appears, choose the "Logo 1" mask from the Using menu. Use subtle Amount and Softness settings (we used Amount, 46%; and Softness, 3.3). Adding Softness will allow you to raise the height of the emboss, but too much softness can make an image blurry. We turned Shine down to 0 (for a matte finish on the sandstone), clicked the top left light button and left the other settings at their defaults.

To produce a wider shadow in our image, we used a stronger Amount setting—138%—when we applied surface texture to the "Logo 2" layer, leaving the other settings alone. Then we used the arrow keys on the keyboard to offset Layer 2 under "Layer 1" so we would see just a small portion of the shadow. Move the "Logo 2" layer 1 pixel to the right and 2 pixels down. The Surface Texture settings and the number of pixels you'll move the lower layer to offset the shadow will depend on the size of your file.

8 Adding the symbol. For the TM symbol, we set 14-point Stone Sans Bold type. We converted the TM type shapes to a selection (as in step 3), and Alt/Option-clicked to make a layer. Since the TM was set in small 14-point type, it required Surface Texture settings with less Softness. Our settings were: Softness 1.0; Amount, 100%; Shine, 0, and we left the other settings at their defaults. ⓦ

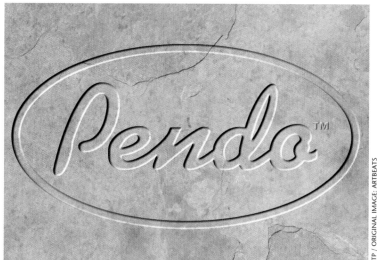

For a variation of the embossed effect using slightly different images with light shining from the bottom right, we used a different sandstone image and checked the Invert box in the Apply Surface Texture dialog box.

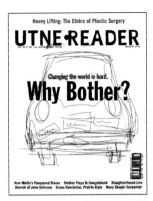

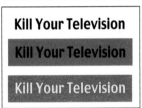

■ "I can't emphasize enough that traditional drawing and rendering skills are indispensable in my approach to digital imaging," says **Mike Reed,** who built this illustration for the cover of *The Utne Reader* magazine. The concept for the cover—how aging baby-boomers' attitudes towards activism have changed—was decided by the art director and editorial staff of the magazine. To begin the image, Reed opened a new file, the exact size of the magazine cover. To import a scan of the art director's page layout, so he could see the type exactly as it would appear in the final printed piece, he chose File, Place. Then he set the Composite Method to Gel in the Layers section of the Objects palette, so he could see through the layout layer. Again using File, Place, he imported a scanned photo of a VW bug and resized it using Effects, Orientation, Free Transform. In the Layers section, he moved the type layer to the top so he could use it as a guide while he

worked. Reed selected the VW bug layer in the Layers section. To simplify and stylize the car, he drew loose brushstrokes over it with the Square Chalk variant of Dry Media. When the VW bug was roughed in, he began adding the bumper stickers to the image. Reed created the bumper stickers using slogans written by the magazine editorial staff. Leaving the main illustration open, he created a new document that measured 1 x 3 inches at 300 pixels-per-inch. Using Dynamic Text in the Dynamic Layers section of the Objects palette, he set type for several bumper stickers, then chose the size and spacing using the controls in the Adjustment tab of the Dynamic Text dialog box. When he was happy with each sticker, he converted each dynamic layer to an image layer. Then to complete each bumper sticker, he used the Rectangular Selection tool to make a selection around the type on the layer. To fill the background outside the type with a color, he

used the Paint Bucket. Again, using the Paint Bucket, he filled each letter of the type with another color. Because Reed didn't want the flat colors of the bumper stickers to contrast with the texture of the final illustration, he added texture to each one with Effects, Surface Control, Dye Concentration, Using Paper. He selected each sticker with the Rectangular Selection tool, and then used the Layer Adjuster tool to drag and drop it into the main illustration file, where he positioned it. He repeated this process until the bumper stickers and the license plate were positioned in the file.

With all of the elements in place, Reed added freehand detail to the rest of the image. He slowly built up textures using the Sharp Chalk, Artists Pastel Chalk, Square Chalk and Oil Pastel variants of Dry Media over the Woodshavings texture, loaded from the Painter 6 Wow! CD-ROM. To see more of Mike Reed's illustration work, turn to the galleries at the end of Chapters 4 and 7.

■ **John Dismukes** of Capstone Studios is well known for his creative logo design and hand-drawn typography. He used similar processes to design and airbrush the three images on these pages. Dismukes begins each design by drawing many sketches, and when the direction is established, he draws a tight visualization of the typography on paper. The approved pencil sketch is then scanned and used as a template in FreeHand to create Post-Script outlines. He imports the outlines into Photoshop and builds elements on layers. Then he opens the file with layers in Painter for the airbrushing. In Painter, some of the layers are duplicated and used to make selections (via Drop and Select from the Layers section bar menu), and they are then saved as masks. (Alternately, outlines can be imported directly into Painter as shapes via File, Acquire, Adobe Illustrator file and then converted

to layers.) Dismukes uses selections to limit paint as he airbrushes using the Digital Airbrush variant of Airbrushes. For a step-by-step description of a similar technique using Painter, turn to "Selections and Airbrush," on page 127.

The *Grand Marnier Metallic Cactus* illustration (top) was commissioned by Alcone Marketing Group and art-directed by Liliana Marchica. Dismukes began with a tight sketch, but he wanted a rough look for this logo, so he did not import outlines. He painted masks for the type, then converted them to selections he could use to limit the paint. Using the Digital Airbrush, Dismukes airbrushed the lettering. To add texture to the leaf, he cloned texture onto a layer from another file: He opened a texture file with the same dimensions as the logo file, defined it as the clone source by choosing File, Clone

Source and used a Cloning brush variant to softly brush the texture onto the layer.

For the packaging of an action game, art director (Mark Rein) and client (Epic Games, Inc.) wanted a logo with a progressive, "Gothic Tech" style. After scanning his tight sketch, Dismukes began *Unreal* (above), by importing the sketch and outlines into a new file. For an underpainting, he filled the type with brown. Using the imported outlines, he made masks for the letter faces and bevels. With selections loaded from the masks to constrain the spray, he carefully airbrushed the shadows and highlights, working from dark to light. To intensify the bronze color, he duplicated the finished layer and set its Composite method to Multiply, with 30% Opacity.

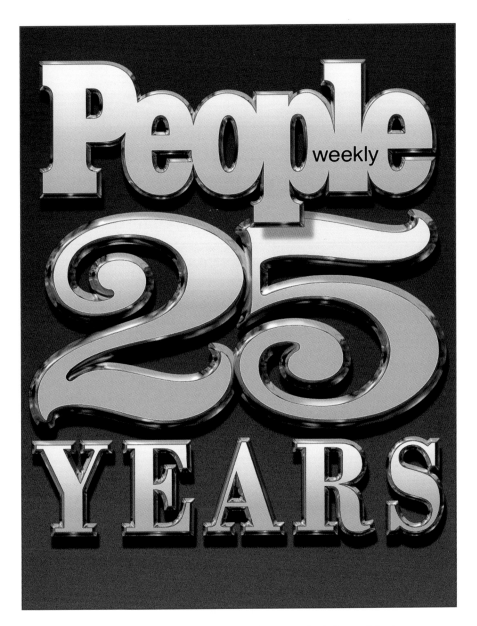

■ For *People's 25th Anniversary logo,* a cover illustration for Time Warner's *People Weekly magazine,* **John Dismukes** and **Jo-Anne Redwood** worked closely with their team at Capstone Studios and the art directors from *People* magazine, Phil Simone and Hilli Pitzer. Making hundreds of sketches, Dismukes and Redwood designed the type to complement the existing *People* magazine logo, make a strong statement, and be legible from a distance. After the design was approved, Dismukes took the time he needed to perfect the letterspacing, and then carefully rendered the realistic reflections. Like a traditional airbrush artist using friskets, Dismukes built a mask for the front face of the type and another for the bevels. After making a new layer, he filled the letters with light gray. Then he loaded the bevel selection and used the Digital Airbrush variant of Airbrushes to paint detailed reflections, highlights and shadows. Finally, he loaded a selection from the face mask again, and with a tiny airbrush, he painted the fine strokes that set off the flat front of the letters from their beveled sides. He finished by adding a drop shadow and background. "For high-quality work, you have to bring artistry to the computer," says Dismukes.

USING
PAINTER
WITH
PHOTOSHOP

When creating Quarry, *Marc Brown used Illustrator, Photoshop and Painter. To see more of his work, turn to page 271.*

MASK MAXIMUMS

A Painter file can contain up to 32 masks in the Masks section, plus one mask for each layer. Photoshop's maximum is 24 channels in a RGB file, but three of the channels are taken up by the Red, Green and Blue color channels (leaving room for 21 masks). If you attempt to open a file with 32 masks in Photoshop, you will be greeted by a polite dialog box asking if you would like to discard the channels (numbers higher than 21 will be discarded).

WITH PAINTER 6 IT'S EASY TO MOVE FILES back and forth seamlessly between Painter and Photoshop. Images can be moved with their layers, masks and paths intact.

And what does Painter have to offer the Photoshop user? Fantastic natural-media brushes that give your images warmth and a multitude of textures and fabulous special effects! In addition to the work showcased in this chapter, several of the other artists whose work appears in this book have used both Painter and Photoshop in the development of their images. If you're an avid Photoshop user and would like to see more examples of how other artists have combined use of the two programs, check out the work of these artists for inspiration: Jeff Burke, Ellie Dickson, John Dismukes, Donal Jolley, and Corrine Okada. The index in the back of this book contains page references for each of their names.

PAINTER TO PHOTOSHOP

Here are some pointers to keep in mind for importing Painter 6 files into Photoshop 5.5.

• To preserve image layers when moving an image from Painter into Photoshop, save a Painter 6 file in Photoshop format. Photoshop will open it and translate the layers with their names and the layer hierarchy intact.

• If a Painter file contains layers that extend beyond Painter's live image area, and that document is opened in Photoshop 4, 5 or 5.5, areas outside of the live area are no longer trimmed off. (Photoshop 3 clipped the layer information outside the image window.)

• Painter offers all of the Photoshop Blending modes, except three—Color Dodge, Color Burn and Exclusion; and it has seven additional

John Dismukes used FreeHand, Photoshop and Painter when building the Risk Game Board for the Parker Bros./Hasbro Games Group, shown here as a detail. See the entire image on page 269.

DYNAMIC LAYERS

When a Painter Dynamic Layer such as Liquid Metal is opened in Photoshop, the layers are preserved but the dynamic capabilities are lost. To keep their dynamic properties, save a copy of your file with live dynamic layers in RIFF format.

A PATH TO PHOTOSHOP

You can store path information with a selection in Painter for import to Photoshop, and the path will appear in the Photoshop Paths palette. When you make a selection with the Lasso, Rectangular or Oval Selection tools or set type shapes and convert them to a selection in Painter (Shapes, Convert To Selection), path information is automatically stored in the file. If you paint a mask or generate one with the Automask or Color Mask functions, you can build path information into the file: Convert this mask-based selection to outline information using Select, Transform Selection. Then if you save the Painter file in Photoshop format, these kinds of outlines will appear in Photoshop's Paths palette.

To import Photoshop paths into Painter, open the file, and choose Yes in the Convert Paths dialog box. The Photoshop paths will convert to shapes, which will appear in the Layers section of the Objects palette.

Compositing Methods of its own. When Photoshop encounters a Painter-native Composite Method (like Pseudocolor or Reverse-out), it converts that layer to Normal. Photoshop converts Magic Combine to Lighten mode, Gel to Darken mode, Colorize to Color mode, and Shadow Map to Multiply.

- To save Painter selections into the Mask List of the Objects palette and use them in Photoshop as channels, save a Painter file in Photoshop format. When you open the file in Photoshop, the named masks will automatically appear in the Channels palette.

- Painter's Shapes cannot be imported into Photoshop with their object-oriented information intact. Saving a Painter file with shapes in Photoshop format rasterizes shapes to Photoshop layers, which appear in the Layers palette using the compositing (blending) method you specified for the shapes in Painter.

PHOTOSHOP TO PAINTER

Here are some pointers for importing Photoshop files into Painter 6.

- If you prefer to begin your file in Photoshop, and the file contains layers, keep in mind that Painter can only open Photoshop format files saved in RGB mode. If you'd like to open a CMYK or Grayscale mode file in Painter, you'll have to save the file in TIFF format.

- Although Painter 6 will now open a CMYK TIFF file, keeping files in RGB color mode when porting files from Photoshop to Painter will make the best color translation, because RGB is Painter's native color model.

- If you save your Photoshop image with layers in Photoshop format, Painter 6 will open it and translate the layers with their names intact. If you are using Photoshop 3, save the file in Photoshop 3 format.

- A Photoshop document made up of transparent layers only— that is, without a Background layer—will open in Painter as layers over a white background in the Canvas layer.

- Painter can recognize all but three (Color Dodge, Color Burn and Exclusion) of Photoshop's Blending modes when compositing the layers. Painter converts Color Burn, Color Dodge and Exclusion modes to Default Compositing method.

- Photoshop Alpha Channel masks will be recognized by Painter 6. The channels will appear in Painter's Masks section. To view a mask in black-and-white, make sure no layers are selected; in the Masks section, click the mask eye icon open and shut the RGB-Canvas eye icon. Also, Photoshop layer masks will convert to layer masks in Painter. To view a layer mask, select the layer in the Layers section, and click the layer mask eye icon open in the Masks section. 🐾

Compositing, Painting and Effects

Overview *Scan a drawing and a sheet of paper and composite the scans; add color and texture with brushes; add a colored lighting effect; open the image in Photoshop and convert it to CMYK.*

JOHN FRETZ

1a

The sheet of speckled Oatmeal paper

1b

The pencil-and-charcoal drawing on paper

2

Compositing the scans of the Oatmeal paper and the sketch

JOHN FRETZ COMBINED TRADITIONAL DRAWING materials and digital ones in Photoshop and Painter to build the composite illustration *AM Exercise* for an American Lung Association calendar.

1 Drawing and scanning. As a basis for his illustration Fretz drew a black-and-white study using pencil and charcoal on a rough newsprint paper. Then he used a flatbed scanner to scan the drawing and a sheet of Oatmeal paper into Photoshop using RGB mode.

2 Compositing the scans. Fretz built the image in Photoshop because he was more familiar with Photoshop's compositing procedures. (His compositing process, which follows, can be accomplished almost identically in Painter.) Fretz copied the drawing and pasted it as a new layer on top of the Oatmeal paper background. To make the white background of the drawing transparent, he applied Multiply blending mode to the drawing layer using the menu on the Layers palette.

For the soft irregular edge on the background layer, Fretz first used the Lasso to draw a selection around the perimeter of the image. He reversed the selection by choosing Select, Inverse and feathered it 30 pixels (Select, Feather), then he filled the border area with 100% white. He saved the file in Photoshop format to preserve the layers for import into Painter.

3 Modifying brushes. At this point, Fretz opened the composite drawing in Painter where he planned to add color and texture. Before beginning to paint, he made two custom Soft Charcoal brushes. The first, for adding soft values, used the Soft Cover subcategory; the second, for subtly darkening color, used the Grainy Soft Buildup subcategory and a low opacity. To make Fretz's

Building up color on the faces using the custom Soft Charcoal brushes

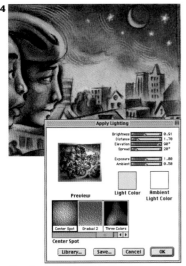

Creating a colored glow in the sky using Apply Lighting

Painting details on the foreground

"darkener," in the Brushes palette, choose the Soft Charcoal variant of Dry Media. In the General section of the Brush Controls palette, change the method to Buildup and the subcategory to Grainy Soft Buildup. A lower opacity will give you more control when building up color, so in the Controls:Brush palette change the Opacity to about 15%. Save your new variant by choosing Save Variant from the Brushes palette's Variant menu. Name it and click OK.

Adding color and texture in Painter. Fretz chose Basic Paper texture in the Papers section of the Art Materials palette. To enlarge the texture to complement the grain of the Oatmeal paper background, he used the Scale slider on the Papers section. He brushed color onto his drawing using two grain-sensitive brushes, the Large Chalk and Square Chalk variants of Dry Media and used his custom Charcoals to deepen color saturation in some areas. Choose a Chalk brush and begin painting color onto your image background; switch to the custom Soft Charcoal variant using Grainy Soft Buildup to darken color. To change the brush size and the opacity while you work, use the Size and Opacity sliders in the Controls:Brush palette.

4 Emphasizing the sky with lighting. For a warm glow in the sky that faded across the people's faces, Fretz applied a colored lighting effect within a soft-edged selection. Begin by choosing the Lasso tool and making a loose freehand selection. Now give the selection a soft edge by applying a feather: Choose Select, Feather, type in a feather width, and click OK. Now apply the lighting effect to make the sky glow as Fretz did: Choose Effects, Surface Control, Apply Lighting. In the Lighting dialog box, choose the Center Spot light. To give the light a colored tint, click on the Light Color box to open the Select Light Color dialog box. Then choose a color by clicking on it in the color picker. (If the circle is black, move the slider to the right.) Click OK. To move the spotlight to a new location in the Preview window, drag the large end of the light indicator. To save the custom light, click the Save button and name the light when prompted, then click OK to apply the light to your image, and deselect (Ctrl/⌘-D).

5 Painting final details. To make the layer and image canvas into one surface on which he could paint details, Fretz merged all the layers. (In the Objects palette, click the right arrow on the Layers section bar to open the menu and choose Drop All.) Then he chose the Scratchboard Rake variant of Pens. Before painting, he modified the Scratchboard Rake, reducing the number of bristles. To build his brush, open the Rake section of the Brush Controls palette. Reduce the number of Bristles to 5. Fretz added finishing strokes in various colors to several places in the foreground, the grass, and highlights on the cars. He also used a smaller brush and more subtle colors to add textured strokes to areas of the background.

Fretz saved a copy of the image as a TIFF file. He opened the file in Photoshop and converted it to CMYK for use in the calendar.

Expressive Painting and Layering

Overview *Make a drawing and scan it; using three versions of the file, add color and blend, and add surface texture; composite the file and add details.*

Howe's pencil sketch

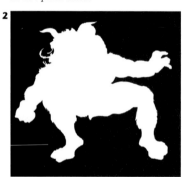

The silhouette mask made in Photoshop

The drawing with reddish-brown tint

PHILIP HOWE

FOR THIS ADVERTISING ILLUSTRATION for Wacom Graphics tablets, Philip Howe created a fantasy portrait of a boy befriended by a wild creature. Howe prefers Painter's brushes and effects for achieving the realistic look of oil paints, but he chooses to make his masks and to do the compositing in Photoshop. In this image, he composited three layers: a soft sepia underpainting with no texture added, a sepia underpainting with surface texture and a painted layer with heavy surface texture.

1 Drawing developmental sketches. After Howe made several pencil sketches, the designer (Paul Nelson), the client (Wacom), and Howe settled on the concept of a young boy riding high on the back of a wild creature that he's befriended.

Howe refined the approved pencil sketch and scanned it. When creating an illustration for print, he prefers working at the final file size needed, because he has more control over the textural effects he wants to achieve in the final print separation without the softening that can occur through interpolation. His scan measured about 5600 x 4600 pixels.

2 Making a silhouette mask. Howe compares his technique to an airbrush artist who saves all of his early masks. Familiar with Photoshop's selections and masking procedures, he prefers to create his masks in that program. Using the Magic Wand, Howe made a selection for the white background in the sketch and saved it as a mask in the Channels palette. He cleaned up the silhouette mask using Photoshop's Paintbrush and Eraser tools.

3 Adding color to build an underpainting. For the sepia underpainting, Howe colored the sketch reddish-brown, as follows: He began by loading the silhouette mask as a selection,

Howe's blending with the Liquid brush

The creature's head showing airbrushed color, blending and surface texture

The completed creature with the boy on his back, airbrushed and blended

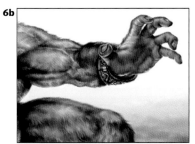

The right arm showing airbrushed sky, and completed composited layers

chose Layer, New Layer Via Copy (to copy the contents to a new layer), turned on Preserve Transparency (to constrain the fill to the existing pixels) and chose Edit, Fill with Normal mode, at 100% Opacity. He set the Blending mode for this layer to Multiply.

To tint the lines in the sketch with sepia, Howe worked on the Background layer. He loaded the silhouette mask again and colored the boy and creature by choosing Edit, Fill, using Color mode, which colored the lines but preserved the gray values. Next, Howe merged the layers to produce a single Background layer with an all-over sepia tint, but still showing the line work.

4 Achieving the effect of oil paint. Howe opened the image in Painter and saved a second version of the file. He wanted an effect similar to oil paint on canvas. Working on one of the two files, he added more color with the Digital Airbrush variant of Airbrushes. He used modified Liquid variants to build up brushstrokes and to blend the creature's hair. For most of the blending and pulling of paint, Howe used a custom Liquid brush based on the Grainy Water variant (in the General section of the Brush Controls palette, he changed the subcategory from Cover to Grainy Drip). While painting, he used a light touch with the stylus to pull the paint expressively. He painted subtle directional strokes, creating a soft oil-like effect over the image.

5 Adding more texture. To emphasize the directional brush-work, Howe used Effects, Apply Surface Texture, Using Image Luminance, with strong settings. He saved the file to use later.

Next Howe worked on the other Painter file. To emboss the hair and hard edges in the drawing, he chose Effects, Surface Control, Apply Surface Texture, Using Image Luminance with subtle settings. As before, he saved the image for use later.

6 Compositing the painted layers and adding details. Back in Photoshop, Howe combined the two files he had saved in Painter and the Photoshop file. With each of the files open in Photoshop, he used the Move tool to drag and drop the lighter textured files from steps 3 and 4 into the painted file with the heavier texture (from step 5). In Photoshop's Layers palette, he set all of the layer blending modes to Normal. Next he used the Eraser tool (in Airbrush mode) to softly erase or wipe out parts of the top layers until the right amount of texture showed through. (The process of compositing and erasing portions of the layers can be accomplished in Painter 6 in the same way.) When Howe was satisfied with the look, he flattened the file and saved a new version, naming it "Pre-final," knowing he could go back and add texture or softness from the individual flat files he had saved, so long as the dimensions of the files remained the same.

Howe airbrushed a loose background landscape, setting the foreground figures out from it and adding a sense of depth. Finally, back in Painter, he cleaned up the transitions between the foreground and background with a small Liquid variant, working much as he would with gouache or oil, careful not to lose the texture effects. 🖌

Collage Using Cloning and Layers

Overview *Scan photos into Photoshop and retouch; use Painter's brushes and textures to build a background image and add textured brushwork to source files; build the composite image in Photoshop; add blending and airbrushed highlights in Painter.*

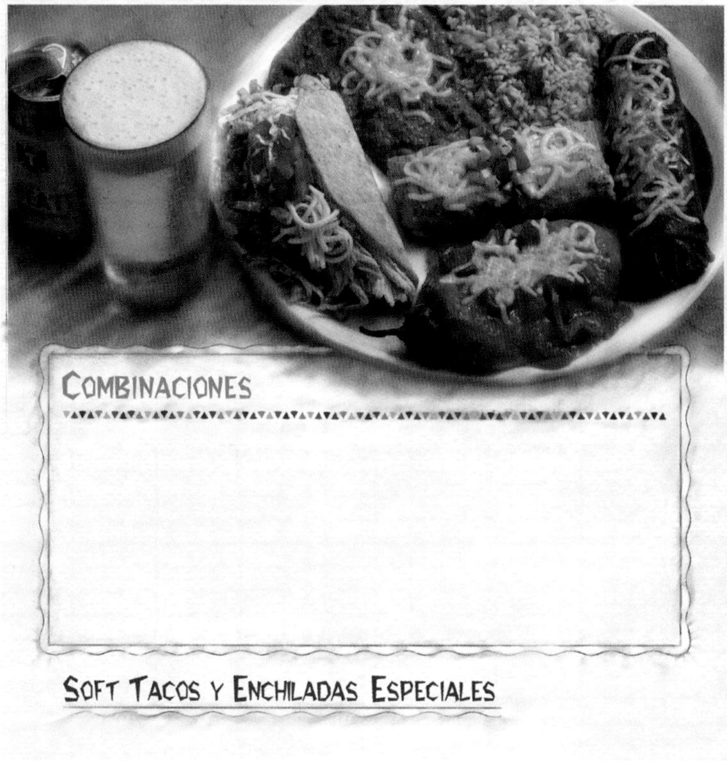

ART DIRECTION AND IMAGES: BURKE / TRIOLO PRODUCTIONS / DESIGN: BOB MARRIOTT, MARRIOTT & ASSAY
CLIENT: ACAPULCO RESTAURANTS

1a

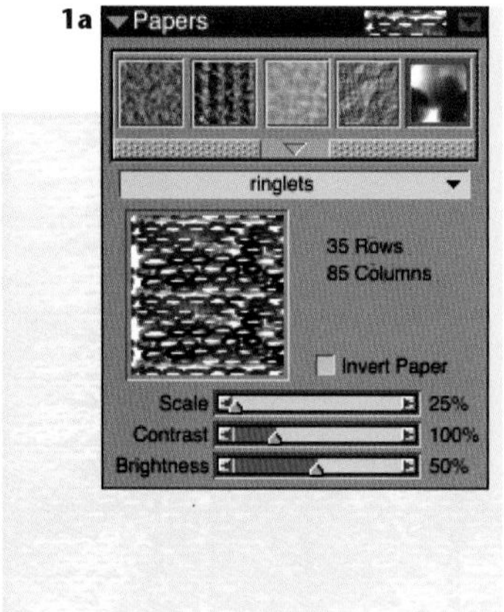

Burke's custom Ringlets texture was used for the background.

1b

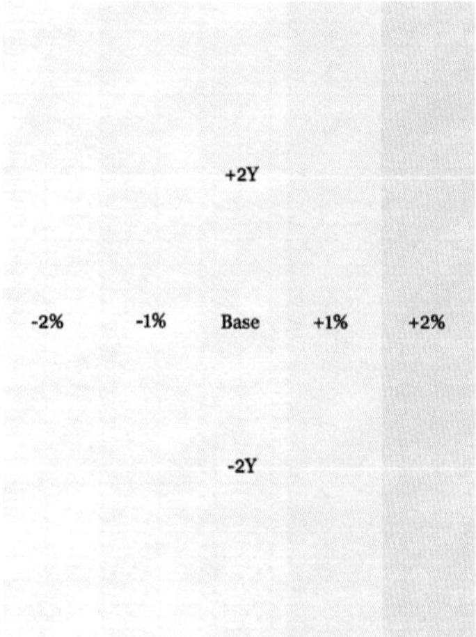

The test file with tonal variations

WHEN JEFF BURKE AND LORRAINE TRIOLO—owners of Burke/Triolo Productions—were commissioned to create new menus for Acapulco Restaurants, they turned to Photoshop for image compositing and to Painter for a textured, painted look. The final composed menu pages are filled with unique, stylized graphics that reflect the texture and style of Old Mexico and suggest the qualities of handmade food and old-world service.

Burke began by exploring techniques in Painter, settling on a rough-edged, textural look with lively brushstrokes, which he presented to the client and the designer. After approval, he built the interior menu pages using several elements: a background paper texture image, textured food images and border graphics. The source files were all composed into a single image file in Photoshop and then opened again in Painter, where more texture and brushwork were added. Later, in QuarkXPress, the type and the dingbat illustrations were placed on top of the composed image as PostScript elements. The folded menu was composed of several panels, built using the same process. The steps that follow use panel 3 as an example. Turn to pages 267 and 268 in the gallery to see a beverage menu panel and the front cover of this menu.

1 Building a textured background. The partners realized that a textured feel would contribute to the old-world atmosphere they wanted to achieve. To accomplish this, Burke created a new

The retouched food photograph

Using the Chalk Cloner brush to paint a rough edge around the elements

Refining the texture around the edge of the plate and beverage

The food photograph with brushwork nearly complete

document in Painter that matched the page size of the menu, measuring 9 x 14.5 inches at 300 pixels per inch. He created a custom paper texture in Painter, called Ringlets. (To read about making a custom paper texture turn to "Applying Scanned Paper Textures" in Chapter 3, on page 78.) Then, using a warm-colored Oil Pastel variant of Dry Media, he brushed the texture over the surface of the page, using light pressure on the stylus. He saved this master texture image for use on each panel of the menu.

Burke converted the light, delicate paper texture to CMYK and created a test file with tonal variations. He sent the test file to his service bureau for a Fuji ColorArt film proof, and when the proof came back, the partners chose the darkest, yellowest variation.

2 Scanning and retouching the images. The team at Burke/Triolo scanned the food images on a Scanview ScanMate 5000 drum scanner, then converted them to RGB. Burke used Photoshop's Rubber Stamp tool to lightly retouch scanning imperfections and to improve details, such as stray rice grains, sauce smears on the plates and dark areas in the food. To whiten most of the background, he made a loose selection completely outside of the elements and reversed it by choosing Select, Inverse. Then he pressed the Delete key.

3 Texturizing the source images. Burke opened each food image in Painter and created a clone by choosing File, Clone. He chose Big Grain Rough paper texture in the Papers section of the Art Materials palette. Using the Chalk Cloner variant of Cloners, with brush sizes varying between 20 and 100 pixels, he gently painted over the image in the clone file along the edges of the plates, the base of the glasses and the stone surface material, in varying densities. This produced a painterly quality in the images reminiscent of painting by hand. By constantly varying the size of the brush and by using a light touch on the stylus, he changed the amount of chalk texture applied. His goal was to add texture to the original without obscuring it completely. As specialists in food styling and photography, Burke and Triolo know that it's important to avoid obscuring the food products in an image.

To add subtly colored brushwork to the edges of the elements, Burke used an Oil Pastel variant of Dry Media. He sampled the color from the image (using the Ctrl/⌘ key) and then painted diagonal strokes. He likes using the Oil Pastel when applying dark colors over a light background or light over dark, because the brush smears color slightly, making the strokes appear to bleed. He carefully applied the treatment consistently over the photo.

Wherever the image became too obscured with brushwork, Burke uses the Soft Cloner variant of Cloners to gently bring back detail from the original, after designating the original retouched photo as the Clone source by choosing File, Clone Source. After completing each individual food image, he saved it for later.

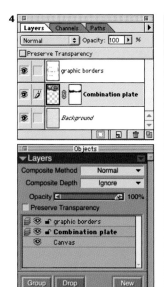

The named layers in the composite file, shown here in the Layers palette in Photoshop (above) and the Layers section of the Objects palette in Painter (below)

Burke painted with the Just Add Water variant to blend the border elements into the page.

A detail of the final image with airbrush highlights added

4 Compositing the menu elements. Because the layout also included border graphics created in Adobe Illustrator, these elements were rasterized (converted from CMYK PostScript elements to bitmapped RGB graphics) so they could be blended into the final page composition. To do this, the designer's QuarkXPress document was modified to remove all of the elements except certain borders (and some headline type, which was retained for position, but later removed). Burke saved the page individually as a separate EPS file from QuarkXPress.

Burke built each panel of the menu as a single image file in Photoshop. However, the elements could have been combined in Painter 6 in almost exactly the same way. He opened the master paper-textured background and the treated food image in Photoshop and dragged and dropped the food image file on top of the background into the position specified in the designer's layout. To blend the images softly into the paper background, he added a layer mask to the food element layer.

Finally, Burke opened the QuarkXPress EPS file and dragged and dropped it into position. To create the illusion of plates and other objects overlapping the graphic elements, he added layer masks for the graphic elements where they appeared to go "behind" the food objects. He also removed the headline type at this point. Because he wanted to use Painter to add brushwork that would blend elements that were currently on separate layers, he merged the layers in the file. Then he saved the file as an RGB TIFF.

5 Adding final details in Painter. Burke opened the file in Painter and prepared to add texture and brushstrokes throughout the image. For editing flexibility he began by creating a clone of the image by choosing File, Clone. To enhance and blend the graphic borders into the image, he used the Oil Pastel variant of Dry Media (sized to about 30 pixels), and roughly filled in the hollow borders with a warm-white color. Then, to gently blur the colored border graphics into the background paper, he used the Just Add Water variant of Liquid. Again, if he overdid the effect, he switched to the Soft Cloner brush (with the original image designated as the Clone Source) and restored detail and clarity.

6 Airbrushing highlights. To complete the menu panel, Burke wanted to embellish the bright highlights on the plate, glass and food. For optimal flexibility, he added a new layer for the highlights by clicking the New button on the Layers section (making sure that Preserve Transparency was turned off in the Layers section). Using the Digital Airbrush variant of Airbrushes and a bright, warm-white color, he softly painted strong, yet natural brushstrokes to "blow out" the highlights. 🐾

■ **Burke/Triolo Productions** is famous for its unique food photography. The team at Burke/Triolo created the illustration above for the *Tequila beverage panel* of the new menu for Acapulco Restaurants. For continuity, they used the same textures and brushwork style throughout all of the menu panels. These techniques are described more fully in "Collage Using Cloning and Layers" on page 264.

For the panel above, Burke/Triolo wanted a composition with a flat perspective, so they chose not to shoot all of the bottles in one photo, but to shoot three photos of the bottles, with a shallow depth of field, then composite the images. **Lorraine Triolo** began by building the still-life arrangements. The team lit the arrangements with dramatic back-lighting that would reflect on and shine though the

bottles. They photographed the elements and then drum-scanned the photos.

Before the Painter treatment and final imaging was done by **Jeff Burke**, a collage was built by **Lew Robertson**, a photographer and digital artist working with Burke/Triolo. Robertson built a composite image of the bottles and table top in Photoshop that incorporated several layers. When the collage was complete, Burke opened a copy of the file, flattened the layers, and saved it as a TIFF file for import into Painter, where he planned to add textured brushwork and highlights.

In Painter, he made a clone of the image (File, Clone) so that he could add brush work to the clone and use the original as a clone source if needed to add back some of the original detail. To make the foreground in the clone white, he made a

loose freehand selection of the area with the Lasso tool, gave it a soft feather by choosing Select, Feather and pressed the Delete/Backspace key.

He chose the Big Grain Rough texture and used the Chalk Cloner to roughen up some of the edges of the foreground bottles and glass. To add light color to the foreground, he used the Oil Pastel variant of Dry Media to paint light-colored, diagonal brushstrokes. For the dramatic highlight glows on the glassware, Burke used the Digital Airbrush and very light color, enhancing the mood of the image while controlling the strokes so that the brand names on the labels remained readable.

The final painted file was saved as a TIFF and laid out with other elements in QuarkXpress. (See page 266 for more about how the panels were completed.)

■ When partners **Jeff Burke** and **Lorraine Triolo** were commissioned to create the new *Acapulco Restaurants menu cover,* several people played important roles: Photography and imaging, Jeffrey Burke; food and prop styling, Lorraine Triolo; art direction, Jeff Burke and Bob Marriott; Design Firm, Marriott & Assay; and Client, Acapulco Restaurants.

To begin the menu cover, Burke built a composite that included several images of food and live models, shot in the studio against a white cove background. To add to the atmosphere, he incorporated a sky image from a recent Caribbean vacation, as well as an outdoor fountain photographed with a point-and-shoot digital camera. He made masks for several of the images in Photoshop using the Lasso and Pen tools and dragged and dropped elements into a composite file. After several preliminary compositions and the client sign-off on a final arrangement, he flattened the file and saved it in TIFF format. (Burke could have brought the file into Painter with layers, but he wanted a flat document with all of the elements merged together so that he could use Painter's brushes to paint over the entire image, completely integrating the elements.)

Burke opened the file in Painter and used much the same process as described in "Collage Using Cloning and Layers" on page 264. He cloned the file and used the Big Grain Rough texture and a pressure-sensitive tablet and stylus. He smudged the edges of some of the elements and added colored brushwork to some areas using the Oil Pastel variant of Dry Media. By selectively blending areas in the image with the Just Add Water brush, and leaving other edges in focus, Burke created a dynamic feeling of movement in the illustration. For instance, in the server's skirt and blouse, the leading and trailing edges are blurred with soft diagonal brushwork, but the sash and ruffle are sharper. To lead the eye to the food tray, Burke airbrushed a glow under the tray and along the sleeve of the blouse. Because the food was the focal point of the composition, Burke avoided adding brushwork here. To balance the design, he left the faces of the mariachis in clearer focus than most of the other elements. It was easy to restore the focus where it was needed by designating the original file as the clone source (File, Clone Source) and using the Soft Cloner.

Finally, Burke airbrushed highlight hints on the image on a separate layer (for editing flexibility), using the Digital Airbrush to "blow out" the highlights, while keeping the look natural.

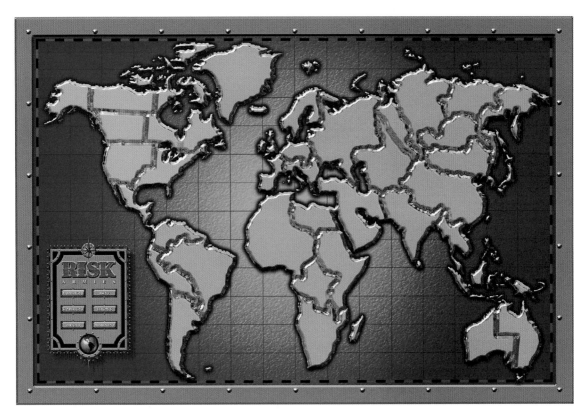

■ **John Dismukes** and **Jo-Anne Redwood,** principals of Capstone Studios, began the *Risk Game Board* for the Parker Bros./Hasbro Games Group, by creating many pencil sketches on paper. After settling on the look they wanted, they presented a tight visualization to the art director of the project, Steve Krupsky. After approval, the pencil sketch was scanned and used as a template in Macromedia FreeHand to create Post-Script outlines, which were saved in EPS format. Because he was more familiar with layers in Photoshop when he built the map, Dismukes imported the outlines into Photoshop, where he made layers for the water, each land region, the legend and the border. (Alternately, the outlines could have been brought directly into Painter as shapes via File, Acquire, Adobe Illustrator File and converted to layers. For a step-by-step description of a similar technique using Painter, turn to "Selections and Airbrush" on page 127.)

To give each element a basic color, he turned on Preserve Transparency in the Layers palette and filled the areas with mid-tone colors. (He planned to add highlights and shadows in Painter with the Digital Airbrush later.) He saved the file in Photoshop format, so it could be opened in Painter with its layers and masks intact.

Dismukes loves the responsiveness of Painter's Airbrushes and their performance with a pressure-sensitive tablet and stylus. When he opened the file in Painter, he turned on Preserve Transparency in the Layers section of the Objects palette and, using the Digital Airbrush variant of Airbrushes, he hand-painted the edge of each individual layer to create a "retro-style" bevel. For each bevel, he first sampled color from the region using the Dropper tool, and then painted

the bevels using light and dark variations of the color. As he worked, he changed the size and opacity of the Digital Airbrush, paying careful attention to detail and spending the time needed to hand-paint realistic highlights and shadows along the edges. He also used the Digital Airbrush to give the chrome studs in the map's border realistic dimension.

For the luminous texture on the water, Dismukes selected a rough custom paper texture in the Papers section of the Art Materials palette, then chose Effects, Focus, Glass Distortion, Using Paper, with Refraction. To strengthen the focal point of the composition, he applied a custom lighting effect to the water layer, by choosing Effects, Surface Control, Apply Lighting. (To see more work from Capstone Studios, turn to pages 256–257.)

■ Graphic designer and artist **Donal Jolley** created twelve images for the *Turning Point 2000 Calendar,* two of which are shown here. To begin the calendar, Jolley worked with his client David Jeremiah to select reference photos from the Corbis Images, PhotoDisc and Stone Images collections. Then he used similar techniques when creating both of these "photo-paintings."

Beginning in Photoshop, Jolley opened the images for *July* (Heeta Head, Oregon, from Stone Images) and *December* (Peggy's Cove, Nova Scotia, Canada, from PhotoDisc). He increased the intensity of the color in the original photos, then removed unwanted elements by cloning using the Rubber Stamp tool. So that he would be able to isolate areas of the images (for instance, the sky, water, rocks and the buildings), he made selections and saved them as masks. Then he saved each image with its masks in Photoshop format, so he could work on them in Painter.

Jolley planned to use Painter's brushes for textured brushwork that would add painterly movement to the images and break up the smooth photographic look. Using many layers and paying careful attention to the volume of the forms, he painted on the images with the Artist Pastel Chalk variant of Dry Media (with a rough paper texture chosen in the Papers section of the Art Materials palette), and several Brushes variants. To blend and pull color while adding texture in the sky in the December image, he loaded a selection from the sky mask he'd saved (Select, Load Selection) and used the Grainy Water variant of Liquid. Then he loaded selections for the building and rocks in turn, and added final colored details with a small Artist Pastel Chalk.

Jolley added more texture to the images as follows: First he made two duplicates of the image by selecting all (Ctrl/⌘-A) and Alt/Option-clicking with the Layer Adjuster. He dragged these copies to the top of the list in the Layers section of the Objects palette. On the first layer, he used Effects, Surface Control, Apply Surface Texture, Using Image Luminance, with subtle settings, to "emboss" the brushstrokes. On the top layer, he used Effects, Surface Control, Apply Surface Texture, Using Paper, also with subtle settings to add paper grain. Then he adjusted the Opacity of both layers to his liking, using the slider on the Layers section.

■ Designer/illustrator **Marc Brown** was commissioned by Angie Lee, art director at Grindstone Graphics, to create *Museum Store* (above). He created *Iron Casters* (right) for Amanda Wilson, art director at The Evans Group Advertising.

Brown employed similar techniques to create both illustrations. He started with a loose pencil drawing, then scanned the drawing and placed it into Adobe Illustrator as a template. In Illustrator he drew the elements on individual layers and filled them with flat color. To rasterize the image, he copied each Illustrator layer and pasted it into Photoshop as a layer. (This process can also be accomplished in Painter by drawing shapes and filling them with color, or by importing Illustrator art into Painter. See Chapters 4 and 5 for more information about using and importing shapes.)

At this point, Brown opened the layered file in Painter. He used Airbrushes variants and the Chalk variants of Dry Media to add colored details to the faces and clothing, blending color with Liquid variants. After he had completed the composite, he merged the layers by choosing Drop All from the Layers section bar's menu on the Objects palette. To finish, he broke up some of the smooth edges by painting them with the Just Add Water variant of Liquid.

■ *Thai Rocks* (above), and *Happy Hula* (right), by **Jack Davis**, were created with much the same style and brushwork as Davis's traditional oils on canvas, which incorporate brilliant colors painted onto a black "ground."

Davis began *Thai Rocks* by taking photos on location. For *Happy Hula,* he began with an original photo taken by Susan Merritt. He scanned the photos into Photoshop, then copied and pasted bits and pieces of the photos into a reference file and increased the saturation of the images. When the composition looked right, he flattened the file and saved it in Photoshop format. Then he opened it in Painter and cloned it (File, Clone). Davis deleted the contents of the clone and filled the background with black. Next, he turned on Tracing Paper (Canvas, Tracing Paper) and chose the Big Wet Luscious variant of Brushes, loaded from the New Paint Tools library on the Painter 6 CD-ROM. To rough in blocks of color based on color in the reference collage, he checked the Clone Color box on the Colors section of the Art Materials palette. After he had laid in the basic composition, he turned off Tracing Paper and the Clone Color option and completed the painting. For the figure and foreground details in *Happy Hula*, Davis also used a small Dry Brush, also from the New Paint Tools library, with Clone Color turned on in the Colors section.

As a last step, he added realistic highlights and shadows to the brushstrokes—building the look of thick paint—using Effects, Surface Control, Apply Surface Texture, Using Image Luminance with subtle settings.

Artist **Pamela Wells** has been using the computer as a creative tool since the first Macintosh was introduced. Her most recent works focus on feminine archetypes and are sold in commercial and fine-art markets.

For *The Gift*, Wells began by collecting photos to use for reference while working on the composition. Then she scanned pieces of the photos into Photoshop and made a rough collage in that program to use as a reference while working in Painter. She merged the layers and saved the file for import into Painter.

In Painter, Wells made a clone of the reference file by choosing File, Clone. In preparation for using Tracing Paper, she deleted the contents of the clone by choosing Ctrl/⌘-A and pressing the Backspace/Delete key. Then she turned on Tracing Paper by pressing Ctrl/⌘-T and used a pressure-sensitive tablet and stylus to draw a detailed black-and-white line sketch with the 2B Pencil variant of the Pencils.

Because she wanted to begin the coloring by filling areas with flat color, she made sure to create a solid line around the exterior of the figure and the gown. She could then apply color fills to these areas using the Paint Bucket from the Tools palette. She filled in as much color as possible using the Paint Bucket before beginning to paint the details.

To model the forms of the figure and the clothing, she carefully painted over the entire illustration using a pressure-sensitive tablet and stylus and the Soft Charcoal variant of Dry Media. Working over the entire image, Wells applied layers of color with the Soft Charcoal, using a light pressure on the stylus. To blend areas, she laid subtly different colors over existing ones. For instance, to render the skin, she brushed the areas with a light tan color, then covered them with a darker orange and finally a peachy red. To add texture to the fabric and brighter colors to the flowers, she used more contrasting values and a tiny Soft Charcoal variant.

When Wells had finished painting the illustration, she saved it as a TIFF file and opened the image in Photoshop, where she applied a few minor color and brightness adjustments. To read about how Wells made a fine-art print of her image, turn to the beginning of Chapter 12, "Printing and Archival Concerns."

MULTIMEDIA AND FILM WITH PAINTER

Film artist Dewey Reid created this pre-production comprehensive for the Nike All Conditions Gear *TV commercial using scanned images and Painter's brushes, effects and Scripts; he worked back and forth between Painter and Adobe Premiere, using Premiere for timing and transitions.*

A Current Script showing the instructions for an application of Surface Texture

WHETHER YOU'RE AN ANIMATOR, film artist, designer, or 3D artist, Painter's multimedia capabilities offer you dozens of practical techniques. Multimedia artists appreciate the creative freedom offered by Painter's brushes, textures and effects. If you're producing an animation or making a movie, many of the techniques and effects shown in this book can be applied to frames in a Frame Stack, Painter's native animation format, or to an imported movie clip. Although it isn't a full-featured animation or film-compositing program, Painter is good for making comps so you can preview motion. And Painter gives 3D artists a wide variety of choices for creating natural, organic textures to be used for texture mapping. In addition, the ability to record painting scripts lets you make tutorials to show others how your painting was built and even lets you batch-process a series of images.

WORKING WITH SCRIPTS

Painter's versatile Script feature lets you record your work, then play the process back, either in Painter or as a QuickTime, AVI or VFW movie. But if you use this feature a lot, you'll soon discover its limitations—for example, its inability to record some Painter operations can change the look of the image during playback.

How did I do that? With Painter's automatic script feature, you can reproduce what you just did using the *Current Script*. While you work, Painter transparently records your actions automatically—saving them as the Current Script in the Painter Script Data file in the Painter 6 folder.

To work with the Current Script, open the Scripts section of the Objects palette, click the

A CURRENT SCRIPT PREFERENCE

You can tell Painter how long to save current scripts by specifying the number of days in the Preferences, General dialog box. (The default is one day.) A word of caution: Saving several days of scripts can use a lot of hard disk space!

To create this animated logo for Fox Television, Geoff Hull built text selections in Painter and used several Brushes variants to add lively brushstrokes and saturated color to his design. Turn to page 293 to see more of Hull's work.

You can use these buttons on the front of the Scripts section to begin recording a single script (center red button) and to stop recording when you're finished (left square button).

Athos Boncompagni saved a series of scripts when creating Luna 1, and played them back at higher resolution to build a larger image. For more information about using scripts in this way, see the tip "Increasing File Resolution With Scripts," on page 9, in Chapter 1.

right triangle on the Scripts section bar and from the menu select Open Script. Choose Current Script from the Painter Script Data file list and click Open. The Current Script cannot be edited, but to use only a specific set of instructions from it, you *can* copy them to the clipboard and paste the instructions into a new script. Then you'll be able to use your new script to re-create just that series of actions. To do this, open the Current Script, Shift-select the instructions that you want to use (you may want to work backwards from the bottom of the list, where the most recent instructions are found), choose Copy from the Scripts menu, and then choose New Script from the menu. Type a name for your new script in the Name the Script dialog box, and click OK. When the empty script window appears, choose Paste from the Scripts menu, and choose Close Script. To play your new script, choose Playback Script from the menu and select the new script by name from the pop-out list in the Scripts section.

Recording a planned script. To record a series of deliberate actions into a script (instead of copying and pasting from the automatically recorded script), click the right triangle on the Scripts section bar to open the menu and choose Record Script to begin recording. When you've finished working on your image choose Stop Recording Script (or click the square Stop button on the left side of the Scripts section). Painter prompts you to name your script. The new script will appear in the pop-out list of the Scripts section, available for later playback. To play the new script, choose Playback Script from the menu, or click the forward arrow button.

Recording and saving a series of scripts. If you want to record the development of a complex painting (so you can use the script to demonstrate how you created the painting) and you don't want to finish the painting in one sitting, you can record a series of work scripts to be played back. First note the dimensions of your file. Click the right triangle on the Scripts section bar, choose Record Script, and begin your painting. When you want to take a break, stop recording (Scripts section bar, Stop Recording Script). Include a number in the name of your script (such as "01") to help you remember the playback order. When you're ready to continue, choose Record Script again and resume working on your image. Record and save as many scripts as you need, giving them the same name and numbering them so you can keep track of the order. To play them back, open a new file of the same dimensions as the original, then choose Playback Script from the menu on the Scripts section bar. Choose the "01" script, and when it's done playing, choose the next script: It will play back on top of the image created by the first script. Continue playing back scripts in order until the image is completed.

Automating a series of operations. A recorded series of actions can save you a lot of time when you need to apply the same effect

To add lighting and a paper texture to this Mediacom video clip, we played a special effects script (using Effects, Surface Control, Apply Lighting and Apply Surface Texture) on each of the frames.

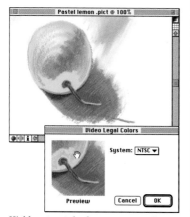

Highly saturated colors can smear when output to video. Choose Effects, Tonal Control, Video Legal Colors to make the colors in your file compatible with NTSC or PAL video color. In the Preview, press and release the grabber to toggle between the RGB and Video Legal Colors previews; click OK to convert the colors in your file.

to several images or to a frame stack. Test a combination of operations (such as a series of choices from the Effects menu) until you get something you like. From the menu on the Scripts section bar accessed by the right triangle, choose Record Script and repeat the series of choices that produces the effect you want. After you've stopped recording and have saved your script, you can apply the operations to a selection, a layer or a still image by selecting your script in the Scripts section and choosing Playback Script from the menu (or by clicking the forward arrow button on the front of the section). To apply your script to a frame stack, choose Movie, Apply Script to Movie, select your script from the Recorded Script list and click the Playback button. Turn to "Automating Movie Effects" later in this chapter for a detailed explanation of this technique.

Playing a script back as a movie. This is a great option if you'd like to play back a painting for someone who does not have Painter. QuickTime movies can be played on Macintosh and PC/Windows computers with a freeware QuickTime projector such as Movie Player (included on the *Wow!* CD-ROM that accompanies this book). First you'll record your work as a script, then you'll play it back on a new file, and then you'll save it as a QuickTime/AVI movie.

Begin by clicking the right triangle on the Scripts section bar and choosing Script Options. In the Script Options dialog box, turn on Record Initial State (otherwise Painter will playback the first few commands or brushstrokes of your script using whatever colors, brushes and textures are active, instead of the ones you actually used during the script). Check Save Frames on Playback, and leave the time interval Painter uses to grab frames from your script at 10, the default. (For future recordings, you may want to experiment with lower settings to get a smoother playback result.)

Next, open a new file of the same dimensions as your eventual movie file. Click the right triangle on the Scripts section bar, choose Record Script from the menu, and make your drawing. When you've finished, from the same menu, choose Stop Recording Script; name and save your script. Now here's when Painter actually converts the script to a movie. First, watch your recorded script played back as a Painter Frame Stack by opening a new file (same dimensions) and choosing Playback Script from the menu. Choose your script from the list, and Painter will prompt you to create a new movie file. Name it, click Save and then specify the number of layers of Onion Skin and color depth by clicking on the appropriate buttons. (For most uses, select 3 layers of Onion Skin and 24-bit color with 8-bit alpha.) Click OK, and your script will unfold as a Frame Stack. When it's finished playing, save it in QuickTime/AVI/VFW (Video For Windows) movie format by choosing Save As, Save Movie as QuickTime. The QuickTime/AVI/VFW file will be smaller than a Frame Stack (if you use a Compressor choice in the Compression Settings dialog box) and will play back more smoothly. (Because most compression degrades quality,

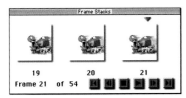

The Frame Stack palette for Donal Jolley's animation Turtle Rockets showing movement in frames 19–21

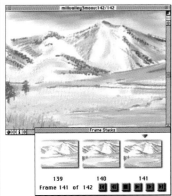

To record the painting process of Mill Valley (360 x 504 pixels, painted with Pastel and Water brushes), we made a movie using Save Frames on Playback and an interval of 10. The resulting movie was 100.6 MB with 142 frames.

compress only once—when you've completed the project. Film artist Dewey Reid suggests using Animation or None as the Compressor setting.) To read more about preserving image quality when working with movies, turn to "Importing and Exporting," on page 279.

Making movies using multiple scripts. Save a series of successive scripts, then play back the scripts as frame stacks and save them as QuickTime movies without compression to preserve quality. Open the movies in a program such as Adobe Premiere, Adobe After Effects or Avid Video Shop and composite the movies into a single movie.

ANIMATING WITH FRAME STACKS

If you open a QuickTime or VFW movie in Painter, it will be converted to a Frame Stack, Painter's native movie format. Frame Stacks are based on the way conventional animators work: Each frame is analogous to an individual transparent acetate cel. You can navigate to any frame within a stack and paint on it or apply effects to it with any of Painter's tools (see "Animating an Illustration" on page 282).

Artists accustomed to specialized animation and video programs such as Adobe After Effects and Adobe Premiere will notice the limitations of the Frame Stack feature (there are no precise timing or compositing controls, for instance). If you use one of these programs, you will probably want to work out timing and compositing in the specialized program, then import your document into Painter to give it an effects treatment.

When you open a QuickTime or VFW video clip in Painter or start a brand-new movie, you'll specify the number of frames and color bit depth to be used in the Frame Stack. You will be asked to name and save your movie. At this point the stack is saved to your hard disk. A Frame Stack will usually take up many more megabytes on your hard disk than it did as a movie (depending on the kind of compression used), so have plenty of space available. Each time you advance a frame in the stack, Painter automatically saves any changes you have made to the movie. When you choose Save As, Painter will ask you to name the movie again. This is not a redundant Save command, but an opportunity to convert

A storyboard frame from the MGM movie Stargate. Peter Mitchell Rubin used Painter to build digital storyboard illustrations for the movie, saving them as numbered PICT files and animating them with Adobe Premiere.

MOVIE "MACRO" TIME-SAVER

Any of Painter's operations such as Auto Mask, or Color Mask (located in the Objects palette's Mask menu), and Effects, Surface Control, Color Overlay or Dye Concentration are good candidates for "macros" that can save you time, especially when working with movies.

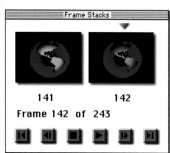

To change the continents from brown to green in this Cascom video clip, we recorded a script while performing the Color Mask procedure and Color Overlay tinting process on one frame, then stopped recording and saved our script. After undoing the effects applied to the first frame, we chose Movie, Apply Script to Movie and took a break while Painter completed the masking and tinting process on all 243 frames. Above: The Frame Stack palette shows frame 141 with the operations applied, and frame 142 as yet untouched.

the file to another format: Save Current Frame as Image, Save Movie as QuickTime or VFW format, or Save Movie as Numbered Files (to create a sequence of frames to composite in another program such as Adobe Premiere).

Creating animated comps. Painter provides a good way to visualize a rough animation. An animatic (a comp of an animation, consisting of keyframe illustrations with movement applied) can be comprised of images drawn in Painter; scanned elements; or numbered PICT files created in Painter, Photoshop or even object-oriented programs that can export PICT files (such as Illustrator). (See "Making an Animated Comp" on page 284, featuring Dewey Reid's illustrations in a demonstration of an animatic technique.) You can also alter individual frames in a movie with Painter's effects or brushes. For a demonstration of frame-by-frame painting, see "Animating an Illustration" on page 282.

Rotoscoping movies. There are numerous ways to rotoscope (paint or apply special effects to movie frames) in Painter. Many of the techniques in this book can be used for rotoscoping—brushwork, masking, tonal adjustment, filters, Effects, Surface Control, Apply Lighting and Apply Surface Texture, or Effects, Focus, Glass Distortion, for example.

Basing an animation on a movie. You can use Painter's Tracing Paper to trace images from a source movie to a clone to create an animation. This feature lets you shoot video and use it as a reference on which to base a path of motion.

COHESIVE MOVIE LIGHTING

Artist Dewey Reid advises using Effects, Surface Control, Apply Lighting to add cohesiveness and to smooth out transitions in a movie. For instance, using Apply Lighting with the same setting on all frames will smooth color transitions between clips and make elements from different sources blend together more successfully. Apply Lighting can also help to cover masking errors.

MANAGING LARGE MOVIE FILES

Because an animation can involve thousands of frames, film artist Dewey Reid advises cutting a large movie into manageable sections using a compositing program such as Adobe Premiere or Adobe After Effects, then importing the sections into Painter to apply the effects. After applying the effects, use a compositing program to recompile the clips. This technique also works for creating an animation in sections in Painter and compiling it in a compositing program.

REAL-TIME COMPOSITING

Painter has no option to set Frames Per Second (FPS) timing; it's better to use Adobe Premiere or Adobe After Effects for compositing, because you can preview motion at 30 FPS so that it appears smooth to the eye.

Reid used Apply Lighting and Apply Surface Texture (using Paper Grain) on the animated character Yuri the Yak for Sesame Street (produced by Children's Television Workshop).

A frame from an animation based on a video clip. We began by using Painter's Water Color brushes to illustrate the frames. Because the Wet Paint sits on top of the entire Frame Stack, we chose Canvas, Dry to merge the Wet Paint onto every frame in the movie when we had finished painting all of the frames. As a final touch, we applied an effects script (with Apply Surface Texture Using Paper Grain) to complete the piece.

EXPORTING A GIF ANIMATION

When your Frame Stack is complete, one option is to export it as a GIF animation for use on a Web page. Choose File, Save As, and when the Save Movie dialog box appears, choose "Save movie as GIF animation," name the movie and click Save. Make choices in the GIF Options dialog box, and click OK. A word of caution: Name the GIF animation a different name so you don't replace the original Frame Stack file. (When a movie is saved in GIF animation format, it is no longer possible to edit it as a Frame Stack in Painter). For more information about using Painter to generate Web graphics turn to Chapter 11.

Choosing the GIF animation option in the Save Movie dialog box

USING A VIDEO CLIP REFERENCE

Painter's cloning function allows you to link two movies—a video clip and a blank movie of the same pixel dimensions—and use the video as a reference on which to base an animation. Open a video clip that you want to use as a reference, then make a blank movie (File, New Movie) of the same pixel dimensions as your video clip. (The second movie doesn't need to have the same number of frames.) Under File, Clone Source, select the video clip. In the blank movie frame, turn on Tracing Paper (Ctrl/⌘-T), and using the clone source as a guide, choose a brush and paint on the frame. To use the Frame Stacks palette to advance one frame in the original, click the appropriate icon (circled in the palette shown below), or press Page Up on your keyboard. Do the same to advance the clone one frame. Use Movie, Go to Frame to move to a specific frame in either clone or original. You can also apply special effects such as Effects, Surface Control, Apply Surface Texture and Color Overlay, or Effects, Focus, Glass Distortion (all using Original Luminance), to your new movie using the clone source.

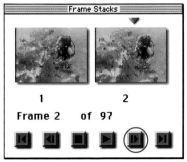

We opened a video clip (shown here in the Frame Stack palette) and a new Frame Stack, both using two layers of Onion Skin to show the position of the diver in both frames. Click on the circled icon to advance one frame in the Frame Stacks palette.

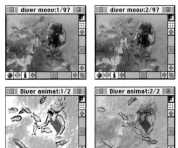

Frames 1 and 2 of the Diver video clip (top row), and corresponding frames in the animation (bottom row), painted with the Sharp Chalk variant. Tracing paper is active on the bottom right image.

IMPORTING AND EXPORTING

With a little planning and understanding of file formats, still and animated files can easily be imported into Painter and exported out of Painter to other programs.

Preserving image quality. Because compression can degrade the quality of image files, when you obtain source files to bring into Painter, choose uncompressed animation and video clips. And because quality deteriorates each time you compress (the degree of degradation depends on the compression choice), save your working files without compression until your project is complete. If you plan to composite Painter movies in another application, such as Adobe Premiere, After Effects or Avid Video Shop, save them without compression. For an in-depth explanation of compressors for QuickTime or for Video For Windows, see Chapter 18 in the *Painter 6 User Guide.*

Importing multimedia files into Painter. Painter can accept QuickTime and VFW movies from any source, as well as still image PICT files and numbered PICT files exported from PostScript drawing programs, Photoshop and Premiere. To number your PICT files

Jon Lee of Fox Television used Painter's brushes and effects to progressively modify the logo for the comedy Martin, *creating numbered PICT files for an animated sequence. The modified files were animated on a Quantel HAL.*

LIGHTS, CAMERA, ACTION!

When you recorded a *session* in previous versions of Painter only your actions were captured. But when you tell Painter to record a script, your "thinking time" (the pauses between actions) is recorded. Keep this in mind if you plan to play back your script as a movie. Recorded "thinking time" can lead to series of "blank" frames. Plan to storyboard your moves so that you'll be able to execute the operations without long pauses. Here's another work-around: After you Record Frames on Playback, check out the Frame Stack, make note of any "blank" frames and use Movie, Delete Frames. Or you can save the Frame Stack as a QuickTime/VFW movie and edit it in Adobe Premiere or Avid Video Shop.

so that they're read in the correct order by Painter, you must use the same number of digits for all the files, and you must number them sequentially, such as "File 000," "File 001," "File 002" and so on. With all files in a single folder, choose File, Open and check the Open Numbered Files option. Select the first numbered file in your sequence and, when prompted, select the last file. Painter will assemble the files into a Frame Stack.

Exporting Painter images to multimedia applications.

Since multimedia work is created to be viewed on monitors and the standard monitor resolution is 72 ppi, set up your Frame Stacks and still image files using that resolution. Most files used in multimedia have a 4 x 3 aspect ratio: 160 x 120, 240 x 180, 320 x 240 or 640 x 480 pixels. Television also has a 4 x 3 aspect ratio, but for digital television the pixels are slightly taller than they are wide. Artists and designers who create animation for broadcast usually prepare their files at "D-1 size," 720 x 486 pixels. Digital television uses a ".9" pixel (90 percent the width of standard square pixels). The narrower pixel causes circles and other objects to be stretched vertically. To create a file for D-1 maintaining the height-to-width ratio (to preserve circles), begin with a 720 x 540-pixel image. Then scale the image non-proportionally to 720 x 486. This will "crush" the image slightly as it appears on your computer screen, but when it's transferred to digital television it will be in the correct proportions.

QuickTime movie files can be exported from Painter and opened in multimedia programs such as Premiere, After Effects and Macromedia Director. If you're using one of these programs to create an 8-bit color production, you'll save processing time if you start with an 8-bit Frame Stack in Painter: Choose the 8-bit Color System Palette option in the New Frame Stack dialog box (after choosing File, New and naming your movie). If you don't set up your file as

IMPORTING AND EXPORTING MOVIES WITH MASKS

You can create a mask in a Painter movie and use it in your Frame Stack, or export it within a Quick-Time movie to another program such as Premiere or After Effects. To make a movie with a mask, choose one of the options with a mask in the New Frame Stack dialog box. (You can also make a Frame Stack from a sequence of numbered PICT files in which each file includes its own mask.) To export the movie from Painter as a QuickTime movie and include the mask, choose Save As and select the QuickTime movie option. When the Compression Settings dialog box appears, in the Compressor section, choose Animation or None from the top pop-up menu to make the mask option available, then choose Millions of Colors+ in the lower pop-up menu. Click OK.

We used a modified photo to create this repeating pattern. To generate seamless, tiled textures for 3D, use any of the commands in the menu of the Patterns section of the Art Materials palette. Turn to "Exploring Patterns" on page 209 in the beginning of Chapter 7 and to "Making a Seamless Tile" on page 306, for more about working with patterns.

8-bit in Painter, you should consider using Photoshop or Equilibrium Debabelizer—both offer excellent color conversion control.

Many experienced artists prefer to export their Painter images as PICT files rather than as movies because they can easily remove frames from the sequence if they choose. To export Painter still images to applications such as Premiere and After Effects, or to other platforms, save them as single PICT images or as a series of numbered PICT files. You can include a single mask in a Painter PICT file that can be used in compositing in Premiere or After Effects. See "Animating a Logo," on page 286, for a demonstration of exporting Painter images to another platform.

You can also import Painter-created QuickTime movies and still PICT images into Macromedia Director. A QuickTime movie comes in as a single linked Cast Member in the Cast Window, which means it will be stored outside the Director file, keeping file size manageable. 🐾

CREATING TEXTURE MAPS FOR 3D RENDERING

A *texture map*—a flat image applied to the surface of 3D object—can greatly enhance the realism of rendering in 3D programs such as Bryce 3D, Strata Studio Pro, Ray Dream Designer or Infini-D. Many kinds of images can be used for mapping—scanned photographs, logo artwork or painted textures, for example. 3D artists especially like Painter's ability to emulate colorful, natural textures (such as painted wood grain or foliage). There are several kinds of texture maps: A *color texture map* is an image that's used to apply colored texture to a 3D rendering of an object. Other types of mapping use grayscale information; for instance, a *bump map* (a two-dimensional representation of an uneven sur-

face), a *transparency map* (used to define areas of an image that are transparent, such as glass panes in a window) and a *reflectance map* (used to define matte and shiny areas on an object's surface). If you're applying more than one of these surface maps to a 3D object, you can keep them in register by using Save As or making clones of the same "master" Painter image to keep file dimensions the same. Remember to save your surface maps in PICT format so the 3D program will be able to recognize them.

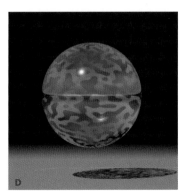

These floating globes were rendered by John Odam in Studio Pro 1.5.2. He created a texture map in Painter using the Wriggle texture from the More Wild Textures library (in the Paper Texture Libraries folder on the Painter 6 CD-ROM) and applied the texture to the objects as follows: color map (A), bump map (B), reflectance map (C) and transparency map (D). The Studio Pro document size was 416 x 416 pixels; the texture map size was 256 x 256 pixels.

Animating an Illustration

***Overview** Create an illustration; open a new movie document; paste the drawing into the movie in each frame as a layer; position and drop the layer into a new, precise position; use brushes to paint on individual frames.*

DONAL JOLLEY

CREATING AN ANIMATION—whether you use Painter or draw on traditional acetate cels—is labor-intensive because of the sheer number of frames required to get smooth motion. But working digitally does have advantages. You can save a lot of time by copying and pasting a single illustration onto multiple frames; corrections to digital art are easier to make than with conventional methods; and, thanks to the Frame Stacks player, you can see results immediately.

To begin *Turtle Rockets*, a cartoon "teaser" used between segments of a youth outreach video, Donal Jolley painted and animated a not-so-pokey turtle with Painter's brushes. Once the basic animation was in place, Jolley painted speed blurs, flame, smoke, and even a wad of gum picked up by one of the skateboard's wheels.

1 Planning the animation and illustrating. It's a good idea to do a quick storyboard sketch on paper to visualize the path of motion for your animation. To keep the process simple, choose a subject that you won't need to redraw in every frame—such as a soaring bird without flapping wings or a speeding car. Jolley sketched a turtle on a skateboard moving from right to left across a 3 x 3-inch frame.

Create an illustration in Painter, choosing a file size no more than a few inches square at 72 ppi. Use Painter's brushes to paint just the essential image; you'll be adding the details to each individual frame later. When you've finished your illustration, choose Select, All, then copy it to the clipboard. It's now ready to be pasted into a movie. To fill his movie more completely with his image, Jolley created an illustration file two inches wider than the movie file would be (5 x 3 inches at 72 ppi). He rendered a line sketch of the turtle, rockets and flame using a small Medium Tip Felt Pens variant. Jolley added color using several Brushes variants, modeled forms with the Digital Airbrush variant of Airbrushes, added linework and shadows using Felt Pens variants and blended color with the Just Add Water variant of Liquid.

2 Starting a new Frame Stack. To open a new movie file, choose File, New. Choose a small size so Painter will play the movie quickly, then click the Movie Picture Type, and enter enough frames to give you a smooth animation. (Jolley created a 3 x 3-inch movie at 72 ppi with 35 frames to start, though he added more frames as he needed them using Movie, Add Frames,

1

Jolley's finished Painter illustration

2

Beginning a new Frame Stack, 3 x 3 inches, 72 ppi, with 35 frames

3

Pasting the layer into the movie

4a

| Layer Attributes |
| Name: Layer 2 |
| Position: Top: 4   Left: 190 |
| Note: |

Entering coordinates for the second layer

4b

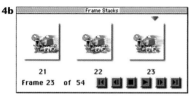

Frame Stacks

21   22   23

Frame 23   of 54

The red marker shows that Frame 23 is active.

4c

Detail of Frame 25, showing motion blur

4d

Frame 28 with Tracing Paper/Onion Skin (three layers) turned on

4e

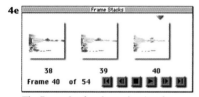

Frame Stacks

38   39   40

Frame 40   of 54

The Frame Stack palette, showing the movement in Frames 38–40

4f

Shaping the flame and adding smoke on Frame 40

so that his finished animation was 54 frames.) Click OK; name and save your movie, and in the New Frame Stack dialog box, choose Jolley's options: three layers of Onion Skin (so you can see three frames back into the stack) and full 24-bit color with an 8-bit mask.

3 Positioning the first layer. Paste your illustration into the movie file—it will come in as a layer. Use the Layer Adjuster tool to move it into its starting position, then double-click on its name in the Layers section of the Objects palette. Jot down the numbers that appear in the Top and Left boxes (Jolley's numbers were Top, 4 and Left, 200) and click OK. Click the Drop button in the Layers section (or press Ctrl/⌘-Shift-D) to drop the layer onto Frame 1.

4 Creating movement by offsetting layers and adding paint. To put a layer into the next frame, go to Frame 2 by pressing Page Up on your keyboard. Paste the illustration again, double-click on its name in the Layers section, and in the Top and Left boxes, add or subtract the number of pixels you want the character to move in the frame. Since Jolley wanted his turtle to move from right to left with no

> **MOVIE AUTO-SAVE**
> Painter saves your movie every time you advance a frame.

vertical variation, he entered 190 in the Left box for Frame 2, leaving the number in the Top box the same as for the first frame. When you've positioned the layer, drop it and advance to the next frame, continuing this paste-and-move process until you have filled all of your frames. To avoid "jumps," add or subtract the same small number of pixels each time. (Remember to drop the layer each time, too.) Jolley used a consistent, 10-pixel difference between frames, resulting in a smooth-moving image.

Look at the Frame Stacks palette to check your progress. You can view previous frames "ghosted" in your main image—much like an animator's light box—by choosing Canvas, Tracing Paper (Ctrl/⌘-T). The number of previous frames displayed is determined by the number of Onion Skin layers you chose when you opened the movie. To change the number of layers, close the file, reopen it, and choose a new number of layers. Use Ctrl/⌘-T to turn the Onion Skin layers on and off as you work.

When the illustration has been positioned and dropped into all of your frames, add to the feeling of motion by painting on individual frames. Jolley painted on his frames to give more life to the animation. He used the Gritty Charcoal variant of Dry Media to paint the dirt—altering it slightly in each frame—and the Opaque Flat variant of Brushes to paint the gum picked up by the first skateboard wheel. He shaped the flame by adding white, then used the Just Add Water variant to smear the pigment. Jolley also created speed blurs by smudging the turtle's back using the Just Add Water variant.

Making an Animated Comp

Overview *Set up a layered illustration file; record the movement of a layer using scripts; play the script back into a movie.*

TO VISUALIZE MOTION in the early stages of creating an animation, Dewey Reid often makes an animated comp (a conceptual illustration with a moving element). Adding motion is a great way to help a client visualize a concept, and it's more exciting than viewing a series of still images. Reid's storyboard, above, shows frames from a movie created by recording a script of a moving layer.

Using scripts and the Record Frames on Playback feature, you can record a layer's movement. When you play the script back, Painter will generate a Frame Stack with the appropriate number of frames, saving you the tedious work of pasting in and moving the character in each frame. After you've made your Frame Stack, convert it into a QuickTime movie (or AVI/VFW on the PC) for easier and faster playback using a freeware utility like Movie Player.

1 Beginning with an illustration. Begin with an image at the size you want your final movie to be. Reid started with a 300 x 173-pixel street scene illustration from his archives.

Painting the mask on the background

The topmost layer showing the dropped-out area that will reveal the background scene underneath

The Dino character showing the painted mask (left), and with the background dropped out

2 Setting up a layered file. Like conventional animation where characters are drawn on layers of acetate, this animation technique works best when all elements in the image are on separate layers. You may want to create masks for the various elements in separate documents, then copy and paste them into your main image. (For more about layers and masking, turn to Chapter 5.)

Reid envisioned three "layers" for this comp: a background image (the street scene) in the bottom layer, a copy of the street scene with a painted mask in the top layer, and a dinosaur positioned between the two street scenes that would move from left to right across the "opening" created by the mask. Reid made a duplicate layer from the Canvas by selecting all and Alt/Option-clicking on the image with the Layer Adjuster tool. To make it easier to see the top layer as you work, hide the Canvas layer by clicking its eye icon shut in the Layers section of the Objects palette. Select the top layer. To remove an area of the layer's mask, choose a brush that will apply opaque color (such as the Scratchboard Tool variant of Pens) and choose white in the Colors section of the Art Materials palette. In the Masks section of the Objects palette, target the layer mask and then paint with white

Reid's original street scene illustration

DEWEY REID

2d

The Dino layer, selected in the Layers section and in starting position, ready to be moved by the arrow keys

3a

Setting up the Script Options to Save Frames on Playback

3b

Saving and naming the script

4

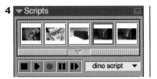

The Dino script selected in the Scripts section of the Objects palette

5

Choosing the QuickTime button in the Save Movie dialog box

to erase. When you've finished, select the RGB-Layer in the Masks section. To see the background layer again, click open the eye icon for the Canvas in the Layers section. You'll see a complete background image, since the lower layer shows through the hole in the top layer.

In a separate file, Reid painted a mask to isolate Dino the dinosaur from the background and turned the mask into a selection by choosing Select, Load Selection. He copied Dino to the clipboard and pasted him into the street scene RIFF file. (An easy way to add a character is to drag an item from the Image Portfolio section of the Objects palette into your image—like the bird, the can or the poser lady, for example.) In the Layers section, Reid dragged Dino down to a position between the two street scene layers. Using the Layer Adjuster and the arrow keys, Reid positioned the dinosaur so that only the red nose was visible behind the left front building, establishing Dino's starting position in the animation.

3 Recording the script. Click the right triangle on the Scripts section bar in the Objects palette to open the menu and choose Script Options; uncheck Record Initial State, check Save Frames on Playback and enter a number for Every 1/10ths of a Second (Reid chose 5), and click OK. Select the layer that will be moving by clicking on its name in the Layers section (for Reid, the Dino Layer). Choose Record Script from the menu on the Scripts section bar (or click the round red button on the front of the Scripts section). Then hold down an arrow key to move the layer smoothly in the RIFF file. When you have completed the path of motion, choose Stop Recording Script from the Scripts section menu (or click the Square button) and name the script. Return the character to its starting position by pressing Ctrl/⌘-Z.

4 Playing back the script into the movie. Click the right triangle on the Scripts section bar to open the menu, choose Playback Script, choose your script from the list, and click Playback. When prompted, name your movie a different name than the RIFF file. Click the Save button and Painter will convert your RIFF image to a movie (leaving the original RIFF intact) and will add the movie frames needed. As the movie is generated, you will see the frames accumulating in the Frame Stack palette. When Painter finishes generating the Frame Stack, turn off visibility for the layers that are above the Canvas by clicking their eye icons in the Layers section. (If you don't hide the layers, you won't be able to see your movie, which is recorded on the Canvas.) Finally, press the Play button on the Frame Stacks palette to play your movie!

5 Converting the Frame Stack to QuickTime or AVI. To play the movie without having Painter loaded, convert the Frame Stack to QuickTime or AVI format: Choose File, Save As, and when the dialog box appears, choose Save Movie as QT/AVI. Give your movie a new name (such as "Dino movie.qtime"), click Save and in the Compression Settings dialog box, select a choice from the top pop-up menu (Reid recommends Animation or None). 🖌

Animating a Logo

Overview *Make a clone of existing artwork and modify it with Painter's brushes and effects; save it, make another clone, and alter the new clone; continue to progressively make and alter clones, restoring the image when needed by pasting a copy of the original logo from the clipboard.*

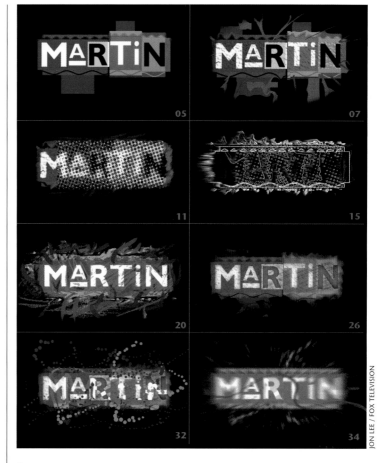

1

Starting with the existing Martin logo

2a

Lee began manipulating the logo by selecting and scaling a portion of the cloned image (left). Then he selected and inverted a portion of the next clone in the sequence (right).

"IMPROVISATIONAL, FRESH, SPONTANEOUS, and very flexible!" says Jon Lee, Director of Art and Design for Fox Television, when describing his artistic experience with Painter. For the Fox TV program *Martin,* Lee built an animated title sequence like a painting, saving frames at different stages of development. He created a wild, hand-done, organic look to express the comedic street sensibility of the TV show.

Lee created a series of 35 keyframes in Painter (keyframes are the frames that establish essential positions in an animated sequence), eight of which are shown above. When he finished, he moved them from his Macintosh to a lightning-fast Quantel HAL system, where he added dissolves to blend one frame into the next. (Dissolves can also be achieved on the Macintosh desktop in Adobe After Effects or Adobe Premiere.)

1 Beginning with existing art. Lee began by opening the existing Martin logo in Painter. He copied and pasted it into a new file measuring 720 x 486 pixels (the aspect ratio of the Quantel HAL) with a black background, then merged the layers by clicking the Drop button in the Layers section of the Objects palette.

2b

Adding colored boxes to Frame 05 with the Rectangular Selection tool and the Fill command

2c

Using a variety of Liquid brushes to pull paint onto the background in Frame 07

2d

A motion blur effect applied in 14 (left), and then cloned and filtered in Frame 15

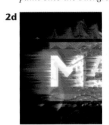

3a

Adding hand lettering and colored brush strokes to a clone of Frame 15 in Frame 16

3b

Restoring readability with a layer in Frame 17

Choose an image that you want to manipulate in your animated sequence and open it in Painter. Save your file in PICT format, naming it "01." In order for a numbered sequence of files to automatically play in numerical order, the files must be named using the same number of digits, such as 01, 02 . . . 10, 11 and so on.

2 Manipulating progressive clones. After planning how many keyframes you'll need and how the artwork will progress through the frames, begin your manipulation. Clone the first document (File, Clone) and use Painter's tools and special effects on your clone. If you don't like the result of a brushstroke or applied effect, undo it and try something else. When you're satisfied with the result, save the file, name it "02," and make another clone from it. The new clone will become the next canvas for your experimentation. Working quickly and intuitively, Lee treated the logo with a wide variety of brushes, filters and effects from the Effects, Surface Control menu, saving progressive versions in a numbered sequence.

3 Restoring the logo. After a few progressively altered clones, your image may become unrecognizable. To restore the original to some degree, go to your original file, select all and copy, then paste it into your current clone. Adjust the Opacity using the slider in the Layers section and Drop the layer. Lee used this technique to periodically restore the readability of the type, working the original logo back into the progressive image.

Outputting the Painter files. When Lee was finished with the series of PICT frames, he used Electric Image Projector (a subprogram within Electric Image) to automatically shuttle the files over to the Quantel HAL platform for compositing and output to Beta videotape for broadcast. The workstation is set up with the Quantel HAL and Mac systems side-by-side; they're connected with an Intelligent Resources card that helps convert the digital imagery from one platform to another. Part of the translation process involved converting RGB color to the NTSC video color system for television.

On the HAL, Lee "stretched" the 35 original frames to 90 frames; the HAL added the appropriate number of frames to achieve the dissolves between each pair of keyframes, keeping the animation even and smooth. To create a 10-second title sequence at 30 frames per second, Lee needed 300 frames total. He made a loop of the 90-frame sequence and let it cycle until it filled the necessary frame count. 🐾

Automating Movie Effects

Overview *Open a video clip; test a series of effects on a single frame; undo the effects; repeat the effects while recording a script; apply the script to the entire clip.*

CTP / VIDEO: MEDIACOM

Frame 1 of the original video clip

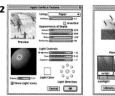

The Apply Surface Texture and Apply Lighting settings chosen for the movie

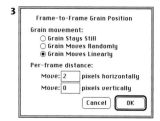

Choosing Movie, Set Grain Position to create a "live" texture on the movie

The Stop button (left) and the Record button (center)

Detail of effects on Frames 35 and 50

WITH PAINTER'S SCRIPTS FEATURE, you can automate any series of recorded effects and apply them to each frame of an entire movie.

1 Starting with a video clip. Tests will be processed faster if you begin with a small video clip like the one we used—320 x 240 pixels with 67 frames. When you open a video clip (a QuickTime or AVI movie), Painter converts it to a Frame Stack. (When you save the Stack, give it a new name so the original clip isn't replaced.)

2 Testing a series of effects on a frame. Before you test a sequence of effects on a single frame, set up multiple Undos so you can return the clip to its original state: Choose Edit, Preferences, Undo, and enter a number that exceeds the number of effects you plan to use. Choose a rough paper texture (we chose Really Thick Paint from the Painted Effects 2 library on the Painter 6 Wow! CD-ROM) and apply it to Frame 1 in your movie with Effects, Surface Control, Apply Surface Texture, Using Paper (we settled on Amount 22%, Picture 90% and Shine 12%). Next, we added a look of cloud-filtered sunlight by choosing Effects, Surface Control, Apply Lighting. We customized the Slide Lighting, named it "sunlight," and saved it. (See Chapter 7 for more about lighting techniques.) When you've finished testing, undo the effects you applied to Frame 1. (Painter will remember the last settings you used in the dialog boxes.)

> **HI-RES MOVIE EFFECTS**
>
> If you want to apply effects to a broadcast-quality (640 x 480 pixels) video, use an editing program (such as Premiere) to create a low-resolution version on which to test a combination of effects. Because it takes a higher setting to get a result in a larger file, you may want to adjust the settings before treating the larger file.

3 Moving paper grain in the movie. To add subtle interest to your movie, you can change paper grain position on a frame-by-frame basis by choosing Movie, Set Grain Position. We chose the Grain Moves Linearly button and a 2-pixel horizontal movement.

4 Recording and playing back the session on the movie. Begin recording the effects by clicking the Record button in the Scripts section (Objects palette); then repeat your sequence of effects. When you're finished, click the Stop button. Give your script a descriptive name, and undo your effects again. To apply your script to the movie, choose Movie, Apply Script to Movie. When the dialog box appears, find your new Script in the list, click the Playback button, and watch as Painter applies the recorded series of effects to each frame. 🖐

■ **Marc Brown** created the splash screen for *The Adventures of Pinocchio Activity Center CD-ROM,* which was based on the 1996 movie *Pinocchio.* Brown began the illustration in Adobe Illustrator. To rasterize it, he pasted each Illustrator layer onto a layer in Photoshop and saved the file in Photoshop format. He opened the file in Painter and used Painter's brushes to render details on each layer, working from the background to the foreground. He laid in color details in the bluish-gray trees in the background using the Round Camelhair variant of Brushes. To blend color, he used the Just Add Water variant of Liquid. To build the shafts of light, he activated a selection (Select, Load Selection) and feathered it (Select, Feather). Then he filled the selection with yellow (Effects, Fill using a 30% Opacity). To paint the midground and foreground, the yellow forest floor, the green bushes and the red trees, he used the Round Camelhair brush. For Pinocchio, Brown referred to reference photos from the movie while painting using the same two brushes.

■ **Lawrence Kaplan** of Hot Tech Multimedia turned to Painter's special effects to "make a painting come to life" in a music video. Working with the New York artist **Crash**, Kaplan co-directed the four-and-a-half minute animated music video *What She Wants* for Warner Bros. Reprise Records. For a series of frames early in the video, he created a "morphing" animation using Painter's Liquid Metal. He began by opening a new movie with one frame and made a Liquid Metal dynamic layer. Using the Brush in the Liquid Metal dialog box (and the Standard Metal Map type), he painted a quantity of Liquid Metal into the first frame and clicked OK to close the dialog box. He copied the Liquid Metal layer to the clipboard, then dropped the layer (Ctrl/⌘-Shift-D) into the first frame. Kaplan added a new frame, pasted the Liquid Metal layer into the new frame and pressed the Enter key to open the Liquid Metal dialog box again. Using the Arrow tool, he selected areas of the metal and deleted them, then added more metal and clicked OK. Kaplan repeated the process of adding frames and editing the layer to complete the series of frames, morphing the dancing figure into a heart that changes into two figures and fades away into the bottom of the frame, then saved the file.

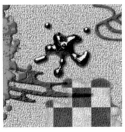

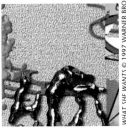

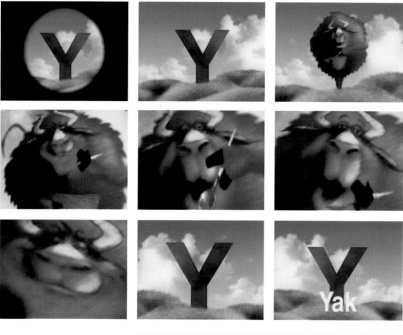

■ **Dewey Reid** of Reid Creative, illustrated the 30-second animation *Yuri the Yak* for Sesame Street, a production of Children's Television Workshop. In the story segment, Yuri travels the countryside eating yellow yams and yogurt, and teaching the letter "Y." Reid stresses the importance of preproduction planning in animation. He created the *Yuri the Yak* animation with a total of only 35 drawings (it could have taken hundreds). His background in conventional animation helped him determine which drawings to make, and which to generate by tweening in an animation program, saving time and a lot of work. Reid used Painter to create individual parts of the Yak, such as the head, body and arms. He opened the illustrations in Photoshop and created a mask for each image, then saved the illustrations as PICT files in a numbered sequence. (He prefers using PICT files rather than QuickTime movies, since PICT files allow higher quality. Also, a sequence of PICT files allows for more flexibility—it's easier to remove a frame or two, if necessary.) He imported the masked files into Adobe After Effects, created animation cycles for each of the Yak parts, then joined animation cycles together. A virtuoso with effects, Reid completed his artistic vision by adding subtle lighting and texture. He opened the animation in Painter as a Frame Stack. After recording a script of Effects, Surface Control, Apply Lighting and Apply Surface Texture, he chose Movie, Apply Script to Movie to add the effects to the frames.

■ *Snuffy 1 and 2* are two compositional layout illustrations by **Cindy Reid** of Reid Creative for a proposed Sesame Street production of Children's Television Workshop. The animation was conceived to accompany the children's song "I Wish I Were Small." In frame 1, Snuffy (who is normally mammoth-size) becomes small enough to fit into a bird's nest; in frame 2, small enough to fit in a buttercup. To create both frames Reid shot photos of a bird's nest, a bee, the sky and clouds, foliage and buttercup flowers for "scrap." She scanned the photos into Photoshop and pasted the images onto layers to build two composite files. When the elements were in place, she opened the layered composite file in Painter, where she added painterly brushwork to each layer using the Grainy Water variant of Liquid. She added details using a small Chalk variant (Dry Media). When the brushwork was complete, she flattened the image by choosing Drop All from the Objects palette's Layer section bar menu.

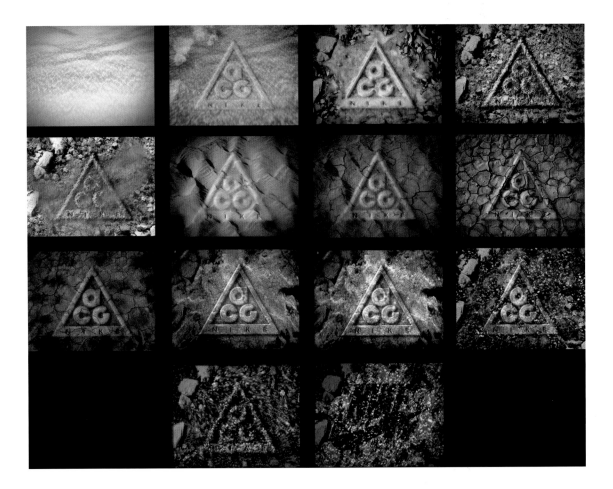

■ Creative director and film artist **Dewey Reid**, working with Colossal Pictures, engineered the preproduction for the *Nike All Conditions Gear* TV commercial. To begin the preproduction visualization, Reid scanned a variety of images. Then he used Painter to create keyframes to establish the essential positions in the animated sequence. He imported the Nike logo (by copying it from Illustrator and pasting it into the Painter file as shapes while both applications were running), converted the logo shapes to selections (Shapes, Convert To Selection) and applied a feather to the selections. He embossed the artwork in stages, with Effects, Surface Control, Apply Surface Texture (Using Mask), creating the illusion that the logo pushes up through the scanned images. Reid saved the keyframes as numbered PICT files,

then used Adobe Premiere to create transitions (such as Cross Dissolves) between the keyframes. He manipulated a few of the masks in Adobe After Effects.

Back in Painter, Reid painted clouds of dust with an Airbrushes variant and used Effects, Surface Control, Image Warp to subtly change the shape of the clouds. He imported the dust image into Premiere and moved the dust across one series of frames.

After working out the timing in Premiere, Reid used Painter to add special effects to the entire movie to increase the 3D look. A whiz with scripts, he opened the movie as a Frame Stack and treated it with an effects script that included Effects, Surface Control, Apply Lighting and Apply Surface Texture, Using Image Luminance.

■ An innovative storyboard artist, **Peter Mitchell Rubin** used a variety of Painter's brushes and compositing controls to create the storyboards for the MGM movie *Stargate.* The Giza, Egypt, sequence is shown here. Rubin outputs his illustrations from Painter as numbered PICT files, then animates them in Adobe Premiere.

Rubin's love of drawing shows in his storyboards. He works very quickly, in gray, at 72 ppi. His document size depends on the amount of detail needed, but is usually under 600 pixels wide. The aspect ratio depends upon how the film will be shot. Rubin organizes the thousands of drawings that he creates for a film in folders according to scene. He sets up QuicKeys macros to automate actions wherever possible, automating the processing of all the files in a folder.

When Rubin adds other elements to an image, he pastes the element, drops it, then paints into it to merge it seamlessly into the composition. He also uses Painter's Cloners brushes. For example, he created the texture in Frame 15 (left column, third frame down from top) by photographing the actual set sculpture used in the movie, scanning it and cloning the scan into his drawing.

■ As both a broadcast designer for Fox Television and a freelance graphic designer, **Geoff Hull** employs a spontaneous, progressive approach when designing with type.

Hull began the *Fox Logo Pattern* with a black background. He imported a file with both solid and outline versions of the Fox logo (using File, Acquire, Adobe Illustrator file—which creates a new file). He copied the shapes from the new file and pasted them into the larger background file, then converted the two logo shape groups into two layers. Working quickly and intuitively, he painted on the logo layers with Brushes variants and saturated color. To build a layered look, Hull made additional copies of the layers and added more brushstrokes. In busier areas, he erased portions of layers by painting the layer masks with white paint.

To create the animated title sequence for the TV show *Wild Oats*, Hull envisioned a hand-done, calligraphic look. He began the image with a white background and set type in Painter using the font Earthquake, a typeface from the T26 foundry. After setting type shapes filled with black, he made a clone (File, Clone) and erased its contents. He chose Canvas, Tracing Paper and expressively traced the letterforms. For the frames of the animation Hull made a series of progressive clones, switching clone sources (File, Clone Source) among the original and several later versions of the title sequence.

Hull created *The Crossing Guard* storyboard for a Miramax Films movie title and trailer. He began with a black background and set individual letterform shapes in Painter using Mason from the Emigré font library. After converting the shapes to layers, he filled them with color and erased portions of the letters by painting the layer masks with white paint. He also used Effects, Orientation, Scale on the layers to vary the size of the elements.

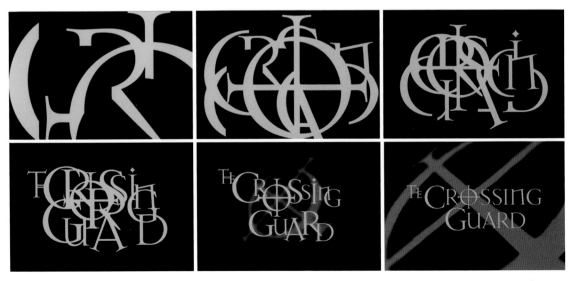

■ Commissioned by Diadem Productions, a producer of multimedia Bible study software, **Ted Larson** created these images as part of a slide show for an educational CD-ROM about the books of Daniel and Zechariah.

Larson used similar techniques to create all three of the illustrations on these pages. He began by sketching in Painter to establish a composition. Then he built a gray-toned composite image that included an environment rendered in Bryce 3D (for instance, the cave wall in *Daniel in the Lion's Den* and the river water in *Vision on the Tigris*), his own photos of cliff rocks and foliage, and stock photos of lions (from a Corel stock-photo CD-ROM). The Messiah, the angel figures, and Daniel seated in the shadows (in the Lion's Den image) were developed from scans of photos Larson took of models in simple-robed costumes. He created the hair and beards with theatrical wigs and crepe hair. He built the angels' wings from two eagle photos from a Corel CD-ROM. When he was satisfied with the composition, he merged the layers and used various brushes in Painter to color the images. In all three images, Larson gave the angels' hands a metallic look by applying a custom bronze gradient using the Express in Image command (located in the menu on the Gradients section bar). To intensify the colors in the image he used Effects, Tonal Control, Adjust Color.

For **Daniel in the Firey Furnace,** Larson began by assembling a black-and-white composite image. He made an empty new layer for the coloring, and to make the layer like a transparent color overlay on top of the gray image, he set the Composite Method of the layer to Color. Then, using warm colors to convey the heat, he loosely painted color in the firey areas using low-opacity Airbrushes variants. He brightened areas of the flames with the Fire and Glow variants of the F/X brush.

Larson wanted to convey a warm Rembrandt-like look in **Daniel in the Lion's Den,** so he chose deep monochromatic earth colors with a touch of gold ochre, making the angel the main source of light. Larson brushed subtle sepia color over the image using the Simple Water variant of Water Color. He also used the Spatter Water variant of Water Color at low opacity settings. To touch up areas, he used a small Digital Airbrush variant of Airbrushes. After the sepia coloring was developed, Larson used Painter's Glow and Fire variants to build special lighting effects around the angel and on the cave wall.

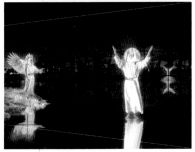

■ To create *The Vision upon the Tigris*, **Ted Larson** began the composition by drawing a color sketch in Painter. He used the Sharp Chalk and Charcoal variants of Dry Media to rough out the position of the three figures and to establish an angle for the river.

Next, in Bryce 3D, Larson rendered a river water image, and placed it in a scene with a perspective grid. He used the grid to help scale the figures and palm trees along the river. He made silhouette masks for the trees and grass banks and scaled the images to fit his composition.

For the figure elements, Larson photographed friends dressed in costume, scanned the photos and opened them in Photoshop, where he applied the Solarize filter. He saved the angel files and opened them in Painter.

After he had pasted the wings into each angel source file, he made silhouette masks for the wings, so he could select and distort them to match the perspective of the figures, using the Distort command.

Larson painted the evening stars, rippled water reflections and light rays in Painter

using Airbrushes and F/X brushes. Then he tinted the finished black-and-white composition with a custom gradient (choosing Express in Image from the Gradients section bar's menu in the Art Materials palette).

To add more color to the figures and clothing, Larson painted transparent washes using the Simple Water variant of Water Color. For more color and texture in some areas, he used the Variable Splatter and Digital Airbrush variants of Airbrushes with low opacity settings.

11

USING PAINTER FOR WEB GRAPHICS

Ben Barbante created Efolio, *an illustration for his Web site's index page. To see the entire image, turn to page 321 in the gallery.*

Ben Barbante created Efolio, *an illustration for his Web site's index page. To see the entire image, turn to page 321 in the gallery.*

ON-SCREEN TYPE AND COLOR

Type on-screen can be difficult to read in small sizes, so it's important that it be as clear as possible. For both type and drawings, flat color with crisp edges often works best. Anti-aliasing and gradations don't compress well—they can become blotchy.

WHAT DOES PAINTER OFFER AN ARTIST who designs graphics for the World Wide Web? In addition to its powerful natural media brushes, compositing tools, mosaics and other effects, Painter can help you prepare images for Web pages. For example, you can set type for titles with the Text tool or Dynamic Text, use shapes to draw polygons, convert the shapes to layers and define the polygons as clickable regions for use on your Web page. Use the Image Slicer to segment an image into smaller parts so the viewer can see the image as it loads, then export some of the slices with JavaScript rollovers. You can open source video in Painter as a frame stack and grab stills to use as graphics or as references for your Web illustrations, or export the frame stack directly from Painter as a GIF animation. (If you need help with the painting techniques or compositing methods referred to in this chapter, you can find more information in Chapters 3, 4 and 5. Turn to Chapter 10 for information on scripts and frame stack animations. And see Appendix E for recommended books relating to Web design.)

CREATING GRAPHICS FOR THE WEB

Painter has tools that make it easy to adapt graphics for the Web. For instance, you can save in GIF and JPEG (the two most popular image formats used on the Web). And you can tell Painter to do some of the coding to help you set up image maps or linked graphics. Here are some tips for creating Web graphics in Painter.

First, there are two basic uses for images on a Web page. One is an in-line graphic or "static" image embedded in the page without a link to another location—for example, an embedded background graphic. The second use for graphics is as "hot spots," or "buttons." A hot spot is a clickable region on your artwork that will allow the user to hyperlink (or travel) to another location on the Web, either within the same Web site or at another site. There are two general

Susan LeVan created images for "Off" and "On" button states, for the Nichole Shoes Web site. To see the entire set of buttons, turn to page 319 in the gallery.

turn to page 319 in the gallery.

Choosing 256 colors in the Monitors and Sound control panel

types of hot spots. The simpler one is a *button* that links to one location (URL, or Uniform Resource Locator). The second is an *image map*—an image that has been divided into regions, each of which lets you link to a different URL.

Making an image map. You can choose any kind of graphic as an image map: title type, a photograph or an illustration you've painted. Define an image map by selecting all or part of an image (by dragging around it with a selection tool and making a layer). Double-click on the layer name in the Layers section of the Objects palette to access the Layer Attributes dialog box. Use the checkbox to make it a WWW map clickable region. In the Save as GIF and JPEG dialog boxes, you can choose to export a client-side image map (directions for the image map are included in the HTML for the page) or server-side image map (directions for the map are stored on the server), by telling Painter to create an image map definition file with dimensions for the hot spots. Client-side image maps are more efficient to use when designing for newer browsers, but if you want your image map to work with older browsers as well, consider including both client-side and server-side directions in the HTML for the image map.

Using Web-friendly file formats. The JPEG and transparent GIF formats that Painter supports are two of the most popular file formats used in Web page design. Transparent GIF files make use of the mask you've saved with the file, allowing a graphic to be placed on the page with an irregular edge or with holes cut into it to reveal the background underneath. You can make a transparent GIF by choosing File, Save As, GIF. In the Save As GIF Options dialog box, use the Output Transparency checkbox. Click the Preview Data button to make sure your mask is working. We suggest using GIF format to save simple line art and flat-color graphics without gradations and soft edges. Save photos and painted artwork in 24-bit JPEG format.

Building small files that load fast. Many Web-savvy designers recommend making graphics files small, between 20 and 30K, because most Web visitors will not wait for images that take a long time to load. Typical modem speed is 56,600 bps and graphics of 20–30K will download within about 3 seconds. To make GIF images small, use Painter's Save As GIF Options dialog box to compress the number of colors from millions to 256 (8-bit) or fewer. Save as GIF in the exact pixel dimensions needed for the page design. When you use JPEG format to preserve the 24-bit color of an image, experiment with the JPEG Encoding Quality settings to determine how much compression an image can withstand. JPEG is a lossy compression (it removes information, which can't be restored), so make sure to use File, Save As to create the new JPEG file with a different name, preserving your master file.

Creating a subdued background. Painter has tools for creating exciting backgrounds, but a busy, contrasty background can

A row of interactive buttons on the Lenny Kravitz *Web site* Music *screen designed by Hugo Hidalgo with BoxTop Interactive for client Virgin Records. The center button features a colored animation, inviting the viewer to click there first.*

EXPORTING WEB-SAFE COLOR

Painter's color set feature can be used in conjunction with GIF export in a similar way that indexed color palettes are used in other programs. To export a GIF from Painter with colors constrained to a Web-safe color set, begin by loading a set (such as the Netscape 216 color set); then choose File, Save As, GIF. In the Save As GIF Options dialog box, under Imaging Method, turn on the Quantize to Nearest Color and Color Set buttons. To read about exporting a GIF with a color set of only three colors, turn to "Reducing Color Using Apply Screen," on pages 302–303.

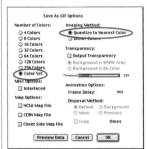

The Save As GIF Options dialog box with Quantize to Nearest Color and Color Set buttons chosen

take attention away from the subject of the screen and overwhelm your audience. Here are two suggestions that will help you make a background more subtle: Turn down the contrast using Effects, Tonal Control, Brightness and Contrast, or desaturate the background (using Effects, Tonal Control, Adjust Colors) to call attention to brighter-colored content. To desaturate, move the Saturation slider to the left. Click OK when you see the look you want in the Preview window.

Adding movie stills and video to your page. You can open a movie in Painter and capture frames to use as static images or hot spots. And you can save a QuickTime or AVI/VFW movie using effective compression such as Cinepak, so it can be played within the Netscape 2.0 (or newer) browser.

Exporting a movie as a GIF animation. Painter makes it easy to add movement to your Web pages with GIF animations! You can open a QuickTime/VFW/AVI movie as a frame stack (or create your own animation in Painter) and export it directly from Painter as a GIF animation. Here are some tips to help you make a GIF animation that loads quickly and plays smoothly on your Web page: Make movies with a small frame size (such as 160 x 120). (Painter doesn't permit movies to be resized. So if you plan to import video into Painter, reduce the frame size in a video editor such as Adobe Premiere before opening it in Painter.) Use as few frames as possible. (You can use the Movie, Delete Frames dialog box to remove any unnecessary frames.) Reduce the number of colors—using black-and-white or just a few, for instance, will help to make a smaller animation file.

To save a completed frame stack as a GIF animation, choose File, Save As, Save Movie as GIF Animation. In the Save As GIF Options box, make the choices you need. **Beware:** Save your GIF animation under a new name so you don't accidently replace your frame stack. Painter 6 will not open a GIF animation as a frame stack.

WEB-FRIENDLY COLOR

Painter 6 ships with several color sets built for Web graphics. To load a Web-friendly color set, open the Art Materials palette, click the right arrow on the Colors section bar and from the menu, choose Load Color Set. Navigate to the Painter 6 Application CD-ROM and open the Color Sets folder. Select a "Hex" Color Set, the Netscape 216, the Macintosh default 256 or the Windows Default 256 Color Set and click Open.

SHRINKING A COPY

If you're doing detailed painting to be displayed on the Web at 72 ppi, you may want to create your art at a higher resolution so you can zoom in and paint the details. Then use Canvas, Resize to shrink a copy of your image down to 72 ppi. Sharpen areas that become soft (Effects, Focus, Sharpen).

Designing a Masthead and Template

Overview; *Choose Web-safe colors; set Dynamic Text in a source file; import this and other source files into a template; export elements from the template in a Web-friendly file format.*

Choosing a light purple color from the Hex 99ffff->880000 Color Set

Creating a small file for the header type

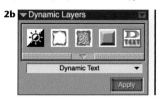

Clicking the Apply button in the Dynamic Layers section of the Objects palette to make a Dynamic Text layer

The Dynamic Text cursor appears centered in the image window.

USING TEMPLATES, DESIGNERS CAN VISUALLY lay out elements within the constraints of a page and make decisions about color and spatial balance. A template can also be a useful guide for HTML programmers when they write code for Web pages. Layers are ideal for building Web page templates because they keep the elements separate so they can be exported later as small individual files, which download and display faster than a single large image.

For our welcome screen above, we avoided overpowering special effects that might distract from the art being shown at this gallery site, instead creating a simple, asymmetrical design with a white background that would showcase the art. Using Painter's versatile Dynamic Text, we set type in a separate file, and then we assembled the type and the other source files in the template.

1 Choosing color for the masthead. For a unified masthead design, we chose an analogous color scheme of blue and purple. (To read more about color theory, turn to the beginning of Chapter 2, "The Power of Color," on page 20.) Several color sets designed for use with Web graphics are available on the Painter 6 Application CD-ROM. These Web-safe colors are designed to be displayed on monitors with 256 colors or less. For this project, we loaded the Hex 99ffff->880000 color set. The set incorporates a hexadecimal value identification for each color. (Hex values are used in HTML code to specify color.) Before beginning your

3a

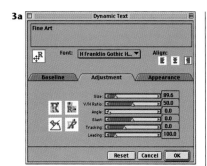

Settings in the Dynamic Text dialog box; the Position icon is in the top section of the dialog box.

3b

Right-aligned text will appear on the left of the center Align mark.

4

Positioning the layer with small type

5

The Layers section showing the open group with the "live" Dynamic Text layers inside. (To open or close a group, click the green arrow to the left of its name.)

SMALLER, FASTER AND EASIER

When you make a Dynamic Text layer, Painter creates a layer to cover your entire image. If you have a large image with several layers, processing can become slow and file size can grow. A remedy: Create Dynamic Text layers in small source files and paste them into your composite image. The small layers will also be easier to position in the layout file.

---

header design, load this color set as follows: On the Art Materials palette's Colors section bar, click the right triangle to open the menu and choose Load Color Set. Navigate to the Hex 99ffff->880000 Color Set. This set can be found on the Painter 6 CD-ROM, in the Color Sets folder. Choose the color set name and click Open to display the set. In preparation for styling the type in step 3, choose a color from the Color Set by clicking on it. We chose a light purple.

2 Setting editable text in a source file. Create a small source file for your dynamic text; you'll paste the contents of the file into the page template later. To match our example, choose File, New, and make a blank file that measures 520 x 100 pixels.

Painter's Dynamic Text allows you to create multiple letters as a single editable layer. (You can also set individual letterforms in Painter using type shapes. For information about shapes, turn to the beginning of Chapter 5 "Using Layers and Shapes," on page 140.)

To set the type, in the Dynamic Layers section of the Objects palette choose Dynamic Text from the resource list. Make a transparent, empty Dynamic Text layer by clicking the Apply button on the front of the section (or choose Apply from the menu on the section bar). When the dialog box appears, Painter will place an alignment symbol at the center of the new layer. To see the text in your image as you type it, drag the large dialog box out of the way. Type your text into the text field at the top of the dialog box.

3 Styling the type. You can choose a font, adjust opacity, scale, apply special shadow effects and much more using the Dynamic Text dialog box. In the Dynamic Text box, select a typeface from the Font pop-up menu (we chose Franklin Gothic Heavy). Next, click on an Alignment style (we chose Right Align). When you click on an alignment method, Painter orients the text in relation to the alignment symbol.

If you'd like to interactively resize the type, click on the Size icon and drag on a corner of the live text in your image. You can also resize the type using the Size slider. At any time during the process you can use the Position icon to reposition the text block.

To color your type, click the Appearance tab to open it. Painter remembers the last color you used to fill type; so to apply the new Web-safe color you've chosen, click the Apply Fill button. When you've finished making adjustments, click OK.

4 Adding more type. We created a layered effect on the header by positioning a second layer directly on top of the first. To make another layer of Dynamic Text, click the Apply button on the section again. When the dialog box appears, click on a color (we chose a darker purple from the Web-safe Color Set) type into the Text field and style the type as you did in step 3. (If your type does not automatically fill with the new color, click the Apply Fill button on the Appearance tab. In the top part of the dialog box, click on the Position icon, then drag the type into position. For

6a

Creating a new file for the page template

6b

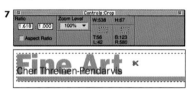

The template in progress, showing most of the elements in place, including the image of a painting

7

Cropping the masthead portion of the file

DYNAMIC TEXT BUG

As of this writing, a Mac/PC bug occurs when a Dynamic Text layer (or a layer that was *previously dynamic*) is pasted using Edit, Paste, Paste Into New Image. The bug causes the background of the new image to be black. Here's a work-around: Avoid the Paste Into New Image command by using the Rectangular Selection tool to select the area you want to paste, reading the dimensions in the Controls: Selection palette, creating a new file of the same size, and copying and pasting into this file.

The width and height of the selection are displayed in pixels

the smaller type, we used Franklin Gothic. We clicked on it with the Size icon in the Adjustment tab and visually scaled it to match the width of the bolder light purple type.

5 Grouping the layers and saving the file. When you've finished making modifications to your masthead type, group the two layers. To group the layers, select them by holding down the Shift key and clicking on their names in the Layers section of the Objects palette. When they're both selected, click the Group button at the bottom of the palette. When you group the masthead layers, Dynamic Text capabilities are preserved, should you need to use the source file again to make changes to the type.

6 Importing source files into the template. We built a 580-pixel-wide page template, because we planned to assemble the page elements later in Adobe GoLive; the program recommends a 580-pixel width for viewing on 14-inch monitors (640 x 480 pixels). To match our example, open a new file that measures 580 x 580 pixels. We imported a collapsed copy of the masthead layer group into the template by copying and pasting. To begin, Alt/Option-click on the group in the image to duplicate it, then press the Collapse button on the Layers section. If the Commit dialog box appears, click Commit All to convert the duplicate, grouped Dynamic Text layers into a single image layer. (Your layers will now become a single image layer without Dynamic Text capabilities.) To name the duplicate, double-click on the closed group in the list and the Layer Attributes dialog box will appear. Type a name in the Name field, and click OK. The name will be retained when you import the layer group into the template.

To copy and paste, use the Layer Adjuster to select the collapsed duplicate layer in the Layers section of the source file and choose Edit, Copy. Make the template file window active and choose Edit, Paste to add a layer to the template file.

7 Exporting. Keep the key elements in your design on individual layers so they can easily be saved as separate images for use on your Web pages. When you're ready to produce files for the Web, export each layer as follows: Click on the layer in the Layers section to select it. Using the Rectangular Selection tool, make a selection close to the edges of the graphics. Read the "H" and "W" dimensions in the Controls:Selection palette and create a new file the size of the selection. (Our masthead was 350 x 70 pixels.) Copy the selection and paste it into the new file. Merge the layer with the canvas by clicking the Drop button on the Layers section. (If you'd like to export the masthead with transparency, instead of using the Drop button, click the right triangle on the Layers section bar and choose Drop and Select.) Finally, save the file as a GIF in Painter; we used a palette of four colors (to export with transparency, turn on Output Transparency in GIF Options). We used Adobe GoLive to assemble all of the elements for our page (shown viewed in Netscape at the top of page 299).

Reducing Color Using Apply Screen

Overview *Choose an image; reduce color using Apply Screen; edit the color to make it Web-safe; export the image.*

1

The original photograph with selection active and background sky made lighter

2a

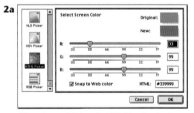

Choosing a Web-safe HTML color in the Select Screen dialog box on a Mac using the System 9 Color Picker

2b

The Apply Screen dialog box with preview showing the new color choices

REDUCING THE NUMBER OF COLORS is a frequently used method for making small files for faster downloading of Web graphics. To create this three-color image, we used Apply Screen—one of Painter's most efficient "color reduction" tools. It allows you to create images composed of only three colors without the anti-aliasing that creates many intermediate colors when it smooths edges.

1 Choosing a photo and making adjustments. Open an image that you want to convert to a three-color composition. In our first attempt to modify color using the Apply Screen function, the skiers merged with the background sky because the sky's value did not contrast enough with the skiers. We undid the Apply Screen, and before trying again, we isolated the sky by making a selection, and then lightened the sky. To make a selection of an area like the sky based on color, click on the area with the Magic Wand. To add areas of noncontiguous color to the selection, turn off the Contiguous checkbox in the Controls:Magic Wand palette; expand or shrink the range of colors by adjusting the Tolerance. (To read more about the Magic Wand, turn to page 111 in Chapter 4.) Then we increased the value within the selected sky using Brightness/Contrast (choose Effects, Tonal Control, Brightness/Contrast). After adjusting the Brightness, we chose Select, None.

2 Reducing color. To apply the color effect to your entire image choose Effects, Surface Control, Apply Screen, Using Image Luminance and choose a color by clicking the middle of the three color squares. In the color picker that opened, we settled on an aqua color, in addition to the black and white. (If you are using a Mac with System 8.0 or later featuring the updated Apple Color Picker, you can choose a Web-safe color at this point using the HTML Picker, and skip steps 3 and 4. If you have this option, check the Snap to Web color box, and select a color.) If your computer does not have the HTML color option, choose a color to

3a

The image showing active selection made with the Dropper and the Auto Select, Using Current Color dialog box

3b

Close-up of the image with selection. The original aqua color shows dithering when viewed on a monitor with only 256 colors.

4a

The Netscape Navigator 216 Color Set, showing the new aqua we used for the fill

4b

Filling with the Web-safe color

5

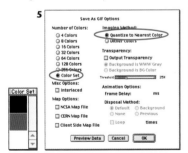

Our settings in the GIF Options dialog box and the Color Set with three Web-safe colors

serve as a preview of the final effect. It doesn't have to be a Web-safe color. In step 3 you can replace it. We adjusted the Threshold sliders to bring out important details in the skiers' faces. The Threshold 1 slider controls the relationship between aqua (the middle color) and white (the color on the right); the Threshold 2 slider controls the amount of black (the left color).

3 Making a selection. As of this writing, Painter's Apply Screen dialog box does not let you directly apply color from a Web-safe color set. To replace our color with a Web-safe color, we first made a hard-edged mask. To make a hard-edged selection based on color, choose the Dropper and click on the colored area you want to mask. From the Select menu choose Auto Select, Using Current Color. Click OK; you'll see a selection marquee appear on your image.

4 Filling the selection with a Web-safe color. Now load the Web-safe Netscape Navigator 216 Color Set as follows: On the Art Materials palette's Colors section bar, click the right triangle to open the menu and choose Load Color Set. Navigate to the Netscape Navigator 216 Color Set. This set can be found on the Painter 6 CD-ROM, in the Color Sets folder. Next, click on a Web-safe color that complements your design (we chose a bright aqua). Choose Effects, Fill With Current Color, and click OK.

5 Making a color set and exporting a GIF file. To preserve the Web-safe colors that you used in your illustration, export a GIF that uses a custom color set that contains the three Web-safe colors in your image. (This process is similar to setting up an Indexed Color palette in Photoshop.)

Before you make the Color Set, open the Color Variability section of the Art Materials palette, choose "In HSV" from the pop-up menu and set the (± H), (± S) and (± V) sliders to 0. Now choose the Dropper tool and click on one of the three colors in your image. The Colors section of the Art Materials palette will display the color. In the Art Materials palette, click on the Color Set section bar to open the Color Set section, and click on the New Set button. A very small Color Set title bar will appear. Click on the Add Color button to add the selected color to the Color Set. Sample and add the two remaining colors by using the Dropper and the Add Color button. To save your colors, click on the Library button in the Color Sets palette, then click Save, name the set and Save. (For more information about making color sets, turn to "Capturing a Color Set" on page 36, in Chapter 2.)

To export a GIF from Painter to use on your Web page, choose File, Save As, GIF. When the Save As GIF Options dialog box appears, under Imaging method, turn on Quantize to Nearest Color and choose the Color Set button. 🖌

Posterizing with Web-Safe Colors

Overview *Open an image; load the Netscape Navigator 216 Color Set; posterize the image using the Color Set; retouch it using flat color fills and Painter's Web safe brushes; export the file.*

CHER THREINEN-PENDARVIS / ORIGINAL PHOTO: CORBIS IMAGES

PHOTO: CORBIS IMAGES

The original photo

The Netscape Navigator 216 Color Set

POSTERIZING CAN ADD AN INTERESTING GRAPHIC LOOK to a photo, and at the same time, simplify color for faster downloading. We posterized the image above using Painter's Netscape Navigator 216 Web-safe color set so the color would not dither on most monitors. Then we exported our GIF file with color constrained by the color set.

1 Choosing a photo. We opened a 512-pixel-wide photo. Select a photo or an illustration with a simple background, such as this snowboarder image.

2 Posterizing using a Color Set. Begin by loading the Netscape Navigator 216 Color Set. On the Art Materials palette's Colors section bar, click the right triangle to open the menu and choose Load Color Set. Navigate to the Netscape Navigator 216 Color Set. This set can be found on the Painter 6 CD-ROM, in the Color Sets folder. Now choose Effects, Tonal Control, Posterize Using Color Set. The command doesn't allow you to have complete control over how color reduction is performed, but it does automatically constrain all of the colors in the image to the Netscape 216-color palette and can be a real time-saver.

3

Making a selection with the Magic Wand

4

Painting with a Web-safe brush

5a

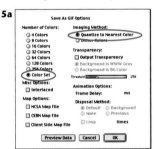

To constrain our GIF to Web-safe colors, we turned on the Quantize to Nearest Color and Color Set buttons in GIF Options.

5b

Detail of our final GIF shows no dithering when viewed using 256 colors.

3 Cleaning up the background. Posterizing with the Netscape Navigator 216 Color Set provided a close match for the important colors in our image (such as flesh tones), but it produced some distracting debris in the sky. We used the Magic Wand to select these areas. Click with the Magic Wand on the color you want to select. To select noncontiguous color, turn off the Contiguous checkbox in the Controls:Magic Wand palette. If needed, adjust the Tolerance slider in the Controls:Magic Wand palette. To read more about the Magic Wand, turn to page 111 in the Chapter 4, "Selections, Shapes and Masks." After making the selection, we filled the area with blue sampled from the sky. To sample color in your image and fill as we did, choose the Dropper tool and click in your image. Then choose Effects, Fill, Fill With Current Color.

4 Touching up with a Web-safe brush. There was still some debris left after we applied the fill, so we painted the area using a "Web-safe" brush. Choose a brush from Painter's WebMedia Brushes library. To load the WebMedia Brushes, select Load Library from the bottom of the brush resource list on the Brushes palette. Navigate to the Brushes folder (located the Contents Sampler folder in the Painter application folder), select the WebMedia Brushes library and click Open.

> **WEB-SAFE BRUSHES**
>
> Painter ships with a WebMedia brush library. The WebMedia Brushes use Grainy Edge Flat Cover and Grainy Flat Cover (two subcategories that incorporate aliased edges). The brushes are ideal for painting when you want to avoid the in-between colors that are generated during anti-aliasing.

We chose the Calligraphic Winner brush variant of the W Thick-n-Thin brush. Then we used the blue, sampled from the sky, to paint over the remaining purple speckles. The sky was now a solid blue.

5 Exporting the image. You can export a GIF from Painter, while retaining Web-safe colors from the Netscape Navigator 216 Color Set chosen in step 2, as follows: Choose File, Save As, GIF, and when the Save As GIF Options dialog box appears, under Imaging method, turn on Quantize to Nearest Color, and under Number of Colors, choose Color Set.

This function works similar to the indexed color palettes supported by Equilibrium DeBabelizer, Macromedia Fireworks and Adobe ImageReady that allow Web-safe colors to be preserved. Our final image is at the top of the previous page. 🖌

> **HELPFUL FREEWARE AND SHAREWARE**
>
> GifBuilder and GIF Construction Set are two nifty applications that are useful for exporting constrained color palettes and for animating GIFs. Both programs are available on the Web. You can find GifBuilder (Mac platform) at http://download.cnet.com/downloads/ and GIF Construction Set (Windows platform) at http://shareware.cnet.com/shareware.

Making a Seamless Tile

Overview *Select an image; use the Kaleidoscope plug-in to make a tile; edit its color; test the tile; and save the tile in JPEG format.*

CHER THREINEN-PENDARVIS

PHOTO: CORBIS IMAGES

The original photograph of palm trees

Image with Kaleidoscope dynamic layer

The new tile image

PAINTER HAS SEAMLESS-TILE-CREATION TOOLS that are unequaled by other programs. To make this background for a Web site welcome screen, we began by using the Kaleidoscope dynamic layer to create a symmetrical design based on a photo of palm trees. After making the seamless tile and testing it in Painter, we saved the finished image as a JPEG file for import into a Web page editor.

1 Choosing an image. For this nostalgic background design, we chose a 768 x 512-pixel image with gold-to-brown colors.

2 Using Kaleidoscope as a lens. A Kaleidoscope dynamic layer acts as a lens: As you move it over your image, it distorts the underlying imagery into symmetrical designs that are ideal for perfect seamless tiles or fabric design. To make a Kaleidoscope layer, in the Dynamic Layers section of the Objects palette, choose the Kaleidoscope plug-in from the resource list pop-up menu. Now, click the Apply button on the front of the section (or choose Apply from the menu, opened by clicking the right triangle on the Dynamic Layers section bar). When the dialog box appears, it will reflect the default size of 100 x 100 pixels. We typed 200 into the field to make a larger "lens." Move the Kaleidoscope layer around your image until you find a "tile" effect you like. (To read more about dynamic layers, turn to Chapter 5, "Using Layers and Shapes.")

3 Making a tile image. Building a background by importing a single repeating tile into a Web page editor is much more efficient than importing an entire background image. That's because the smaller tile image downloads faster, and it can be repeated very quickly by the browser. Here's the quickest way to prepare your tile: Open the Layers section of the Objects palette, choose the Layer Adjuster and select the Kaleidoscope dynamic layer by clicking on its name in the Layers section. To capture the Kaleidoscope imagery into the layer, use the Commit command to convert the dynamic layer

4

Lightening the color for a subdued look

5

Naming the pattern in the Capture Pattern dialog box

6

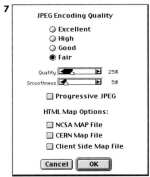

The Painter image filled with the Golden Palms pattern

7

Saving the tile as a JPEG with Fair quality and a Smoothness setting of 5%

SOFTEN WITH SMOOTHNESS

When low-quality JPEG settings are used, square artifacts can appear in an image. The Smoothness setting in the JPEG dialog box can help to soften artifacts. Use Smoothness with care, however, because a setting that's too high can blur the image. A bonus: Smoothness can further reduce the size of the file.

into an image layer: Click the right triangle on the Dynamic Layers section bar to open the pull-down menu and choose Commit. Copy the layer (Edit, Copy), and then choose Edit, Paste into New Image.

4 Lightening the tile image. We lightened the new image to make a background that would not compete with text and other elements on the page by choosing Effects, Tonal Control, Adjust Colors. One way to lighten is to move the Value slider in the dialog box to the right. Our setting was 121%.

5 Making a pattern. Select the entire tile image by choosing Select, All. Now you can capture the tile as a pattern and test its tiling in Painter. On the Art Materials palette, click the right triangle on the Patterns section bar to open the menu and choose Capture Pattern. When the dialog box appears, name your pattern. For a Rectangular tile with no Horizontal or Vertical Shift (like ours), leave the other settings at their defaults.

6 Testing the tile. To see the overall effect of your pattern in Painter, create a new 600 x 600-pixel document. Now choose Effects, Fill, and in the dialog box, click the Pattern button. Click OK to fill the new document with the pattern.

7 Exporting the seamless tile. At this point we saved our full-color file (File, Save). Always remember to keep your original file in a format that preserves its image quality, such as TIFF, RIFF or Photoshop. Because the audience for this site would be viewing its images using millions of colors, we didn't want to limit the colors in our image to a Web-safe palette. So we also saved the tile in JPEG format, a Web format that preserves the 24-bit color depth. (GIF format limits the number of colors to a maximum of 256.) To save a copy of your file as a JPEG, choose File, Save As, JPEG, and remember to add the proper file extension (.jpg) to its name. To make the image small, we chose the Fair setting and applied a Smoothness of 5% in the JPEG dialog box. (Smoothness can soften JPEG artifacts.) Our final background (viewed in Netscape) is shown at the top of page 306.

BRACKETING TO COMPARE JPEG IMAGE QUALITY

Most designers export continuous-tone images for the Web using JPEG format. Often, a low JPEG setting will provide adequate quality (and a tiny file size).

JPEG settings: Excellent (top left), High (top right), Good (bottom left), and Fair (bottom right).

To know for sure, test the file by "bracketing," or saving it using several different quality settings. Begin by opening the image you want to compress. To duplicate the image, choose File, Clone, and save it using the lowest quality setting (Fair). Name the file so you can compare results later. Select your original file, choose File, Clone again and save the second image using Good quality. Repeat the process twice more using High and Excellent quality settings. Close the images, and reopen to compare the results. (JPEG compression artifacts are not visible until an image is closed and reopened.)

Creating a Web Page with an Image Map

Overview *Scan elements; build a patterned background using the scanned elements; create layers and designate an image map in Painter; finish the HTML.*

LYNDA WEINMAN, THE AUTHOR OF SEVERAL BOOKS about web design, creates graphics and animation for movies, TV commercials, music videos and Web sites. To build the Web site *Sequoyah Online* for an alternative elementary and junior high school in Pasadena, Weinman used Painter to create a background pattern, a logotype, graphics, and image map buttons for the index page (including some of the HTML code for the image map). Weinman made a small tile, using the browser's tiling function to repeat it, so it would download quickly. She designed the site to be viewed with any browser and used her own site, http://www.lynda.com, to develop the prototype.

1 Preparing to set up the page. In preparation for the page layout process, Weinman had made a pattern in Painter that consisted of a hand graphic which she had rotated, scaled and repeated. Then she colored and textured the tile using Effects, Surface Control, Color Overlay and Apply Surface Texture. When the tile was complete, she captured the pattern, so she could use it as a fill later. (For information about making a pattern tile, turn to "Making a Seamless Pattern Tile" on page 306.) She also captured the tile as a paper texture that she could use in conjunction with Apply Surface Texture Using Paper when she wanted to add textured highlights and shadows to the graphics in step 3, after the pattern fill was applied. (For information about how to make a paper texture, turn to "Applying Scanned Paper Textures," on page 78 in Chapter 3). After making your pattern tile, save a copy as a GIF by choosing File, Save As, GIF. Choose the number of colors and click the Quantize to Nearest Color radio button. (For advice on reducing Web page color palettes, see pages 297–298.)

2 Setting up the page. This step sets up the home page for the Web site. There are no absolute size restrictions on Web pages. They can be any length, because the viewer can scroll. But it's

1a

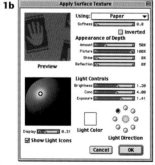

Positioning a hand layer by dragging with the Layer Adjuster tool

1b

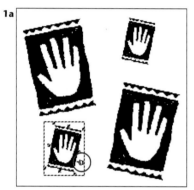

Adding relief to the colored tile with Apply Surface Texture Using Paper

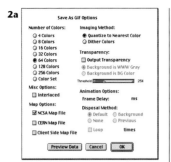

Saving the file as a GIF with 64 colors

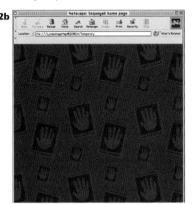

The background pattern tile was set up to repeat in the browser.

3

The logo mask (top) and hand graphic with type mask (bottom) shown by opening the mask eye icon and shutting the RGB-Canvas eye icon in the Masks section

4

The finished hand graphic with type; relief added with Apply Surface Texture

best to make the page no wider than 640 pixels (the width of the average monitor screen display). Weinman created her new page file at 500 x 600 pixels, to fit within the default page size of the popular browser, Netscape.

For your prototype Web page design, create a new file. To see how your pattern will look as a background, fill the image by choosing Effects, Fill, Pattern. The pattern will be removed from the file before the final export is done and a single pattern tile will be exported as a GIF file with a reduced color palette, to be repeated by the browser's tiling function for the finished page.

3 Creating a logotype and graphics. It's often easier to build source graphics in separate files and paste them into the final screen image when all of the elements are done. Start a new file the same width as the page and as high as the graphic you want to add. Using the Text tool with black as the current color, set large bold letters for a logotype. Weinman made a 500 x 100-pixel file and typed "Sequoyah" using Hot Coffee, a font by Ethan Durham at Fonthead Design (http://www.fonthead.com).

Since you'll be treating all the letters as a unit, group the selected type shapes (Ctrl/⌘-G) and merge them to make one layer (Collapse button, in the Layers section). In preparation for the fill to come, turn on Preserve Transparency in the Layers section of the Objects palette, so only the areas of the layer that contain pixels will be filled. To fill the logotype layer with a gray version of her pattern, Weinman used Effects, Fill, Pattern and then stripped the color out by using Effects, Tonal Control, Adjust Colors, and dragging the Saturation slider to the left. She added texture to "Sequoyah" (Effects, Surface Control, Apply Surface Texture Using Paper) using the Paper she had saved in step 1, so it lined up perfectly with the pattern fill. Then she added the subhead type to the logotype file with the Type tool, in a gray color she sampled from the logotype using the Dropper.

Weinman created another new file (416 x 283 pixels), copied and pasted her original hand graphic into it, and merged it with the Canvas. At this point, she used the Text tool to set type for several buttons—the "Mission Statement," for example. As she set type for each word, she grouped the type shapes, collapsed them and merged them with the Canvas.

She masked the hand and type (from the Objects palette, Masks section bar menu, choose Auto Mask using the Current Color, black). Then, as she had done for the logotype, she filled it with the pattern, grayed it out, and added text. (Choose the Layer Adjuster tool and click inside the active selection to make a layer.)

4 Embossing. For the logotype and the graphic, Weinman built a crisp-edged embossed effect that would display well on the screen, using a limited number of colors so the file would be smaller. To do this you'll need to make two copies of your graphic. Select the layer

The logo, graphic and button type on top of the test background image

The Layers section with the named layers

The Layer Attributes dialog:
Name: mission
Position: Top: 237 Left: 257
URL: http://www.lynda.com/mission/html

Layer Visibility Mask: ○ Disabled ● Normal ○ Inverted
☑ WWW Map Clickable Region
Region: ● Rectangle Bounding Box
○ Oval Inside Bounding Box
○ Polygon Region
Cancel OK

Entering the URL into the information field

by clicking on its name in the Layers section with the Layer Adjuster tool. Now, Alt/Option-click twice on the image to make two more copies, one for the highlight (the middle one in the Layers section list) and one for the shadow (the bottom one in the list). Select the shadow layer in the Layers section and use the arrow keys to offset it a few pixels to create a hard-edged shadow (Weinman moved hers to the left and up, simulating lighting from above left of her cut-out hand design). Then darken it by choosing Effects, Tonal Control, Adjust Colors and dragging the Value slider to the left. Now select the highlight layer in the Layers section, move it a few pixels down and to the right, and lighten it (this time the Value slider goes right).

To merge the three graphics layers, while saving a mask so it can be selected, proceed as follows: After combining the layers (Shift-select all three layers in the Layers section, press the Group button, and then press the Collapse button), merge the layer with the Canvas, by clicking the right triangle on the Layers section bar to open the pull-down menu and choosing Drop and Select. Then choose Select, Save Selection to save the selection as a mask.

5 Completing the layout and making the image map.
Open the background file (from step 2; this was Weinman's 500 x 600-pixel file). Then copy and paste your logotype and graphics images into it (from steps 3 and 4; for example, the completed "Sequoyah" file and the file with the hand graphic and button type).

If you want to paste the source files into the final file with transparency (in Weinman's example, the background needed to show through the counters of the "e," "q," "o" and "a" in "Sequo-yah" and through the hand in the graphic), load the selection you saved by choosing Select, Load Selection and choose Edit, Copy. Make the destination file active and choose Edit, Paste. Select the Layer Adjuster tool, turn on the Auto Select Layer box in the Controls:Adjuster palette and drag with the Layer Adjuster to position the elements over the background. To save a mask, needed to export the final GIF with transparency, she targeted all the graphic layers in the Layers section (but not the background layer), clicked the right triangle on the Layers section bar and chose Drop and Select from the menu. She saved the selection (Select, Save Selection).

Painter allows you to define an image file as an *image map* (a document that's divided into non-overlapping clickable regions, each of which lets you link to a different URL or location on the Web). In the finished layout, target the layer with the button type and drag with the Rectangular Selection tool to create a marquee around one of the elements that will become a clickable region. Type "F" to switch to the Layer Adjuster tool and click to a make a new layer for the item. Target the button type layer in the Layers section again, type "R" to switch to the Rectangular Selection tool, make another rectangular selection and turn it into a layer. Repeat this process for as many clickable regions as you need.

5d

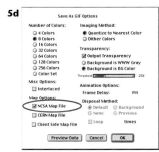

Checking the Server-Side Map File box to generate the map definition file for the server-side version of the image map

5e

Checking the Client Side Map File box to generate the map definition file for the client-side version of the image map

6a

```
# mission ——— name of the hot spot
rect http://www.lynda.com/mission/html
184,19 430,80
```

coordinates of upper left and lower right corners of the rectangle   **URL that hot spot links to**

The anatomy of one of the clickable regions in the server-side map definition file that Painter automatically generates

Now it's time to tell Painter what to include in the image map definition file (Weinman's included the type buttons, but omitted the tiled background layer; it would instead be tiled in the browser). For each layer you want to include in the image map, double-click the layer name in the Layers section to open the Layer Attributes dialog box. In the Name field, enter the name you want the layer to have on export. Use the checkbox to select WWW clickable map (the Region button will default to Rectangle), and type the URL into the URL field.

Some designers include directions for both server-side and client-side versions of an image map in the HTML, so the page can be viewed by both older and newer browsers. (Older browsers require server-side image maps, with instructions for the map stored on a server. But client-side image maps are more efficient for newer browsers. Instructions for client-side image maps are included in the HTML for the page.) For a server-side image map, choose File, Save As, GIF, and when the Save As GIF Options dialog box appears, use the NCSA map or CERN map box, depending on which type your Web server requires. To export a map description file for a client-side version of the image map, click the Client Side Map File box in the GIF Options dialog box. For both options, if you'd like to export elements with a clear background (as Weinman did) turn on Output Transparency.

6 Finishing the HTML. Painter will make the map definition file for you—which lists the name of each region, defines its position using *x* and *y* coordinates and lists the URL it links to. Instructions for client-side image maps are downloaded with the file when it is viewed in newer browsers. For server-side maps, ask your service provider where the CGI script for image maps is stored and how to use it (CGI is an acronym for Common Gateway Interface, and CGI script is the external programming script used by the Web server). Check out these URLs on the World Wide Web to learn how to set up programming for client-side and server-side image maps: http://www.ihip.com/cside.html and http://www.ihip.com. You'll also need additional HTML programming to make the links work. To see an example of HTML code used for tiling a background in a browser, turn to "Adding Interactivity" on page 312.

6b

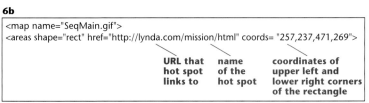

```
<map name="SeqMain.gif">
<areas shape="rect" href="http://lynda.com/mission/html" coords= "257,237,471,269">
```

URL that hot spot links to   **name of the hot spot**   **coordinates of upper left and lower right corners of the rectangle**

The anatomy of one of the clickable regions in the client-side map definition file that Painter automatically generates

Adding Interactivity

Overview: *Open a layered image in Painter; use the Image Slicer to segment the image; make masks for On and Off states; use the Image Slicer to export the image pieces with JavaScript for rollover effects.*

SHAWN GRUNBERGER

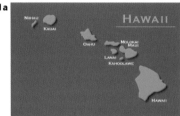

The Hawaii map, ready to be sliced

The Layers section of the Objects palette showing the Hawaii map elements, with no layers selected

WITH PAINTER'S IMAGE SLICER you can divide large images or navigation graphics into separate but precisely fitting elements, each of which can be its own hot spot. The slicing process also generates the HTML code for the slices, naming and positioning each slice on the HTML page. The Image Slicer plug-in can also be used to generate and export the JavaScript code for rollover effects. (A rollover is a simple animation that is played when the cursor moves over a button or graphic, or when the button is clicked. During a rollover, a different image of the same dimensions is swapped in. Most fourth-generation browsers, such as Netscape 4 and Internet Explorer 4, can display JavaScript rollover effects.)

An innovative Web designer, Shawn Grunberger created the interactive map of Hawaii above using Painter's Natural Media tools and effects. He wanted each island to display its name and to change color when the mouse was moved over it and this required On and Off versions of each of the islands (a two-state mouseover). He used Painter's Image Slicer plug-in to divide the image into pieces that he could export from Painter with JavaScript rollovers. Because the irregularly-shaped islands would be shown over a tiling background, he created two masks to achieve the transparency for each state.

1 Opening the map image. Grunberger opened the Painter RIFF file that contained the map elements. When making the file, he had saved two versions of the island images as two layer groups—"Islands On" and "Islands Off." The island name text labels were also organized in a layer group. Other elements were on separate

2

The Image Slicer dynamic layer affects the layers below it in the Layers section.

3a

Choosing the Vertical tool in the Image Slicer dialog box

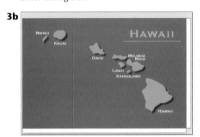
3b

Click the Vertical tool in the image to place a vertical line.

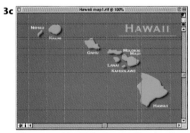
3c

The map with all the image slices in place, before grouping some of the slices

4a

Choosing the Select tool

4b

Dragging with the Select tool to create a group of slices

layers. To read more about working with layers using the Layers section, turn to page 140 in Chapter 5, "Using Layers and Shapes."

2 Making an Image Slicer layer. If you'd like to slice your entire image (as Grunberger did), make sure no layers are selected in the Layers section of the Objects palette. (The Image Slicer doesn't perform properly when it is applied to an existing layer.) To use the Image Slicer, open the Dynamic Layers section of the Objects palette. From the Dynamic Layers resource list choose Image Slicer and click the Apply button. Painter will generate an empty, transparent Image Slicer layer. When the slices are drawn in this layer, the slicing will affect all layers below it in the Layers section.

3 Setting up a grid of image slice lines. Before creating any slices, Grunberger set the File Type menu in the Image Slicer dialog box to "No export." Since all new slices inherit the settings of the first slice, this meant that all slices in the image would be set to "No Export" by default. He planned to export only the slices of the image that contained the islands and thus would have two different versions. Since most of the slices were open areas of the ocean, they wouldn't be exported, so using the "No Export" setting saved some time later. (Instead, the open ocean would be filled in with a tiled background tiled in the browser, which would make the total size of the page and graphics smaller.)

The fewer slices, the simpler the HTML table will be. Sometimes the process can require experimentation in the Image Slicer dialog box, with frequent repositioning of slice lines and with grouping of unused slices. The benefits of rollover effects and quick downloading have to be balanced against code complexity. To set up a grid of Image Slicer lines for your image, use the Vertical tool to place vertical lines and the Horizontal tool for horizontal ones. To quickly divide an image into quadrants, use the Combined tool.

4 Repositioning elements and grouping. While Grunberger was setting up the image slices, he had to adjust the position of the text captions, which had to fit within the slice boundaries. You can adjust the position of a layer to better fit within a slice boundary as follows: Close the Image Slicer dialog box by clicking OK, use the Layer Adjuster to select the layer's name in the Layers section and use the arrow keys

MOVING SLICE LINES

To move a horizontal slice line, select the Horizontal tool and click on a horizontal slice line on the Image Slicer layer. A small horizontal arrow will appear on the cursor. Move the slice line to a new position. (Use the Vertical tool in the same way to move a vertical slice.)

DELETING SLICE LINES

To delete a vertical Image Slice line, choose the Vertical tool, hold down the Ctrl/⌘ key, and click on a vertical slice line on the Image Slicer layer. (Use the Horizontal tool to delete a horizontal slice line.)

5a

The Hawaii map with final grouped slices and with the Kauai slice activated with the Image Slicer Select tool

5b

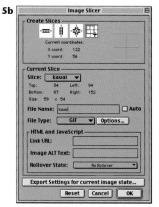

"Test" settings for the Kauai slice in the Image Slicer dialog box, with Rollover State set to No Rollover

5c

Make sure to check that the HTML table location path and the image location path are pointed to the same location.

USE SHORT NAMES

Painter adds location information to directions included in the HTML table. So, when naming the HTML table file and the folder you want to export to, use very short names, especially when working on the Mac. On the Mac, Painter can not process names with more than 31 characters; you will be greeted by a warning dialog box as you attempt to export and the table will not work.

on your keyboard to nudge the layer into position under the slice boundary. To open the Image Slicer dialog box again, double-click the Image Slicer layer in the Layers section list.

To make a slice for the area with the four small closely associated islands, Grunberger selected and grouped them to create a single slice. (Grouping makes a single larger slice from multiple smaller slices in the grid.) He planned to make a separate image map for this area later so it could include a hot spot for each island. He also grouped the large areas of the ocean that did not contain islands since they would not be exported at all.

To group slices (as for the small islands), choose the Select tool in the Image Slicer dialog box, click on the top left slice in the area you want to group and drag the tool to the right and down to create a rectangular shape around the cells you want to combine. To ungroup, hold down the Shift key and click in the group with the Select tool.

5 Testing the HTML export. With all of the slices in place, it was time to test the HTML export of the sliced image table. To export each of your slices as a GIF file for testing the way Grunberger did, click on each slice you want to export with the Image Slicer Select tool. In the Image Slicer dialog box, change the File Type from No Export to Mouse over-out. Now click the Options button to open GIF Options and set the Number of Colors, Imaging Method and Transparency options. Grunberger used 32 colors (enough to make the map look good), no Transparency (so he could see the position of the entire slice) and no Interlacing (interlacing makes each graphic appear in stages, which can be more interesting for the viewer, but it creates a larger file). Under Imaging Method, he chose Quantize to Nearest Color. To preview the color in your image, click the Preview button, then click OK to exit the Preview (if you need to adjust the color settings, do so in GIF Options and Preview again if needed). When you're satisfied with the Preview, click OK again to accept the settings in GIF Options and return to the Image Slicer dialog box.

Back in the Image Slicer dialog box, Grunberger set Rollover State to No Rollover for this test, because he wanted check the image slice table in a browser before adding the complexity of rollover effects to the HTML code. Click the larger button labeled "Export Settings for Current Image State" to access the Export Slices Options dialog box. Under "Location where HTML table will be created," click the Select button to browse and locate the folder where you want the HTML table and images to be stored. Under "Location where images will be exported," click the Select button and navigate to the same folder. (The table file and images must be in the same folder for the interactivity to work.) Then click the Export button. All of the slices set up for export will be exported at once, and will appear in the folder with the HTML document. Any slice whose File Type remains as No Export will not be saved.

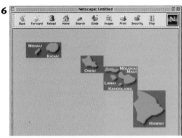

6

7

Opening the test file in Netscape 4.5 revealed the island slices in position over the default gray background.

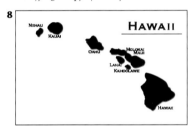

The original "Islands Off" mask, made by modifying a copy of the layer mask

8

The "Islands On" layer mask

9a

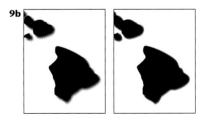

Using Equalize to make the "Islands On" mask denser at the edges so it would export well as a 1-bit mask for the GIF

9b

The original (left) and final "Islands Off" mask (right) showing a narrower, crisper edge on the shadow and larger dark areas that would keep the mask from eliminating the drop shadows.

6 Testing the page in a browser. Once he had exported the slices, Grunberger opened the HTML page in a browser. Since only the island slices had been exported, other areas showed the default gray background of the browser. To view the HTML page in a browser, launch your browser, then choose File, Open and navigate to the folder where you stored the exported GIF images and the HTML table document, which is a text file that will be read by the browser to display the page. Select the HTML table file and click Open to view the table with images.

7 Making the "Islands Off" mask. If your image does not include irregular elements that you need to mask in order to display correctly over a tiled background, you can skip steps 7, 8 and 9, and proceed to the exporting directions in step 10.

Having completed his initial test, Grunberger now wanted to make the blue rectangle around each island transparent so the islands would be silhouetted against the background of the Web page. Because Painter uses the active or most recent selection to define GIF transparency, he needed to make a selection around the contours of the islands. Since he wanted the island captions to appear only in the rollover "On" state, he created two masks: one for the On state and one for the Off state. (If he'd used only one selection for both states, the image caption areas would always be present, or always absent, the same in both states.) So before he exported a state, he used Select, Load Selection to make a selection from the correct mask, which he had made and stored in the Masks section of the Objects palette as follows:

Grunberger created the Off mask first. This mask needed to contain the islands, their shadows and the Hawaii title text. With Painter it's not easy to make a mask from multiple layers in one step, so he used the following method: Shift-select all the relevant layers (leaving the Canvas unselected) and group them by clicking the Group button at the bottom of the Layers section (or type Ctrl/⌘-G). Choose the Layer Adjuster and Alt/Option-click on the layer group in the image to duplicate the group in place. Next, click the Collapse button on the Layers section to merge the layers in this duplicate group. You can now make the single mask you're interested in from the resulting collapsed layer. Check to make sure the collapsed layer is selected and click the left triangle on the Masks section bar to open the Masks section. A layer mask for this layer will appear in the list in italics. Select this mask, and from the menu (opened by clicking the right triangle on the Masks section bar) choose Copy Mask. Clicking OK will create a new independent mask identical to the layer mask. (You need to copy the mask because Painter does not currently allow you to directly load a selection based on a layer mask.) To give the new mask a descriptive name, double-click on its name in the Masks section (to access the Mask Attributes dialog box) and type a new name in the field (Grunberger called this mask "Islands Off"). You can now

INCREASING CONTRAST

You can use the Equalize dialog box to increase contrast, reducing a graduated mask to black-and-white. Choose Effects, Tonal Control, Equalize and move the Black and White point sliders under the Histogram close together.

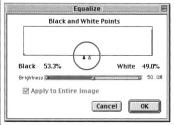

To increase the contrast, move the Black and White Point sliders closer together

10a

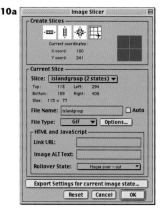

The Image Slicer dialog box with the settings for the island group slice

10b

Settings in GIF Options for the Number of Colors, Imaging Method and Transparency

use Select, Load Selection to create an active selection based on this mask. (To read more about working with selections and masks, turn to Chapter 4, "Selections, Shapes and Masks" on page 106.)

8 Making the "Islands On" mask. To make the mask for the On state, Grunberger made a composite mask that included the "Islands Off" mask and the island captions. To begin, he created a new mask containing just the island captions (using the procedure in step 7 above). Then he duplicated the "Islands Off" mask by selecting it in the Masks section and choosing Copy Mask (from the menu opened by clicking the right triangle on the Masks section bar). Finally, he added these two masks together to create the final composite "Islands On" mask: Choose Select, Load Selection, and when the dialog box appears choose the Off mask in the Load From menu. (Leave the Operation button at the default option, Replace Selection.) You'll see an animated marquee on your image. Now add to the selection by choosing Select, Load Selection again; but this time choose the "island" captions mask and set Operation to Add to Selection. To preserve the new composite selection as a mask in the Masks section choose Select, Save Selection.

9 Adjusting contrast of the masks. GIF transparency masks are 1-bit (black-and-white), while Painter's native masks are 8-bit (256 shades of gray). So Grunberger's mask needed to be modified. Without adjusting the contrast, Slicer-exported GIFs wouldn't show the island drop shadows at all; the shadows would be masked out along with the background.

To avoid this, Grunberger edited each of his two masks using Painter's Effects, Tonal Control, Equalize function. (With this procedure you can accomplish the same goal as with the Mask Threshold slider that's available when you use File, Save As to make a GIF. The Mask Threshold isn't available in the Image Slicer.) Grunberger increased the Brightness to a setting of 85, which produced the masks he wanted.

To use the Equalize function on a mask, begin by targeting the mask in the Masks section. To view the mask in black-and-white without the RGB-Canvas, toggle the mask's eye icon open and toggle the RGB-Canvas's eye icon closed. Select the mask's name and choose Effects, Tonal Control, Equalize. Use the Brightness slider to control the relative amounts of black and white in the mask. Note that increasing the Brightness will also make the edge of the shadow crisper and the gradation in the shadow will be less noticeable.

10 Making the final export and testing. Grunberger's map images were now ready for the final Image Slicer export. He set each of the island slices to GIF file type with 32 colors, as he had for the test, but this time with transparency. In the GIF Options dialog box he clicked the Preview button to check the GIF Output Preview; the Preview revealed that the transparency worked correctly.

10c

Checking GIF Output Preview to make sure the transparency is working

10d

Using the Export Slices Options dialog box to Export the Current Image State for the "Islands On" group

11a

The map viewed in Netscape 4 showing the islands in their "Off" state and the background image in place

11b

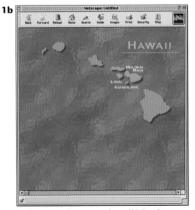

Rolling over the group of small islands turns them on as a unit. Grunberger planned to create an image map for them which would allow On and Off states for each island in this group.

He also set each of the island slices to a two-state rollover (Mouse Over-out), and gave each island a URL pointing to the island's page on a NASA Web site.

To export the images and code for two-state JavaScript rollovers, Grunberger did two separate export operations, one for each rollover state. His steps while exporting the rollovers were as follows: After hiding all layers except for those needed for the Off State, by turning off their icons in the Layers section, he used Select, Load Selection to load the "Islands Off" mask as a selection. Then he opened the Image Slicer dialog box and exported with Include JavaScript checked and "Current image state" set to the default Mouse Out. He clicked OK to close the Image Slicer dialog box.

For the On state Grunberger hid all layers except the "Islands On" group. Then he used Select, Load Selection to load the "Islands On" mask as a selection. He opened the Image Slicer again and set Export Settings for Current Image State to Mouse Over and clicked OK. Finally, he loaded the new HTML page into a browser to test, as described in step 6.

11 Defining the background color using HTML. The map test was successful, but as exported from Painter, the map page didn't have a designated background color or background image. To add these instructions, Grunberger opened the HTML file in a text editor and modified the <body> tag to read as follows, using a tile (oceantile.jpg) he had designed and stored in the HTML folder:

```
<body background="oceantile.jpg" bgcolor="#4861C9">
```

The process of applying a single tile using the browser's tiling function offers flexibility (the browser window can be resized to fill a large screen, with the ocean tiles covering the entire area). When specifying a tiled background or a background image, it's a good idea to also provide a background color (*bgcolor* in HTML). The bgcolor value is specified in the hexadecimal color format used in HTML. The background color will make the page more attractive and readable if there's a delay in loading the real background. It's usually best to set the background color to the average color of the background tile or image. For the interactive Hawaii map, Grunberger chose a medium-blue from his tile.

Finishing the page code. To complete this phase of the map production, Grunberger wrapped the HTML table in a <center> tag. This HTML tag ensures the map will always appear in the horizontal center of the page, regardless of the browser window size. The finished interactive map of Hawaii is shown at the top of page 312 and can also be seen on the Web (http://beta.peachpit.com/wow/painter/map/part3.1/hawaii.html). 🖌

■ When working with Boxtop Interactive, Web designer **Hugo Hidalgo** built the graphics for the *Lenny Kravitz* Web site for client Virgin Records. The site features many exciting pages that work together in a unified design. Hidalgo used tiled patterns built from images he had captured from video. He opened each video clip in Painter as a frame stack, and saved single frames by choosing File, Save As, Save Current Frame As Image. He also used the video grabs and photos supplied by the client to build button graphics in Painter.

To make it more inviting to enter the site, Hidalgo created an animated color button for the *Main Hub* (top). He put together a simple low-memory color animation for the button by making different color versions, saving the series as numbered files, and animating them in GIF Builder, a freeware program that animates GIF 89a files, written by Yves Piquet (yvespiquet@ia.epfl.ch). First, Hidalgo applied a red color to the button with Effects, Color Overlay, Using Image Luminance and Dye Concentration and saved the file as "01." He cloned the file and used Effects, Tonal Control, Adjust Colors to change the Hue from red to purple. He saved the second file as a numbered file ("02"), and repeated the process to save the other files, moving around the color wheel.

For the *Videos* screen (bottom), Hidalgo drew a vertical, irregular shape with the Pen tool in a separate source file that included a pattern made from a montage he had built from video grabs. He converted the shape to a selection and used the selection to capture a section of the montage that he could paste into the final *Videos* screen image. The vertical pattern also appears on several other screens within the site. He designed the *Videos* screen to take advantage of Netscape's ability to play movies with sound in response to clicking a button on a Web page.

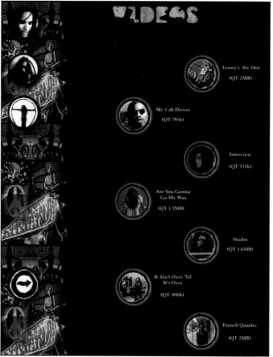

■ When **Karen Dodds** was looking for something lively and hip for the launch of a Web site Dodds Design had developed for *Nicole's Shoes*, she commissioned **Susan LeVan** of LeVan/Barbee Studio to create a series of colorful on-off buttons.

LeVan began by choosing a saturated color palette from Painter's default color set, including warm oranges and yellows, accented by blues and greens. (Painter's default color set is composed of Web-safe colors.) LeVan applied colorful textures to the backgrounds using a variety of favorite textures from earlier versions of Painter (such as the Simple Texture library, located in the Paper Textures Libraries folder on the Painter 6 CD-ROM). She applied the textures with Color Overlay, Using Paper and Hiding Power. LeVan drew the shoes, flower and face with the Scratchboard Tool variant of Pens. For the abstract elements, she drew shapes using the Pen tool (Tools palette) and filled the shapes with color. When she was satisfied with the arrangement of colored shapes, she merged the layers by selecting their names in the Layers section of the Objects palette, pressing the Group button and then the Collapse button. To finish, she set the layer's Composite method to Gel.

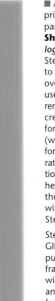

■ Arthur Steuer and Even Steven Levee, principals of i~potato production company, commissioned artist/animator **Sharon Steuer** to create the *i-potato logo* and the cover of their pop-music CD. Steuer used Painter's Water Color brushes to loosely paint the sky, clouds and water over a rough textured paper. Then she used Brushes and Airbrushes variants to render the potato, figures and beach. Steuer created an animation of the eye blinking for the Y2K launching of the website (www.i-potato.net). She created the cels for the eye-blink in Painter 6, using a separate layer to draw each stage of the animation. So the animation would load quickly, her client chose to use only two of the three stages. (See a QuickTime 4 movie with music that includes all three stages in Steuer's folder on the Wow! CD-ROM.)

Steuer produced the *i-potato* as an animated GIF. To export a GIF animation from Painter, put the stages for the animation into a frame stack by creating a new frame stack with as many frames as the stages. Copy and paste an animation stage into each frame. After pasting into a frame, make sure to click the Drop button in the Layers section before you advance to the next frame. To export the frame stack, choose File, Save As, Save Movie as GIF Animation and name the movie. When the GIF Options box appears, choose the Number of Colors and Imaging Method and click OK.

■ **Judy Miller,** web developer and artist for Fall River Decorative Arts, designed and built graphics for the *Painter World Web site* using Painter 6, then exported the files to Macromedia Fireworks.

Miller made several seamless tiles by importing imagery, painting with brushes and applying special effects. She created the Painter World logo with Painter's type tools. After applying Surface Texture effects and beveling to the elements, she saved the tiles and logo as TIFF files and opened them in Fireworks. Miller assembled the banners in Fireworks and added other text and live effects to complete the banners.

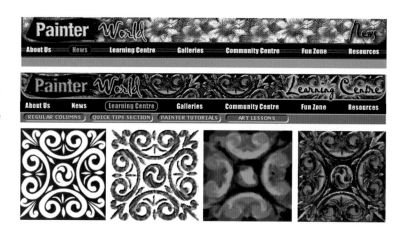

■ Designer and artist **Debi Lee Mandel** created *DT-Car* and *DT-Space* (top), two proposed animated banners for the DigitalThink Web site and two screens for the DuraFlame Web site, *Campsite* (middle) and *Hearth* (bottom).

Mandel began the banner animations by drawing the elements (the cars and buildings in *DT-Car* and the rocketship and planets in *DT-Space)* using the Pens variants, custom Brushes variants and Painter's frame stacks, finally adding the type with Dynamic Text.

For *Campsite* and *Hearth*, she began by sketching in Painter with a custom "indigo-color crayon" (based on the Waxy Crayon variant) on a black background. Both screens incorporate animations. Mandel began by painting elements for the animations (the comet and fire in *Campsite*, and the fire in *Hearth*) using Painter's frame stacks. When she was pleased with the progression, she saved each frame stack as a GIF animation.

After completing the crayon drawing for *Campsite*, Mandel painted crisp-edged brushstrokes using flat color. To build up deep color saturation, she used custom Brushes variants with oval-shaped tips for a calligraphic feel.

To complete *Hearth*, Mandel smoothed the crayon drawing with the Just Add Water variant of Liquid. She used a custom Water Color brush with an oval tip to lay in large, loose areas of color, then she switched to a smaller brush to add details. When she was satisfied with the watercolor, she dried the image (Canvas, Dry). Then she added deeper color and more detail using her own custom Oil Paint brushes. See another example of Mandel's animation work in her folder on the Painter 6 Wow! CD-ROM.

■ Art director **Ben Barbante** designed and illustrated *Efolio* for his Home page using a combination of Painter, Illustrator and Photoshop. He used Painter's Image Slicer to separate the picture into both GIF and JPEG files for optimal file compression, then he exported HTML code (including navigational buttons with JavaScript rollovers) and a GIF animation from Painter for the final page.

To begin the slicing and export process, Barbante opened the completed layered illustration, which included the efolio case with a light bulb (for the "off" state). He made a new layer and created a black screen on top of the lightbulb, for the rollover "on" state, because he needed a second state. (Later, the "on" state graphic would be replaced by a GIF animation.) Then he hid the layer that would show the Mouse "on" state (the efolio with the black screen) by turning its eye icon off in the Layers section. He targeted the image canvas and chose the Image Slicer from the Dynamic Layers section of the Objects palette and clicked the Apply button to make an Image Slicer layer. In the Image Slicer, Barbante used the Horizontal and Vertical tools to divide the image, and used the Select tool to group some of the slices. Then using the File Name menu in the Image Slicer box, he named each slice that he planned to export and chose a compression method

(File Type) for the slices, choosing GIF format to save slices with flat areas of color in the gray border outside the illustration, and JPEG format to save the slices within the illustration, which included airbrushed color gradations.

For most slices in the image, Barbante selected a slice that would not be exported and Under Export HTML and JavaScript, he set the Rollover State to No Rollover. Next, he selected the efolio case slice that would be the Mouse "off" state, set the Rollover State to Mouse over-out and clicked the Export settings for Current Image State button. When the Export Slice Options dialog box appeared, he chose the Mouse out button, turned on Include JavaScript and clicked Export. He clicked OK in the Image Slicer, temporarily leaving the dialog box so he could turn on the hidden layer that would be the Mouse "on" state (when the cursor is over the button). He reopened the Image Slicer, selected the slice he wanted to export for the mouse "on" state and repeated the process he had used for the "off" state, but this time, he chose the Mouse Over button. Painter saved the images and generated the JavaScript and the HTML.

For the final Home page, Barbante substituted a GIF animation for the "on" state image (the black screen). After slicing the image and creating the JavaScript rollover,

he noted the exact pixel dimensions of the mouse-over slice in the Image Slicer. He made a frame stack in Painter with five frames (featuring his illustration portfolio) using the exact dimensions of the efolio screen with the lightbulb. He exported a copy of the frame stack as a GIF animation and gave it the exact name of the "on" image so the HTML would replace it in the Home page. The rollover displays the animated GIF when the cursor is placed over it. Barbante's Home page can be viewed at http://www.barbante.com.

12

PRINTING
AND
ARCHIVAL
CONCERNS

Wise Woman is a part of the series Journey of the Spirit *by Dorothy Simpson Krause. The image was printed on the Roland HiFi Jet on Concord paper using the Roland 6-color pigmented ink set. The 35x28-inch print was printed in an edition of 20, coated with encaustic (beeswax) and rubbed with pearlescent pigment.*

PAINTER AND CMYK TIFFS

Painter 6 can now open CMYK TIFF files, but in doing so, it converts them to RGB, Painter's native color space. You can also save a CMYK TIFF from Painter.

HOW WILL YOU PRESENT YOUR PAINTER ARTWORK to the world? Will it be as a limited-edition digital painting, printed on archival paper by a print studio or service bureau, then matted, framed, and hung on a gallery wall? Or as an illustration in a magazine, where it's part of a page layout that's output by an imagesetting service bureau, to printed on an offset press? Or as a desktop color print? Or as part of a slide show? For each of these and other output options, there are things you can do to prepare your Painter file so the output process runs smoothly. We hope the tips that follow help you as you plan your own project.

COLOR FOR PRINTING

Most types of printing involve the use of four-color process, or CMYK (cyan, magenta, yellow, black) inks and dyes. Painter's native color mode is RGB (red, green, blue), which has a larger color *gamut* (range of colors) than the CMYK color model. (An illustration that compares RGB and CMYK color gamuts is on page 10 in Chapter 1.) Although Painter doesn't let you specify CMYK color mixes like Adobe Photoshop and some other programs do, it does allow you to work in Output Preview mode, using only those colors within the RGB gamut that are realizable in CMYK. You can also output CMYK TIFF and EPS files for color separation directly from Painter.

Using Output Preview. Before you turn a file over to an imagesetting service bureau or printer for output in a form that will be used for CMYK printing, consider using Output Preview. Painter's Output Preview incorporates the Kodak Color Management System. With this system you can set up a monitor-to-printer calibration loop that will allow you to see an on-screen approximation of how your printed image will look. (A word of

Click the Output Preview icon to toggle between RGB and the Output Preview.

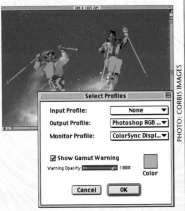

For an approximation of how a default Photoshop CMYK conversion of a Painter RGB image will look, choose the Photoshop RGB to CMYK Output Profile. Check the Gamut Warning box to show colors that are beyond the color range of the selected Output Profile. In our example, bright, saturated colors on the skiers' clothing are out of range for the Photoshop RGB-to-CMYK color conversion. The out-of-gamut colors are identified here covered by a bright green overlay.

caution: There are many variables besides the RGB-to-CMYK conversion that will affect how a color print will look—for instance, the color cast of your particular monitor and the color of your paper.) Begin by choosing Canvas, Output Preview and selecting Kodak Color Correction. Now choose Canvas, Preview Options, and in the dialog box, choose a Monitor Profile and an Output Profile. When you perform a Painter Easy Installation, the program automatically installs a selection of Output Profiles into your system folder. And you'll find more profiles in the Kodak ICC folder on the Painter 6 Application CD-ROM. (If you don't see your monitor or printer profile in the list, it can often be obtained from the manufacturer.) To add profiles to your system, run a Custom Installation, choosing the Additional ICC Profiles option; or copy them from the Painter 6 CD-ROM as follows: Macintosh users should drag the profiles into the System Folder, Preferences, ColorSync™ Profiles folder. And Windows users should copy profiles into the Windows\Color folder.

To toggle between the broader-gamut RGB image and the Output Preview, click the Output Preview icon above the right scroll bar. Remember to change the Device Color Profile settings if you plan to print to another device. For more information about Painter's color management tools see "Color Management," in Chapter 19 of the *Painter 6 User Guide*.

Making CMYK conversions in another program. Some Painter artists prefer to work in the broader RGB color gamut and convert their finished images to CMYK in another imaging program such as Photoshop or Equilibrium DeBabelizer, because these programs allow more control of how the conversion is made. There are several good resources that give detailed explanations of color conversion using Photoshop, including the *Adobe Photoshop User Guide* and *The Photoshop 5/5.5 Wow! Book* and *Photoshop in 4 Colors* (both from Peachpit Press). Some printing studios—for example, Cone Editions—prefer to receive RGB files from artists and make the conversion themselves using custom color tables they create in Photoshop especially for that image. (See "Making a Fine Art Master Print" on page 336 for an explanation of Cone Editions' process.) Check with your printer or service bureau to work out a conversion method.

Writing EPS-DCS files from Painter. Many illustrators prefer to have control over the prepress process by ordering their own four-color film for illustrations that will be printed on a four-color sheet fed press at a printing plant. Rather than an electronic file, they send the film separations and a laminated proof (a Matchprint, for example) to the client. Whether you or someone else will be ordering the film, check with the service bureau operator who will be doing the output. They should be able to tell you the correct setup for the equipment that will output your job.

Detail of The Gift, *by Pamela Wells. When making the fine art print of her image, Wells calibrated her computer system to the profile of the Iris inkjet printer at the service bureau she planned to send it to. Turn to page 273 in Chapter 9 to view the entire image.*

When saving a file as an EPS-DCS, remember to preserve your original Painter file by giving the EPS file a different name. Although the program cannot open EPS files, Painter can save in EPS format.

Dorothy Krause and Bonny Lhotka printed Krause's image, Procession, *on the Alpha Merics Spectrum printer. The large-format printer is outstanding for printing on thick material. The Spectrum's variable "Z" axis can be adjusted to the thickness of the substrate, allowing it to print on materials up to .75-inch thick (such as the wood shown in the photo above).*

FINE ART PRINTING AT A SERVICE BUREAU

Many artists prefer to choose a service bureau or master printer who specializes in output for fine art printmaking. Rather than attempt to print an edition in their studio, they rely on fine art service bureaus for high-quality equipment—for instance, an Iris inkjet printer is very expensive, and is not affordable for most artists. (Iris prints are accepted by many galleries and museums; they are no longer thought of as "experimental prints.") The expertise needed for a fine art print studio differs greatly from that of a commercial service bureau accustomed to making film and proofs for offset printing. Choose a printer who has experience working with artists and who understands archival and editioning issues. (See Appendix C for a list of service bureaus that specialize in working with artists.)

Printing digital watercolors with the Iris. Iris printers are special inkjet machines capable of producing images with luminous color and no visible dot, making the output desirable for fine art printmaking. The Iris sprays water-based CMYK dyes or pigment-based inks (similar to watercolors) through four extremely narrow nozzles. The paper or other substrate is taped to a rotating drum in the machine and sprayed with millions of droplets per second. Many fine art printers modify the Iris 3047 (the largest of the Iris printer line) so it can handle thicker substrates. Cone Editions and Nash Editions were among the first printers to pioneer this technique; they moved back the printing heads, allowing 400-lb. watercolor paper, canvas or metal to be taped onto the drum.

More large-format inkjet printers. Some service bureaus offer prints from the Hewlett-Packard DesignJet 2000 and 3000 CP series, using the new Hewlett-Packard CP UV archival inks. The 600 dpi printers can accept rolled watercolor paper and canvas. With these 600 dpi printers, sometimes images with very light, graduated tones can produce areas with tiny dots in a dither or scatter pattern. Printing on canvas can help hide these dots. Wilhelm Imaging Research Inc. reports that the HP DesignJet CP ink systems UV inks will hold true color for 150+ years.

Outputting to large canvas. Richard Noble is a traditionally trained artist and commercial illustrator who has worked with the computer for several years. He researched large-output options and discovered Vutek, a large-format, low-resolution technology originally devised to print billboards. Noble established a partnership with Vutek and adapted the technology to print large-format fine art. The machine sprays acrylic-based pigments through four nozzles simultaneously, producing soft-edged images very much like an airbrush painting on canvas. Once they dry, the acrylic-based pigments are not water-soluble and offer permanency similar to that of acrylic paint. Images can be printed up to 4 feet wide

Pulling a print on the Vutek system (top), and a close-up view of the nozzle heads on the Vutek machine (bottom)

and as long as you like, with enough canvas remaining around the perimeter of the image for stretching around a frame. Although the prints look good right off the Vutek, you can add even more dimension by working back into them with conventional brushes and acrylic paint. Since the Vutek prints at 18 ppi, files can be fairly small. For example, to produce a 4 x 6-foot painting, you'll need to set up an 864 x 1296-pixel file (only about 5 MB).

Outputting to a digital positive. Major advances are being made in the area of direct digital photographic prints. In general, the three printing methods discussed below use a laser to image the digital file onto a photographic substrate.

Prints made from the Fujix Pictrography 3000 and 4000 (up to 12 x 18 inches) offer better registration and permanency and more natural color than a dye-sublimation print such as the Kodak XL7700 or 3M Rainbow. The Fujix uses a laser to image the digital file onto a "donor" sheet, which is then printed onto photographic paper using a single-pass, silver-halide printing process. The appearance and permanency (about 20 years) of the Fujix are similar to those of a photographic Cibachrome (C-print). Prints can be laminated with a coating that includes an ultraviolet inhibitor, extending their life further.

The Cymbolic Sciences Lightjet 5000 also uses a laser, imaging the digital file to large-format archival photo paper and creating a continuous-tone print without visible dots, as large as 48 x 96 inches. Because the Lightjet 5000 uses 36-bit RGB color, the broad color gamut in these prints is comparable to that in photographic "R" prints. To prepare Painter files for the LightJet 5000, set up your file at its final output size, using a resolution of 150–200 ppi and save it as an uncompressed RGB TIFF file. The LightJet's software incorporates an interpolation algorithm that makes it possible to increase the resolution of the image while retaining its sharpness. Artist and photographer Phillip Charris often outputs his Painter-enhanced photographs using a Lightjet 5000, then carefully strips the print from its backing paper and mounts it on canvas.

Another recommended photo-slick, archival printmaking method is the Durst Lamda system. (Using a laser, it images to archival photo media, such as paper, color negative media or color reversal media.) It's also a 36-bit RGB system. The Durst Lamda 76 can print seamless 32-inch-wide images up to 164 feet long. Durst Lamda prints are reported to be lightfast for a minimum of 50 years. Some

To check color and detail before printing on a Hewlett-Packard 2500CP with archival UV inks, Cher Threinen-Pendarvis proofed Forked Path *as an 8 x 10-inch Fujix Pictrography print. (Fujix Pictrography prints are described on page 325.) The final print was made at 15 x 17 inches on Arches cold-pressed watercolor paper and framed with UV-protective glass.*

A LENTICULAR SERVICE

Some service bureaus specialize in making lenticular signs. (A lenticular is an image that uses a lens to produce stereo 3D or video-motion-like effects.) These companies (for instance, Lenticular Development, www.lenticulardevelopement.com and Durst Dice America, www.durstonline.com) can print a lenticular using an artist's files. They also offer proprietary software and training in the process.

John Derry printed Graffiti Bridge, *shown here as a detail, on an Epson 1270 six-color printer using Epson's archival ink set. Turn to page 344 in the gallery to view the entire image.*

artists (Italy's Lorenzo Paolini, for instance), strip the prints, mount them on canvas then finish them with glazes of UV protectant varnish (such as Golden Varnish, described on page 328) to protect the print from humidity and to add a hand-finished look.

PHOTOGRAPHIC IMAGING OPTIONS

Many new technologies are available for Painter output at graphic arts service bureaus and photo labs that use digital equipment.

Imaging to transparencies using a film recorder. Small- and large-format film recorders are used to image digital files such as Painter artwork to transparencies ranging from 35mm to 16 x 20 inches. For output via a film recorder, images should be in landscape orientation (horizontal) to take advantage of the width of the film.

To avoid *pixelation* (a jaggy, stair-step look caused by lack of sufficient resolution) on transparencies generated by a service bureau's film recorder, here are some guidelines from Chrome Digital and Photodyne (San Diego) and The Digital Pond (San Francisco) for creating or sizing your files. Most professional-quality 35mm film recorders (such as the Solitaire 16 series) use a minimum resolution of 4000 lines; for this resolution, your image should be 4096 x 2732 pixels (about 32 MB). The minimum resolution for 4 x 5-inch transparencies is 8000 lines, requiring an 8192 x 5464-pixel (approximately 165 MB) file. For even more crispness, devices such as the Solitaire 16XPS will image at a resolution of 16,000 lines (a 16,384 x 10,928-pixel file, of approximately 512 MB). Two powerful film recorders used to create 4 x 5-inch, 8 x 10-inch and larger-format transparencies are the LVT (from Light Valve Technology, a subsidiary of Kodak) and the Lightjet 2080 (from Cymbolic Sciences, Inc.). Plan to create huge images (up to 15000 x 18000 pixels and approximately 800 MB) to take full advantage of the resolution capabilities of these machines.

Printing your images as Fujichrome. For fine art images, Fujichrome prints made from transparencies offer excellent detail and saturated color, and can be ordered with a high gloss. Prints can be made from 35mm slides or 4 x 5-inch transparencies. To print to the maximum size of 20 x 24 inches, a 4 x 5 transparency is recommended. The permanency of the Fuji print is 40–50 years, and this can be extended by adding a lamination with an ultraviolet inhibitor. Diane Fenster, a noted fine artist and photographer, produces much of her digital work as large-format Fujichrome prints.

FINE ART PRINTING IN THE STUDIO

Today, many exciting alternatives are available for artists who want to proof their images, or make fine art prints in their own studio using archival ink sets and papers.

Printing digital watercolors with desktop printers. Desktop inkjet printers can deliver beautiful color prints if they are set up properly. The affordable HP printers (such as the 1220c) and

Detail of Indigo, *an experimental Fresco print by Bonny Lhotka. To view the entire image, turn to page 343 in the gallery.*

image, turn to page 343 in the gallery.

PAPER-AND-INK COMBOS

The correct paper-and-ink combination can contribute to the greater longevity of your prints. Check out Henry Wilhelm's Web site, www.wilhelm-research.com for suggested paper-and-ink combinations.

Sometimes Philip Howe uses his digital paintings as templates for oil painting, as he did here for Profile. *Howe printed the digital painting onto canvas using an HP 2500 CP printer and archival inks. Then he painted over the entire image with oil paint. To see another of Howe's paintings using this technique, turn to the gallery on page 339.*

the Epson Stylus series are great printers not only for pulling test prints before sending images to an Iris, but also for experimental fine art prints. Most inkjet inks are water-soluble, so you can try painting into a print with a wet brush. Although most desktop printers work best with slick paper, archival-quality cotton papers produce excellent results on some machines. For example, the Epson 1520 and 3000 print on thicker acid-free papers if you feed the paper manually. (Two papers to try are 80–120 lb. Arches cold-pressed watercolor paper and Rives BFK printmaking paper.)

New inks and substrates for desktop art prints. With the increased interest in desktop art-making, new inks and papers keep coming out. Henry Wilhelm has done important research regarding the longevity of different ink and substrate combinations. A comparison of color gamut and longevity with the different inks is also available through Wilhelm Imaging Research, Inc., on the Web at www.wilhelm-research.com.

New inks with better longevity and waterproof characteristics are becoming available for many inkjet printers. For information about products for use with the Hewlett-Packard printers, check out www.hp.com; for information about Epson products, contact its company Web site at www.epson.com. Also, InkJet Mall (a sister company of Cone Editions) is another good resource for information and you can buy sets of archival inks (such as Lumias) for several desktop printers; it's found on the Web at www.inkjetmall.com. Several other companies offer new archival inks sets for desktop printers. One of the most notable is Media Street, offering Generations Inks, found on the Web at www.mediastreet.com.

Several traditional art papers are now manufactured for digital printmaking—for instance, Somerset Enhanced and Concorde Rag, both available from Cone Editions' Ink Jet Mall. Also check out Somerset photo-enhanced paper and other new papers on the Web at www.dygraphics.com. And there are many canvases available for use with inkjet printers. For instance, check out the artist-grade canvases available from Sentinel Imaging, located on the Web at www.inkjet.com, and the pure-white artist-grade-canvas from Dr. Graphix Inc. at www.drgraphix.com.

Ink jet receivers and protective coatings. To seal custom substrates (like hand made papers), so the ink will hold better, paint thin rabbit skin glue on the substrate with a brush and dry it thoroughly. Then make your print.

INCREASING LONGEVITY

A few fine art printers (notably, Cone Editions and Nash Editions) have developed their own silk-screened coatings to protect Iris prints from fading. The coating merges with the ink on the substrate and doesn't change the appearance of the print. (Many ink sets developed for inkjet printers use water-soluble inks. Keep the print dry unless you purposely want to spot or mix the color with water.)

Bonny Lhotka creates one-of-a-kind "monotype" substrates to use as unique surfaces in the printing of her digital images.

IRIS PRINT AND MONOTYPE

Master printer David Salgado has developed a process that combines monotypes with Iris prints, using the 39 x 52-inch Mailänder flatbed hand-fed offset press at Trillium Press. After a mylar-coated aluminum plate is painted with lithography inks, the plate is mounted on the press and the press roller pulls ink from the plate to transfer to the Iris print. Depending on the image, seven to ten prints can be pulled in what is known as an *edition variée*. Some artists use an Iris print as a starting point, while others use cutout pieces of an Iris print as elements in collage work, then the collage is run through the press. Salgado feels they've just begun to discover the possibilities. Trillium has printed editions of artwork that have combined Iris printing, silk-screen, monotype and lithography in edition numbers of 50 and more.

You can treat prints yourself so the color will last much longer. Several protective coatings are available at your local art supply store, from Daniel Smith via mail order, or from Media Street on the Web at www.mediastreet.com. One of our favorites is Golden MSA Varnish with UVLS (soluble with mineral spirits). Use a protective respirator and gloves for the process because the fumes from this coating are *very* toxic. To minimize contact with dangerous airborne particles, dilute the varnish and apply it with a brush. Golden Varnish is also available in a spray can, as is Krylon UV Protectant spray.

DIFFERENTIAL AGING

If you plan to add another medium (such as acrylic or pastel) to a digital print, keep in mind that different pigments and dyes can age at different rates. So the strokes you carefully hand-work into the print may begin to stand out over time.

Caring for prints. After a UV-protective coating has been applied, treat your print as you would a watercolor and avoid displaying it in direct sunlight. Frame it using UV-resistant glazing (glass or Plexiglas) and preserve air space between the surface of the print and the glazing.

EXPERIMENTAL PRINTMAKING

In today's world of experimental printmaking, anything goes if it works with your vision of the image you're printing. For instance, many different substrates can be used successfully with inkjet printers; among the favorites are archival-quality papers with a high cotton content. Browse your local art store for Saunders handmade watercolor paper, Arches hot-press and cold-press watercolor paper, Rives BFK printmaking papers, and Canson drawing and charcoal papers. You can hand-feed these papers into a studio desktop printer, or request that a fine art print studio create an Iris print with paper that you supply. Fine art print studios often keep special papers in stock—Cone Editions, for instance, has about 80 different fine art papers on hand. Some print studios also print on canvas, film or metal.

Mixing media. Prints from an Iris or another inkjet printer can be modified with traditional tools and fine art printing processes, such as embossing, intaglio and silkscreen. (Turn to page 332 to read about Carol Benioff's technique of overprinting a copperplate etching on top of an Iris print.) If you plan to hand-work an inkjet print with media such as pastels, pencils or oil paint—make the print on rag paper with enough body to hold together when you apply the traditional media to the print. Arches 140-pound watercolor paper and Rives heavyweight printmaking paper are good choices.

Making Translite transfers. The Translite transfer technique was pioneered by Jon Cone. First, he printed a digital image onto Translite film using an Iris printer. He soaked archival-quality paper

Flint by Dorothy Simpson Krause, includes elements collected during a journey to Tibet. After the collage was complete, Krause prepared the surface of the substrate (dimensionally stable spunbond polyester) for printing, by painting it with Golden Molding Paste. When the surface was dry, she added a coat of gel medium mixed with pearlescent pigment. To provide a receiver for the inks, she painted the substrate with rabbit skin glue, dried it, then compressed it by running it though a Coda laminator. The final print was made on a Roland Hi-Jet using their pigmented 6-color inks.

CERTIFICATE OF AUTHEN

Title **Swimmers 2**

Image Size **12 x 18"**   Edition # **2/50**

Edition Size **50**   Artist Proofs **5**

Date Created **July 1, 1995**   Date Purchased **July 14,**

Art Media **Iris print on Rives BFK**

Uniqueness of this Print **This print is hand-worked with pe**

Artist

The above information contains all the information pertaining to this Edition. As t
or watercolor, do not display this artwork in direct sunlight. Frame it under UP3 pl

Detail of a sample certificate of authenticity. You'll find a PageMaker 6.5 file and a PDF of this sample certificate on the Painter 6 Wow! CD-ROM.

IRIS PRINT OR GICLÉE?

Some businesses in the fine art print-making community have adopted the name Giclée (which can be loosely defined as *spray*) when referring to a fine art print made on an Iris inkjet. Most artists who create their work digitally prefer to leave the Giclée term to the traditional fine art reproduction industry that originated it. Artists who create work digitally do not want their work confused with a traditional reproduction, because each direct digital print has its own unique value and, in fact, is not a reproduction.

(such as Rives BFK) in water, and when it was partially dry, he transferred the image from the Translite "plate" onto the dampened printmaking paper using an embossing press—producing a monoprint with softly graduated color.

Overprinting a digital file onto a monotype. To create a surface that she would later use for printing *Day Job* (shown at left), Bonny Lhotka created a one-of-a-kind monotype "plate" by applying acrylic paint onto prepared acetate. She laid a piece of rag paper onto the "plate" and used a custom-made 40-lb. roller to transfer the painted image onto the paper. After transferring, she lifted the paper off the "plate" and allowed it to dry. Then she used a Novajet inkjet printer to overprint the digital file on top of the monoprint. She believes that the overprinting process produces a broader range of color than is possible with a standard inkjet print, resulting in a print with more depth.

FINE ART EDITIONS FROM DIGITAL FILES

Some artists scan finished, traditionally created artwork and then print it on an Iris. This process is actually *replicating* an original piece of work and is not original digital art. When artwork *originates* as a digital file—using a program such as Painter—and is then printed to an Iris, that print becomes an original. (Think of your Painter image as a kind of "digital printing plate" stored in your computer.)

Advantages of digital editions. Printing a digital edition has advantages over traditional, limited-run printing methods. Any number of multiple originals can be made from a digital file without loss of quality: The "digital plate" won't deteriorate. Also, the setup charge for the digital process is usually much less than when an edition is printed conventionally. And while an edition printed with traditional methods needs to be printed all at once, with digital editions, an artist may request prints from the fine art service bureau as needed.

Planning an edition. An edition should be carefully tracked and controlled, just as it would be if printed with traditional methods. It's wise to make a contract between the master printer and artist, stating the type of edition, the number of prints in the edition and that no more prints will be made. When an original is sold, the artist should give the buyer a certificate of authenticity that contains the name of the artist and the print, the date sold, the edition size, the print number, the number of artist proofs, the substrate, and any details of hand-working done on the print. Once the edition is complete, the artist should destroy the digital file, just as the screen would be destroyed after a silkscreen edition. (See "Making a Fine Art Master Print" on page 336.)

Building an Experimental Desktop Print

Overview *Create colorful, textured elements for a collage; roughen and coat the paper prior to printing; print the final image on a desktop inkjet printer.*

BONNY LHOTKA

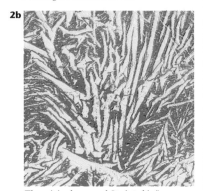

Lhotka's color sketch, created in Painter

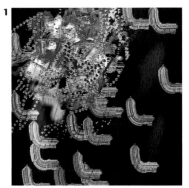

Painting on the scanner bed

The original scanned "paint skin"

"MOST OF MY ORIGINAL WORK has a strong tactile quality," says Bonny Lhotka of her printmaking experimentation. She often uses traditional printmaking equipment to prepare rich, complex surfaces for her digital collage work. To create *Old World*, Lhotka used three digital source files and composited them into a collage, then wrinkled and coated the paper before feeding it through her desktop inkjet printer. You may want to loosely follow Lhotka's image-making process and also experiment with your own effects.

1 Sketching with color. Open a new file and make a colorful, abstract sketch. Lhotka opened an 8-inch-wide, 100-ppi file with a black background. She created an abstract, color sketch using a variety of brushes in Painter, in much the same way she would paint an image with traditional tools. She saved the image for use later in the process.

2 Making a "paint skin." To create source images that she calls "paint skins," Lhotka applies paint directly on the glass surface of her scanner (or to a sheet of acetate) and scans it. To create your own paint skin in a process similar to Lhotka's, paint a textured design on a piece of clear acetate with acrylic paint. If you like, make marks in the paint with a palette knife or flat brush. When the paint dries, place the acetate on the scanner bed and scan it.

3 Compositing in Photoshop. Lhotka began the composite in Photoshop, though she could have done the work in Painter. Without a preconceived idea, she opened the Painter file (from step 1) in Photoshop where she flipped, inverted and distorted the image. She copied and pasted the paint skin image (from step 2) into the developing, 11 x 11-inch, 300-ppi Photoshop composite as a layer. She turned the skin negative (Image, Map, Invert) to

3

4a

The image showing the emerging map-like design

The boat scan, ready to paste into the composite

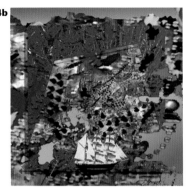

4b

The image as sent to the desktop printer

5a

Ironing the dampened, crumpled paper

5b

Painting a dark acrylic wash onto the paper to enhance the wrinkled effect

5c

Positioning the paper on the etching press to flatten it before printing

change the color spectrum to blue tones. As the image evolved, a map-like configuration emerged. She selected some of the dark areas in the skin layer with the Magic Wand and deleted them to make those areas transparent. (These tasks could have been done in Painter in much the same way.)

To give her image more depth, Lhotka created a new background image for the composite by copying a portion of her original sketch and resizing and softening it. She pasted the working composite into the new background image, combined the two layers using the blending modes, then flattened the image.

4 Refining the image in Painter. To make the evolving image appear more like a map, Lhotka opened the image in Painter and used the program's brushes and effects. She used the Magic Wand to select areas based on color in the top and right side of her image and filled the selections with blue (Ctrl/⌘-F, Current Color) to create a sky and bodies of water. Then she painted an island chain in the lower right using a variety of brushes. She gave the sky and water more depth by reselecting all of the solid blue areas with the Magic Wand and filling the selections with a blue-to-white Two-Point gradation (Effects, Fill, Gradation). Lhotka created drop shadows beneath the "land masses" in her map and added linear elements and arrows to suggest an abstract compass. She chose a scanned photo of a model boat from her archives and pasted it into the composite image. As a final step to finish the image, she used Effects, Tonal Control, Adjust Colors and experimented with the Hue Shift, Saturation and Value sliders.

5 Preparing the paper and printing. Many desktop inkjet printers will accept thicker papers that have been pretreated for more uniform printing. If your printer can do this, try using an archival-quality paper with a high rag content such as Rives printmaking or Arches watercolor paper. Lhotka used a cream-colored, heavyweight Rives paper. To give the paper an antique look that enhanced the Old World feel, she dampened and crumpled the paper, then flattened it with a steam iron. To add to the wrinkled look, she applied a wash of acrylic that soaked into the creases. She dried the paper and ran it through an etching press to flatten it.

As a final step before printing, she precoated the paper with diluted rabbit skin glue to enhance the uniform application of the inks and maintain color fidelity. She printed the 11 x 11-inch image on a Hewlett-Packard XL300 inkjet printer. She set the XL300 to print without PostScript software, which allowed the device to print the inks in a scatter pattern similar to that of an Iris inkjet printer, but coarser. The inks soaked into the paper and helped integrate the image with the character of the prepared paper itself. To protect the print from fading, Lhotka brushed a UV varnish (from Golden Varnishes) onto the finished print. 🖌

Combining Digital and Intaglio Printmaking

Overview *Make a print using a traditional printmaking method; scan the print; use the scan as a guide to create a colored image in Painter; output the digital file to an Iris printer; overprint the traditional print on top the Iris print in register.*

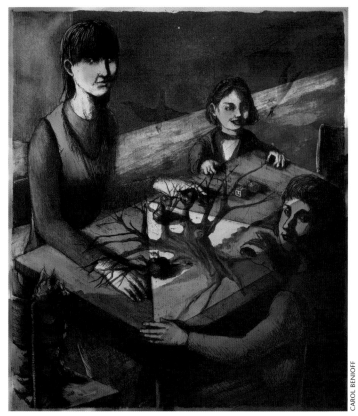

CAROL BENIOFF

Photograph of the copperplate etching. The composition is created in reverse.

Grayscale scan of the black-and-white intaglio print

CAROL BENIOFF'S INNOVATIVE PRINTMAKING method combines classic intaglio techniques with digital printing. An award-winning fine artist and illustrator, she has illustrated for magazines such as *Atlantic Monthly* and *Parenting*—and her work appears in the *CA Illustration Annual*. Currently she works with The Graphics Arts Workshop in San Francisco. One of the oldest artists' cooperatives in the United States, it has been in existence since the 1930s. To create *The Game*, a self-promotional piece, Benioff overprinted a copperplate etching on top of an Iris inkjet print made on Daniel Smith archival printmaking paper.

1 Making an intaglio print. Benioff planned the 6 x 7-inch copperplate knowing that she would be adding a dimension of colored imagery created in Painter. Using primarily a hard ground etching technique, she etched fine lines with a fine-point diamond stylus. When making a classic hard ground etching, an artist scribes lines into an acid-resistant coating, exposing the metal underneath. Then the plate is soaked in a acid bath to etch the drawing deeper into the plate. The acid-etched lines hold the ink, yielding warm, velvety black lines when printed.

Benioff rolled black ink onto the plate, working it into the lines with a cardboard dauber, then rubbed off excess ink with tarlatan (starched open-weave muslin). Next, she chose a piece of archival

2

The two images: A painted landscape (left), and a watercolor tint image to match the etching (right)

3

Photograph of the Iris print composite

4a

Inking the plate (left) and making registration marks on a clear acetate sheet to help align the copperplate to the Iris print (right)

4b

After lifting the press felts on the intaglio press, Benioff carefully pulled the finished print off the copperplate.

printmaking paper and soaked it, so it would absorb the ink better. After letting the paper partially dry, she made a print using an etching press.

When the print was dry, she scanned it and saved the scan to use as a guide to help develop two color images (described in step 2). Benioff's grayscale scan measured 2400 x 2800 pixels.

2 Creating color images and compositing. Open your scan, make a clone (File, Clone), and delete the contents of the clone (Select, All, and press the Backspace/Delete key). Now, turn on Tracing Paper (Ctrl/⌘-T). Using the scan as a guide, paint a colorful image that will complement your traditional print.

Benioff created two images: a painted landscape and a loose watercolor version of the etched composition. The landscape was designed to add dynamic tension to the composition. To begin the landscape, she sketched larger shapes with the Simple Water Watercolor brush, then added details with the Chalk variants of Dry Media and Brushes variants. When the image was complete, she saved it for use later in the process.

To paint a second image, which would add colored tints to elements in the etching, she made a second clone of the scan, again deleting the contents. Using the scan as a guide, she painted a loose color composition with the Simple Water brush.

Benioff composited the images in Photoshop by merging the second image with the first using the Image, Apply Image and the Multiply blending mode. To merge two color images in Painter, open both images and make the second image active. Select, All, Copy, and Paste it into the first image. In the Layers section of the Objects palette, choose a Compositing Method that complements your image.

3 Choosing paper for the print. To achieve a good ink impression of the copperplate, paper should be softened by dampening so that it will mold to the detail etched into the plate. This poses a problem when printing over an Iris print, because Iris prints bleed when wet. To resolve this problem, Benioff experimented extensively with different papers. She found that some very soft papers will soak through—even when you spritz the back of the paper to dampen it slightly—destroying the water-based Iris image. The paper she chose to print *The Game* (Daniel Smith archival printmaking paper) is fibrous enough to soften and swell when slightly moistened but thick enough that the dampness did not soak through to the inks on the front.

4 Overprinting the etching. After preparing the copperplate with ink, Benioff made an acetate template to register the image on the paper and plate. The elements in the Iris print needed to align perfectly with the copperplate, so she carefully traced the position of the figures and table onto the acetate. She aligned the template, the plate and the paper (Iris print) on the press bed and pulled the print.

Constructing a Lenticular Work

Overview *Build textured elements and layer them into a collage; set up multiple versions of the file for the lenticular; print the images on an inkjet printer; glaze the wood mat and embellish its surface.*

BONNY LHOTKA

1

The handmade paper, the letterpress type block with the radio tower image and the tray filled with "lava"

2

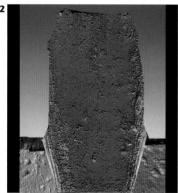

The lava and paper elements with the Apply Surface Texture emboss added

3

An impression of the photo of sand and foam was embossed into the working image.

"A LENTICULAR IMAGE SUSPENDS TIME, space and movement. It adds a level of ambiguity that engages the viewer's attention," says artist Bonny Lhotka. (A lenticular image is actually several images sliced into strips and alternated. A plastic sheet with a series of parallel lens strips, or lenticules, embossed into one surface is applied over the assemblage, so the different images are seen one at a time, as a viewer moves past the artwork.) To create *Ancient Echo*, Lhotka scanned elements, applied textural effects, then composited the source files into a collage. To build the lenticular, she created eleven variations of the file. As a viewer walks past *Ancient Echo*, the central portion of the image turns to black. At the same time, the background rotates through a rainbow of color shifts and the lower portion appears to recede. You may want to loosely follow Lhotka's process and also experiment with your own effects.

1 Preparing the source images. Lhotka chose squares of painted handmade paper from an earlier project, and a letterpress type block with a radio tower image. For one of the background layers, she built a surface using modeling paste and painted it with acrylics to look like lava. Lhotka scanned and touched up the source images. She created the rings in Painter and colored them with a gradient. To give the rings wirelike dimension, she used Glass Distortion.

2 Adding texture to elements. Lhotka likes to emulate the look of handmade paper, using Painter's Apply Surface Texture feature. For this work, she embossed several elements (including the lava and paper elements) with Apply Surface Texture Using Image Luminance and subtle settings.

The composite in progress

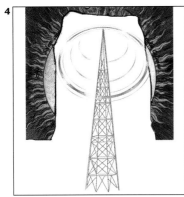

Printing the images

Preparing the transfer board

Mixing the gel and applying it to the board

Preparing to transfer the mat print

Burning the mat surface to crackle the glaze

3 Giving the colored fields texture. She wanted to add texture to more colored areas in the image. So she opened an original photo of beach sand and used Apply Surface Texture, Using Original Luminance to emboss the pattern of the foam and sand into her image. To ensure that the emboss effect will apply to your entire image, choose as your clone source an image with the same pixel dimensions as your working file. Make the image that you want to emboss active, target a layer you want to emboss and designate the clone source by choosing File, Clone Source. Choose Effects, Surface Control, Apply Surface Texture, Using Original Luminance.

4 Assembling the composite. After all of the elements were embossed with Apply Surface Texture, Lhotka copied and pasted the elements into Photoshop, where she completed the composite. After the image was finished, she created eleven different color variations of the central portion of the file, which would become the lenticular.

5 Processing and printing the lenticular. For the next step, Lhotka used SuperFlip software (available from www.flipsigns.com). Using a sophisticated mathematical formula, the software sliced the images into linear strips and reassembled them according to the specifications for the lenticular that Lhotka had chosen. When the assemblage was complete, Lhotka printed it on a Roland Hi-Fi Jet. The six-color printer uses a CMYKOG archival pigment set with saturated colors. After the interlaced image was printed, it was aligned with the lens.

6 Setting up a gel transfer for the glaze. When building the fine art mat for the lenticular, Lhotka chose Baltic birch. As she planned to pour liquid onto the wood, to prevent the wood from bowing, she temporarily attached a one-by-three-foot board to the back of the birch mat. To hold the liquid, she placed duct tape around the sides to make a tray. Then she made a gel: She dissolved rabbit skin glue in water, warmed it, and allowed it to return to room temperature, then added powered pearlescent pigment to it. She used a strainer to remove undissolved colorant and large bubbles, then poured the mixture onto the wood.

7 Printing the image for the mat. Lhotka printed the image for the mat on Rexam white film. After printing, she transferred it to the gel on the wood. Placing the printed film on the gel caused the image to transfer immediately without pressure. When the gel dried, the image was permanently bonded into the wood.

8 Embellishing the surface of the mat. To give the glaze a crackled effect, Lhotka used a torch to burn the surface of the mat after it was dry. This caused the glue to bubble, creating a crackled glaze surface. The completed presentation of *Ancient Echo* measures 34 x 28-inches; the 28 x 22-inch center of the image with the 3D animated lenticular sits inside a one-half inch recession on the glazed mat board.

Making a Fine Art Master Print

Overview *Make a custom color conversion of a Painter image; choose a textured, handmade paper that will enhance the image; after a first, light printing, paint an iridescent polymer onto some areas of the print; print the image a second time; apply a UV-protective coating to the print; document the edition.*

CHER THREINEN-PENDARVIS / PRINTED BY JON CONE, CONE EDITIONS PRESS

1a

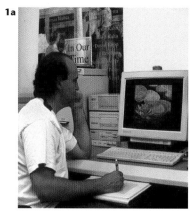

Cone at the Power Mac that's connected to the Iris system

1b

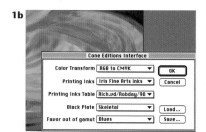

One of Cone's custom ink settings

JON CONE OF CONE EDITIONS PRESS has been making prints and editions for artists since 1980. In 1985, Cone Editions began using computers in printmaking, pioneering techniques such as digital gravure, digital silkscreen and various digital monotype techniques. The firm has made Iris inkjet prints since 1992 and has become a leader in Iris printing technology, sharing methods, materials and techniques with other fine art service bureaus.

When he makes a fine art Iris master print, Cone interprets the artist's image in a collaborative manner. Often the selection of a paper, a special color transformation or perhaps even an experimental printing method can enhance an image. Cone used all three of these to realize the Painter image above.

1 Resizing and converting the color mode. An image may need to be resized to take advantage of the Iris printer's resolution (300 dpi) and replication capabilities. The Iris achieves the look of a much higher resolution because of the way the ink sprays onto the paper. Although the optimal resolution for files that will be printed on the Iris is 300 ppi, the printer can interpolate resolutions of 150 ppi or 100 ppi to produce high-quality prints.

Cone prefers to use Adobe Photoshop for a monitor-to-output calibration loop. He has written a proprietary color transformation engine for Photoshop that he uses to convert images from RGB to CMYK. This interface also helps him calibrate the Iris, allowing the monitor to show a close approximation of the printed image. After converting this image, Cone used Photoshop's Image, Adjust, Curves

IRIS FACTS

The Iris printer's drum spins at 110 inches per second; up to 1 million droplets of ink per second are sprayed at 90 mph through each of its four nozzles. Using only cyan, magenta, yellow and black inks, it can simulate millions of colors.

Positioning the paper on the Iris drum

Carefully painting the iridescent polymer coating on the print

Drying the iridescent solution

Stopping the printer to show how the cyan, magenta, yellow and black inks are printed in sequence on the substrate

Using a silkscreen process to add a protective archival coating

dialog box to compensate for out-of-gamut blues that had been lost. (Since RGB has a broader color gamut than CMYK, out-of-gamut colors are dulled when an image is converted to CMYK.) The black plate was adjusted separately to bring out detail in the darkest areas of the image. Finally, a proprietary plug-in Iris format RIP (raster image processor) was used to save the image in a form that the Iris can use for printing.

2 Choosing a paper and setting up the Iris. Cone selected a sheet of heavy, handmade paper with a very soft, large surface grain and an exaggerated deckled edge that would complement the vivid color and lively brushstrokes in the image. He taped the paper to the drum of the Iris.

3 Printing, painting and drying. Cone used the Iris to print this particular image twice. For the first pass, he adjusted the ink tables in the Iris's RIP to print a faint version of the image. With the print still taped to the drum, Cone brushed an experimental iridescent solution (composed of titanium dioxide–coated mica and hydroscopic polymer) onto the lily only. Then he dried the hand-painted coating with a hair dryer.

4 Printing the image a second time. Cone loaded a new set of rich-printing color ink tables into the Iris's RIP and made a second printing pass. The transparent Iris inks adhered to the polymer coating on the lily as easily as they did to the uncoated paper; the iridescent polymer provided a subtle reflection, adding luminance to the lily.

5 Applying a protective coating to the print. Michael Pelletier, Systems and Production Manager for Cone Editions, applied a silkscreen coating of hindered amine light stabilizers (HALS) and ultraviolet absorbers (UVA) to the finished print. This solvent-based coating developed by Cone carries the protective additives deep into the printed image where they fully encapsulate the dyes, helping to produce what Cone Editions says is "the longest-lasting archival Iris print available today."

Documenting the edition. The artist now signs the finished print to make it the "right-to-print proof" against which future prints in the edition will be compared. After the artist has signed approval, an edition can be printed on demand while the image file is stored safely on CD-ROM at Cone Editions. A documentation sheet signed by both master printer and artist details the size of the edition, number of proofs printed, methods used and dimensions. Most importantly, it specifies that no other proofs or prints can or will be made. (After completing an edition, Cone destroys all copies of the image file.) Each print will bear a unique print identification number and will be signed and numbered in pencil by the artist.

■ For **Laurence Gartel,** *Guggenheim* would not be the same without the sequential mixing of media—from scanned photos and painting in Painter, to print, back into Painter and out again at mural size. He began the work by scanning a few of his own photographs, then he painted over other photos with real paint and scanned them. "People really respond to this piece because of the paint," says Gartel. He opened the scanned images in Painter, assembled them into a composition and added more brushwork and special effects (such as Apply Surface Texture and Liquid Metal) to the painted areas. To create more depth in the upper right of his composition, he created a 3D woman in the Poser program, applied a foreshortened perspective to her and pasted her into the working image.

When he was happy with the composition, Gartel printed the image on canvas using a Colorspan printer. Then he painted over areas of the 16 x 24-inch print. He scanned the print in sections, reassembled them in Painter and applied brushwork and a few more effects. He printed the image on the Colorspan again and this time at approximately 8.5 x 5.6 feet. To keep the surface of the final print stable, Gartel applied several thin coats of Lukas fixative.

■ Inspired by legends of aliens who trav-
eled the galaxy in early history, **John
Dismukes** created *Lost Tribe Warlord.*
He began the image by drawing a pencil
sketch on paper. Then the pencil sketch
was scanned and used as a template for
setting up layered elements for the
image. He painted many fine details (the
warrior's braids, for instance) with a tiny
Digital Airbrush. (For a step-by-step

description of a similar technique, turn to
"Selections and Airbrush" on page 127.)
To print this work, Dismukes set up an
on-demand Iris edition of 500 prints with
50 artist proofs, made with archival inks
on Arches paper. To add final touches,
Dismukes hand-works each print as it is
made with PrismaColor pencil, pastel and
a traditional airbrush using acrylic paint.

■ Artist **Judi Moncrieff** created *Traditions* (above) and *Generations* (right), two works in her series called *First Nation*, for a New York art exhibition. She began by taking photos of the people, artifacts and landscape surroundings at Spirit Days in Anchorage, Alaska. Spirit Days is a celebration of Native Americans from southeast Alaska to central and Northern Alaska, and she had been invited to photograph people at the event. After the shoot, she used both Photoshop and Painter to create composite images from bits and pieces of many photographs, then added textures, more color and brushwork in Painter. "Nothing you see is real and, yet, *it is real*," says Moncrieff.

For the exhibition at the A.I.R. Gallery in SoHo, she created the main series as "one of a kind" (instead of members in an edition) because the images were presented using a complex printing, transfer and installation process that allowed Moncrieff to achieve a unique multidimensional look. To begin, the images were printed onto heat transfer paper on a Hewlett-Packard 2500CP with HP's pigment-based light-fast ink set. Then the resulting images on the heat transfer paper were applied to leather using heat and pressure. For the exhibition, the works were hung on the wall behind free-standing Plexiglas pieces on pedestals that were prepared with a black-and-clear image (printed onto a clear cling by the HP 2500 CP). Placing the Plexiglas elements one-half-inch away from the leather created a multidimensional effect.

■ *Heart of the Tree* is the second work in **Philip Howe's** series of angel paintings. It suggests that there is a life energy in everything and the ancient angel senses the old tree's history. Howe began the image by roughing out the concept in Painter—sketching and assembling finished drawings and photos from his archives into a composition. He turned the assemblage into an underpainting, using sepia-toned color, which he printed out on canvas to use as a base for working with oil paints. Then he printed the underpainting using a Hewlett-Packard DesignJet 2500CP printer, with Hewlett-Packard's archival ink set. To seal the canvas before painting on it, Howe used Liquin, which he had purchased from the Daniel Smith art store. The Liquin brought out rich values in the darker areas of the image and provided a good surface to paint over. When the sealer was thoroughly dry, he tacked the canvas up on the wall and applied oil paints over its entire surface. The tight, accurate underpainting allowed him to paint more loosely and concentrate on final effects. Howe used mostly wet-into-wet oil techniques, although he did let the image dry a few times, and painted translucent glazes over some areas of the canvas.

■ Fine artist **Dorothy Simpson Krause** created the collage *Primordial Fear* as the subject for a 35 x 28-inch lenticular. Krause assembled the image from six scanned objects and set each one up on its own layer: a photograph by Viola Kaumlen of a dramatic sky, a diagram of Babbage's computing engine, an early transistor, a photograph by Jan Doucette of the model Linda Serafin, a drawing of celestial alignments at Stonehenge and a compass.

Krause created several versions of the image, with elements in different positions, that would "animate" in the lenticular. To make objects recede in space, Krause moved elements in small increments to the left. To make an object come forward in space, she moved it in small increments to the right. Greater increments and a larger number of steps created more depth. Krause saved eight "frames" as TIFF files. Then she used the Flip program to interlace the eight frames into vertical strips. She printed the interlaced image using a Roland HiFi Jet onto Roland PETG white film with Roland's six-color archival inks. Then she used a CODA laminator to apply the print to a plastic lenticular lens.

As a viewers moves past the completed image, they see one "frame" at a time and the image changes with each frame, creating the illusion of depth and movement. For instance, the transistor rises and sets (like a sun or moon) behind the woman, who is frozen with fear and does not move, the compass covering her face becomes a mask, and the lines of the azimuth and one circle from the Babbage diagram come forward in the picture plane.

■ *Indigo* is a 28 x 35-inch fresco transfer, and a member of **Bonny Lhotka's** *Heartland* series. The artist found inspiration for the work while visiting her hometown in Illinois in a unique store that had items left over from garage sales, the discarded possessions of everyday life. This mosaic of commonality inspired Lhotka, and she took many photographs while at the store. To create the image, she used the photos and also made scans of actual elements. For instance, she captured the position of a fragment of cheesecloth and her hand holding the marigolds. For another source image, she dyed the integra branches purple, and when then were dry, she laid them on a large-format Epson scanner and covered them with cheesecloth. When the collage was complete, she printed it onto clear film with an Encad printer using the GO pigment ink set. Then she transferred the clear film print to a plaster fresco surface. (In her search for ways to apply her images to walls, Lhotka researched old masters' ways of creating gesso grounds and frescos. She made a fresco-like surface by applying a strained mixture of rabbit skin glue and calcium carbonate to a board.) When the fresco was nearly complete, she wanted to add a darker, metallic and iridescent look to the image's center (using a portion of the image she had printed earlier). So she coated a piece of translucent silver fabric with diluted rabbit skin glue (as an inkjet pre-coat), and when it was dry, printed the fabric on an Epson 3000 using Lysonic archival dye-based inks. Then she attached the print to the center of the fresco.

■ *Capitola* (top) and *Graffiti Bridge* represent a new approach to image-making for artist **John Derry.** His purchase of a Sony DSC-F505 digital camera and the speed with which he could see the source images on screen opened some exciting possibilities.

To begin *Capitola,* Derry shot several digital photos of the colorful, quaint beach-front homes in Capitola, California. Back at the studio, he assembled the photos into a wide panoramic montage. He built the decorative border by copying embellishments from a few of the home fronts and assembling the pieces using layers. The panorama measures 24 x 3.7 inches.

Derry was walking on a railroad trestle near his home after taking the Capitola photos when he spotted the inspiration for *Graffiti Bridge.* As he walked, he noticed that the supports for the trestle's protective railing were covered with intriguing graffiti. He took a series of individual images, photographing all 35 of the supports. Back at his studio, he organized them into a tightly spaced arrangement in Painter. When the composition was complete, he printed the 18 x 8.5-inch image on his six-color Epson 1270 using Epson's archival ink set on sheets of Epson matte-finish paper. Derry also plans to print his *Capitola* image larger on roll paper, to take advantage of the printer's ability to load a roll of 13-inch wide media, and print images up to 44 inches long.

■ **Chet Phillips** created these larger-than-life-size vehicle graphics (top and middle left) for *Dallas Photo Imaging*, using the "Colorizing Scratchboard" technique described on page 29. To make sure the three images would fit the truck exactly, he used a full-size template of the Suburban's shape (provided by the service bureau) to plan each panel. He created individual panels for the driver's side, passenger's side and the truck's back. Phillips built the original files at a resolution of 65 ppi; each file was over 100 MB. When the illustrations were complete, they were output on Dallas Photo Imaging's Idanit inkjet printer onto Avery fleet graphic vinyl with adhesive backing, then attached to the truck.

■ As the principal and creative director for Cinco de Mayo Design Studio, **Mauricio Alanis** conceived and built the *Shouting Bucket* vehicle graphics (bottom left) for Abigarrados, a service bureau in Monterrey, Mexico, which specializes in large-format printing. Using Painter, he created a layered image that included the paint can photo, the circular shapes around the can image and the exploding paint. To give the paint more realistic dimension, he added a semi-transparent layer of Liquid Metal brushstrokes. To add to the relief, he used Apply Surface Texture with Image Luminance. The final 65 ppi image was output onto adhesive-backed vinyl media using a large-format inkjet printer, and mounted on the Abigarrados van.

Appendix A Images on the *Wow!* CD-ROM

These vendors provided photos or video clips from their collections for the Wow! *CD-ROM in the back of this book.*

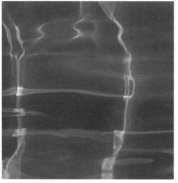

Artbeats
Volumes of backgrounds and textures, including Wood and Paper and Leather and Fabric; sizes to 16.5 MB; Reel Textures, a collection of 40 animated backgrounds

Corbis Images
Extensive collection of royalty-free images, available on CD-ROM or online. Business, lifestyle, nature, backgrounds and more; sizes to 32MB.

Fabulous Fonts
Volumes 31–36 (e.g. Friz Quadrata Book, Corroded Rust and Vidigris; Shelley Volante, Gold and Platinum); picture fonts in sizes to 2.6 MB, designed by John Dismukes and Jo-Anne Redwood of Capstone Studios

Digital Wisdom
Body Shots: One volume of photographs shot with twelve models in various business situations against a white background; sizes to 4 MB

Image Farm
Volumes including Arizona Desert, Berlin Walls, Cottage and Country, Real Rock, Streets of London, and Industrial Backgrounds and Objects; high quality photographic textures and backgrounds; sizes to 18 MB.

Mediacom
Adclips: One volume (2 CDs) of video clips including Recreation, Corporate, Historical, Lifestyles, Wildlife; sizes to 320 x 240 pixels

PhotoDisc
85,000 images downloadable from the Web; over 190 thematic CD-ROM discs; including Signature Series; Object Series (with clipping paths); Fine Art series and Background Series discs; sizes to 28.5 MB

PhotoSpin
Premiere Series and Photo Objects (images with masks); sizes to 25 MB; 50–100 images per disc

Visual Concept Entertainment
Pyromania 1, 2 and Pyromania! Pro:
3 volumes of digitized video of explosions,
fireworks, smoke, and other incendiary
displays; sizes to 640 x 480 pixels

Appendix B Vendor Information

IMAGE COLLECTIONS

Artbeats, Inc.
2611 S. Myrtle Road
Myrtle Creek, OR 97457
541-863-4429 541-863-4547 fax
www.artbeats.com

Corbis Images
15395 S.E. 30th Place, Ste. 300
Bellevue, WA 98007
800-260-0444
425-641-4505
www.corbisimages.com

Digital Wisdom, Inc.
300 Jeanette Drive, Box 2070
Tappahannock, VA 22560
800-800-8560 804-443-9000
804-443-3632 fax

Fabulous Fonts
c/o PhotoSpin
29916 South Hawthorne Blvd.
Rolling Hills Estates, CA 90274
310-265-1313 888-246-1313
310-265-1314 fax
www.photospin.com

Image Farm, Inc.
309 Adelaide Street, Suite 1004
Toronto, ON
Canada M5V 1S7
416-504-4161 416-504-4163 fax
www.imagefarm.com

Mediacom
9210 Arboretum Pkwy. Ste. 150
Richmond, VA 23236
804-560-9200 804-560-4370 fax

PhotoDisc, Inc.
701 North 34th Street, Ste 400
Seattle, WA 98103
800-528-3472
206-268-2001 fax
www.photodisc.com

PhotoSpin
29916 South Hawthorne Blvd.
Rolling Hills Estates, CA 90274
310-265-1313 888-246-1313
310-265-1314 fax
www.photospin.com

Visual Concept Entertainment
P.O. Box 921226
Sylmar, CA 91392
818-367-9187 818-362-3490 fax
http://www.vce.com

HARDWARE

Apple Computer, Inc.
800-767-2775

Hewlett-Packard / *Desktop color printers*
16399 West Bernardo Drive
San Diego, CA 92127
858-655-4100
www.hp.com

Epson America / *Desktop color printers*
P.O. Box 2854
Torrance, CA 90509
800-289-3776 800-873-7766
www.epson.com

Iomega / *Removable drives*
1821 West Iomega Way
Roy, UT 84067-9977
800-456-5522 801-778-3000

Mitsubishi Electronics Inc. / *Monitors*
5665 Plaza Drive, P.O. Box, 6007
Cypress, CA 90630
800-843-2515

Wacom / *Drawing tablets*
115 Century Road
Paramus, NJ 07652
800-922-6613

INKS AND SUBSTRATES

Charrette Corporation / *Substrates and Inks*
800-367-3729
www.inkjet.com

Dr. Graphix Inc. / *Substrates*
www.drgraphix.com

Epson / *Substrates and Inks*
www.epson.com

Hewlett-Packard / *Substrates and Inks*
www.hp.com

ilab Corporation, Inc. / *inks for Epson, Iris and Novaget*
P.O. Box 1030
Atkinson, NH 03811
603-362-4190 fax 603-362-4191
www.ilabcorp.com

InkJet Mall / *Substrates and Inks*
www.inkjetmall.com

Luminos Photo Corporation / *inks for Epson and other printers*
P.O. Box 158
Yonkers, NY 10705
800-586-4667 fax 914-965-0367

Media Street / *Substrates and Inks*
888-633-4295 fax 888-329-5991
www.mediastreet.com

TSS Photo / *Substrates and Inks*
801-363-9700 fax 801-363-9707
www.inkjetart.com
www.tssphoto.com/sp/dg/

Wilhelm Imaging Research, Inc. / *Ink and paper longevity information*
P.O. Box 775
Grinnell, IA 50112-0775
fax 515-236-4222
www.wilhelm-research.com

SOFTWARE

Adobe Systems / *After Effects, Dimensions, GoLive, Illustrator, PageMaker, Photoshop, Premiere*
345 Park Avenue
San Jose, CA 95110
800-833-6687

Auto F/X / *Photographic Edges*
31 Inverness Parkway, Ste. 270
Birmingham, AL 35242
205-980-0056
www.autofx.com

Corel Corporation / *Corel Painter 6, CorelDRAW 9 Suite (graphics), CorelDRAW 9 Suite Professional Color Edition, Corel Photo-Paint 9, Corel Knock-Out 1.5, Corel KPT 5, Corel KPT 6, Corel Bryce 4, Corel KPT Vector Effects 1.5*
1600 Carling Avenue
Ottawa, ON
Canada K1Z 8R7
613-728-0826
www.corel.com

Macromedia / *Director, Dreamweaver FreeHand, Fireworks, Flash*
600 Townsend Street, Suite 310-W
San Francisco, CA 94103
800-989-3762
415-252-2000

Netscape Communications Corp.
Netscape, Netscape Navigator
501 East Middlefield Road
Mountain View, CA 94043
415-528-2555

Strata, Inc. / *Studio Pro*
2 West St. George Boulevard, Suite 2100
St. George, UT 84770
800-787-2823
801-628-9756

Appendix C
Fine Art Output Suppliers

These bureaus specialize in making large format prints for fine artists, using the Iris inkjet and other printers. More are listed on the Wow! CD-ROM.

Cone Editions / *Iris fine art prints*
East Topsham, VT
802-439-5751

Cone-Laumont Editions, Ltd. / *Iris fine art prints*
333 West 52nd Street
New York, NY 10019
212-245-2113

Chrome Digital / *Fujix Pictrography prints; film recorder output*
858-452-1588

Color Reflections / *Durst Lamda and Fujix Pictrography prints; film recorder output*
www.colorreflections.com

Dallas Photo Imaging *LightJet 5000 prints; vehicle graphics*
3942 Irving Blvd.
Dallas, TX 75247
800-852-6929 214-630-4351
www.dpitexas.com

Digicolor / *Iris fine art prints*
Seattle, WA
206-284-2198

Digicolorado / *Iris fine art prints*
610 South Lipan Street
Denver, CO 80223
303-777-6720

Digital Output Corp. / *Hewlett-Packard DesignJet 3500CP prints; Iris fine art prints*
2121 5th Avenue
San Diego, CA 92101
619-685-5800 fax 619-685-5804
www.digtialoutput.com

Durst Dice America / *Lenticular prints*
16 Sterling Road
Tuxedo, NY 10987
914-351-2677

Electric Paintbrush / *Iris fine art prints*
Hopkinton, MA
508-435-7726

Foto 1 Imaging / *LightJet 5000; Fujix Pictrography prints*
800-761-3686
www.foto1.com

High Resolution / *Iris fine art prints*
Camden, ME
207-236-3777

Imagestation / *Iris fine art prints*
Kihei, HI
808-536-1718

Lenticular Products / *Lenticular prints*
www.lenticulardevelopement.com

Nash Editions / *Iris fine art prints*
Manhattan Beach, CA
310-545-4352

Paris Photo Lab / *Iris fine art prints*
Los Angeles, CA
310-204-0500

Photodyne / *Hewlett-Packard DesignJet 3500CP prints; film recorder output*
7012 Convoy Court
San Diego, CA 92011
858-292-0140

River City Silver / *LightJet 5000 prints*
800-938-2788

Salon Iris / *Iris fine art prints*
Vienna, Austria

Trillium Press / *Iris fine art prints; monotypes; silk screen*
91 Park Lane
Brisbane, CA 94005
415-468-8166 fax 415-468-0721

Urban Digital Color / *Iris fine art prints*
San Francisco, CA
415-626-8403

Appendix D
Contributing Artists

Mauricio Alanis
c/o Cinco de Mayo
5 de Mayo Pte., Monterrey, N.L.
Mexico, 64000
malanis@mail.cmact.com

Ben Barbante
1176 Key Avenue
San Francisco, CA 94124
415-657-9844

Caty Bartholomew
198 Seventh Avenue #4R
Brooklyn, NY 11215
718-965-0790

Kathleen Blavatt
4261 Montalvo Street
San Diego, CA 92107
619-222-0057

Ray Blavatt
4261 Montalvo Street
San Diego, CA 92107
619-222-0057

Athos Boncompagni
Via Desenzano, 14
20146 Milano, Italy
bonathos@iname.com

Carol Benioff
2226 11th Avenue #4
Oakland, CA 94606
510-533-9987

Richard Biever
117 N. Frederick
Evansville, IN 47711
812-437-9308

Marc Brown
2786 South Monroe
Denver, CO 80210
303-758-9411

Ginny Bobrink (Jinny Brown)
Cupertino, CA
408-996-8469
jinbrown@pixelalley.com
www.pixelalley.com

Jeff Burke
8755 Washington Blvd.
Culver City, CA 90232
310-837-9900

Steve Campbell
1880 Fulton #5
San Francisco, CA 94117
415-668-5826

Phillip Charris
27184 Ortega Highway
San Juan Capistrano, CA 92675
949-496-3330

Gary Clark
823 Lightstreet Road
Bloomsburg, PA 17815
717-387-1689

James D'Avanzo
(11/2/73–5/28/96)
Family of James D'Avanzo
1446 Jennings Road
Fairfield, CT 06430
203-255-6822

Linda Davick
4805 Hilldale Drive
Knoxville, TN 37914
615-546-1020

Jack Davis
1315 Belleview Avenue
Cardiff, CA 92007
619-944-7232

John Derry
Aptos, CA
pixlart@mac.com

Ellie Dickson
185 West End Avenue #3L
New York, NY 10023
212-724-3598

Matt Dineen
1465 Dougmar Road
Santa Cruz, CA 95062

John Dismukes
949-888-9911
www.dismukes.com

Mary Envall
1536 Promontory Ridge Way
Vista, CA 92083
760-727-8995

Grace Ferguson
2226–11th Avenue
Oakland, CA 94606

John Fretz
707 S. Snoqualmie Street, #5D
Seattle, WA 98108
206-623-1931

Laurence Gartel
P.O. Box 971251
Boca Raton, FL 33487
561-477-1100

Kerry Gavin
154 East Canaan Road
East Canaan, CT 06024
203-824-4839

Jack Gold
12939 Indian River Drive #6
Sebastian, FL 32958
561-388-2620

Helen Golden
460 El Capitan Place
Palo Alto, CA 94306
415-494-3461

Steven Gordon
136 Mill Creek Crossing
Madison, AL 35758
256-772-0022

Francois Guerin
33 Rue Alexandre Dumas
75011 Paris, France
0-11-331-43-73-36-62

Shawn Grunberger
415-552-0367
shawn@deepstorm.com

Andrew Hathaway
805 Page Street
San Francisco, CA 94117
415-621-0671

Brent Houston
brenthouston@earthlink.net

Hugo Hidalgo
9014 Reichling Lane
Pico Rivera, CA 90660
310-942-7526

Philip Howe
12425 68th Avenue SE
Snohomish, WA 98296
425-385-8426
dooder1@aol.com

Geoff Hull
4054 Cartwright Avenue
Studio City, CA 91604
818-761-6019

Donal Jolley
c/o Studio 3.0
1506 Black Spruce Court
Lilburn, GA 30047
770-923-6480

Rick Kirkman
11809 N. 56th Drive
Glendale, AZ 85304
623-334-9199

Dorothy Simpson Krause
P.O. Box 421
Marshfield Hills, MA 02051
781-837-1682
www.dotkrause.com

Ted Larson
7718 Corliss Avenue North
Seattle, WA 98103
206-525-0588
theoneson@earthlink.net

John Lee
2293 El Contento Drive
Los Angeles, CA 90068
213-467-9317

LeVan/Barbee
P.O. Box 68
Jamestown, NC 27282
lvbnc@earthlink.net

Bonny Lhotka
5658 Cascade Place
Boulder, CO 80303
303-494-5631

Michele Lill
2503 Kieffer Court
Valparaiso, IN 46383
219-531-4728
lill@netnitco.net

Patrick Litchy
8211 E. Wadora NW
North Canton, OH 55720
330-494-5593

Debi Lee Mandel
www.catsprite.com
530-886-8910

Janet Martini
4857 Biona Drive
San Diego, CA 9211
619-283-7895

Craig McClain
9587 Tropico Drive
La Mesa, CA 91941
619-469-9599

Pedro Meyer
1333 Beverly Glen #1004
Los Angeles, CA 90024
pedro@zonezero.com

Judy Miller
31 Martin Drive
Fall River, NS
B2T 1E7 Canada
902-861-1193
judy@creativeartist.com

Judi Moncrieff
16125 Juan-Wdvl Wy NE #104
Bothell, WA 98011
425-483-8008

Brian Moose
P.O. Box 927
Capitola, CA 95010
831-425-1672

Wendy Morris
4876 Orchard Avenue
San Diego, CA 92107
619-222-5044
wendydraw@aol.com

Bill Niffenegger
1007 Grand Boulevard
Cloudcroft, NM 88317
505-682-2776

Richard Noble
899 Forest Lane
Alamo, CA 94507
510-838-5524

Louis Ocepek
1761 Pomona Drive
Las Cruces, NM 88011
505-522-0427
505-646-7550

John Odam
2163 Cordero Road
Del Mar, CA 92014
858-259-8230

Corinne Okada
657 Evert Avenue, Apt. 1
Palo Alto, CA 94301
415-325-3549

Dennis Orlando
79 Brookline Road
Ivyland, PA 18974
215-355-5524
dorlando@voicenet.com

Dott. Lorenzo Paolini
Rome, Italy
conor@mware.it

Chet Phillips
6527 Del Norte
Dallas, TX 75225
214-987-4344
www.chetart.com

Jean Francois Podevin
5812 Newlin Avenue
Whittier, CA 90601
310-945-9613

David Purnell
c/o New York West
8145-100th Street W
Lonsdale, MN 55046
507-744-5408

Abbie Rabinowitz
7 Yellow Ferry Harbor
Sausalito, CA 94965
415-331-0878

Mike Reed
1314 Summit Avenue
Minneapolis, MN 55403
612-374-3164

Cindy Reid
11018 122nd Lane NE/91
Kirkland, WA 98033

Dewey Reid
c/o Microsoft Corporation
1 Microsoft Way, 13/1052
Redmond, WA 98052-6399

Lew Robinson
Photography and Digital Imaging
310-837-7009

Peter Mitchell Rubin
c/o Production Arts Limited
310-915-5610

Cecil Rice
5784 Salem Terrace
Acworth, GA 30102
770-974-0684

Chelsea Sammel
PO Box 30132
Oakland, CA 94604-6332
510-628-8474

Larry Scher
11821 North Circle Drive
Whittier, CA 90601
310-699-8797

Don Seegmiller
c/o Saffire
754 West 700 South
Pleasant Grove UT 84062
801-785-3016
don@saffire.com

Karin Schminke
5803 NE 181st Street
Seattle WA 98155
425-402-8606

Nancy Stahl
470 West End Avenue
New York, NY 10024
212-362-8779

Sharon Steuer
205 Valley Road
Bethany, CT 06524
203-393-3981

Jeremy Sutton
415-626-3871
jeremy@portrayals.com
www.portrayals.com

S. Swaminathan
P.O. Box 1547
Capitola, CA
408-722-3301

Margaret Sweeney
12939 Indian River Drive #6
Sebastian, FL 32958
561-388-2620

Lorraine Triolo
8755 Washington Boulevard
Culver City, CA 90232
310-837-9900

Ayse Ulay
146 South Michigan Avenue, #101
Pasadena, CA 91106
818-796-4615

Stanley Vealé
zetar@yahoo.com

Pamela Drury Wattenmaker
17 South Palomar Drive
Redwood City, CA 94061
415-368-7878

Pamela Wells
136 Verdi Avenue
Cardiff, CA 92007
760-632-8495

Lynda Weinman
P.O. Box 789
Ojai, CA 93024
www.lynda.com

Hiroshi Yoshii
1-2-13-304, Tamagawadai, Setagaya-ku
Tokyo 1580096, Japan
tel/fax 81.3.5491.5337
hiroshi@yoshii.com

●

Appendix E Reference Materials

Here's a sampling of recommended references for both traditional and digital art forms.

ART BOOKS

Art Through the Ages
Fifth Edition
Revised by Horst de la Croix and Richard G. Tansey
Harcourt, Brace and World, Inc.
New York, Chicago, San Francisco, and Atlanta

The Art of Color
Johannes Itten
Van Nostrand Reinhold
New York

Drawing Lessons from the Great Masters
Robert Beverly Hale
Watson-Guptill Publications
New York

Mainstreams of Modern Art
John Canaday
Holt, Reinhart and Winston
New York

Printmaking
Gabor Peterdi
The Macmillan Company
New York
Collier-Macmillan Ltd.
London

The Natural Way to Draw
Kimon Nicolaïdes
Houghton Mifflin Company
Boston

The Photographer's Handbook
John Hedgecoe
Alfred A. Knopf
New York

TypeWise
Kit Hinrichs
with Delphine Hirasura
North Light Books
Cincinnati, Ohio

COMPUTER IMAGERY BOOKS

Creating Killer Web Sites
Second Edition
David Siegel
Hayden Books
201 West 103 Street
Indianapolis, IN 46290

Elements of Web Design
Second Edition
Darcy DiNucci with *Maria Giudice* and *Lynne Stiles*
Peachpit Press
Berkeley, CA

Deconstructing Web Graphics
Second Edition
Lynda Weinman and Jon Warren Lentz
New Riders Publishing
Indianapolis, IN

Designing Web Graphics 3
How to Prepare Images and Media for the Web
Lynda Weinman
New Riders Publishing
Indianapolis, IN

Non-Designers Web Book
Robin Williams and John Tollett
Peachpit Press
Berkeley, CA

The Illustrator 8 Wow! Book
Sharon Steuer
Peachpit Press
Berkeley, CA

The Photoshop 5/5.5 Wow! Book
Linnea Dayton and Jack Davis
Peachpit Press
Berkeley, CA

PUBLICATIONS

Communication Arts
Coyne & Blanchard, Inc.
410 Sherman Avenue
Palo Alto, CA 94306

Design Graphics
Design Editorial Pty. Ltd.
11 School Road
Ferny Creek
Victoria 3786 Australia

Electronic Publishing
Ten Tara Boulevard, Fifth Floor
Nashua, NH 03062

Graphis
Graphis US, Inc.
141 Lexington Avenue
New York, NY 10016

How
Ideas and Techniques for Graphic Design
104 Fifth Avenue
New York, NY 10011

Print
RC Publications
104 Fifth Avenue
New York, NY 10011

Step-by-Step Graphics and
Step-by-Step Electronic Design
Step-by-Step Publishing
6000 Forest Park Drive
Peoria, IL 61614

Index